CRT

BN 708789·6

The GUINNESS Book of the

BUSINESS WORLD

William Fortnum and Hugh Mason opened a grocery shop about 1707 close to the present site of the store (see page 140); the monumental clock inaugurated on 4 November 1964 was made by Thwaites & Reed, established in 1740 (see page 72); the bronze founding was executed by James Gibbons Ltd established in 1670 (see page 77), and the bells came from the Whitechapel Bell Foundry, dating from 1570 (see page 67)

The GUINNESS Book
of the
BUSINESS
WORLD

by

Henry G Button, MA

and

Andrew P Lampert, BSc

GUINNESS SUPERLATIVES LIMITED

2 CECIL COURT, LONDON ROAD, ENFIELD, MIDDLESEX

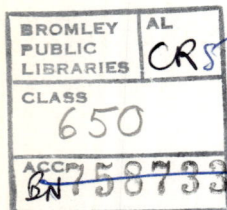

© Henry G Button and Andrew P Lampert
and Guinness Superlatives Ltd 1976

Published in Great Britain by
Guinness Superlatives Ltd, 2 Cecil Court,
London Road, Enfield, Middlesex

ISBN 0 900424 32 X

Guinness is a registered trade mark of
Arthur Guinness Son & Co Ltd

Set in 'Monophoto' Plantin Series 110

Printed and bound in Great Britain by
Jarrold and Sons Ltd, Norwich

OTHER GUINNESS SUPERLATIVES TITLES

CONTENTS

Contents continued overleaf

Contents continued

ACKNOWLEDGEMENTS

This book could not have been written without the ready co-operation, over a number of years, of many of the businesses and institutions mentioned in the following pages. The authors trust that they will be forgiven for not listing them all again here, but a special word of thanks must go to the people and institutions listed below:

SECTION I

Baker Library, Harvard University; Bodleian Library, Oxford; British Museum; Business Archives Council, London; Cambridge University Library; Christ's College Library, Cambridge; *Daily Telegraph*; *Economist*; Eleutherian Mills-Hagley Foundation, Wilmington, Delaware; *Financial Times*; Flour Milling and Baking Research Association, Chorleywood, Hertfordshire; *Fortune*; French Embassy, London; German Embassy, London; Goldsmiths' Company, London; Guildhall Library, London; *Guinness Book of Records*; Miss Etna M Kelley, New York; Marshall Library, Cambridge; Professor Peter Mathias, Oxford; Ministry of Agriculture, Fisheries and Food Library, London; Naval Historical Library, Ministry of Defence, London; Netherlands Economic and Cultural Documentation, Amsterdam; Philadelphia Free Library; Public Archives, Halifax, Nova Scotia, Canada; Records Office, Guildhall, London; *Shell Book of Firsts*, Patrick Robertson; Spanish Embassy, London; Swedish Embassy, London; *The Times*; *The Times 1000 (1975–6)*; Tolson Memorial Museum, Huddersfield; Toronto Public Libraries; Trades Union Congress; *Whitaker's Almanack*; *Who Owns Whom*.

Thanks are due to the Goldsmiths' Company and to the Keystone Agency for the pictures of the hallmarking of platinum (pages 167 and 168), and to John Blomfield for the picture of the Mustard Shop, Norwich (page 29). The London Records Office and the British Museum kindly arranged for the photographing of the extract from the Rolls of the Mayor's Court (page 171) and of the Egibi tablets (page 114).

SECTION II

Stephen J Lewis and Chris Anthony – Philips and Drew.

William J Hall – *Banker Magazine*.
Brian A Johnson – London Stock Exchange.
D R Bramwell – Press and Information Service, Central Statistical Office.
John Stockley – Media Expenditure Analysis Limited.
David Jones and Brian Naylor – *Investors' Chronicle*.
Tony Lyons – *Sunday Telegraph*.
Diana Fisher – *Observer*.
B J Hales-Dutton – Department of Trade.
Alan Hughes – Sidney Sussex College, Cambridge.
Mrs B M Evans – National Farmers' Union.
Mary Gegelys and Anthony Rau – J Walter Thompson Company.
Margaret Strong – Institute of Chartered Accountants in England and Wales.
TAF Atkins – Lloyds of London.
Jean E Tobin – Librarian, New York Stock Exchange.
Chris Booker and Bennie Gray – *Observer*.
F M Shaw – Britannia Building Society.
J K Galbraith – 'The Great Crash'.
M Boleat – Building Society Association.
Michael Crosbie – Save and Prosper Group Limited.
Barry Goldsmith – M and G Unit Trust Group.
George Stevens – Slater Walker.
J J Sturgess and J W Rath – Association of Investment Trust Companies.
Anthony Bambridge – *Observer*.
Keith Lewis – *Financial Times*.
The Union Bank of Switzerland, London.
L. Faulkner – Philips and Drew.
Mervyn Emery.
W J Eiteman, C A Dice, D K Eiteman – 'The Stock Market'.

Some of the information contained in the following pages is bound to be out of date by the time the book appears in the shops. Chairmen retire or die, firms cease to exist or lose their identity in amalgamations, and so on. The authors would be glad to be notified of any such changes.

Finally, the authors wish to record their indebtedness to their collaborators at Guinness Superlatives Ltd, notably Norris McWhirter, Beatrice Frei, David Roberts and Sue Gullen.

GLOSSARY

(As recorded in the
Oxford English Dictionary)

Accept (a bill or letter of exchange) – to agree or promise to pay (1665).

Account – a reckoning as to money (c 1300).

Balance of payments – the difference of value between payments into and out of a country (1844).

Balance-sheet – a tabular statement of assets and liabilities (Cobden, 1849).

Bank – an establishment for the custody of money (1526, Tindale, *Luke* 19: 23).

Bear (Stock Exchange) – a speculator for a fall (1744).

Bull (Stock Exchange) – one who endeavours by speculative purchases, or otherwise, to raise the price of stocks (1761).

Cartel (originally in Germany) – an agreement or association between two or more business houses for regulating output, fixing prices, etc (1902).

Conglomerate – a large business group or industrial corporation resulting from the merging of originally separate and diverse commercial enterprises (1967).

Critical path – the most important sequence of stages in an operation (1959).

Day-book, for commercial transactions (1660).

Director – a member of a Board (1632).

Firm – a commercial house (1817).

Ledger – principal book for recording mercantile transactions (1588).

Merger – United States, the combination or consolidation of one firm or trading company with another (1889).

Office – a place for the transaction of business (Chaucer, c 1386).

Overdraft (banking) (1878).

Profit and loss account (1588).

Share (commercial) – (Ben Jonson, 1601).

Stag (Stock Exchange) – a speculator on new issues (Thackeray, 1845).

Stock – the subscribed capital of a trading company (before 1692).

Section 1

BUSINESS HISTORY

Henry G Button, MA

INTRODUCTION

This section is principally concerned with the oldest and largest businesses of various kinds in different parts of the world. The largest businesses, because of their size, are usually well known and well documented, so that it is a simple matter to collate already published information about them. Some of the oldest businesses, on the other hand, are relatively small undertakings, and this is partly the story of a quest for them. Nothing quite like this seems to have been attempted before.

There is no lack of general economic histories, and there are many studies of individual industries, but these are written from a different point of view and are not usually concerned with the fate of the *individual* businesses that make up an industry. The Reports of the Working Parties appointed by the President of the Board of Trade just after the Second World War are a case in point.

Again, there are many histories of individual firms and institutions, often written to celebrate a notable anniversary such as a centenary, bicentenary or even a tercentenary, but histories of this kind tend to be focused, quite rightly, on the individual business rather than on its relationship to other similar businesses. These individual histories have furnished much of the material for this section, but they seldom provide the answer to some of the questions with which we are here concerned. Much of the information on which the text is based has, therefore, had to be obtained by inquiries directed to librarians, firms and individual correspondents both in this country and abroad. Without their help, this book could not have been compiled. Information about a business that is not attributed to a named source has generally been supplied by that business, sometimes in the course of correspondence and sometimes by way of leaflets or brochures.

The importance attached to age varies from industry to industry. Breweries, for instance, often indicate the date of their foundation in their advertisements and on their labels. Firms in the clothing industry, on the other hand, seldom do so. Banks and insurance companies often draw attention to their age in their advertisements and on their buildings. Age is no doubt regarded as a guarantee of the quality of the firm's products, or as a sign of integrity and financial stability.

Firms which have been established for 100 years or more often draw attention to the fact on their notepaper and in their advertisements, and at times incorporate a reference to their age in the name of their products. Well-known examples are Younger's 'Double Century' ale and Pedro Domecq's 'Double Century' sherry.

Earlywarm blankets boasted of having been 'Famous through 15 reigns' (namely, since the days of King Charles II). In 1973 the Tollemache & Cobbold Breweries, of Ipswich, marked their 250th anniversary with the production of Tolly Cobbold's '250 Strong Pale Ale'. One of the most famous advertisements in the world is that for Johnnie Walker whisky – 'Born 1820, still going strong'.

A good deal of the information contained in these pages has been obtained by following up such indications of the age of a firm. Some firms and institutions also proclaim the fact that they are the oldest of their kind in their country, or even in the world.

The publication of this book may possibly bring to light some old firms whose records can challenge those of the old firms mentioned in these pages. Further studies of old firms may disclose that some of them are even older than they think they are – a complaint rare, I am told, among human centenarians.

What explains the survival of the old firms

that we shall be describing? There is no obvious reply to this question. In general, it can be said that these firms have ministered to common and unchanging needs. Men still want bells, books and candles. They still drink beer, tea and coffee. Occasionally, as with the Durtnells of Brasted or the Hoares of London, a family provides the thread of continuity which carries a business through the centuries. But the stories of the Smiths of Thirsk and of the Ottways of Ealing show that a family business that has survived for more than three centuries may not reach its 400th anniversary.

In some cases, as we shall see, new families have come in to an established business and carried on its traditions. And we shall find more than one instance of the industrious apprentice who married his master's daughter and inherited the business when his father-in-law died.

What is a business?

There is not usually much doubt as to whether a big business is in fact a business. Because of their size, most big businesses have a corporate character, being registered under the company legislation of the country or countries where they operate, or deriving their powers and privileges and duties from a Royal Charter or some such instrument, for example, a Papal Bull. With the old businesses, however, we cannot reach even a provisional conclusion as to the oldest business of any kind without first deciding what we mean by a business.

According to H C Wyld's *Universal Diction-ary of the English Language*, a business is 'a regular, habitual, occupation, trade, profession, followed for a livelihood'. On this definition, hunting or fishing (or flint-knapping) might be counted among the oldest businesses, but taken by themselves they lack what Theseus, in *A Midsummer Night's Dream*, called 'a local habi-tation and a name'. The same dictionary gives a further definition of a business as 'a particular commercial enterprise'.

For the purpose of the London Guildhall Library's *Handlist of London Business House Histories,* 'a business house is defined as a commercial or industrial concern whose aim is to make a profit'. *The Shorter Oxford English Dictionary* gives 19 definitions of the word 'business', the last one being 'a commercial enterprise as a going concern'. It is with identifiable, individual enterprises as going concerns aimed at making a profit that we shall be dealing.

In the *Manchester Guardian* (as it was then called) of 1 February 1957, a critic who was dealing with a book about furs wrote: 'The fur trade is the oldest trade in the world, initiated by the first cave man to find himself with a surplus skin.' This argument, however, is self-defeating. Our hypothetical owner of the first surplus furskin must, according to this theory, have come across one of his fellows with a surplus of, say, fish or flints that could be exchanged for his furskin. It would, therefore, be equally correct, on this hypothesis, to regard the fish trade or the flint trade as the oldest trade in the world.

Agriculture, again, has frequently been des-cribed as our oldest industry, although both hunting and fishing are older. We now have it, on the authority of the *Guinness Book of Records,* that the oldest known industry is flint-knapping. There is no evidence that agriculture was practised before about 11 000 BC whereas, to quote the *Encyclopaedia Britannica,* man made his tools of stone and other materials such as bone and antler for 'several hundreds of thousands of years' before he discovered metals. Primitive man had learnt the art of knapping flints long before he cultivated a crop or tended a flock.

CHAPTER 1

FOOD AND DRINK

A. BUSINESSES IN THE BRITISH ISLES

Brewing

Any historical account of the brewing industry in the British Isles must draw on Alfred Barnard's magnificently produced work entitled *The Noted Breweries of Great Britain and Ireland*, which was published in four volumes between 1889 and 1891. Barnard spent a number of years visiting the main breweries in the British Isles and writing an account of his visits. Taking each brewery in turn, he gives a description of the town in which it is situated, his journey to it, a history of the owners and a lengthy description of the premises and of the processes of manufacture.

In connection with his visit to Oxford he writes: 'In former times every college had its brewery, but during the last few years (i.e. before 1890) several have been abolished, among them the famous brew-houses of Brasenose and Magdalen'. Barnard was, however, able to visit the brewhouses of All Souls and of Queen's. At the latter college he saw the so-called 'Chancellor's ale', which was 'so strong that two wineglasses would intoxicate a man'. G V Cox, in a delightful work entitled *Recollections of Oxford* (published in 1868), describes the visit of Queen Adelaide in 1835, when the Queen's horn was handed round, well filled with good beverage, and the Provost of Queen's remarked to Queen Adelaide that the College 'had been brewers for 500 years'. (The College was founded in 1340.)

A number of breweries are on the site of old monastic brewhouses. The **Ardee Street Brewery** in Dublin, for instance, which Barnard described as the oldest in that city, was erected on the site of what was formerly the brewhouse of the Monastery of St Thomas.

The **Guinness Brewery** in the same city, 'the largest and most renowned brewery in Europe' as Barnard called it, was founded by Arthur Guinness (1725–1803), an ancestor of the present Chairman, in 1759, but there was an old brewery on the present site which Arthur Guinness took over. The Guinness Brewery in Dublin still occupies the original site, although it has been greatly extended since its early days.

The second Earl of Iveagh, who represented the fifth generation of the Guinness family, was Chairman of the company from 1927 to 1962. He died in September 1967 at the age of 93. His grandson, Viscount Elveden, who had taken over from him as Chairman of the company, succeeded to the title as the third Earl and represents the seventh generation of the family to be associated with the business.

In the 19th century, Guinness grew to be the largest brewery in the world. The London brewery at Park Royal was started in 1934 and the first brew was made there in 1936.

A letter from a cavalry officer who was wounded at Waterloo provides interesting evidence that the export of Guinness must have begun before 1815. 'When I was sufficiently recovered to be permitted to take some nourishment, I felt the most extraordinary

Road tanker specially designed to carry Guinness stout in bulk – capacity 4680 gallons. *(Arthur Guinness Son & Co (Dublin) Ltd)*

desire for a glass of Guinness, which I knew could be obtained without difficulty.'

Several other famous breweries were established about the middle of the 18th century. The firm of **Worthington** was founded by William Worthington in 1744. The firm of **Bass** was founded in 1777 by William Bass, the great-grandfather of the Lord Burton who was the Chairman of the firm at the time of Barnard's visit.

Somewhat earlier in the century, in the year 1730, Mr Salmon and Mr Hare built a brewery in Limehouse. In the course of time this became the Barley Mow Brewery of **Taylor, Walker & Company Limited.**

Another London brewery dating from the middle of the 18th century is **Whitbread's.** Samuel Whitbread (1720–96) established the business which still bears his name between 1740 and 1742. According to *Whitbread's Brewery,* a short history published in 1951, 'the latter year is generally claimed as that which saw the foundation of his brewery'.

Samuel Whitbread II (1758–1815) was a noted Member of Parliament. One of his daughters married Charles Shaw Lefevre, later Viscount Eversley (1795–1888), who was Speaker of the House of Commons from 1839 to 1857. It is to Lefevre that Whitbread's Brewery owes 'the proud privilege of providing horses for the historic Speaker's coach on State occasions'. The coach, now more than 250 years old, weighs $2\frac{3}{4}$ tons.

The breweries already mentioned are by no means the oldest in the country, and Barnard does not tell us explicitly which is the oldest.

Writing of the brewery at Stone in Staffordshire belonging to **John Joule and Sons,** Barnard does say that 'it is said to be the oldest brewery in England, having been founded early in the 17th century'; before that time the monastery at Stone had been 'renowned for the quality of its brew and the potency of its ale'. He also tells us that the **Cannon Brewery** of Benskins at Watford was in existence in 1750, that **Pike, Spicer and Company's** brewery at Portsmouth dated from 1719, and that the **Lion Brewery** at Chester was 'of great antiquity, having been founded in the year 1642'.

Barnard refers to the **Red Lion Brewery** in Lower East Smithfield, near the Tower of London, as 'the oldest brewery in London,' adding that it 'can be traced back to the 16th century'. At the time of Barnard's visit the brewery belonged to Hoare and Company, of the same family as the bankers in Fleet Street (see page 109), who had taken it over in 1802. Sir John Ellerman later acquired a controlling interest in the company, became its Chairman about the end of the First World War and subsequently sold his interest to Charrington and Company. The brewery was demolished some years ago.

Anchor Brewery, Mile End, London E1, belonging to Charrington and Company, was built in 1757. The founder of the business was John Charrington (1739–1815).

Of the **City of London Brewery,** formerly in Upper Thames Street, Barnard writes:

'The date of the foundation of this brewery goes back to such a remote period, that it would be difficult to fix the exact year. From various ancient documents in the archives of the brewery, there is no doubt that it was in existence in the year 1580, and, therefore, it was built prior to that date'

Walking down Upper Thames Street from Cannon Street Station, you would see on your right hand, between Upper Thames Street and the river, a half-derelict stretch of land used mainly as a car park. A few years ago there was a small board on a post with the inscription 'Site of the Hour-Glass – City of London Brewery and Investment Trust Ltd. Fully Licensed. Licensee . . .', but the name of the licensee was obliterated. This small notice-board was the last remaining indication that this plot of land was once occupied by the City of London Brewery – the Hour-Glass was the sign of the brewery as well as of the tavern, and hence it was sometimes called the 'Hour-Glass Brewery'. The name lingers on in the Hour Glass Investment Company, a subsidiary of the City of London Brewery and Investment Trust. In 1967 the company sold its Thames-side property, then described as 89/92 Upper Thames Street, and in 1968 it sold off its 20 'Patmac' pubs, including the one known as the 'Coal Hole' in the Strand.

Mrs L B Ellis has given an interesting account of the City of London Brewery in the *Transactions of the London and Middlesex Archaeological Society* (Volume IX, Part 2, pages 165–79). It is said to have been 'the oldest brewery in the City of London'. In July 1941 the City of London Brewery and Investment Trust moved its offices to Kensington Gore 'and severed, at any rate temporarily, its long connection with the City'.

An assignment of the year 1431 contains a list of brewing utensils which were then in the custody of John Reynolds, brewer, at the Heywharf in Heywharflane (now renamed Campion Lane).

In 1744 the brewery was owned by Sir William Calvert. Before being taken over by the City of London Brewery Company in 1860, the firm was known as 'Felix Calvert and Company'. Brewing ceased in the 1920s, and in 1932 the company was formed into an investment trust.

When the City of London Brewery closed down, the Anchor Brewery of Barclay, Perkins and Company Limited became the oldest brewery in London. The following account is based mainly on their booklet *Three Centuries – The Story of our Ancient Brewery*.

The brewery, situated in Park Street, Southwark, traces its origin to the year 1616, when James Monger the Elder started a brewhouse there, next to the Globe Theatre. The site of the brewery was later extended and covered the ground where the Globe Theatre once stood.

About 1729, Ralph Thrale (1698–1758) bought the brewhouse from the executors of his uncle, the previous owner. On his death, in 1758, the brewery passed to his son Henry Thrale, the friend of Dr Johnson. The connection of Dr Johnson with the Thrale family

This tun, *left*, (designated 26M) at the Guinness Brewery in St James's Gate, Dublin, is the largest fermenting vessel in any brewery. It can ferment 8000 bulk barrels of stout (2 304 000 pints) at one brewing. *(Arthur Guinness Son & Co (Dublin) Ltd)*. The first beer tanker, *right*, the converted *Lady Patricia*. Capacity 224 000 gallons or the equivalent of 3·5 million bottles of stout. *(Arthur Guinness Son & Co (Dublin) Ltd)*

and with the brewery is recalled by their sign and their 'Doctor's Ale'.

Henry Thrale died in 1781 and the business was sold to the Barclays, who thus make their first appearance on the scene. Henry Thrale's Manager, John Perkins, was taken into partnership, and by 1782 the partners were four, namely two Barclays, Perkins, and Sylvanus Bevan, each with a quarter share of the profits. In 1797 the name of the firm was changed to Barclay, Perkins and Company. From that day to 1951, when the booklet was written, through six generations, there was always a Barclay, a Perkins and a Bevan in the firm, 'a record probably unequalled in London' (or, probably, anywhere else in the country). Older family connections admittedly are to be found, but this triple-barrelled record is astonishing.

In 1748 the output of Thrale's brewery was only about two-thirds that of Calvert's (later known as the City of London Brewery – see page 15). By 1776, Thrale was second to Whitbread and in 1802 second to Meux. In 1809, however, Barclay's output (205 328 barrels) exceeded that of any other London brewery.

The firm's first recorded export order dates from 1695, when 15 tuns of 'XX beer' were shipped to 'Beerbados' (an understandable misspelling).

In 1929, several other breweries, among them the **Royal Brewery** at Brentford, became associated with Barclay, Perkins and Company. The Royal Brewery and the Dome at Brighton are said to have the unique distinction of holding 'the only two grants of

Royal Coats of Arms which need not be renewed upon the death of the reigning sovereign'. William IV granted the arms to the brewery in 1832 in recognition of the services of the owner, Sir Felix Booth, in fitting out an expedition under Captain Ross to explore the Polar seas.

In 1955, Courage and Company and Barclay, Perkins and Company came together to form **Courage and Barclay Limited.** Several other companies have since joined them. John Courage bought a small brewery on the south bank of the Thames in 1787, and his name is perpetuated in the bottles of John Courage beer. H and G Simonds, of Reading, another member of the group, was founded late in the 18th century, and the Bristol Brewery, formerly the Bristol Porter Brewery, was founded in 1788.

The Southwark Brewery is a brewery no longer. After the merger it was transformed into the Globe Bottling Store, which is said to incorporate 'the most advanced mechanical handling system of any brewery in the world'. It has an output capacity of more than a million bottles a day.

Another old brewery that reached the end of the road a few years ago was **Lacon's Brewery** at Great Yarmouth, which had become part of the Whitbread Group. It was announced in December 1967 that the 330-year-old brewery was to close.

Yet another brewing firm dating from the 17th century was **Truman, Hanbury and Buxton,** now part of the Grand Metropolitan Group. This brewery firm and **Mann, Crossman and Paulin** are the only three-barrelled names given by Barnard, although such names later became much commoner in this industry. About 1890, **Ind** and **Coope** were already joined, but not yet with **Allsopp.** Although the names of Ratcliffe and Gretton appeared among the Bass directors, Bass was still the name of the firm. **Watney, Combe** and **Reid** were then three separate firms. Thornbury mentions Alderman Combe, Mayor of London in 1799, 'whom some saucy citizens nick-named "Mash-tub"'.

The history of Truman, Hanbury, Buxton and Company has been told in Lionel Birch's *The Story of Beer* and later in the tercentenary volume *Trumans the Brewers 1666–1966.* Although, as the tercentenary history explains, there is no existing documentary evidence for the year 1666, it goes on to say that 'there seems every reason to accept the traditional belief, based on papers now lost but referred to in a letter of nearly 100 years ago, that Joseph Truman first set up in business in 1666'.

The Trumans were in sole charge of the business for about 100 years. Joseph's son, Benjamin Truman, was knighted by George III, and is commemorated in the firm's 'Old Ben' ales. About the year 1800, Sampson Hanbury and Thomas Fowell Buxton both joined the firm, and gave it its three-barrelled name.

The brewery firm of **Watney Mann** also forms part of the Grand Metropolitan Group. It was in June 1972 that Grand Metropolitan Hotels made a bid of £438 million for Watney Mann, a bid which figures in the *Guinness Book of Records* as 'the largest take-over in commercial history'.

Mention must also be made of the firm of **Tomson and Wotton Limited,** of Ramsgate, Kent. According to their notepaper, the brewery at Ramsgate was established prior to 1634 and was bought by Thomas Tomson in 1680. Mr D J Martin-Tomson informed the author in 1960 that the date of the first brewery on the site was no longer known, but that brewing had certainly been continuous on the site since 1634. Two of the directors of the company at that time were descended from the Thomas Tomson who bought the brewery and two others from the Thomas Wotton who became Brewer at the firm in 1854 and was taken into partnership in 1867.

When Barclay, Perkins gave up brewing at Southwark (see above), Tomson and Wotton assumed the mantle of Britain's Oldest Brewery, and so described themselves on their labels.

Peter Mathias, in *The Brewing Industry in England 1700–1830* (1959), cites Tomson and Wotton as 'perhaps the most remarkable example of continuity of ownership and site' in the brewing industry in this country.

Turning now to Scotland, the **Abbey Brewery** of William Younger and Company in Edinburgh dates its origin from the year 1749, and Younger's 'Double Century' ale commemorates the 200th anniversary of the firm. (Domecq's 'Double Century' sherry was

MILESTONES IN THE HISTORY OF BREWING

Beer originated in Egypt and Babylon some 5000 years ago.

In Egypt liquor called *hek* made from fermented barley.

Hops used in Babylon pre AD 200.

Wooden casks originated in Switzerland during the Bronze Age.

Ale was introduced into Britain by Celts about 2000 years ago.

1267 Henry III established the Assize of Ale to fix the price of ale in the light of the rising price of malt.

1277 An Assize directed that 'no brewster henceforth shall sell except by true name, namely the gallon, the bottle and quart . . .'.

1437 The Brewers' Company incorporated – new Charter received from Elizabeth I in 1560.

14th–15th century Bottom fermentation originated in Germany.

1552–3 Licensing of alehouses, inns and taverns dates from Acts of 1552 and 1553.

1562 Izaak Walton attributes the discovery of bottled beer to Alexander Nowell, Dean of St Paul's.

1722 Porter may have been originated in Bell's Brewhouse, Shoreditch.

Mid 18th century Many major brewers started their businesses about the middle of the 18th century – including Whitbread 1742, Worthington 1744, Guinness 1759, and Bass 1777.

1876 Louis Pasteur proved fermentation was brought about by yeast.

1880 Finance Act required anyone producing beer for sale to obtain an Excise licence. In 1881 16 798 such licences were issued.

Between 1881 and 1900 the number of breweries fell by almost half to 6 447.

1933 Present method of paying duty on beer introduced.

1933 Watney developed and marketed keg beer, although it was not then so called. Not until the mid 1950s did Flowers become the first company to use the term 'keg' for this kind of beer.

1960 By the end of the 1960s, after the mergers which left only seven main brewing companies, some 75 per cent of UK beer production was in the hands of these seven companies. There are now less than 200 breweries.

similarly 'selected specially to celebrate the 200th birthday of the famous house of Pedro Domecq'.)

As for Ireland, the **Cork Porter Brewery** at Cork was described by Barnard as 'the most ancient porter brewery in Ireland . . . dating as far back as the 17th century'.

Cider

The **Showering** family have been cider-makers at Shepton Mallet in Somerset for more than 200 years, but it was the marketing of 'Babycham' on a national scale in 1950 that laid the foundation of the Showering Group. Following the takeover by Allied Breweries in 1968, Showerings, Vine Products and Whiteways, which had merged in a £17 million combine in 1961, became responsible for all the wine, spirit, cider, perry and soft-drink interests of the Allied Group.

Bulmers of Hereford began as a small family business in 1887 and became the largest cider-making concern in the world. In *The Times 1000 (1975–6)* list of the 1000 largest UK industrial companies, Bulmers ranked No 939, with sales of nearly £15 million.

Cocoa and chocolate

The firm of **J S Fry and Sons Limited,** of Somerdale, Bristol were the 'founders of the British cocoa and chocolate industry'. They have also been called 'the world's oldest chocolate manufacturers'.

The business was founded by Dr Joseph Fry, a Quaker physician. 'He bought a small shop which had been established in 1728 by a Mr Walter Churchman, and with it he acquired patent rights and recipes for the manufacture of drinking chocolate'. Dr Fry was succeeded as head of the business by his wife, Anna, and then by his son Joseph Storrs Fry, who gave his name to the firm.

Eating chocolate, as distinct from drinking chocolate, was introduced early in the reign of

Queen Victoria. The exact date of the introduction is not known, but Fry's were selling it in 1847 and claim to be one of the first firms to have done so.

'Fry's Cream Bar' is still made in the pattern of a mould designed by Francis Fry in the year 1875, although it could not be wrapped for another 50 years. The 'Cream Bar', made from a recipe evolved more than 100 years ago, first appeared, as 'Fry's Cream Stick', in 1853, and is said to have been 'the first chocolate confectionery ever to be made on a factory scale and sold as a luxury which everybody could afford'.

In 1725, three years before Mr Churchman opened his shop in Bristol, a Quaker woman named **Mary Tuke** opened a small grocer's shop in Walmgate, in the City of York. In *The Romance of a Great Industry – A Commercial and Family History*, G H Mennell has described how this small business developed into the well-known firm of Rowntrees (now Rowntree Mackintosh).

In 1733 Mary Tuke married, and soon afterwards moved to Castlegate in the centre of the city. When she died, in 1752, the business passed to her nephew William Tuke, who had been apprenticed to her in 1746.

William's son, Henry, became a partner in the business in 1785. Up to that year the business seems to have remained a grocer's. Earlier price-lists make no mention of cocoa and chocolate, but a surviving list dated March 1785 quotes prices for them.

The business was divided in 1862 and the cocoa manufactory was acquired by **Henry Isaac Rowntree,** another Quaker. A circular issued at the time said that the old firm 'had relinquished the manufacture of Cocoa, Chocolate and Chicory in favour of our friend H. I. Rowntree, who has been for some time practically engaged on the concern'.

In 1864 the cocoa and chocolate business was moved to Tanner's Moat, where it remained till 1908. In 1869, H I Rowntree was joined by his brother Joseph (1836–1925). The main product at this time was 'Tuke's Rock Cocoa', and no confectionery was made at all. (Rock cocoa was a blend of cocoa and sugar, used to make a drink.)

Packing Edward VII coronation tins – 1902, York Factory. *(Rowntree Mackintosh Ltd)*

In 1881 the firm began to make crystallised gums and soon 'Rowntree's Fruit Pastilles' were introduced. 'Clear Gums' were introduced in 1893. H I Rowntree died in 1883 and Joseph, having carried on the business alone for a while, was later joined by his sons J W Rowntree and B Seebohm Rowntree. In 1890 an estate on the outskirts of York was bought, and new buildings were erected.

This brief account of two of the oldest firms in the cocoa and chocolate industry shows how difficult it is to give a simple answer to the question of which firm is the older of the

Part of the modern-day Kit Kat plant. (*Rowntree Mackintosh Ltd*)

two. On the one hand, Rowntree's can trace a connection back to the shop that Mary Tuke opened in 1725. But cocoa and chocolate do not appear in their story until 1785, and in one sense the business that became Rowntree's might be said to date only from 1862, when Henry Isaac Rowntree took over the cocoa manufactory. On the other hand there is Fry's, whose history begins in 1728, but who were concerned with cocoa from the beginning and who can point to a family connection with the founder of the business lasting for well over 200 years.

Another of York's old firms is **Joseph Terry and Sons Limited,** of The Chocolate Works, Bishopsthorpe Road. The firm was founded in 1767, under the name of Baildon and Berry. In the early 19th century Joseph Terry (1793–1850) joined the partnership, and in 1828 the business passed entirely into his hands. The firm's '1767' assortment of chocolates is a reminder of the year in which its story began.

Crumpets and muffins

'Their crumpet secret is a century old' was the title of an article in the *Middlesex County Times* of 2 February 1957. It began: 'Every Sunday afternoon, from September till Easter, **Ern Payne,** of Acton, walks through the streets of West London and Middlesex selling crumpets made by a secret recipe more than a hundred years old.' The recipe was said to have been invented by his great-great-grandfather, and even Mr Payne's son did not know it.

In 1939 the business had to be suspended. For one thing, muffin-bells were no longer allowed to be rung after the outbreak of war because the ringing of bells was to be a signal that enemy parachutists had landed. Only one firm, it was said, still made those bells and they cost 28s 6d in 1957, as compared with 3s 6d before the war.

The origin of the word 'crumpet' is unknown, but can be traced back to the 17th century. The earliest use of 'crompid' was in 1382 by Wyclif. Oscar Wilde in *The Importance of Being Earnest*, published in 1899, alludes to Lady Harbury partaking of crumpets. The use of the word for desirable females is very modern, dating only from 1936.

Muffins – perhaps in some way connected with Old French *moufflet*, meaning soft (bread) – has also got an obscure origin. 'Moofin' was first used in 1703. The name 'muffin' was Canadian slang in 1856, when an unmarried gentleman selected a young lady to be his companion in the numerous amusements of the season – when she agreed, she was called a 'muffin'.

Essences

In the year 1777 a chemist named Langdale established a distillery in Holborn Hill, close to the entrance to Leather Lane. On 7 June 1780, during the Gordon Riots, the distillery was burnt to the ground by the mob, and the unfortunate proprietor suffered a loss of £100000. A picture of the burning factory was used as the firm's trademark.

E F Langdale, a descendant of the unfortunate chemist, is said to have been 'the first who offered to the public the great boon of purified essences retaining all of their original delicious flavour'. These essences have been marketed since the middle of the 19th century by the firm known as 'E F Langdale Limited'. The distillery was then at 72 Hatton Garden, London, EC but later moved to Croydon.

Fish

The letter-heading of **George Tabor Limited,** oyster producers and fish merchants, of Imperial House, Pudding Lane, Billingsgate carries the inscription 'Established over 400 years'.

The company have an oysterlaying on a 999-year lease dating from about 1550. The company is mentioned in the Faversham Oyster Fishery Act of 1930 (see page 165) as having a lease of part of the oyster fishery near Faversham in Kent, although their main oyster-beds were at Brightlingsea, in Essex. An article in the *London Chamber of Commerce Journal* of 1933 described the company as 'sole agent for the frozen and pickled fish of the Hudson's Bay Company'.

Fish and chips

In 1965 the National Federation of Fish Friers began a search for the oldest fish and chip business in the world. At that time the most favoured candidate for the title was a 102-year-old business at Mossley, in Lancashire, that claimed to be the oldest chip-potato restaurant in the world. What the Federation was seeking, however, was the business with the longest unbroken record of selling both fish and chips.

The Federation's investigations established that the trade in fried fish began about 1850, but that it was not until towards 1870 that the chips began to be sold with the fish. At the end of their inquiries the Federation decided that the oldest established fish and chip business was not, as might have been expected,

in the north of England, but in London.

In 1968 Mr Cledwyn Hughes, who was then the Minister of Agriculture, Fisheries and Food, formally presented a plaque made by the Federation to **Malin's,** of Old Ford Road, Bow, which bore the wording 'The world's oldest fish and chip business – Malin's – presented 1968 by the National Federation of Fish Friers to mark 100 years of fish and chips'. The plaque was received by Mr Dennis Malin, the great-great-grandson of the man who founded the business in 1865.

Flour-millers

The vans of **Marriage and Sons,** of Chelmsford, show that the firm was established in 1824.

Just over half a century later, in 1875, **Joseph Rank** rented his first mill, at Holderness Road, Hull. In 1933, when Joseph Rank Limited announced that it was to become a public company, a holding company, Ranks Limited, was floated, with a capital of £7 million, to acquire Joseph Rank Limited.

In 1962, Ranks Limited acquired the Hovis-

Joseph Rank's first mill. *(Ranks Hovis McDougall Ltd)*

Macdougall company and changed its name to **Ranks Hovis McDougall Limited.** Six years later it acquired Cerebos. In the course of 100 years, the business had grown from one young man milling flour in Hull to a food group with annual sales of £700 million and a payroll of 64000 men and women in 15 countries. It is said to be Britain's largest bread-maker with about a quarter of the market.

Another old milling business, with roots in the 18th century, is that of the **Andrews,** of Comber, Northern Ireland. Thomas Andrews was born in 1698, and was working the Upper Mill in Comber on lease or sub-lease grinding corn in 1722. His son John, in 1769, became the owner of the second mill in Ireland to make flour, as distinct from meal. The first such mill had been built in 1765 at Glenoak, Crumlin, County Antrim.

Food-manufacturers

Crosse and Blackwell, of London, dating from 1706, is one of the oldest firms in the food-manufacturing industry. The firm celebrated its quarter-millenary one day after Twinings the tea-merchants had celebrated theirs.

The business began in what is now known as Shaftesbury Avenue, on the site of the old Shaftesbury Theatre. A firm known as 'West and Wyatt' began trading there as 'oilmen' in 1706, and during the following 100 years or so they became famous for their pickles, sauces and condiments. In 1819 two boys, both aged 15, were taken on as apprentices. One was Edmund Crosse, the grandfather of Mr Victor M Crosse, and the other was Thomas Blackwell. In 1829 William Wyatt decided to retire, and the two young men bought the business in 1830 for £600. In 1839 the business was moved to Soho Square.

MILESTONES IN MILLING AND BAKING

Milling

3000 BC   Bread wheats made their appearance. Saddlestones introduced in place of pestles and mortars for grinding grain.

500 BC   Combined flour-mills and bread-bakeries built in Athens.

200 BC   Introduction of rotary mills that were turned by horses or donkeys and also hand-operated rotary mills known as 'querns'.

100 BC   Invention of the water-wheel and its use to grind millstones.

AD 1100   Introduction of wind sail mills in western Europe.

18th century   Transformation of flour-milling into an integrated automatic process.

1860   Invention of the middlings purifier – a step that had an enormous impact on future development of the industry.

c. **1874**   General introduction of the roller mill.

1960   Introduction of air classification, a method of effecting protein displacement whereby from one wheat flours of markedly different protein contents could be obtained.

Baking

4000 BC   Pieces of bread found in the remains of a lake dwelling in Switzerland.

3000–1000 BC   Numerous samples of bread salvaged from Egyptian tombs.

240 BC   Treatise 'Art of Breadmaking' by Chrysippus of Tyana, a city of Cappadocia.

160 BC   Some public bakeries appeared in Rome and became incorporated as a trade guild known as 'Collegium Pistorium'.

1912   Introduction of first non-adjustable bread over-wrapping machine.

1925   Introduction of first adjustable over-wrapping machine. Not until this time did the sale of wrapped bread become considerable.

1928–30   First sliced bread appeared.

1950   Introduction of continuous bread production based on the mechanical ripening of dough.

1960   Activated dough process which permits the use of mechanical ripening without high-speed mixing because of the addition of a blend of reducing and oxidising agents.

1961   Introduction in the UK of the Chorleywood Bread Process in which means of employing mechanical dough ripening (thereby eliminating lengthy bulk fermentation) was adapted to batch production in small bakeries.

Compiled by Dr A J Amos

A modern flour-mill, Selby, Ranks Hovis McDougall Ltd. (*Kershaw Studios*)

Qualiotti, one of the firm's chefs, perfected and marketed the first 'Piccalilli', which appeared in 1838. At the time of the Vienna Universal Exhibition of 1873 the firm was described as 'the largest firm in the world in this branch' (i.e. preserved meats, etc.).

One of the firm's factories at the old Vinegar Brewery in Caledonian Road had one of the largest vats in the world. It held 115 000 gal ($\frac{1}{2}$ million l).

Crosse and Blackwell now forms part of the Nestlé Group, having been taken over in 1960.

Lea and Perrins Limited, of Worcester, were the pioneers of Worcester sauce. William Perrins and John Whealey Lea founded the firm on 1 January 1828. The famous sauce made its first appearance in the 1830s and the recipe is said to have come from Lord Sandys of Ombersley Court, a former Governor of Bengal.

Another old firm in the food-manufacturing industry is **C Shippam Limited,** of Chichester, Sussex. This family business was founded about 1750 and has had at least six generations in the firm. To begin with, the business dealt mainly with provisions, and during the Napoleonic Wars it was constantly sending goods to Portsmouth for the victualling of the dockyard and ships at Spithead.

The firm supplied some of the provisions for Scott's expedition to the South Pole in 1910/12 and other Polar expeditions. In 1924 they supplied a case of miniature jars of meat and fish pastes for the Queen's Doll's House.

Almost as old as Shippam's is the firm of **John Burgess and Son Limited,** of London. They were established in the year 1760. William Burgess, who was a country grocer, sent his son John to London in 1760 to enter the trade of 'Oilman and Italian Warehouseman'. In the Strand he opened what would nowadays be called a delicatessen. His business prospered, and he soon moved to larger premises, from number 101 to 107.

The first issue of *The Times*, which appeared on 1 January 1788, advertised some of

Nestlé Administrative headquarters – Vevey, Switzerland. *(Nestlé-Alimentana)*

Burgess's numerous delicacies. The firm used to claim that, 'of all the commercial undertakings advertised in the First Issue, the House of Burgess alone survives'.

John Burgess invented some of the products that he sold, the most famous of these being his 'Original and Superior Essence of Anchovy'. Lord Nelson took some of Burgess's products with him to the Battle of the Nile, and supplies were also sent to HMS *Victory* in 1805.

The firm received the Royal Warrant as suppliers to Queen Victoria in 1853. Two years later, in 1855, they were sending supplies to Lord Raglan, who was then besieging Sevastopol. In 1910, like Shippam's, they supplied some of the goods for Scott's expedition to the Antarctic.

Another food business dating from the 18th century is **Wall's.** In 1786 Richard Wall, after serving his apprenticeship to a pork butcher in St James's Market, established his family business close by, in Jermyn Street. Until a few years ago the shop still bore his name. It sold meat products and was also used as a simple restaurant. The family of the foun-

der, however, no longer has any connection with the business, which now forms part of Unilever.

The architect of the firm's greatness was Thomas Wall, the grandson of the founder (1846–1930). Wall's was famous for sausages long before the name was associated with ice-cream.

The ice-cream factory in Acton, north London, is said to be the largest ice-cream factory in the world. This was built soon after the First World War, on the site of an old monastic house, and is still known as 'The Friary'.

The Times 1000 (1975–6) shows **Unilever** lying fifth in the list of the 1000 largest UK industrial companies, with sales of more than £2400 million. In the *Fortune* list of August 1976, however, Unilever appears as No 4 in the list of the 500 largest industrial corporations outside the USA, with sales in 1975 of well over $15000 million. As *Fortune* gives Unilever a dual nationality (Britain-Netherlands), the inclusion of the Dutch element may account for the difference in the figures (apart from the difference in the year). In March 1976, the English papers reported Unilever's sales in 1975 as £6760 million, as compared with £5843 million in 1974.

Gelatine

B Young and Company Limited, of Grange Road, London SE1, 'the oldest name in gelatine manufacture', was founded in 1818 for the production of glue and glue size. Although Benjamin Young auctioned the business in 1861, it was known under his name for another 100 years, and is still referred to as Youngs.

It became the headquarters of BGC Gelatine division with Research and Development Department and produced nearly all types of gelatine.

The firm has been taken over by Croda.

Gin

It is commonly believed that gin was first made in Geneva. In fact, the word 'gin' is derived from *genièvre*, the French word for juniper, the berries of which are a main ingredient in the manufacture of gin.

The **Curtis Distillery** in London was founded by John Curtis in 1769. In 1879, the connection between the distillery and the Curtis family was severed, and the distillery became known as the 'Mile End Distillery'. In 1896 the Cannon Brewery bought all the shares of the distillery, and in 1930 the brewery firm of Taylor, Walker and Company acquired the Cannon Brewery. In 1948 the name of the Mile End Distillery was changed back to the Curtis Distillery.

Booth's Distilleries, in Turnmill Street, London, EC1, date their origin from the year 1740. The age of the firm is not in dispute, but the precise significance of the year 1740 is difficult to discover.

Coates and Company, of the Black Friars Distillery at Plymouth, describe themselves as 'Gin Distillers since 1793'. According to a report in the *Daily Telegraph* of 7 July 1958, their 'Plymouth Gin' was made from a recipe which was a family secret handed down from father to son. Only the head of the firm knew the formula and himself conducted the special flavouring.

Coates and Company is now owned by **Long**

John International, the Scotch whisky and gin distillers. There is no longer any connection with the Coates family. The name 'Long John' commemorates 'Long John' Macdonald, who built a distillery at Fort William in the year 1825. But, to quote *The Romance of Long John*, a booklet by Jack House,

'The great whiskies sold under the Long John labels today have no connection with the distillery which still exists at Fort William, below Ben Nevis. Due to the ramifications of modern business, it was the name which has been carried on when it passed into the hands of Long John International.'

Grocers

John James Sainsbury (1844–1928) opened his first shop in 1869, at 173 Drury Lane where, together with his wife Mary Ann (daughter of a dairyman), he established a dairyman's business. J J Sainsbury was a man with a passion for work, order, thrift and

Sainsbury's Drury Lane shop in 1958. (*J Sainsbury Ltd*)

Part of Sainsbury's supermarket in Coldhams Lane, Cambridge, opened in December 1974. *(J Sainsbury Ltd)*

self-discipline. Business started growing and from 1876 he established several branches in London. In those days working conditions were hard everywhere, and Sainsbury's was no exception. His staff started work at 7.30 am every day except on Sunday. On Tuesday, Wednesday and Thursday trading ended at 9.15 pm, on Friday at 10.45 pm and on Saturday the shop was open till midnight.

In 1906 his sons John Benjamin, George, Arthur and Alfred Sainsbury were working with their father, while Frank became a farmer in Suffolk. He started an egg-collecting round, regularly buying fresh eggs from local farms which he then sent to Sainsbury's – graded and tested. He was the pioneer in this field.

In 1914 Sainsbury's had been selling tea, coffee, cocoa, sugar, jam, syrup, canned fruit, salmon, sardines and milk; in 1920 J B Sainsbury introduced 'own label' groceries in a separate department and they also began to develop their meat trade.

After J J Sainsbury's death in 1928 John Benjamin Sainsbury, a single-minded man of immense vitality, became Chairman and Governing Director of the company.

In 1936 a large sausage- and pie-making plant was built at Blackfriars, London, and in 1938 James Sainsbury became responsible for its direction.

In 1938 J B Sainsbury handed over the management of the firm to his two sons Alan (now Lord Sainsbury) and Robert (now Sir Robert). Alan was responsible for trading matters while Robert concentrated on administration, finance and personnel. Alan went to the USA in 1949 to study the deep-frozen food industry and there became interested in their self-service technique of retailing. On his return the Croydon branch was adapted for self-service trading in 1950, and by 1954 there were four self-service shops established.

After the war, staff had desired shorter

working hours and the pattern of trading began to change. In 1961 Sainsbury's pioneered the five-day trading and working week and became the first retail food company in England to introduce a computerised stock replenishment system.

Lord Sainsbury's three sons John, Simon and Timothy are directors; and Sir Robert's only son David joined in 1963.

Sainsbury's became a public company in July 1973 and in the same year made two important range extensions into textiles and hardware. In 1974 they opened the first of a chain of freezer centres and in 1975 announced that they were joining with British Home Stores to form a company to develop a new concept in hypermarket trading.

Associated companies include Haverhill Meat Products Limited (jointly owned by J Sainsbury Limited and Canada Packers Limited of Toronto), Sainsbury-Spillers Limited (a joint venture to strengthen further Sainsbury's trading position in the egg and poultry industries), Sainsbury's Pauls and Whites Limited (a joint venture to undertake commercial production of quality pigs).

Sainsbury's operate two farms in Scotland, one at Kinermony, where the Kinermony herd of pedigree Aberdeen Angus cattle was founded in 1945 while the other is a commercial fattening farm of 1000 acres at Inverquohomery.

About 31 000 people are employed in the company, of which 15 600 are part-time. The average supermarket turnover is about £55 000 per week, compared with a national supermarket average of about £15 000. The total number of lines stocked is approximately 3800.

Total selling area in Sainsbury's supermarkets stands at 198 528 m² (2 136 935 ft²) as at March 1976.

Sainsbury's now have 214 stores, of which 175 are supermarkets and 18 are freezer centres.

The name **Allied Suppliers** could hardly be said to be a household word, but it covers such well-known shop names as **Lipton's,** the merry-sounding **Maypole** and the harmoniously dactylic **Home and Colonial.** The Maypole derived from a provision business in Birmingham that was in existence in 1819. Thomas Lipton opened his first shop in 1871.

The old grocer's shop of **Paxton and**

Whitfield in Jermyn Street, London, not far from Piccadilly Circus, proclaims its age both outside and inside. The firm dates its foundation from the year 1797 and is, therefore, a later arrival in Jermyn Street than Floris (see page 92). The railings outside, to guard the front of the shop, are similar to those still standing outside the chemist's shop of Savory and Moore in Bond Street (see page 89).

Vye and Son Limited, of Ramsgate, 'the Kentish grocers', date their history from 1817, when Sarah Vye and her son Jesse set up in business together in a shop at the junction of Queen Street and Cliff Street. In the course of time, a number of branches were opened, and in 1955 the business was taken over by Allied Suppliers. Mr N G H Taylor, the great-great-great-grandson of Sarah Vye, remained as Managing Director of Vye's.

The wholesale grocery firm of **Alfred Button and Sons Limited,** of Uxbridge, Middlesex, developed from a grocery shop that was opened by Alfred Button in the High Street, Uxbridge, in 1798. It grew into one of the largest grocery wholesalers in the south of England, and in 1957 it became part of the Booker Group (see the *Middlesex County Times* of 17 March 1967 and page 29).

A much older grocery business than any of those so far mentioned in this section, the splendidly named firm **Upward and Rich,** of Newport, Isle of Wight, was founded in 1650 and held the distinction of being the oldest established wholesale grocer in Great Britain. Although they moved, a few years ago, to new premises in Petticoat Lane, their subsidiary companies continued to trade from their original site in Pyle Street, Newport. The company still had the original documents proving the sale of land in 1650. In 1974, after an existence of more than 300 years, Upward and Rich were taken over by Associated Food Holdings Limited, of London.

Yet another old firm of wholesale grocers is **Fitch Lovell Limited,** of London. They were established in 1784.

Inns

Most old inns should probably be regarded as old buildings rather than as old businesses in the sense in which we have defined the term.

There are various claimants to the title of the UK's oldest inn. The foremost claimants include **The Angel and Royal** (*c.* 1450) at Grantham, Lincolnshire, which has cellar masonry dated 1213; the **George** (early 15th century) at Norton St Philip, Somerset; the oldest Welsh inn, the **Skirrid Mountain Inn,** Llanvihangel Crucorney, Gwent recorded in 1110; **The Trip to Jerusalem** in Nottingham, with foundations believed to date back to 1070; **The Fighting Cocks,** St Albans, Hertfordshire (an 11th-century structure on an 8th-century site) and the **Godbegot,** Winchester, Hampshire dating to 1002. An origin as early as AD 560 has been claimed for **Ye Olde Ferry Boat Inn** at Holywell, Cambridgeshire. There is some evidence that it antedates the local church, built in 980, but the earliest documents are not dated earlier than 1100. There is evidence that the **Bingley Arms,** Bardsey, near Leeds, West Yorkshire, restored and extended in 1738, existed as the **Priest's Inn** according to Bardsey Church records dated 905.

Liqueurs

The liqueur 'Drambuie' is made by the **Drambuie Liqueur Company** of Edinburgh. The following account of 'Prince Charles Edward's liqueur' is based on an article in the *Wine and Spirit Trade Record* of 16 August 1955, entitled 'The Romance of Drambuie'.

After the Rebellion of 1745, Prince Charles Edward (Bonnie Prince Charlie) fled for his life to the Isle of Skye. When he left for France, in 1746, he left to Mackinnon the secret formula of his personal liqueur. For nearly a century and a half the Mackinnons kept the treasure to themselves. It was used at the annual Gathering of the Clan, but the name was not registered as a trademark until 1892. (The name comes from the Gaelic *An dram buidheach* meaning 'the drink that satisfies'.)

In 1906, Malcolm Mackinnon decided to produce the liqueur on a commercial scale on the mainland. The name was transferred to the Drambuie Liqueur Company, and Mackinnon went to Edinburgh, where he began to make the liqueur in a cellar under Union Street. The base of the liqueur is a blend of Highland malt whiskies, but the formula still remains a family secret.

During the first year of the business, only twelve cases of the liqueur were sold. Since then, however, it has developed into the largest liqueur-producing plant in the British Commonwealth and Empire.

Mustard

In the year 1814 a miller named Jeremiah Colman, who had been milling flour for ten years, leased a mill at Stoke Holy Cross, about four miles south of Norwich, whose owner had started to make mustard. The mill had also been used for paper-making, but Jeremiah opted for flour-milling and mustard-milling. The firm of **J and J Colman** dates from 15 February 1823, when Jeremiah, who had no family, entered into a partnership with his nephew James.

The company's history up to the Second World War has been told by Dr S H Edgar in *The History of J & J Colman* (unpublished). Dr Edgar describes the rise of Colman's from a small country mill to a world-wide enterprise, a development not unlike that of the enterprise started by another miller, Joseph Rank (see page 21 and illustration page 29).

Sausage Casings

C Edwards and Son, of 33/35 Charterhouse Square, London, are described as sausage-casing processors, and their letter-heading shows them to have been established in 1600. According to Mr G W Edwards, the Managing Director, the firm is believed to have been started by an Edwards and to have been in the family ever since it began.

Smoked Salmon

Barnetts of Frying Pan Alley, London, E1, claim to be 'the oldest private salmon curing company in Great Britain'. An advertisement in *Signature* for December 1967 offered 'Sides of Scotch Smoked Salmon from their 90-year-old smoke holes'.

Sugar

The growth in the number and scope of what are hideously but aptly called 'multinational

Mustard shop – J and J Colman, Norwich. (*John Blomfield*)

conglomerates' creates problems of classification in a work such as this. At one time the names of Tate and Lyle, and of Booker and McConnell, were almost synonymous with sugar, but this is no longer the case.

Tate and Lyle, for instance, took full-page advertisements in the papers in January 1975 to explain how relatively unimportant the refining of sugar had become. Their Mr Cube was depicted as a 'Man of Many Parts', with interests in shipping, international trading, engineering, tank farming and road transport as well as in sugar-refining. The accounts for the year ending 30 September 1974 showed that the production and refining of sugar accounted for little more than a quarter of the total profits for the period.

Generations of both Tates and Lyles have been concerned with sugar. The two businesses merged in 1921. Tate had specialised in cubes, Lyle in syrup. One of the relatively unchanging things in a changing world is the design on the tin of 'Lyle's Golden Syrup', with its picture of the insect-infested lion and the caption 'Out of the strong came forth sweetness.' The words are taken from the Book of Judges (14 : 14).

For the greater part of the 19th century the Tate and Lyle businesses were headed by Abram Lyle (1820–91) and Sir Henry Tate (1819–99). Sir Henry Tate lived long enough to see the opening, in August 1897, of the Gallery named after him. He had presented to the nation a collection of pictures valued at £75 000 and contributed £80 000 towards the cost of erecting a gallery in which to house them. (See illustrations pages 30 and 33.)

Another name long associated with sugar is that of **Booker McConnell.** Like Tate & Lyle, it presents a problem of taxonomy. While its origins were in sugar production and trading with Guyana, its operations have extended into engineering, shipping and general trading services. It operates in a number of countries.

MILESTONES IN THE HISTORY OF SUGAR IN THIS COUNTRY

1264   First recorded use of sugar in England, ordered by the King for the Royal Household.

1544   First sugar-refinery opened.

1813   Invention of the vacuum pan, shortly to be used for boiling sugar.

1843   Adoption of the centrifugal machine by the refining industry.

1878   Henry Tate opened a refinery at Silvertown, London E16, primarily for the production of cube sugar.

1882   Abram Lyle built a refinery at Plaistow, London E16, where 'Golden Syrup' was the speciality.

1921   Formation of Tate and Lyle Limited.

1924   First successful beet-sugar processing factory opened. Many earlier attempts had been fated.

1936   Formation of British Sugar Corporation by the Government.

1949–52   Birth of 'Mr Cube' and the refining industry's successful defence against nationalisation.

1950   First delivery of bulk granulated sugar to industrial users.

1951   Commonwealth Sugar Agreement negotiated.

1952   Start of bulk shipments of raw cane sugar to the UK, and gradual phasing out of jute bags.

1961   Tate and Lyle Refineries Limited formed as the main subsidiary of the parent company, Tate and Lyle Limited.

1975   End of Commonwealth Sugar Agreement.

Compiled by Tate and Lyle Limited

Tate & Lyle's parcel tanker *Anco Sceptre. (Tate & Lyle Ltd)*

The factory and part of the nucleus estate of the Mumias Sugar Company in Kenya, in which Booker McConnell have a 5 per cent share of the equity and which is both managed, and technical services provided, by Bookers Agricultural and Technical Services. The factory produced 59000 tons of sugar in 1975 and is currently being expanded to produce 75000 tons of sugar a year. (*Booker McConnell Limited*)

In Britain alone, it operates nine engineering factories, 72 wholesale depots and 423 supermarkets and shops.

In 1815 Josiah Booker went out to British Guiana (then known as 'Demerary'), which had been ceded to Britain by the Dutch in 1814. He was later joined by two of his kinsmen, and together they founded the firm of Booker Brothers.

John McConnell went out to Demerara in 1846. In 1874 he founded the firm of John McConnell and Company in London. This business had a close association with George Booker and Company, a firm that George Booker had established in Liverpool in 1832, and in 1900 the businesses were merged to form Booker Brothers, McConnell and Company. In 1939 Booker's merged with Curtis

Campbell and Company, who had been engaged in trade in Demerara and London since the end of the 18th century, when Demerara was still a Dutch possession.

In May 1976, Booker McConnell's sugar and other businesses in Guyana were acquired by the government. Its interest in the growing and manufacturing of cane sugar continues, however, through the provision of agricultural management and technical services to a number of other developing countries around the world. Its trading interests range from health foods to rum. The subsidiary company United Rum Merchants markets such well-known brands as Lamb's Navy rum and Lemon Hart rum, the latter having been first produced by a gentleman named Mr Lemon Hart in 1804.

Sweets

The firm of **S Parkinson and Son (Doncaster) Limited,** whose address is Royal Butter-Scotch Works, Doncaster, was established in the year 1817. Like Rowntrees (see page 19) it started its career as a firm of family grocers, and among the commodities it sold in those early days were butter-scotch and baking powder. Queen Victoria accepted a gift of butter-scotch when she visited Doncaster in 1852, and from that time the product has been known as 'Royal Doncaster Butter-Scotch'.

The name 'butter-scotch' is derived from the manner in which the ingredients were cooked: 'It was said that the butter and sugar were scorched or scotched, hence Butter-scorched or scotched, which through the years has become shortened to Butter-scotch'.

Tea

In October 1956, **R Twining and Company Limited,** of 216 Strand, London, celebrated their quarter-millenary, having been founded in the year 1706. The Mayor of Westminster

Thomas Twining 1675–1741, after the original painting by Hogarth. *(Antony Miles Ltd)*

unveiled a plaque in honour of the founder of the business, and said that he believed Twining's to be the oldest ratepayers in the City of Westminster. (This claim might be challenged by Berry Brothers and Rudd, the wine-merchants, see page 39.) The firm gave a luncheon at the Hyde Park Hotel to celebrate '250 years, the same family, on the same site, in the same business'.

Thomas Twining (1675–1741) (see portrait, below) started business at Tom's Coffee House in Devereux Court, off the Strand, in the year 1706. Thomas Twining soon turned his attention to the sale of tea, and in 1711 he was Purveyor of Tea to Queen Anne. His first ledger was begun in 1712. This is now lost, but ledgers from 1718 can still be seen. Houses in those days were not yet numbered, and Thomas Twining chose for his sign the Golden Lion.

In 1783 Richard Twining I, the third generation to take over the business, advised William Pitt to reduce the heavy duty on tea, because of which large quantities of tea were smuggled into the country. In the Commutation Act of 1784 the old duty was replaced by a small *ad valorem* duty of $2\frac{1}{2}$d to $6\frac{1}{2}$d (1p to 3p) a pound; this made smuggling no longer worth while, and the revenue actually increased.

Through seven generations the Twining family has carried on the business founded by Thomas Twining in the year 1706.

The great change in the 19th century was the gradual displacement of China tea. As late as 1867 the tea from Assam represented only 5 per cent of the tea consumed in this country, but by 1887 it had risen to 50 per cent. In the year 1928, India provided about 56 per cent of our tea and Ceylon 28 per cent, while China provided less than 2 per cent.

In 1910, Twining's celebrated their bi-centenary, for it was then believed that the business had begun in 1710. In 1924, Twining's provided models of a tea-chest and a coffee-tin for the Queen's Doll's House.

Aytoun Ellis wrote in *The Penny Universities*, his book about London's coffee-houses, 'There must be few if any family businesses with an uninterrupted history covering nearly three centuries; there is none with a more romantic one.' There are, in fact, a number of such businesses. Only a few days after Twining's

Tate & Lyle's Thames Refinery. *(Tate & Lyle Ltd)*

MV *Booker Vanguard*, one of the cargo liners of the Booker Line, the merchant-shipping fleet of Booker McConnell, loading sugar by night at the Demerara Sugar Terminal, Georgetown, Guyana. *(Booker McConnell Limited)*

quarter-millenary luncheon, Mr Cooper of Scott's (see page 86) wrote to *The Times* to point out that his own firm had been in the same family and in the same line of business – basket-making – since 1661. He had, however, to admit that his firm had moved three times in its existence. Twining's record, remarkable as it is, nevertheless had to yield pride of place until the year 1971 to that of B Smiths (Thirsk) Limited, who had been on the same site, in the same family and in the same trade since 1580 (see page 61).

Mr Early of Witney, in a letter that appeared in *The Times* of 9 November 1956, also challenged Twining's record. One of the mills of Charles Early and Company at Witney has been used for the manufacture of blankets since the firm's history began in 1669, and had in fact been used for the same purpose even earlier (see page 63). There are one or two other firms that beat Twining's record.

A younger firm, **W H Whittard,** describe themselves as 'tea and coffee merchants since 1886'. Is it always 'tea and coffee', like 'Oxford and Cambridge' or 'ham and eggs'?

The firm of **Davison, Newman and Company,** formerly at 14 Creechurch Lane, London, EC3, is said to have been founded in 1650 by Daniel Rawlinson, grocer. The sign of the Crown and Three Sugar Loaves still indicated the nature of the business, and a sign outside the shop carried the inscription 'the oldest tea-men in the world'. Some of the firm's tea was thrown into the sea at the famous Boston Tea-party of 1773, and the tins of tea now sold by the firm carry a reproduction of the firm's petition to the Crown for compensation.

Until 1890 the business was at 44 Fenchurch Street. The Daniel Rawlinson who is said to have started the business was a friend of Samuel Pepys (see the Diary for 28 September 1660) and is said to have been the first English grocer to sell a pound of tea. The London Hospital has been a customer of the firm since 1754.

The firm's own book, *At The Three Sugar Loaves and Crown* by Owen Rutter (1938), says that the earliest printed reference to the firm is in Henry Kent's *Directory* for 1736, which mentions 'Rawlinson, Thomas, grocer, Fenchurch Street'. Rutter also says: 'A tradition handed down from generation to generation gives 1650 as the year in which Davison, Newman and Co. was founded.'

According to C G Harper's *Queer Things about London*, this was 'the oldest business actually in the City of London'. The Whitechapel Bell Foundry (see page 67) is admittedly older, but lies just outside the City. Skilbeck's, however, also date from 1650 (see page 143) and were still in the City in 1923 when Harper was writing, but he does not mention them.

Davison, Newman and Company is now incorporated in the West Indian Produce Association Limited.

Brooke, Bond and Company was established in 1869. David Wainwright's centenary history *Brooke Bond – a Hundred Years*, might have been sub-titled *The Man Who Never Was.*

Arthur Brooke, born in 1845, was the son of a wholesale tea-merchant, and in 1869 he set himself up in business as a retailer of tea, at 29 Market Street, Manchester. There never was a Mr Bond, but Arthur Brooke added the name to his own because it 'seemed to him to sound well'.

The year 1968 saw the merger with **Liebig** to form Brooke Bond Liebig, one of the largest food-manufacturing and distributing companies in the UK. Liebig's Extract of Meat Company was the slightly older partner in the merger, having been incorporated in London in 1865. Brooke Bond Liebig ranked No 67 in *The Times 1000 (1975–6)* list of the largest UK industrial companies with a turnover of nearly £380 million.

Vines and Vineyards

The famous vine at Hampton Court was planted in the year 1769, and has been producing grapes for some 200 years. It has, therefore, a right to be counted among the oldest productive enterprises in the country.

According to Lewis Wilshire's *The Vale of Berkeley*, the Roman soldiers cultivated a vineyard at Tortworth in Gloucestershire, near the Camp of Bloody Acre. This vineyard survived well into the 19th century when, as the result of a dispute over tithes, the owner had it destroyed rather than let the local rector have a tenth of his grape-crop.

Lincoln Corporation used to claim that its vineyard in the grounds of the Old Bishop's Palace was the most northerly in the world, but this title has now passed, by a margin of three minutes of latitude, to **Mr Reresby Sitwell's** vineyard at Renishaw Hall in Derbyshire, lying at 53° 18′ North.

Whisky and Whiskey

According to Sir Robert Bruce Lockhart's *Scotch – The Whisky of Scotland in Fact and Story*,

'the history of malt whisky lies shrouded in the mists of the Celtic dawn. . . . Some romantic writers have gone even so far as to claim that uisge-beatha was the tipple of Noah and that Dionysos was the god of whisky before he was the god of wine!'

We cannot hope to trace our story as far back as this, but there was undoubtedly a good deal of illicit distilling before the trade became organised after the passing of the Act of 1825. One of the few dates that almost everybody knows – 1820 – relates to the year in which **John Walker** established himself as a grocer and wine- and spirit-merchant in Kilmarnock. The famous poster about Johnnie Walker – 'Born 1820, still going strong' – was first used in 1908.

As in the case of old breweries, it is not possible to say definitely which is the oldest whisky-distillery in the country. For many years a good deal of whisky was made illicitly by the smugglers (who were manufacturers as well as distributors). A number of distilleries which later became respectable enterprises were originally carried on by the smugglers, who naturally left few records of their activities behind them. It was only after the Act of 1825 had brought some semblance of order into the distilling industry that many of them assumed their formal organisation. There were illicit stills in Ireland as well as in Scotland.

In 1887, Alfred Barnard published a work on *The Whisky Distilleries of the United Kingdom*. (See also page 13). In all, he described 129 distilleries in Scotland (including no less than 21 in Campbelltown), 28 in Ireland and four in England. There were apparently no distilleries in Wales. Here, briefly, are the oldest distilleries in the three countries, arranged as

Worker at the Cardow Distillery J Walker & Sons Ltd. *(Cryer & Marchant Limited)*

far as possible in chronological order according to the information given by Barnard:

Scotland

At the time of Barnard's visit, the Cameron Bridge Distillery at Windygates in Fifeshire was in charge of **Hugh V Haig,** the son of the John Haig who worked the distillery from 1824 to 1877, the year when it was merged into the **Distillers Company Limited.** Hugh V Haig represented the 'sixth successive generation engaged on distillation'. Barnard says that the distillery was in operation 'many years' before the time of John Haig, and that 'the whisky made here is said to have no rival in the world'.

According to Sir Robert Bruce Lockhart, the connection of the Haig family with whisky goes back to the year 1623, when Robert Haig left Bemersyde. The label on the bottles of 'Haig's Gold Label Scotch Whisky' describes the producers as 'the Oldest Distillers of Scotch Whisky in the World'. The label also states that 'Whisky has been a study with us, not only for a lifetime, but for generation upon generation.'

James Laver has recounted the history of the business in *The House of Haig*, published in 1958. It was a Robert Haig who left the ancestral estates at Bemersyde about 1627 (not 1623, as Bruce Lockhart has it) and settled at Throsk in Stirlingshire. Like most farmers in those days he carried on a little distilling, and he had in fact studied the most modern methods of distilling in Holland, where he had relations. The John Haig who gave his name to the business built the Cameron Bridge Distillery in 1824. He was the great-great-great-great-grandson of Robert. John's youngest son, born in 1861, was the future Field-Marshal Earl Haig of Bemersyde. One of John's daughters, Henrietta, married William Jameson, thus forging another link between the two famous distilling families, as the eldest daughter of an earlier John Haig (who died in 1773) had married John Jameson, the founder of John Jameson and Son, of Dublin.

The **Lagavulin Distillery,** Islay, according to Barnard, 'is said to be one of the oldest distilleries in Islay, the business to a certain extent having been founded in 1742'.

The **Glenochil Distillery** near Stirling was established in 1746. This distillery also made 'an enormous quantity of what is called German yeast'. The **Langholm Distillery** at Langholm was established in 1765.

The **Dundashill Distillery** at Glasgow was founded in the year 1770 by John Harvey, who was 'one of the first three licensed Distillers in Scotland'. Dundashill 'may claim to be one of the very first distilleries established in Glasgow'. Since 1770, too, the **Yoker Distillery** near Glasgow had been in the hands of the Harvey family, and 'was in existence previous to that remote date'.

The **Glenturret Distillery** near Crieff was 'said to be one of the oldest in Scotland, having been established in 1775'. The **Grange Distillery** at Burntisland was established in 1786, and the **Oban Distillery** at Oban was built in the year 1794.

Barnard said that distilling was carried on in the neighbourhood of the **Rieclachan Distillery,** Campbelltown, 'from the remotest days of antiquity'. He is inclined to use words such as this to denote any period before the 19th

century. The distillery itself dated from 1824.

The **Milton Duff Distillery** at Elgin, mostly rebuilt in 1824, was yet another distillery on a site previously used by the smugglers.

Barnard says that the **Caledonian Distillery** at Edinburgh, which was built in 1855, had an annual output of more than 2 million gal (0.1 hl), and was at that time 'the second largest grain distillery in the United Kingdom'.

Ireland

The Brusna Distillery at Kilbeggan, belonging to **John Locke and Company,** was 'said to be the oldest in Ireland, having been founded in the year 1750'.

Almost as old was the Thomas Street Distillery in Dublin, nearly opposite the main buildings of Guinness and Company. This distillery, belonging to **George Roe and Company Limited,** was bought by Peter Roe in 1757, when it was 'quite a small concern',

Still House – the very heart of new Midleton. *(Irish Distillers Ltd)*

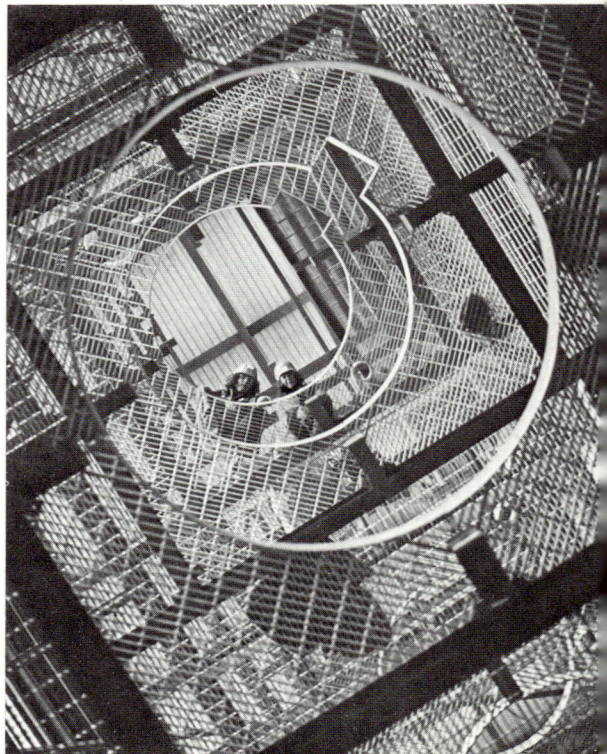

but it had since developed into a vast undertaking covering 17 acres (7 ha) of ground and with an annual output that had reached nearly 2 million gal (o.1 m. hl), although, says Barnard, this 'lately has been reduced considerably'.

The Marrowbone Lane Distillery in Dublin, belonging to **William Jameson and Company,** was bought by the ancestors of the owners in 1779. In that year also was erected the North Mall Distillery at Cork, which once belonged to **Francis Wise,** the producer of 'Wise's Old Whisky'.

The Bow Street Distillery of **John Jameson** in Dublin is 'one of the oldest in Ireland', having been established about the year 1780, although the grandfather of the Jameson who was in charge of the business when Barnard visited it did not buy the distillery until the beginning of the 19th century. Its output was about 1 million gal (0.05 m. hl) a year.

Although Barnard referred to the Brusna Distillery as 'the oldest in Ireland', this does not prevent him from writing about the **Bushmills Distillery** at Bushmills, County Antrim:

'The first record we have of this, no doubt the eldest Distillery in Ireland, is in the year 1743, when it was in the hands of a band of smugglers; but in 1784 we find it recognized as a legitimate Distillery'.

Clearly it depends on which of these dates is taken whether this distillery is to be regarded as older or younger than the Brusna Distillery, which was founded in 1750.

The 'Old Bushmills' whiskey from the distillery at Bushmills, County Antrim, Northern Ireland, is advertised as 'the oldest whiskey in the world', although the label on the bottle tells us that the distillery was established as comparatively recently as 1784.

The explanation of this apparent discrepancy is to be found in the booklet entitled *Old Bushmills*, of 1938. In order to control the manufacture of whiskey in Ireland in the reign of Henry VIII, an Act was passed in Drogheda in 1556 to restrict its manufacture to licensed sources. The King's Deputy of the Plantation of Ulster was authorised to grant licences, and in 1608 he granted a licence to himself to distil whiskey at the place now called Bushmills.

The date on the label, 1784, was the year in which distillers came under Excise Survey, the duty (originally at the rate of 4d (2p) a gallon) that had first been imposed in 1661 having been 'honoured in the breach far more than observance'.

An article in the *Financial Times* of 6 September 1972 stated that the Bushmills Distillery (now part of the Bass Charrington Group) produces the only Irish whiskey in the UK and 'is said to be the oldest distillery in the world'. The omission of 'whisky' or 'whiskey' before 'distillery' leaves this statement open to question. Even if we accept the date of 1608 for the origin of Bushmills, we shall find at least one firm of distillers laying claim to this title, with a history going back to 1575, as well as another firm dating from the 16th century, although not always on the same site (see pages 46 and 48).

The **Abbey Street Distillery,** in Londonderry, was said to be 'the largest in Ireland; the buildings alone cover eight acres of ground'. The Thomas Street Distillery in Dublin, however, covered 17 acres (7 ha) of ground, but Barnard does not say how many of the 17 acres were covered with buildings.

A curious old book entitled *Truths About Whisky*, published in 1878, was issued by four firms of Dublin distillers to explain how genuine whisky was made and to warn the public against the inferior stuff known as 'silent spirit'. The book also contains a brief history of the four firms.

It says of **John Jameson and Son** that 'its origin cannot now be traced', but that it must have been before 1802, when the distillery passed into the hands of the ancestors of the present proprietors. The distillery of Wm Jameson and Company is said to have been in the possession of the family of the present proprietors since the year 1779. The John's Lane Distillery of **John Power and Son** was established in 1791, while the Thomas Street Distillery of George Roe and Company 'was founded before the middle of the 18th century, and became the property of an ancestor of the present proprietor, Mr. Henry Roe, junior, in the year 1757'.

The information about Wm Jameson and Company seems to be contradicted by the reproduction of one of their labels at the end of the book. This gives their date of establishment as 1799, not 1779. John Jameson now date their origin from 1780.

John's Lane Distillery, Dublin. *(Irish Distillers Ltd)*

England

Barnard does not mention a single distillery in Wales, and even in England there were only ten licensed distillers, 'most of them confined to the manufacture of Plain Spirit for rectifying or manufacturing purposes'. Only four of the English distillers were deemed to fall within the scope of Barnard's book; two in Liverpool (Vauxhall and Bank Hill), one in Bristol and one in London.

The **Vauxhall Distillery** in Liverpool was founded in 1781 and had an output of 2 million gal (0.1 m. hl) a year. The **Lea Valley Distillery** at Stratford, London, was 'the only Malt Distillery in England'. The Bristol Distillery was 'said to be the most ancient in England . . .', a few lines later it is described as 'one of the oldest in England having been founded in the 17th century'.

Wine bar

The **Wine Shades** in Martin Lane, just off Cannon Street, in the City of London, was described in the *Daily Telegraph* of 27 December 1974 as 'probably the oldest wine bar in the world', although no date was given. It must, however, have been older than the **Jamaica Wine House** in St Michael's Alley, off Cornhill, also mentioned, which was said to be well established in 1720.

An article in *The Times* of 22 March 1972 dealt with a public inquiry at Guildhall that was examining an application to demolish Ye Olde Wine Shades. It was said that a notice above the black wooden front claimed that the establishment had been 'established here since 1663', but nobody at the inquiry had offered any evidence to support that date.

Wine-merchants
(For wine-shippers, see page 54)

Hedges and Butler Limited, the wine-merchants of Regent Street, London, celebrated their 300th anniversary in 1967. In the course of the celebrations they entertained some of their fellow tercentenarians to lunch. An account of that event is given on page 175.

The business has not always been in Regent Street. It was established in the year 1657 by Edmund Harris in Hungerford Street, off the Strand. On Harris's death the business passed to William Hedges, who had married a great-granddaughter of Harris. The Butlers appeared in the 19th century, when James Butler married the daughter of a second William Hedges.

The business was transferred to Regent Street in 1811. The present shop dates only from 1922, but some of the cellars beneath it date from the 17th century and are, therefore, older than Regent Street itself. The firm obtained its first Royal Warrant, as suppliers of wine to William IV, in 1830.

There are several other firms of wine-merchants with a history or tradition going back to the 17th century. **Christopher and Company** lost all their old records in the war, but the emblem on the outside of their catalogue describes them as 'Wine Merchants in the Parish of St. James's, Est. since the Great Fire of 1666'.

Christopher's, formerly of Jermyn Street and now of 4 Ormond Yard, St James's (which is partly the same building approached from a different direction) once claimed to be London's oldest established independent wine-merchants. The firm is said to have been founded by a smuggler called Mr Christopher, who specialised in running cognac and Dutch gin. He worked from a base on the Isle of Dogs opposite Greenwich, but later he turned respectable and moved to Bloomsbury. The firm's first premises are said to have been destroyed in the Great Fire of 1666.

In August 1972 it was announced that Christopher and Company, described as London's oldest independent wine-merchant, had been taken over by Scottish and Newcastle Breweries.

The *Financial Times* of 31 August 1972 went on, somewhat rashly, to say that the founding of the firm in the 17th century, 'probably in 1666', gave them a claim to being 'Britain's and indeed Europe's and the world's oldest wine merchants'. A letter in the *Financial Times* of 8 September 1972 suggested that Christopher's themselves made no such claim to

pre-eminence in the matter of age, and went on to mention Stallards and Oldfields in this country, as well as the Trier business of 1377 and the Würzburg business of 1319 (see page 54).

J and G Oldfield Limited, of York, were 'established 1664 in the reign of Charles II'. The notice outside the premises at 3 St Sampson's Square, York, proclaims them to be 'Wine Merchants – the Oldest in England'. Very little, unfortunately, seems to be known about their history, and it is, therefore, difficult to verify this claim.

Associated with Oldfield's is the firm of **Josiah Stallard and Sons Limited,** of Worcester. According to the records of Worcester Cathedral, a member of the Stallard family supplied Communion wine to the Cathedral in the years 1642–3, and the firm's price-list, therefore, proclaims it to have been 'established prior to 1642'. This date is prominently displayed on the shop-front of their premises in Worcester.

Yet another firm of wine-merchants with a foot in the 17th century is **Henekeys Limited,** 22 and 23 High Holborn, London WC1, who claim to have been established in the year 1695. Mr George Henekey, who gave his name to the business, did not come upon the scene until the early 1830s, but the premises now occupied by the firm or, rather, the premises that used to stand on this site, have a much longer history than that. At the end of the 17th century a wine-house stood here, which was much frequented by the lawyers from the neighbouring Gray's Inn as well as by merchants and tradesmen from the City.

Another interesting old firm, whose shop-front proudly announces that it was 'established in the XVIIth century', is **Berry Brothers and Rudd Limited** of 3 St James's Street, London SW1. The history of the firm has been admirably told by H Warner Allen in *Number Three Saint James's Street*.

Berry Brothers, wrote Warner Allen in 1950, is a business 'with a connection of kinship and affairs unbroken through nearly two and a half centuries'. The business was not always that of a wine-merchant, for it began as an 'Italian Warehouseman or Grocer, at the Sign of the Coffee Mill'. The old sign outside the shop still portrays a coffee-mill, and the name is

Berry Brothers and Rudd Limited – the interior of No 3 St James's Street, London from the drawing by Sir Muirhead Bone. *(Berry Brothers & Rudd Ltd)*

still to be found on the beautifully balanced weighing-beam inside the shop which may well be 300 years old.

The exact year of the firm's origin is unknown; it may have been started in 1696 'but it seems safer to date its origin from 1699, when the rates were being paid by the Widow Bourne whose family name was a year or two later absorbed by marriage in the patronymic of Pickering – Pickering, a name that was for over a century to be the hall-mark of the highest quality coffee and tea'. The quaint little 18th-century court behind the shop is called Pickering's Court still. William Pickering married the daughter of the Widow Bourne, and took over the business about the year 1702.

'Little Ealing', an article which appeared in the *Middlesex County Times* for 22 September 1956, mentioned William Pickering.

'This latter gentleman had a high-class grocery and wine business at "The Coffee Mill" in St. James's Street. The pretty cul-de-sac near the bottom of that street, known to-day as Pickering Court, perpetuates his memory.'

The writer of the article has confused this William Pickering with his father, the first William Pickering, who died in 1734. It was the father who gave his name to the court, which was built between 1731 and 1734. Further, although the business of 'Number Three' is now devoted exclusively to wine, there is no evidence that it was anything other than a high-class grocer's shop in the days of the Pickerings.

John Clarke, who seems to have been a relation of the Pickerings, was taken into partnership and his name was added to the firm's title by 1761. It was about this time that the firm began the custom of weighing its distinguished customers on the great scales, and for 200 years the weighing-books have provided a record of the weights of some of the best-known families in the country. The earliest surviving entry dates from the year

1765, but there seem to have been earlier books, now lost.

John Clarke died in 1788. His daughter Mary had married John Berry, a wine-merchant of Exeter. Clarke intended the business to pass to her son, George (1787–1854), and so a relation, John Browne, was brought in to act as caretaker. The name Clarke on the shop-front gave place to Browne in 1788, and in 1813 George Berry took charge of the business. He had been working in the business since 1803, when he came up to London from Exeter.

Two of his sons, George Berry II and Henry Berry, succeeded him, and carried on the business under the name of George and Henry Berry, later shortened to Berry Brothers and Company. They in turn were succeeded by a son of each, and by the end of the 19th century the business was in the hands of one grandson of George Berry II and one grandson of Henry Berry. Mr Anthony Berry, the present head of the firm, is thus a direct descendant of the John Clarke who came into the business about 200 years ago.

The shop appears today much as it appeared in the time of William Pickering, the damage done by German bombs having been skilfully repaired. To enter it is to step back through 200 years. (See illustration, page 40.)

It is not known just when 'Number Three' began to deal in wines as well as in groceries, but it appears to have been some time in the 1830s. The grocery side of the business was finally given up in the year 1896, when the remaining stocks of tea, coffee and cocoa were sold to Fry's, the grocer's shop in Duke Street, not very far away.

When the Queen's Doll's House was being equipped, Berry Brothers were given the task of supplying the tiny bottles of wine for the cellars.

Justerini and Brooks moved to 61 St James's Street from 153 New Bond Street. This is another firm of wine-merchants which has been 'established over 200 years'. The history of the firm has been told by Mr Dennis Wheatley in *The Seven Ages of Justerini*. The shop in Bond Street carried the date 1749 but the associated firm of **Chalié Richards and Company,** of the same address, dated from 1700 – it has now been wound up.

Although we shall be dealing with wine-shippers later in this section, this is an appropriate place at which to say a word about the London premises of **Geo G Sandeman, Sons and Company Limited,** a business founded in 1790. They occupied their premises at 20 St Swithin's Lane in the City of London from 1805 until a few years ago.

Among the fittings and fixtures taken over with the buildings in 1805 was 'a Capital Patent Crane with three iron wheels, Jib Roller, Rope, Pulleys and Jigger'.

According to Dr Glyn Daniel's *Lascaux and Carnac*, the wine trade between Bordeaux and the western ports of Britain 'goes right back to Roman times'. It is not, therefore, surprising to find a number of old wine-merchants in the West Country. The firm of **Zachary and Company,** of Cirencester, according to its advertisements, was established in 1760.

Avery and Company have been established at their present address since 1793, and possibly for a much longer period. According to its advertisements, the firm was established in 1793 or 'before 1793'. The site has been considerably extended during the lifetime of the firm, but parts of the cellars are believed to belong to the original structure.

John Harvey and Sons Limited, of 12 Denmark Street, Bristol, was founded in the year 1796. The business still occupies its original site, although the old building was destroyed in 1940 by bombing. The cellars survived, and are older even than the firm.

The firm was founded by William Perry, who established it in a 15th-century house. He took as a partner Thomas Urch, whose sister had married Thomas Harvey, a sea-captain. Thomas Harvey's son John was taken into the wine business by his uncle and the business was controlled by the Harvey family until comparatively recent times, when it was taken over by Showerings (see page 18). The firm's 'Bristol Milk' and 'Bristol Cream' must be counted among the most famous sherries in the world.

The third firm of wine-merchants in Bristol, **J R Phillips and Company Limited,** claims in advertisements displayed on London Underground stations to have been 'established before 1789'. An advertisement in the *Listener* of 24 April 1958, however, stated that the firm was established 'circa 1739'. The discrepancy is explained by the fact that documents in the company's possession are dated 1789, but that one of the partners of the company, William George, is known to have been established in Bristol as a wine-merchant and distiller in 1739.

His two sons took over the business about 1775; Philip George became a maltster, while James George continued to run the distilling and wine-merchant's business with his son and James Rouquet Phillips. After the death of James George I in 1821, Phillips took over the leadership of the firm, which was renamed J R Phillips and Company in 1823.

The **House of Gilbey** is a comparative newcomer in this field. The brothers Walter and Alfred Gilbey started business as retail wine-merchants in February 1857, and the firm has, therefore, celebrated only its first centenary. Its story has been well told by Alec Waugh in *Merchants of Wine*.

The visitors to the firm's Centenary Exhibition held at the Café Royal from 21 May to 7 June 1957 could see copies of the old Customs returns showing that by 1872 Gilbey's were importing more wine than any other firm in London.

B. BUSINESSES IN OTHER LANDS

Biscuits, cakes and gingerbread

The old Dutch firm of **Jb Bussink's Koninklijke Deventer Koekfabrieken** was established in 1593. The bakery remained on its original site until 1952, when a new factory was built. Although the factory is new, the recipe for Bussink's cake is said to be still the same as it was years ago.

The oldest Basler 'Leckerli' (gingerbread) firm in Switzerland, **Karl Jakob,** was founded in 1753.

The packets of Aachen 'Printen' (described as 'Spiced Cake' but also known as 'gingerbread') made by the firm of **Henry Lambertz** at Aachen (Aix-la-Chapelle), Germany, inform us that the firm has been in existence since 1688, and that its premises at Aachen are the oldest and biggest 'Printen' factory in the world.

Packet of Aachen 'Printen' (Spiced Cake). *(Henry Lambertz)*

Brewing

The Bavarian State Brewery **Weihenstephan,** at Freising, not far from Munich, proclaims itself to be the oldest brewery in the world. Recent researches have provided evidence that beer was brewed at the monastery as early as 1040, a quarter of a century before the Battle of Hastings. The brewery was taken over by the State, in 1803, and now forms part of the Faculty of Brewing of the University of Munich.

Only a few miles from Freising, at Scheyern, is another brewery of monastic origin, the **Klosterbrauerei Scheyern.** The labels on its bottles show that it has been brewing 'seit 1119' ('since 1119').

Bottles, cans and beer-mats can be useful sources of information. They put the author on the track of **Münchner Löwenbräu** (1383) which advertises itself as the biggest brewery in Bavaria and producer of the world's most expensive beer, and of two other Munich breweries of about the same age: **Spatenbräu** (1397) and **Hackerbräu** (1417). Almost as old is the **Grenzquell-Brauerei** of H Günnel, Wernes-

Some bottles from the author's collection. From left to right: Weihenstephan brewery, Germany (1040); Pasquier-Desvignes, France (1420); Bols, Netherlands (1575); Danziger Goldwasser, Germany (1598); Krambambuly, Germany (1606); Henri Maire, France (1632); Tomson & Wotton, England (1634); Rocher Frères, France (1705). *(Ramsey & Muspratt)*

Bavarian State Brewery, Weihenstephan

A few beer-mats from the author's collections. From left to right: Weihenstephan brewery, Germany (1040); Moy brewery, Germany (1160); Augustiner brewery, Germany (1328); Löwenbräu, Germany (1383); Spaten (Spade) brewery, Germany (1397); Hacker brewery, Germany (1417); Grenzquell brewery, Germany (1436); Hofbräuhaus, Germany (1589); Three Horseshoes brewery, Netherlands (1628); Kronenbourg brewery, France (1664); Oranjeboom (Orange-tree) brewery, Netherlands (1671); Fürstenberg brewery, Germany (1705). *(Ramsey & Muspratt)*

grün iV, boasting of 'Braurechte seit 1436' ('brewing rights since 1436'). The **Augustiner-Bräu** in Munich was founded in 1328. By comparison with these, the **Fürstenberg Bräu** is a mere youngster, dating as it does from 1705.

The famous **Urquell** Brewery at Pilsen in Czechoslovakia dates from 1295.

In Holland, the Orange-tree Brewery **(Oranjeboom)** at Rotterdam was established in 1671. The Three Horse-shoes Brewery **(De Drie Hoefijzers)** at Breda dates from 1628. The Key Brewery **(De Sleutel)** at Dordrecht dates from 1433, and is said to be 'Holland's oldest industrial establishment still in full production'.

At the **Kronenbourg Brewery** in Strasbourg, the Hatt family have been 'brasseurs de père en fils depuis 1664'.

The **Molson** Brewery in Montreal dates from 1786 and celebrated its 175th anniversary in 1931. The company has a modern brewery in Toronto, in the entrance to which is displayed a stone taken from the old brewery in Montreal. The **Dow Brewery,** also of Montreal, is nearly as old as Molson's, having been established in 1790.

Another old Canadian brewery is that of **John Labatt,** of London, Ontario, with a history going back to 1828.

According to an advertisement in the *Boston Sunday Advertiser*, the first **Narragansett Brewery** was established in the 1800s, at the corner of Fountain and Jackson Streets in Providence. The Narragansett Brewery of today is located in Cranston, not far from the centre of Providence, and calls itself 'One of America's Great Breweries.'

Cafés

The **Café Procope,** 13 rue de l'Ancienne Comédie, Paris, describes itself as the oldest café in the world. It was established in 1686 by Francesco Procopio dei Coltelli, a gentleman from Palermo.

Coca-Cola

Dr John S Pemberton, an Atlanta pharmacist, launched Coca-Cola in 1886 as a tonic. Asa Griggs Candler, another druggist, acquired control of the product and formed the Coca-Cola Company, in Georgia, in 1891. The famous bottle was patented as a trademark in 1915. Over 175 000 000 drinks were sold per day at the end of 1975 in more than 130 countries.

Cocoa and chocolate

The **Walter Baker Company** in Dorchester, near Boston, Massachusetts, USA, was milling chocolate as long ago as 1766, ten years before the American Revolution. In 1927 it was purchased by the Postum Company, a name changed in 1929 to General Foods Corporation. It was gradually merged with the Corporation, and manufacturing at Dorchester came to an end in 1964. The entire chocolate production was moved to Dover (Delaware), where Walter Baker products are now made. (See also 'Food-Manufacturers', page 51.)

An article that was published in 1948 described the Walter Baker business as the oldest concern in the USA with a record of

Old factory of the Walter Baker Company, Dorchester, Near Boston, Massachusetts, USA. (General Foods Corporation)

La Belle Chocolatière by Jean Etienne Liotard (Walter Baker's trademark). (General Foods Corporation)

having made the same type of product continuously in its original location. (The Rhoads family, see page 101, had been tanning leather for longer, but not at their original location.)

The company was an early advertiser. In 1777, Hannon, who founded the firm, was publishing a money-back satisfaction guarantee. About half a century later, in 1833, Abraham Lincoln and his partner, William Barry, were selling 'Walter Baker's Breakfast Cocoa' in their store in New Salem, Illinois – the only packaged and advertised food product they carried.

The picture entitled La Belle Chocolatière by Jean Etienne Liotard (1702–90), a famous Swiss portrait-painter, has been used as a

trademark for about a century. The picture was formally registered as a trademark in 1883, but it was said at that time that the picture 'had appeared on Baker's products many years earlier'. (Liotard's picture La Belle Chocolatière is reproduced in the Encyclopaedia Britannica, opposite the article on pastels. Another of his portraits, La Liseuse, appeared on the United States 10 cent stamp that was issued in 1974 to commemorate the centenary of the Universal Postal Union.)

Coenraad Johannes van Houten, who founded the firm in Holland that still bears his name, was granted Letters Patent on 4 April 1828 for his method of removing superfluous

The ancient distillery ʼt Lootsje', Amsterdam. *(Lucas Bols, Amsterdam)*

fat (or cocoa-butter) from cocoa-beans. In the same year he began to sell his 'powdered chocolate', i.e. soluble cocoa-powder.

In 1815 his father had started a chocolate factory in Amsterdam, and it is from the year of Waterloo that the firm dates its history. In 1842 the business was transferred to Leyden, and in 1850 Coenraad took premises at Weesp. In 1889 a Royal Warrant gave the firm the title of 'De Koninklijke van Houten's Cacao-fabriek'.

Distilling (liqueurs and spirits)

The distillery of **Erven Lucas Bols** in Amsterdam, known as ''t Lootsje' (meaning 'shack'), had been on its original site since the year 1575. According to the firm's own account of its history it is, 'in so far as can be ascertained, the oldest existent distillery in the world'.

Lucas Bols began distilling aniseed and caraway-seed liqueurs in 1575, in the small wooden building that is still pictured on the firm's notepaper. Because of the danger of fire, the business had to be carried on outside the city walls. In 1612 the wooden 'Lootsje' was replaced by a brick building, but the location and the name of the business remained the same. The business remained in the Bols family from its foundation until the year 1815,

The bottling hall of the Royal Distilleries Erven Lucas Bols, Nieuw-Vennep (Holland). *(Erven Lucas Bols)*

when the Bols family died out and the name of the firm was changed to Erven Lucas Bols. ('Erven' means 'heirs'.)

It was Lucas Bols who created 'the typically Dutch product, V.O. Geneva'. This 'Very Old Geneva' (or gin) is made by passing distilled alcohol 'through the pungently scented juniper berries and thereby giving that special aroma which characterizes the beverage he then named "Jenever"'. (See also 'Gin', page 25.)

In 1964 the Bols Board of Management decided to look for a new location. They found a suitable site in Nieuw-Vennep, about 20 miles south of Amsterdam and it was here, on 11 September 1970, that His Royal Highness Prince Bernhard opened the new Bols plant. To mark the occasion, the title 'Koninklijke' ('Royal') was conferred on the concern by Her Majesty Queen Juliana, so that Bols joined the select company of Bussink (page 42), the Golden Hand Soap Works (page 104) and Van Houten (page 45).

Bols is not the only old maker of liqueurs in Holland. There is also **Warninks,** another Amsterdam firm, founded in 1616; **Wynand Fockink,** dating from 1679, and **Johannes de Kuyper en Zoon** in Schiedam, established in 1695.

The French firm of **Rocher Frères,** makers of 'Cherry-Rocher' and other fine liqueurs, carries on its bottles and on its notepaper the words 'Maison fondée en 1705, la plus ancienne de France.' This must mean the oldest business of its kind in France.

The Rocher family came from Pierrelatte, a small town half-way between Orange and Montélimar. Barthélemy Rocher was born in 1677 and, being left an orphan, he was brought up by an uncle. He was interested in botany, and began to make elixirs, to be used as medicines. In order to disguise their bitter taste he hit on the idea of sweetening them, and thereby found a market for his products among the healthy as well as among the sick.

Barthélemy Rocher established a small factory at La Côte Saint-André, where the present premises now stand. Eight generations of the family have been connected with the business since it began, more than 260 years ago. They thus beat Twining's record by one year (see page 32). The exact date at which the business began is unknown but in the year

1705, from which the business is dated, Barthélemy received an order from the town of Grenoble in connection with the celebration of the birth of the duc de Bretagne.

Barthélemy Rocher was succeeded by his son, François; François in turn was succeeded by three of his sons, Joseph, Antoine and Louis, who gave the business its present name of Rocher Frères. The three brothers took as their sign the Three Rocks which symbolised their close association and also recalled three curiously shaped hills near Pierrelatte.

The official report of the Paris Exhibition of 1855 describes the firm as 'la première qui ait généralisé l'usage des liqueurs en France'. It was said of the firm that

'tout en dotant le Trésor d'un impôt considérable, elle a affranchi la France du tribut qu'elle payait à l'Autriche pour son Marasquin, à la Prusse pour son eau-de-vie-de-Dantzig. à la Suisse pour son absinthe, à l'Italie pour son Alkermès, à la Hollande pour son curaçao'.

Towards the end of the 19th century the firm was producing more than 100 different products, but its chief product, then as now, was 'Cherry-Rocher'.

Marie Brizard of Bordeaux, who gave her name to the famous firm of distillers which celebrated its bicentenary in 1955, was born in Bordeaux in the year 1714. The following brief account of the firm's history is based on its bicentenary booklet, *Deux Siècles de Prestige 1755–1955.*

In her youth, Marie Brizard spent a good deal of her time visiting the sick and the poor. During an epidemic she tended a West Indian native and, as a token of his gratitude, he gave her a recipe for an elixir which, he said, would cure many ills. The basis of this elixir was aniseed, and it proved so successful that many of Marie's patients wished to continue taking it after they had been cured.

So great was the demand for the elixir that Marie had to engage staff to help her, and in 1755 the firm was launched. A lease of new premises that were taken in 1762 is still in existence. Marie had taken into partnership with her Jean-Baptiste Roger, who later married Anne Brizard, Marie's niece. The firm was registered under the name of Marie Brizard et Roger.

Other products were introduced too, such as 'Cacao Chouao', 'Apry', 'Blackberry', and 'Crème de Menthe'.

Jean-Baptiste Roger died in 1796, and Marie handed over her interest in the business to his widow. When Marie died in 1801 Jean-Baptiste Roger's son took charge of the business. Six generations have been concerned with the business, counting from Jean-Baptiste Roger himself.

Of the brandy firms in Cognac, the oldest is **Augier Frères et Compagnie,** dating from 1643.

An advertisement in *Country Life* of 26 December 1963 for **Rouyer** cognac refers to a tradition that the Rouyer business was founded by the Mayor (presumably the Maire) of Cognac in 1701.

The Augier firm has a comfortable lead in the matter of age over **Martel (1715), Rémy Martin (1724)** and **Hennessy (1785).**

In order to celebrate the 250th anniversary of the House of Rémy Martin, a cognac of unique quality was specially blended and limited to 38 709 bottles. The price was a mere £50 a bottle.

A brief account of the history of **Pernod** was given by Denis Morris in the *Field* of 20 October 1966. A French doctor, Pierre Ordinaire, was treating his patients with it about 1790, when he had taken refuge at Coutet in Switzerland from the French Revolution. After the Doctor's death in 1821, Henri Louis Pernod acquired the secret of the drink's composition from the old man's housekeeper. By 1830 the drink was known as 'Pernod'. Later, a factory for its manufacture was built at Pontarlier, in France, not far from the Swiss frontier.

The Spanish firm of Osborne, producers of the brandy **Viejo Veterano,** dates from 1772.

J A Gilka KG, now of Hamburg, announce on their labels 'Seit 1836 – 4 Generationen' ('Since 1836 – 4 generations'). The firm was established in Berlin in 1836, lost its premises by bombing in the war, later found itself one street too far to the east (that is, in the Russian Zone of Berlin) and re-established itself in Hamburg, where it still produces the Kümmel in the square bottles.

At Flensburg, near the Danish frontier, the **Bommerlunder** concern now unites the Bommerlunder Aquavit business of Herm G Dethleffsen, founded in 1760, and the old rum and grog business of **O C Balle,** dating from 1717. The establishment of the distillery at Flensburg is said to be due to a recipe for Aquavit given to the landlord of a local inn by a French officer wounded in the course of the Seven Years War. This was in June 1760. That part of Germany is known as 'Bommerlund', and the spirit became known as 'Bommerlunder'. The old recipe of 1760 is still in use. The Balle part of the business goes back to 1717, and is named after Ole Christian Balle, a merchant of Flensburg trading in rum from Jamaica.

Mampe, of Berlin, dating from 1831, are the makers of the oldest German 'Halb und Halb'.

Older than all the others in this group, and perhaps second only to Bols as a distillery, is the Danzig Goldwasser firm of **Isaac Wedling Wwe und Eydam Dirck Hekker,** brandy and liqueur distillers, the makers of the liqueur with small pieces of gold-leaf floating in it. The firm was established in Danzig in 1598, when Ambrosius Vermöllen, a Dutch Mennonite, who had fled from religious persecution in his own country, was admitted as a citizen of Danzig. In 1708, his grandson, Solomon, gave the distillery to his brother-in-law, Isaac Wedling, whose name still appears on the firm's labels. Isaac moved the business, in 1704, to a house in the Breitgasse decorated with a salmon, which soon gave its name to the distillery. Isaac died in 1711. His widow carried on the business with the help of her son-in-law, (Eydam) Dirck Hekker, whose name also lives on in the label.

The firm had to move when Danzig became a Free City, in 1921. With its famous trademark of a salmon, it moved to Berlin in 1922.

The business formerly conducted under the sign of 'Der Lachs' ('the salmon') in Danzig and then in Berlin now forms part of the Gräflich von Hardenberg'sche Kornbrennerei Vertriebs KG at Nörten-Hardenberg, in the *Land* of Lower Saxony. The business of the Counts von Hardenberg is itself an enterprise of some antiquity, dating from 1700. In addition to the famous 'Goldwasser', the firm also produces

More bottles. From left to right: Kronenbourg brewery, France (1664); Berry Brothers & Rudd, England (1699); Tollemache & Cobbold, England (1723); Ruinart Père et Fils, France (1729); Guinness, Ireland (1759), bottled by Tollemache & Cobbold (1723); Jim Beam, United States (1795); Brotherhood Corporation, United States (1839); Jack Daniel Distillery, United States (1866). *(Ramsey & Muspratt,*

'Krambambuly', a cherry-based liqueur. According to the label on the bottle, the recipe for the liqueur is taken 'aus dem Rezeptbuch D.Fa.Lachs A.D.Jahre 1606', which makes it almost as old as the 'Goldwasser' itself. (See illustration, page 43.)

The Danzig 'Goldwasser' firm issue a facsimile of an 'Avertissement' (or broadsheet), written in German and dated 1776, warning their customers that unscrupulous people were imitating their signs and asking their customers to make sure that they got the genuine article. (See illustration, page 163.)

Stobbe and **Rückforth,** are two other old family businesses, Rückforth dating from 1742 and Stobbe from 1776. Heinr Stobbe, of Oldenburg, moved from Danzig, where the firm was established in 1776. Rückforth, at Siegburg in the Rhineland since 1945, is another firm that was driven west as a result of the war. Its history began in Stettin in 1742.

The **Buchholzer Kornbrennerei KG** (distillery) of Klein-Buchholz, in Hanover is known to have been in existence in 1715, but is probably even older.

Underberg, the pick-me-up that comes in small bottles wrapped in brown paper and tastes something like cough mixture, has been 'produced from a secret family recipe since the year 1846'. The secret recipe is said to be known only to the Underberg family. It is 86 degrees proof and is made at Rheinberg am Niederrhein, in Germany.

In Denmark, the firm of **Peter F Heering,** makers of cherry brandy, dates from 1818.

The **Jack Daniel Distillery,** Lynchburg, Tennessee was founded in 1866. Jack Daniel built his distillery in the Hollow and began the tradition of making 'Tennessee sippin' whiskey' that has not changed to this day. According to the label on the bottle, this is 'the oldest registered distillery in the United States'. A further distinction claimed by the Jack Daniel Distillery is that it is the first distillery to be placed in the National Register of Historic Places by the United States Government.

The **James B Beam Distilling Company,** of Clermont, Kentucky, USA dates from 1795. Its notepaper carries the heading 'The World's Finest Bourbon Since 1795'. The label on the bottles of 'Jim Beam' informs us that 'Beam Whiskey' has been made from a formula since

1795 by six generations of distillers. Mr T Jeremiah Beam, whose signature appears on the label along with his father's, was President of the company from 1944 to 1967, when he retired. Jacob Beam started his distillery in Washington County, Kentucky, where it remained until 1884. In 1884 the business was carried on from Nelson County. The present plant, at Clermont in Bullitt County, was built by Mr Jeremiah Beam's father after the repeal of Prohibition.

The **Brown-Forman Distillers Corporation,** of Louisville, Kentucky, celebrated its centenary in 1970. It was in 1870 that a young wholesale drug salesman named George Gavin Brown set up in business as a distiller. In the years following the American Civil War there was a shortage of Bourbon whisky of a reliable quality in the USA and, in order to ensure that his whisky was not tampered with in the barrel, Brown packaged it in bottles with a tamper-proof closure. His 'Old Forester Bourbon' whisky was the first American whisky ever sold exclusively in a distiller-sealed bottle. Bourbon is made from a mixture of corn (maize), rye and malted barley and it must contain at least 51 per cent of corn. In the days of Prohibition in the USA, Brown-Forman was one of only ten distillers to be licensed by the Treasury Department for the production of whisky for sale through druggists against a doctor's prescription.

The oldest producers of Bourbon whisky in the USA, according to Etna M Kelley's *Business Founding Date Directory*, are **James E Pepper and Company,** of Lexington, Kentucky. They were established in 1740.

The **Gooderham and Worts** Distillery in Toronto, dating from 1832, is said to be the oldest distillery in Canada which is still in existence. It is now used principally to produce industrial alcohol. The Gooderham and Worts Company is a wholly owned subsidiary of Hiram Walker and Sons, of Walkerville, Ontario, who were established in 1858.

An article in the *Sunday Times* of 17 September 1967 carried a photograph of Robert Siegert, the boss of **Angostura Bitters,** whose great-grandfather invented the bitters as a cure for the stomach-ache afflicting Simon Bolivar's troops in Venezuela. Angostura was said to be Trinidad's biggest secondary manufactured product. It was also reported that Angostura had a secret recipe known to only four people, and that Robert Siegert's grandfather had taken elaborate measures to preserve the secrecy 'when manufacture was transferred to Trinidad from Ciudad Bolivar where the bitters were first sold, in 1846'.

A letter in the *Daily Telegraph* of 15 March 1965 from a Director of Coates and Company of Plymouth, makers of the original **Plymouth Gin** used for making a pink gin, referred to angostura bitters as 'a digestive tonic created by Dr. Johann Siegert in Venezuela in 1824'. The bitters were exported to Trinidad and 'the "marriage" between Coates's Plymouth gin and angostura bitters, to form a pink Plymouth or pink gin, is thought to have taken place in Trinidad during 1830'.

There has evidently been some confusion about the date of the invention. Simon Bolivar died in 1830, having liberated Venezuela some years earlier, and would not have had much use for a product invented in 1846. The label on the bottle states clearly that the bitters was first made in 1824 in the town of Angostura, which was renamed Ciudad Bolivar in 1846.

It was stated in the *Daily Telegraph* of 7 July 1958 that 'Coates's Plymouth Gin' was made from a recipe which was a family secret handed down from father to son. Only the head of the firm knew the formula. (See also page 25.)

Pierre Smirnoff established his distillery to produce vodka in Moscow in the year 1818. By 1914, a million bottles of **Smirnoff Vodka** were being sold each day, and the family was reputed to be the richest in the world. With the Revolution of 1917 came exile for the family and confiscation of their properties in Russia, but production was restarted in Paris and 'Smirnoff Vodka' is now said to be the largest selling distilled liquor in the world.

Bacardi Rum has a somewhat similar history. Facundo Bacardi began to distil rum in Santiago de Cuba in 1862, but the Castro Revolution led to the confiscation of all the Bacardi properties in Cuba. By that time, however, the Bacardi organisation had set up distilleries in several other countries, starting with Puerto Rico, and its international headquarters is now to be found in Hamilton, Bermuda. 'Bacardi Rum' is claimed to be one of the top three selling spirit brands in the world.

The **Distillers Corporation-Seagrams Limited,** of Canada, describe themselves as 'the world's largest distilling organisation', with plants and facilities in fifteen countries. Joseph E Seagram and Sons of Waterloo, Ontario, were established in 1857, but the architect of the Corporation was Samuel Bronfman (1891–1971).

Samuel Bronfman, with his three brothers, formed the Distillers Corporation in 1926, and acquired Seagrams in 1928. The Corporation's Annual Report of 1971 contained a history of the Corporation and a biography of 'Mr Sam'.

The Corporation covers many famous names, such as 'Chivas Regal Whisky', 'Captain Morgan Rum' in Jamaica and the Paul Masson vineyards in California. It owns the Strathisla-Glenlivet Distillery at Keith, in Banffshire, said to be 'the oldest operational malt whisky distillery in the Scottish Highlands', and Augier Frères, of Cognac, the oldest cognac firm (see page 48). Seagram's 'Seven Crown Whiskey', made in the USA, is claimed to be 'the largest selling brand of whiskey in the world'.

Fishing

Baine, Johnston and Company, of St John's, Newfoundland, trace their history back to 1780, although almost all their records were lost in two great fires, in 1846 and 1892. A firm known as 'Lang, Baine and Company' was operating at Port De Grave in 1780, and was removed to St John's about 1800. Fishing, sealing and shipping were their main concerns.

Another Canadian firm dating from the 18th century is **Zwicker and Company** of Lunenburg, Nova Scotia. The company was founded in 1789 and has been engaged in fishing and in trading with the West Indies.

Food – manufacturers

In 1925 the **Postum Cereal Company** entered into the first of a series of consolidations resulting in the organisation which in 1929 took the name of **General Foods,** whose head office is now at White Plains, New York. A number of the businesses that now form part of General

Foods already had a considerable history at that date. The oldest of all was the Walter Baker chocolate business (see page 45). In the 1975 *Fortune* list of the 500 largest industrial companies in the USA, General Foods ranked 58, with sales of nearly $3000 million.

The first of the amalgamations that led to the formation of General Foods took place in 1925, and involved the Postum Cereal Company Incorporated. This business traced its history back to 1895, when C W Post first marketed 'Postum', a new cereal beverage. Two years later, he introduced 'Grape-Nuts', one of the first ready-to-eat cold cereals.

The Igleheart Brothers had started milling flour (later known as 'Swans Down') in Evansville, Indiana, in 1856. The beginnings of 'Maxwell House Coffee' date from the 1890s, and 'Jell-O' from 1896. It was the Jell-O Company that the Postum organisation acquired in 1925. After other acquisitions in 1926, 1927 and 1928, the Postum Company acquired a controlling interest in all the Birds Eye rights, patents and operations in 1929.

Apart from Birds Eye, most of the companies in the organisation were established businesses. It is perhaps surprising to learn that, such was the prejudice against cold-storage foods at the outset, that it was not until eleven years after General Foods first marketed quick-frozen foods that Birds Eye showed a profit. The first sales were at Springfield, Massachusetts, in 1930. It was a scientist named Clarence Birdseye who developed the process of freezing food quickly to preserve it.

It was Marjorie Post, the daughter of C W Post, who saw the possibilities inherent in the new process. In 1926, when Birds Eye was on the verge of bankruptcy, Mrs Post's chef served a quick-frozen goose on one of her yachts, and Mrs Post was impressed with its flavour. It took her three years, however, to persuade her Board of Directors to invest in Birds Eye, by which time they had to pay ten times what they would have had to pay in 1926. Marjorie Post, who died in 1973 at the age of 86, was said to have been worth $250 million, and was one of the richest women in the world. She had her footmen change their livery three times a day.

Another famous food company, the **Quaker Oats Company,** has a history going back to the last quarter of the 19th century. Henry Parsons

Twinings Coffee Shop, 216 The Strand, London. (*John Addey Associates/R Twining & Co Ltd*)

Crowell was selling oats under the brand-name 'Quaker' from his mill at Ravenna, Ohio, in 1886, and possibly earlier. According to the curiously named work *Brands, Trademarks and Good Will*, sub-titled *The Story of the Quaker Oats Company*, by Arthur F Marquette, 'Quaker Oats' was the largest-selling breakfast food in the world in 1966, the year before the book appeared.

The figure of a man in Quaker garb was registered as a trademark in 1877, America's first registered trademark for a breakfast cereal. Crowell bought the Ravenna mill in 1881.

The Quaker product 'Puffed Rice' was launched in 1904. It was introduced as a novelty rather than as a breakfast food.

The **Del Monte Company,** of San Francisco, advertise themselves as the world's largest canner of fruits and vegetables. In the 1975 *Fortune* list of industrial companies in the USA they rank 192, with sales of just over $1000 million.

In the *Fortune* list of 1976 giving the 500 largest industrial corporations outside the USA the Swiss firm of **Nestlé,** with headquarters at Vevey, ranked No 19 and, with sales of $7000 million, also ranked as the largest such corporation in Switzerland.

Food-retailers

The **Great Atlantic and Pacific Tea Company** ('A&P'), of Montvale, New Jersey, describe themselves as 'America's Dependable Food Merchants since 1859'. In the *Fortune* list of 1975 of the 50 largest retailing companies in the USA, A & P ranked No 4, with sales of nearly $6900 million, while Safeway Stores, of Oakland, California, ranked No 2, with sales amounting to nearly $8200 million.

Maltsters

The **Perot Malting Company** of Philadelphia, USA, traced its history back to 1687 and boasted that it was older than the Bank of England. When Etna M Kelley published her *Business Founding Date Directory* in 1954, the Perot Malting Company was the only one with a founding date earlier than 1700.

In 1962 the tangible assets of the Perot Malting Company were sold to Canadian Breweries of Toronto, and the old family company was completely liquidated. The mantle of the oldest company in the USA then passed to J E Rhoads and Sons, of Wilmington, Delaware (see 'Leather and belting', page 101).

The founder of the Perot Malting Company, Anthony Morris II, erected a malt-house and brewery in 1687, in Front Street, Philadelphia. Five generations of the Morris family were connected with the business. Francis Perot (born in 1796) was apprenticed to the last of the Morrises family and later married the daughter of his old master.

In 1889, 100 years after the inauguration of George Washington as the first President of the United States of America, there was formed an association of firms and corporations in the USA that were controlled by descendants of the original founder who controlled them 100 years before. It was then found that the Perot firm was the oldest in continuous existence in the USA at that time, and so it remained until 1962.

Soy sauce

'Kikkoman Soy Sauce', 'backed by more than 300 years of experience in the manufacture of quality soy sauce', is made by the **Noda Shoyu Company** of Tokyo. Their labels are marked 'since 1630', and the company are still manufacturing 'from the same location' as in 1630. The President and majority of the Managing Directors are descendants of the original founders, the Mogi family.

Spices

D & L Slade, of Boston, Massachusetts, appear in Etna M Kelley's *Directory* as importers and manufacturers of spices and other food specialities. The business was established as long ago as 1734, and controlled by the Slade family since 1827.

Vermouth

The House of **Carpano** at Turin, Italy, maker of the famous vermouth 'Punt e Mes', was established in 1786. According to its labels and circulars, it is 'La Più Antica Fabbrica di Vermuth' and 'the world's earliest Vermouth manufacture'.

The House of **Cinzano** – described as

'distillers, confectioners and vermouth producers' – traces its history back to 6 January
1757, the date of the document in the records
of the Confectioners' and Distillers' Guild of
Turin in which appear the names of two
brothers, Carlo Stefano Cinzano and Giovanni
Giàcomo Cinzano. Until recently, the firm's
origin was dated only from 1816, the year when
Giovanni Francesco Cinzano, the grandson of
Giovanni Giacomo, was known to have been a
distiller in Turin.

The French firm **Noilly Prat,** of Lyon and
Marseille, was established in 1813.

Vines and vineyards

An article in the *New Statesman and Nation* of
9 March 1957 referred to Cyprus wine and
mentioned a strange liqueur-like wine called
Commanderie St John. It went on to say:
'The vineyards which produce this wine are
the same which provided the wine for Richard
Coeur de Lion. . . .' (One hopes that their
history was stronger than their grammar!)

A booklet entitled *The Wine Industry*,
published by the Wine Advisory Board of
San Francisco, California, contains a picture of
'the oldest winery in California', a little adobe
building where the Mission Fathers made wine.
It is at the **Mission San Gabriel,** founded
near Los Angeles in 1771. Two years before, in
1769, the Franciscans had established the
Mission San Diego and planted wine grapes
there, so laying the foundation of the Califor-
nian wine industry. Until 1824, however, the
Franciscan Fathers were the only wine-growers
in California. It was at San Gabriel that the
famous Trinity Vine, planted by the Franciscan Fathers in 1775, flourished for over 170
years.

Another report says that the wine industry
of California was founded by a Hungarian
nobleman, Count Agoston Haraszthy, who
brought 100000 vine cuttings from Europe in
1857 and planted them at Sonoma, north of
San Francisco. His vineyard, **Buena Vista,**
has been called America's oldest winery.

There seems to be some dispute about the
relative age of American wineries. The labels of
the **Brotherhood Corporation** at Washing-
tonville, in the State of New York, carry the
words 'America's Oldest Winery', but do not
indicate the date of the winery's establishment.
It was 1839. (For whiskey and whisky, see
'Distilling', page 46.)

Wine-growers, -shippers and -merchants

If this section of the book is not to swamp
the rest, we can do little more than mention
here some of the old firms that have been
producing and shipping wine for centuries.

On a journey that the author made from
Harwich to the Hook of Holland, the 'cellars'
of the ship yielded up a bottle of Moselle
wine, a 'Piesporter'. The label on the bottle
showed that it came from the firm of **Josef
Milz** and from a vineyard that had been 'in der
Familie seit 1520'.

Another old family business is **Gustav
Adolf Schmitt'sches Weingut** at Nierstein
am Rhein. The Schmitt family has lived in
Nierstein for more than 300 years, and their
notepaper is inscribed 'Weinbau seit 1618'.

Other old family businesses from that part of
the world are **Richard Langguth,** of Traben-
Trarbach (1620) and **Adolph Huesgen,** also of
Traben-Trarbach (1697). The latter firm has a
splendid label showing six generations of the
family, the earliest one looking remarkably like
Johann Sebastian Bach. About a century younger is the firm of **Hellmers und Söhne,** of
Reil an der Mosel (1785).

The **Bürgerspital zum Heiligen Geist**
('The Citizens' Hospital of the Holy Ghost')
in Würzburg – a charitable foundation – was
founded and endowed with vineyards in the
year 1319, the date which appears on its labels.
Not many undertakings of this kind, or indeed
businesses of any kind, have been able to
celebrate a 650th anniversary.

The vineyards of the **Reichsgraf von
Kesselstatt** at Trier, in Germany have been
in the family for more than 600 years, but
they date the foundation of the enterprise from
1377.

F E Hugel et Fils, of Riquewihr, France,
date from 1639.

The London *Evening Standard* of 8 April
1965 carried an advertisement for a wine called
'The General', a hock shipped by Nassauer
Brothers and stocked by numerous shops,
including Fortnum and Mason. The wine was
being launched to celebrate the 500th anni-

Dom Thierry Ruinart. *(Ruinart Père & Fils)*

versary of the **von Simmern** vineyards in Eltville, Germany.

The General thus commemorated was General Ernst Eberhard Kuno Baron Langwerth von Simmern, who fought against Napoleon and led the Royal English Legion in the Spanish Peninsular campaigns. Recent attempts to obtain a bottle and to find out more about the vineyard have proved vain.

The vineyards of **Friedrich Priesteroth** at Braubach am Rhein, Germany, have been owned by the family since 1690.

The **Pieroth** family of Burg Layen, near Bingen, has been in existence for 300 years but is content to claim 'a wine tradition' of only 270 years.

The oldest German Sekt ('champagne') firm – Deutschlands älteste Sektkellerei – is to be found at Esslingen, not far from Stuttgart. The business was founded in 1826 but, according to the labels on the bottles, it was in 1823 that **G C Kessler** produced the first German Sekt. G C Kessler who gave his name to the firm was born in Heilbronn in 1787 and

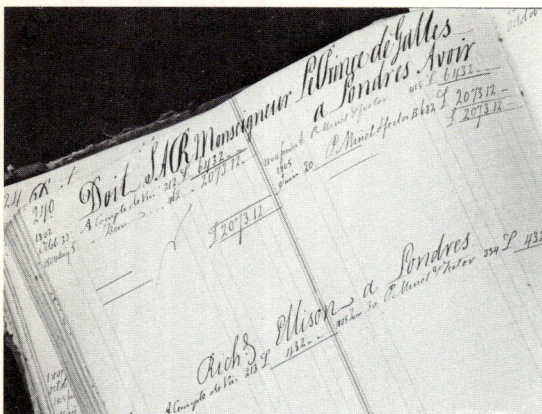

Old Ruinart ledger. *(Ruinart Père & Fils)*

spent 16 years as a book-keeper with the champagne firm of Veuve Clicquot in Reims, in which he became a partner. He returned to Germany in 1823, and severed his connection with the House of the Veuve Clicquot in 1826.

The House of **Moët et Chandon** at Épernay dates from 1743 and **Ruinart père et fils** at Reims, 'la maison la plus ancienne' de Champagne, dates from 1729. Both these champagne firms have old ledgers recording sales to the crowned heads of Europe and other distinguished customers long before the days of the French Revolution. Ruinart is said to have been the first champagne house to send supplies to the UK. (See illustration above.)

The second oldest champagne house is **Chanoine,** founded in Épernay only a year after Ruinart.

Yet another old champagne firm dating from the same period is **Taittinger,** of Reims, founded in 1734 by a certain Jean Fourneaux. Pierre Taittinger, the father of the present head of the business, came on the scene after the First World War.

Lanson père et fils, also of Reims, was founded in 1760. The House of **Piper-Heidsieck** was founded in 1785.

Veuve Clicquot-Ponsardin ('The Widow'), another business woman of renown, who lived from 1777 to 1866, took charge of the firm that now bears her name in 1805, on the death of the husband whom she had married only six years previously.

Beaune, in Burgundy, is the home of a

number of old firms. The firm of **Chanson père et fils,** 'propriétaires et négociants en vins', was founded in 1750. (Another firm which dates from 1750 is **Bouchard Aîné et fils,** of Beaune, while **Bouchard père et fils,** of Le Château, Beaune, proclaim themselves to have been 'propriétaires et négociants depuis 1731'.) **Poulet père et fils,** who have been established at Beaune since 1 October 1747, boast 'deux siècles et sept générations de probité commerciale et d'expérience bourguignonne'.

Far older than these are the two firms **Raoul Clerget et fils** and **Clerget-Buffet et fils.** The two firms evidently had a common founder, for they both date from the year 1270. The first of these firms, at Saint-Aubin, near Beaune, describe themselves as 'vignerons de père en fils depuis 1270', and the second as 'viticulteurs de père en fils à Volnay depuis 1270'. (Volnay lies a few miles south of Beaune.)

Yet another firm with an aura of the past about it is **Joseph Drouhin** of Beaune, still proclaiming its old glories – 'anciens celliers des rois de France et des Ducs de Bourgogne'.

Monsieur **Marc Pasquier Desvignes,** the head of the Burgundy house of that name at St Lager en Beaujolais, traces his ancestry back to the founder of the firm in 1420. Its products are frequently advertised in our papers, with the words 'Au Marquisat depuis 1420'.

Moving west to Sancerre on the Loire, there is **Alphonse Mellot**, 'de père en fils depuis 1513'. One of the firm's labels supplied by Monsieur Mellot tells us that César Mellot was 'Conseiller du roi en 1698'.

Another old family business is that of **Henri Maire** at Arbois in the Jura. The business goes back to 1632 and describes itself on its labels as 'le plus grand domaine viticole du Jura'.

Château Grillet, in the Rhône Valley, has been called the rarest of all French white wines because of its extremely limited production. Until comparatively recently it was impossible to obtain the wine outside the circle of the family who have owned the vineyard for the past 300 years, except at the two famous restaurants of the Pyramide at Vienne and the Beau-Rivage at Condrieu.

The French firm of **Nicholas** have been

called the biggest wine-merchants in the world.

The House of **Pedro Domecq SA** of Jerez de la Frontera, Spain, was established in 1730 and is one of the oldest businesses in the sherry trade. One of the firm's circulars describes them as 'the oldest firm of sherry growers and shippers'. Its 'Double Century' sherry commemorates the 200th anniversary of the firm. Another well-known sherry firm, **Garveys,** was established in 1780 by an Irishman. The wine firm of **Scholtz Hermanos** at Málaga was founded in 1807.

George Sandeman (1765–1841) founded the business which still bears his name in 1790 (see page 41). When George Sandeman died, in 1841, he was succeeded by his nephew, George Glas Sandeman (1792–1868). He in turn was succeeded by his eldest son, Albert George Sandeman, who took his three brothers into partnership. One of these, Colonel John Glas Sandeman, with the aid of a mechanic, one Everett, invented the penny-in-the-slot machine.

The Italian firms of Cinzano and Carpano have already been mentioned, under 'Vermouth'. To them we should add the House of **Melini,** a Chianti-producer, whose labels carry the inscription 'Casa fondata nel 1705'.

The **Antinori** family of Florence date their history as wine-growers from the year 1385, when the family gained admittance into the official wine guild of that city. Giovanni di Piero Antinori was enrolled as 'vinattiere novizio'.

The history of **Woodhouse and Company,** of Marsala, in Sicily, goes back to 1773. A brief history of the firm that appeared in the *Wine and Spirit Trade Record* of 14 May 1930 mentions the record of a shipment of 70 pipes (7350 gal; 33000 l) of wine from the port of Trapani for the account of John Woodhouse, and the firm accordingly dates its beginning from that year. It was William and John Woodhouse, the sons of the former John, who established themselves as wine-merchants in Marsala in 1796. They were able to supply Nelson with wine for his ships, and it was Nelson who suggested that one of their wines might be named 'Bronte Marsala' after the estate of Bronte that had been conveyed to him.

The Reverend Samuel Woodhouse, the

Nelson's order for Marsala wine from John and William Woodhouse, 1800. *(Rev. S Woodhouse)*

Archdeacon of London, kindly supplied a facsimile of an order for 'five Hundred Pipes of the best Marsala Wine' for His Majesty's ships off Malta that was placed with John and William Woodhouse by Rear-Admiral Horatio Lord Nelson on 19 March 1800. Immediately above the signature 'Bronte Nelson' at the foot of the contract, the following sentence has been added in Nelson's own hand: 'The Wine to be delivered as expeditiously as possible and all to be delivered within the space of five Weeks from this date, a Convoy will be granted for the Vessel from Marsala but all risks are to run by Mr. Woodhouse.' (See illustration above.)

Hunt, Roope and Company, of London and Oporto, is one of those firms whose origins are lost in the mists of time. Their notepaper says simply 'Established Previous to

1679', but the story goes back much further than that.

The history of **Newman, Hunt and Company,** of London, can be traced back to 1395, but it was in 1679 that the Newman and Roope families formed a partnership, trading in port wine from Portugal and cod from Newfoundland.

An advertisement in the *Manchester Guardian* of 14 November 1957 for **Croft and Company,** of London and Oporto, mentioned 'Croft's Port. Established 1678. Nearly Three Hundred Years of fine reputation for quality goes with every bottle.' The firm began as Phayre and Bradley, and it was not until 1736 that a Croft joined the Board. **Taylor's** was founded in 1692, although the Taylor family did not appear on the scene until 1816; and **Cockburn's,** a comparative newcomer by the side of these, was not founded until 1815.

A letter in the *Daily Telegraph* of 18 January 1958 pointed out that 'the oldest Oporto shippers are **Messrs. C. N. Kopke & Co.,** established in 1638'.

Two years earlier, in 1636, Nicolau Kopke went to Lisbon as Consul-General for the Hanseatic Free Towns. In 1638 his son, Christian, the founder of the firm, went to Oporto to establish himself in business there. Not long afterwards he became interested in the export of the sweet wines of Portugal, now universally known as 'port wine'. In 1882, all the old records of the firm were destroyed in a fire, and the last of the Kopkes died in 1895. An English partnership was then formed to take over the Portuguese company.

Warre's, of Vila Nova de Gaia, Portugal, the oldest British port-shipper, dates its history from the year 1670, when two young Englishmen who had gone to Portugal to seek their fortune bought some wine grown in the heart of what is now the officially delimited port country to ship down the Douro to England. The Warre family, however, was not associated with the firm until 1729, when William Warre was admitted as a partner, and the last Warre retired from the firm in 1955. Hence, despite their age, Warre's do not qualify for membership of the Tercentenarians' Club (see chapter 11).

The actual foundation date, 1670, 'is so registered with the Associacao Comercial of Oporto (the local Chamber of Commerce), who have before now produced Certificates to this effect'. One cannot help wishing that other old firms had sometimes taken as much trouble to authenticate their origin.

Warre's is unique. As well as being the oldest British port-shipper, it is still a private company and is still controlled by a single family (now the Symingtons); it still operates solely from Portugal and it still deals only with port. The trademark of its 'Warrior' port (an obvious play on words) is over 200 years old, the oldest on any port-wine label.

Another port firm that should be mentioned here, if only for the sake of its Royal Charter, is **Royal Oporto** (Real Cia Velha, Real Companhia dos Vinos do Porto), founded by Royal Charter in 1756. It is not quite as old as **Offley, Forester and Company,** founded in 1729.

The **Paul Masson Vineyards** at Saratoga, California, claim to be 'one of the oldest wine producers in the United States'. Paul Masson himself, who was born at Beaune in 1859, came to California in 1878, but the history of the firm goes back to 1852.

Saratoga is about an hour's drive south of San Francisco. About as far to the north of the city lie the vineyards of the **Christian Brothers,** in the Napa Valley. The Christian Bothers are a teaching Order founded in France in 1680, and they have been growing wine in California since 1882.

It is perhaps more surprising to come across a wine firm in New York State that is more than 100 years old. The **Pleasant Valley Wine Company,** of Hammondsport, describes itself as 'U.S. Bonded Winery No. 1', and as 'Organized 1860'. Mr Walter S Taylor, the Assistant Managing Director of the company, is a fourth-generation wine-maker and grape-grower, and he has arranged the original winery, his great-grandfather's house, as the Finger Lakes Wine Museum. (See also 'Vines and Vineyards', page 54.)

Schieffelin and Company, of New York, 'Wine and Spirit Importers Since 1794', appear in Etna M Kelley's *Business Founding Date Directory,* where they are described as drug distributors, 'the oldest drug house in America'. An article about their history appeared in *Beverage News* of October 1966, when the Chairman of the Board was W J Schieffelin III, the seventh generation of his family to head the firm. According to this article, the origins of the firm go back to 1781, the year of the Battle of Yorktown. Since that date the firm has operated as wholesale druggists in the New York metropolitan area, manufacturing, importing and distributing drugs and cosmetics. Its Wine and Spirit Division acted as exclusive US distributors for many well-known imported wines and spirits. The business had been founded by a merchant called Effingham Lawrence, who sold it to Jacob Schieffelin in 1794, which explains the two dates.

Australia, too, bears witness to the preservative power of wine. The firm of **B Seppelt and Sons Pty, Limited,** with vineyards in South Australia and Victoria, was established in 1851 and surrounds its coat of arms with the words 'One Family, One Tradition'.

The island of Madeira has a number of old wine firms: **Cossart, Gordon and Company** was established in 1745 and is described on its labels as 'the oldest and the largest Shippers of Madeira' (i.e. of Madeira wine). The firm was founded by Francis Newton in 1745, and its records, letter-books and accounts are complete back to 1748. The Cossart family came originally from Rouen, and have been connected with the firm for more than 150 years. They are related to the Du Pont family of the USA.

Other old Madeira-shippers are **Leacock and Company,** founded in 1760; **Rutherford and Company,** founded in 1814, and **Blandy Brothers and Company,** dating from the early part of the 19th century.

Madeira wine is said to be the longest lived of all. This chapter may fittingly close with a mention of the very rare old Malmsey that was shipped and bottled for **Hedges and Butler** at the time of their tercentenary.

There are only 300 bottles in the whole world, and the guests at the tercentenary luncheon mentioned on page 175 were each given a bottle of the precious fluid. They were told that it was drinkable now, but 'will improve for another hundred years'. Each bottle is numbered, like a special edition of a rare book, and some of the bottles were offered for sale at a special tercentenary price of £15 a bottle.

The Prime Ministers' Chair at Hedges & Butler, London (see page 175). *(Hedges & Butler)*

CHAPTER 2

TEXTILES

A. BUSINESSES IN THE BRITISH ISLES

Carpets

One of the few firms in this country which have their origin in the days of Oliver Cromwell is the **Wilton Royal Carpet Factory,** of Wilton, Wiltshire. The oldest part of the factory was built in 1655, and the firm is still on its original site.

King William III granted the firm its Royal Charter in the year 1699. In 1720 the ninth Earl of Pembroke, impressed by the quality of the carpets that he saw in France, decided to bring some French weavers to England to ply their craft here. As expert French craftsmen were at that time forbidden to leave France, the Earl smuggled two of them out of France in empty barrels.

In 1835, all the weaving plant that had been used in Axminster for weaving Axminster carpets was moved to Wilton, but the name 'Axminster' survives to denote a particular kind of carpet.

Cotton

According to A P Wadsworth and J de L Mann's *The Cotton Trade*, the firm of **J and N Phillips and Company,** of 35 Church Street, Manchester 4, was founded in 1747 by a member of the family still then represented in it. The business is compendiously described as 'Textile manufacturers. Merchant converters. Warehousemen. Narrow Fabric Manufacturers.'

Three years after the establishment of J and N Phillips, the firm of **William Heaton and Sons** began spinning cotton in Bolton. They describe themselves as 'spinners since 1750'.

A booklet (undated, but probably issued between 1918 and 1939) from **Crosses and Winkworth Consolidated Mills Limited** and **Crosses and Heatons' Associated Mills Limited** gives some interesting information about the development of the cotton industry in general and about the firm in particular. Cotton was first used in England in the year 1298, but then only for candlewick. About half a century earlier, in 1251, Bolton had been made a borough, but nobody then foresaw that Bolton would become 'the supreme centre of fine cotton spinning'.

When Samuel Crompton's spinning mule was being introduced, it was a Heaton, in 1800, who was one of the first to use it. The firm of **Dobson and Barlow Limited,** also of Bolton, makers of textile machinery, who were established in 1790, have placed on record that the first mule jenny that they made was for Heatons.

The finest yarns produced by the mills in the group were those spun by William Heaton and Sons Limited at Lostock Junction, near Bolton. They produced yarns 'suitable for the Manufacture of Fine Muslins, Crochet, Embroidery, Dress Goods, Voiles, Poplins, Velvet, Net, Lace, Gloves, Hosiery, Tyre Fabric, Aeroplane, Balloon and Airship Fabrics'.

Another well-known firm in the cotton industry is **Horrockses** of Preston, dating from 1791.

Drapers

The year 1971 witnessed the demise of **B Smiths (Thirsk) Limited,** which had figured for some years in the *Guinness Book of Records* as the oldest retail business in Britain.

The firm had carried on business as drapers, outfitters, furnishers and caterers in the Market Place at Thirsk. They claimed only that theirs was the oldest *drapery* business in Great Britain. In 1951 this claim was challenged by Mr **Gayner** of Thornbury (see below). After the disposal of the Gayner business, however, it would seem that Smiths of Thirsk had a good claim to be regarded as the oldest retail business of any kind in the country, not merely as the oldest drapery business.

Smiths' notepaper used to carry the inscription 'established 1580', but Mr Roderic Smith Hall, the last Chairman of the firm, added that the parish records show that Bartholomew Smith, tailor, died in that year. It is not known how long he had carried on business as a tailor.

The age of the firm was not the only remarkable thing about it. Ever since 1580 it had been on the same site, and the cellars were partly in their original state. There was also a family connection running back to 1580.

The *Universal British Directory* published in 1798 gives Smith, Joseph, as 'draper and grocer'. Half a century later, the *General Directory and Topography of Kingston-upon-Hull* (and of a wide adjacent area), published in 1851 by Francis White and Company, shows 'Smith, Bartw.' (i.e. Bartholomew) in the 'Mkp.' (i.e. Market-place) at Thirsk, under the headings 'Grocers and Tea Dealers', 'Hatters', and 'Linen and Wool Dps' (i.e. Drapers) but not under 'Tailors'.

Up to August 1954 the title of the oldest drapery business in the country was claimed by Gayner's in the High Street at Thornbury, near Bristol. The Gayner family were weavers and drapers in Thornbury for 431 years, from 1523 to 1954. In 1523 Michael Gayner paid an annual tithe to the Lord of the Manor; in 1954 Mr Sidney H Gayner, the last of his line, sold his business to the Bristol Co-operative Society. As the *Thornbury Gazette* said, this is 'a remarkable record which few can possibly equal'. Unlike the Smiths of Thirsk, the Gayners had not always been in business on the same site, having moved to their last premises in the year 1890.

Mr Gayner's grandmother was a corset-maker as well as a draper. She died in 1955, aged 98.

A few years after the sale of the Gayner business, the *Drapers' Record* of 2 March 1957 asked if there were any traders who had been established for more than 150 years. Nobody responded to this challenge, and the *Drapers' Record* itself had apparently forgotten about the draper's shop at Thirsk to which it had referred six years previously (see above). A fortnight later, however, the *Drapers' Record* reported that **Green's Stores** at Stansted in Essex were celebrating 270 years of trading by extending their premises. This business was founded in the year 1687, in the reign of James II, by John Day.

The wholesale drapers, **Cooks** of London, celebrated their 150th anniversary in 1957 with a dinner at the Savoy, where the speakers included Lord Bruce and Lord Hollenden. Lord Bruce spoke of the humble beginnings of the business that had been founded by the Cooks of Norfolk. Lord Hollenden remarked that his own firm **(I and R Morley Limited)** had been in existence a decade before Cooks, i.e. since 1797.

Nets

Joseph Gundry and Company Limited, of Bridport, makers of fishing-nets, were established in the year 1665. In 1963 the Gundry business and a number of similar enterprises came together to form Bridport-Gundry Limited, but the Gundry family is still strongly represented on the Board of Directors.

Gundry's have been in Bridport since 1665, and the premises which were occupied in the early 1700s still form part of the company's present site. This may well be, therefore, another example of a firm that is in a position to challenge the claim of Twining's (see page 32) to be the oldest firm to be on the same site, in the same family and in the same line of business.

A letter in *The Times* of 15 February 1966 from Mr C W Edwards, who was then the

Gieves & Hawkes, Savile Row, W1. *(Gieves & Hawkes Ltd)*

Chairman of Bridport-Gundry Limited, brought the story up to date:

'The record is quite clear, Samuel Gundry having set up in the flax and hemp trade in Bridport in 1665, and his descendants continued in it here independently until 1963, when they amalgamated with Bridport Industries Ltd., the name of which was then changed to Bridport-Gundry Ltd. Even today there are three Gundrys on the board of the company, and two more otherwise employed in it.'

Shirt-makers

The business of **Beale and Inman Limited,** shirt-makers, hosiers and outfitters, was established by James Beale at 131 New Bond Street in the year 1828. The Inman family joined Mr Beale at a later date.

Tailors and outfitters

Several old tailoring firms in Bond Street are described in Ivor Halstead's *Bond Street* (1952), but the information given in the text of the book is not always consistent with the information given in the advertisements that also appear in the book. For example, Halstead describes **Flights Limited** as 'Britain's earliest Military Tailors', and says that William Pyke Flight 'opened the doors of the now famous family business' at Winchester in the year 1746, 'over 200 years ago'. In their advertisement, however, Flights Limited put their date of origin as 1770.

There is a similar inconsistency in the information about **Gieves Limited.** The firm was founded in Portsmouth by Melchizedeck Meredith, George Meredith's grandfather. According to Halstead, 'Mel' started his career as tailor and naval outfitter in 1784, but the firm's own advertisement gives the date of its establishment as 1785. Mel's son sold the business to John Galt, and in 1852 James Gieve was taken into partnership.

In September 1974 it was announced that Gieves were to merge with **Hawkes** of Savile Row, who, according to their advertisements, were established in 1771, which makes them junior by one year to **Flights Limited.**

Tissiman and Sons Limited's notepaper described this firm as 'Ladies' and Gentlemen's Outfitters since 1601'. The beautiful Tudor shop at 10 High Street, Bishop's Stortford, is even older than the business, which had descended from father to son all through the years.

An interesting feature of the shop is the pane of glass let into the floor in the living-room over the shop, which enables anyone in the upper room to see what is going on in the shop below. Some of the old order-books, dating from the last century, show what a flourishing business the supply of mourning dress and equipment must have been. (See also chapter 11, page 175.)

Textile-finishers

Going along Threadneedle Street one day, the author noticed a van standing outside the old office of the Sun Insurance Company. The inscription on the building showed that the Sun was founded in the year 1710. The inscription on the van showed that it belonged to **Perrotts (Nicol and Peyton) Limited,** cloth-finishers, of Bermondsey, and that they, too, were established in 1710. They are more compendiously described as 'London Shrinkers, Finishers and Waterproofers of Woollen and Worsted Fabrics, Fireproofers of Cotton Cloths'.

The *Financial Times* of 3 July 1967 carried the following sad little item of news:

'Historic Mill to Close

Haslingden, Lancs. July 2.

This week sees the closure of what is believed to be Lancashire's oldest and certainly its most historic textile mill. Higher Mill at Helmshore, near Haslingden, where woollen cloth has been fulled and finished since 1789, will cease production because of falling orders.'

Wool

Among the old firms that were mentioned in Skinner's *Wool Trade Directory of the World* are **Wm Hollins Limited,** of Viyella House, Nottingham, the makers of 'Viyella' fabrics, who were established in 1784; **C F Taylor and Company Limited,** of Shipley, described as 'worsted spinners since 1788'; and **Jeremiah Ambler Limited,** of Midland Mills, Bradford, spinners of worsted yarns, who were established in 1789. (The *Wool Trade Directory* has now been replaced by the *British Textile Register.*)

Older than all of these is the firm of **Charles Early and Marriott Limited,** of Witney, Oxfordshire. They have been making blankets ever since 1669 or, as their advertisements used to say, through 15 reigns. Starting with Thomas Early (1655–1733), eight generations of the family, from father to son, have carried on the business. It is estimated that members of the Early family had served the blanket trade in different generations for the astonishing length of time of 723 years. The

Wool Record of 4 May 1950 reported that Mr J H Early, the Chairman, would complete 50 years' service with the company that year (see also chapter 11, page 175).

Blankets were made at Witney by the Saxons, and 'Domesday Book' recorded the existence of two mills at Witney in the year 1085. The business of Messrs Early claims no direct connection with the Saxon weavers, but their Woodford Mill has been in their hands for as long as anyone can remember.

Another of the oldest firms in the textile industry and, like the Earlys of Witney, a founder-member of the Tercentenarians' Club, is **James Kenyon and Son Limited,** of Bury, Lancashire. They now make a variety of fabrics in wool, cotton and man-made fibres. These are mainly used in industry, such as paper-maker's felts and filter cloths.

At the time of the Hedges and Butler luncheon in 1967 (see page 175), when the company was represented by its Chairman, Mr C D Kenyon, there were still four members of the Kenyon family in the company, and ten generations of the family had been associated with it.

Mr Derek Kenyon was succeeded as Chairman by his cousin, Mr James Kenyon. On 4 July 1968 the company was sold to the big American corporation Albany International, who built a new factory on the outskirts of Bury. They refused to call the new building a mill because they did not like the dark, satanic connotations of the word, so it was said.

Among the more unusual Kenyon products was the first cotton filter cloth ever used by the Atomic Energy Commission. This was woven at the Kenyons' Roach Bank Mills, Bury.

D Ballantyne Brothers and Company Limited, of March Street Mills, Peebles, announce with proper pride that they 'have made fine cloth for eleven generations'. The firm as at present constituted is of recent origin, but the Ballantyne family have been manufacturers of cloth for nearly 300 years.

The woollen manufacturers **A and J Macnaughton,** of Pitlochry, Scotland, were established in 1835. On 18 June 1960, on the occasion of their 125th anniversary, they set out to beat the old 'Throckmorton Record of

MILESTONES IN TEXTILES

BC

4000 onwards Wool used by Neolithic man. Flax used in ancient Egypt, also grass and hemp.

3000 onwards Cotton used in India.

2640 Chinese Empress Hsi Ling Shi encourages sericulture, which remains a Chinese monopoly for about 3000 years.

AD

1589 The Reverend William Lee's stocking-frame, the first knitting-machine.

1719 John and Thomas Lombe's silk-throwing mill, Derby.

1733 Kay's flying shuttle.

1764 James Hargreaves's spinning jenny ('jenny' probably means 'engine' – cf. 'gin' below).

1769 Richard Arkwright's water-frame for roller-spinning.

1779 Samuel Crompton's spinning 'mule'.

1785 The Reverend Edmund Cartwright's power loom.

1785 James Watt's steam-engine applied to spinning-machinery.

1793 Eli Whitney's cotton 'gin' ('gin' means 'engine' or 'machine' – cf. 'jenny' above).

1805 Joseph-Marie Jacquard's loom.

1813 Horrocks's steam loom.

1891 Beginning of manufacture of rayon, invented by Chardonnet in France.

1935 Nylon discovered by W H Carothers at E I du Pont de Nemours, USA.

1940 Commercial production of nylon began.

1940 Terylene discovered by J R Whinfield and J T Dickson, Manchester.

Manufacturing Celerity whereby wool was manufactured into cloth and made into a coat in thirteen hours twenty minutes on the 25th of June 1811'. Blair Macnaughton's 'Jaiket' was successfully produced in six hours and ten minutes, and its proud owner was able to wear it at the 125th anniversary dinner that same evening. One of the men who was present to congratulate him and the workers was Mr Nicholas Throckmorton, a descendant of Sir John Throckmorton. The coat made for Sir John in 1811 was also on show. (For the Early blanket record, see chapter 11, page 176.)

There are a number of old wool firms in the west of England, a part of the country that has long been famous for its cloth. The firm of **Wm Playne and Company Limited,** of Longford Mills, Minchinhampton, Gloucestershire, dates from 1759.

Not far away, at Stroud, are the Lodgemore and Frome Hall Mills of **Strachan and Company Limited.**

Lodgemore Mill and Frome Hall Mill are 'two of the oldest cloth mills in the Stroud Valley'. Seventy per cent of their output was exported. At home, the cloth was used for naval officers' uniforms – the naval uniform worn by the Duke of Edinburgh at his wedding was made from cloth produced at Lodgemore

Mill – and Strachan's produce the scarlet worn at the Trooping of the Colour by the Queen and the guardsmen.

In 1830 the two mills were in the possession of Nathaniel Marling and, after several changes of ownership, Josiah Greathead Strachan bought them in 1865 for £30000. Strachan and Company Limited, as a firm, may be said to date from that year.

Another Gloucestershire firm, **Hunt and Winterbotham Limited,** of Cam Mills, Cam, Dursley, proclaim themselves to have been manufacturers of woollen cloth for 400 years. Cloth has in fact been made on the site of the Cam Mills for as long as that, as is shown by a Deed of Conveyance dated 1532. The present firm of Hunt and Winterbotham was established in 1887. Even before that date the cloth from these mills had been awarded medals at exhibitions in London (1862), Dublin (1865), Paris (1867), Melbourne (1881) and Calcutta (1884).

A Laverton and Company Limited, of Westbury, Wiltshire, dates from 'about 1750'. The firm owns two mills: Bitham Mill, which dates from 1772, and Angel Mill, which dates from 1874.

Fox Brothers and Company Limited, of Wellington, Somerset, is another old firm of wool manufacturers in the West Country. In the year 1745, Edward Fox of Wadebridge married into the families of Berry and Were, which were well known in the wool trade more than 300 years ago. Thomas Fox, a son of Edward Fox, became a partner in the business in 1772. Since that date, the control of the business has remained in the Fox family.

John Brooke and Sons Limited, woollen and worsted manufacturers, of Armitage Bridge, Huddersfield, claim to be the oldest family firm in Britain, with a history going back more than 400 years. The business has been handed down from father to son since the Dissolution of the Monasteries by Henry VIII, and Mr Edward Brooke, the present Managing Director, is the 14th generation to direct the business.

According to a letter in *The Times* of 7 February 1966, the family have always milled their cloth in the waters of the River Holme. The 'New Mill' in Wooldale was leased by Homfray Brooke in 1541, the firm moved to Honley early in the 18th century and to Armitage Bridge in 1798. (See also chapter 11, page 176.)

B. BUSINESSES IN OTHER LANDS

Haute couture

About a century before the European Economic Community was established, giving formal approval to freedom of movement within its boundaries, a young Englishman **Charles Frederick Worth** (1825–95) went to Paris in 1845 and founded a business that became a household word, at least in aristocratic households. He worked for some years with Gagelin et Opigez – a shop in the rue de Richelieu noted for its fine materials. Gagelin et Opigez made him their *premier commis* and later he was appointed as *Couturier* to the Empress Eugénie.

Worth married one of the shop-girls, Marie Vernet, who then inspired him to create models which gained increasing success. One day he had the completely new idea of preparing a collection in advance and presenting it to his clientele, and his wife thus became the first mannequin. He then set up his business at 7

rue de la Paix in 1858 as a maker of dresses and mantles.

Three years before Worth opened his establishment in the rue de la Paix, the English tailor **Henry Creed** had opened his Paris house in the rue Royale, and been appointed tailor to the Empress. Queen Victoria had recommended Henry Creed, who was her tailor, to Napoleon III and the Empress Eugénie when they had visited Windsor earlier in the year 1855.

Silk

The French silk-weaving firm of **Tassinari et Chatel,** Lyon, celebrated its bicentenary in 1962. Their customers have included Louis XVI, Napoleon, Catherine II of Russia and Charles IV of Spain.

Some years ago, when it was decided to restore the State Bedchamber of the Prince's Palace (Arvfurstens Palats) in Stockholm to its original condition, it was discovered that Tassinari et Chatel still held the pattern of the 18th-century green silk. However, the price was somewhat higher nowadays.

Wool

Simonius, Vischer and Company, of Basle, are said to be 'the oldest wool-merchants in Switzerland', but they must presumably rank among the oldest wool-merchants anywhere in the world.

It was on 1 March 1719 that the Basle commercial register recorded that 'Johann Fürstenberger has taken his son Johann Heinrich Fürstenberger into his Company as from March 1st, 1719.' The entry itself implies that Fürstenberger I had been in business before that date, and the company of today was clearly on safe ground in taking 1969 as its 250th anniversary.

In its early days, the firm not only bought and sold wool but also manufactured and traded in cloth.

The frontispiece to their book is a beautiful reproduction of the memorial tablet in the head office at Basle which shows the various names under which the firm has traded from 1719 onwards. (See illustration, page 69.)

Another textile business dating from the 18th century is the Dutch firm of **J P Wyers'**

Industrie- en Handelsonderneming, of Amsterdam, established in the year 1797. Its 150th anniversary, in 1947, was marked by the publication of a splendid *Gedenkboek*, with many illustrations, put together by Otto van Tussenbroek, which must be one of the largest business histories ever compiled. French and English translations have been incorporated for those readers who might have difficulty with the Dutch original text.

The **Calwer Decken- und Tuchfabriken,** of Calw, Germany, trace their history back to 1650, the year of the founding of the Calwer Zeughandelscompagnie. The company was dissolved at the end of the 18th century. Several of its constituent members subsequently came together in 1895 under the name of 'Vereinigte Deckenfabriken Calw, Zoeppritz, Wagner und Co KG'. The present name was adopted in 1959.

CHAPTER 3

EXTRACTIVE AND METAL-USING INDUSTRIES

A. BUSINESSES IN THE BRITISH ISLES

Arms

Vickers, Sons and Company Limited had been incorporated in 1867 to take over the assets and liabilities of Naylor, Vickers and Company, of Sheffield which traced its history back to 1829. Mr J D Scott, in his history of Vickers (1962), has much to say about the rivalry between Vickers and Armstrong-Whitworth, ending in the merging of the two companies.

Atomic energy

Every industry, however new, must have its oldest representative. The atomic power station at **Calder Hall,** Cumberland, which was opened by Her Majesty the Queen on 17 October 1956, when power was first fed into the grid of the Central Electricity Authority, might be regarded as the oldest business in our newest industry. It is Britain's – and the world's – first full-scale nuclear power station. Calder Hall was designed to generate some 90 000 kW of electrical power and at the same time to manufacture plutonium, a trans-Uranic nuclear fuel, for military purposes.

Bell-founding

In *Queer Things about London* (published in 1923), C G Harper wrote:

'What and where is the oldest business in London? I will declare, without fear of contradiction, that

it is the bell-founding business of Messrs. Mears and Stainbank.'

The **Whitechapel Bell Foundry** has been on its present site, at 32 and 34 Whitechapel Road, London E1, since 1738, but its origins can be clearly traced back to 1570, when the foundry was situated about 200 yd (200 m) from the present address.

The firm is undoubtedly among the oldest in the country, not merely in London.

'Big Ben' – cast at the Whitechapel Bell Foundry 10 April 1858. (*Whitechapel Bell Foundry*)

'BIG BEN' the great bell of Westminster. Cast at the Whitechapel foundry April 10. 1858.

MILESTONES IN NUCLEAR ENERGY

1938   First observed nuclear fission, discovered by the German chemist Professor Otto Hahn and radiochemist Fritz Strassmann. Hahn was awarded the 1944 Nobel Prize for Chemistry.

1942   First nuclear reactor constructed at University of Chicago; the building was directed by Enrico Fermi.

3 July 1944   Neils Bohr, the Danish physicist, sent his memorandum to Roosevelt and Churchill stating that the nuclear bomb would be 'a perpetual menace to human society'.

16 July 1945   First man-made nuclear explosion at 'Trinity' in the Alamogordo Desert New Mexico, USA.

6 Aug 1945   First atomic bomb dropped on Hiroshima, Japan, killing nearly 100 000 people. The bomb 'Little Boy' weighed 9920 lb (4500 kg) (a 10.5 ft (3.2 m) long cylinder 28.7 in (73 cm) in diameter) containing 132 lb (60 kg) of U235 yielding a 13.5 Kt explosion.

9 Aug 1945   Second atomic bomb dropped over Nagasaki, Japan, killing between 39 000–74 000 people (bombs and radiation exposure). The bomb 'Fat Man' weighed 8818 lb (4000 kg) (an egg-shaped ellipsoid with axes of 10.5 ft (3.2 m) and 4.9 ft (1.5 m) containing 17.6 lb (8 kg) of Pt. 239, yielding a 22 Kt explosion.

Mar 1946   US Strategic Air Command (SAC) formed with B-17 and B-29 medium bombers. SAC peak strength 2000 – reduced to 450 by 1975.

1947   First British reactor at Harwell, England.

21 Aug 1949   First USSR atomic explosion at Semipalatinsk, Central Asia. Yield 20 Kt – world's ninth nuclear detonation.

Jan 1950   President Truman ordered develop-ment of thermonuclear weapons.

May 1951   First thermonuclear reaction at Eniwetok Atoll with 200 Kt yield by US Task Force.

1952   Construction of largest atomic plant in the world: Savannah River project, near Aiken, South Carolina, USA, extending 27 miles (43 km). Total area 315 miles² (816 km²).

Nov 1952   Largest ever fission bomb exploded by US – yield 500 Kt.

Nov 1952   First fission bomb at Elugelab Island, Eniwetok a 200 ton (100000 kg) plus 21.6 ft (6.6 m) long cylinder yielding 10000 Kt or 10 mt.

12 Aug 1953   First USSR thermonuclear device with a yield of 400 Kt.

1954   First atomic power station established at Obninsk, near Moscow: electrical current produced for industrial undertakings and agricultural purposes on 27 June. Output 5 MW.

1 Mar 1954   First deliverable US H-bomb exploded at Bikini Atoll. Yield 15 mega tons (mt) (US record).

23 Nov 1955   First deliverable USSR H-bomb exploded. Yield 2 mt.

1956   USSR Strategic Tu-20 (Bear) and Mya-4 (Bison) bombers deployed.

1956   First large-scale atomic power station in the world was Calder Hall, Cumberland. Output 90 MW.

Oct 1961   Largest ever nuclear device exploded in Novaya Zemlya. Yield about 60 mt.

1973   World's largest atomic station is the Ontario Hydro's Pickering station which, in 1973, attained full output of 2160 MW.

The foundry itself, it should be added, makes no such claim in the booklet *Church Bell Founding during four Centuries at the Whitechapel Bell Foundry*, which contains a short account of its history. The first Master Founder, Robert Mot, began making bells in Whitechapel in the early part of the reign of Queen Elizabeth I and many of Mot's bells are still in existence. They are obviously made to last, as the author discovered that a Mot bell (cast in 1597) which was being repaired would need no further repairs for 300 years!

In 1606, Robert Mot was succeeded by Joseph Carter, a kinsman. Carter had learned his craft at the 14th-century Wokingham Foundry and thus provides a link with an even older business, now no longer in existence.

All the eight bells at Westminster Abbey came from the Whitechapel Bell Foundry, the first in 1583 and the last in 1919. They were recently rehung in new bearings, so that we have here a connection between customer and supplier extending over nearly 400 years.

The well-known Bow bells came from the Whitechapel Bell Foundry in 1762, and were recast there after being damaged in the war. The

anno Dom. 1719   1719

Werdegang der Firma seit der ersten Eintragung im Basler Ragionenbuch primo Martÿ 1719

Fürstenberger

Simonius

Vischer

1719-1742 Johann Fürstenberger	1887-1901 Fürstenberger und Cie.
1742-1757 Joh. Fürstenberger und Söhne	1902-1912 Haerle, Simonius, Strohl u. Cie.
1757-1783 Joh. Heinrich Fürstenberger	1913-1918 Simonius, Strohl und Cie.
1783-1800 Joh. Fürstenberger und Sohn	1918 Simonius, Vischer und Cie.
1783-1886 Hans Georg Fürstenberger	

Memorial tablet in the head office of Simonius, Vischer and Company, Basle (see page 65)

"GREAT PAUL"
T. C. Q. LBS.
WEIGHING 16 14 2 19
(37,483 LBS.) EN ROUTE
FROM LOUGHBOROUGH TO
LONDON. MAY. 1882

THIS GREAT BELL, THE LARGEST
IN THE BRITISH EMPIRE, WAS
FOUNDED BY
JOHN TAYLOR & CO.,
LOUGHBOROUGH
AND HANGS
IN THE S.W. TOWER OF ST.
PAUL'S CATHEDRAL.

'Great Paul' – the largest bell in the British Empire. *(John Taylor & Company)*

most famous of all the bells that have come from this foundry is 'Big Ben'. This huge bell, weighing 13 tons, 10 cwt, 3 qr, 15 lb, was cast on 10 April 1858. (See illustration, page 67.)

Bells from the foundry have been exported all over the world. The 'Liberty Bell' at Philadelphia, which proclaimed the Declaration of Independence on 4 July 1776, was first cast at Whitechapel in 1752 but was broken soon after it was hung. It was recast, using the same shape and lettering, by Pass and Stow of Philadelphia, and was placed upon the hall in which the Congress of 1776 assembled. The bell cracked again when being tolled for the death of Chief Justice Marshall, in 1835. The prophetic inscription on the bell, taken from Leviticus 25, reads: 'Proclaim liberty throughout all the land unto all the inhabitants thereof.'

The only other surviving bell-foundry in this country is at **Loughborough.** According to the section on bell-ringing in the third volume of

Our National Heritage, published by the National Benzole Company, 'The making of bells is one of the oldest industries and an existing bell foundry in Leicestershire dates back to the 14th century.'

The first half of this statement is correct but the second half is more open to question. There was a bell-foundry in Leicester (not Loughborough) in the latter half of the 14th century. At the end of the following century we come across another mention of a bell-founder in Leicester. This business seems to have died out in the 17th century, or to have been carried on in Kettering by the Eayre family, who were also clock-makers. The business later moved to St Neots, in Huntingdonshire, and it was here that Robert Taylor (1759–1830) was apprenticed.

Robert Taylor had two sons, William (1795–1854) and John (1797–1858), who worked with him for some time but afterwards set up in Oxford. John married in 1825 and went to

Buckland Brewer in Devonshire, where he built a foundry. Eight years later he returned to Oxford, which he left again in 1840 to come to Loughborough, where the foundry has since remained.

When John died, in 1858, he left the foundry to his son, John William Taylor. The latter and his son, another John William (1853–1919), cast many bells and peals, including 'Great Paul' for St Paul's Cathedral in London. This is the largest bell in the British Commonwealth, weighing as it does more than 16 tons. It was cast in November 1881 and dedicated in 1882 (see illustration, page 70).

Many cathedrals and town halls have been supplied with bells from the Loughborough Foundry. 'Great George', for Liverpool Roman Catholic Cathedral was cast in 1940 (see illustration below). (The bells in the Anglican Cathedral at Liverpool came from the Whitechapel Bell Foundry and are the heaviest bells in the world that are hung for change ringing. The tenor weighs 82 cwt (4.1 t), and the ring of 13 bells totals 16½ tons.)

'Great George' – Liverpool Cathedral. (*Wayne Photographs Ltd*)

Bricks

The **London Brick Company,** Peterborough, is the world's biggest manufacturer of bricks. They announced in October 1974 that production was to be *reduced* by 11 million bricks a week. At that time they had a stockpile of 300 million bricks. Stewartby is the company's largest production unit and the capacity is about 15 000 000 bricks a week.

The business was established in 1897 by Mr B J H Forder, and took the name of London Brick Company Limited in 1936. In August 1975 the British brick-making industry as a whole was said to have 748 million bricks lying stockpiled.

Builders

The notepaper of **R Durtnell and Sons Limited,** of Brasted, Kent, carries the heading: 'Durtnell: Builders since 1591'. The firm has been carried on from father to son for twelve generations since that time.

Unlike some other old firms, Durtnell's are still on their original site in Brasted. The Smiths of Thirsk, an even older family firm, were also on their original site until they closed down a few years ago (see page 61). So these are two firms founded within a dozen years of each other, in the reign of Elizabeth I, who were in a position to beat by more than a century the claim of Twining's the tea-merchants to be the oldest firm still in the same family on its original site and in the same line of business (see page 32).

In an article, 'The Unusual Archives of Richard Durtnell & Sons Ltd., Builders since 1591' in *Business Archives* of June 1974, Lieutenant-Colonel C S Durtnell pointed out that he had been able to prove, with the help of church registers in Kent, that the Durtnell family had been occupied in the building trade in Brasted for twelve generations since 22 July 1591, when John Dutnell (*sic*) of Brasted, a carpenter, had married Ann Herst of Westerham. The history of the family, however, had been traced back to 1131. (See also chapter 11, page 175.)

Chains

According to Charles Wilkins's *History of the Iron, Steel, Tinplate, and other trades of Wales,* iron chains were introduced in the Royal Navy in 1810, but a full complement of hempen ropes was also carried on board until 1844. (By that time Their Lordships at the Admiralty were presumably satisfied that the newfangled iron chains could be relied upon.)

The iron chains for the Royal Navy were made by **Brown, Lennox and Company** at Pontypridd, 'the oldest contractors to the War Office, Indian Government, Trinity Corporation' and also 'the oldest firm in the trade'. The works at Pontypridd were opened in 1818, but the firm also had works at Millwall, which had been opened in 1812.

According to H L V Fletcher's *South Wales*, the Newbridge Ironworks at Pontypridd 'made the anchor chains for the ships of Nelson's fleet, and they are still making chains and anchors for battleships and liners'. But, if 1810 saw the introduction of iron chains in the Royal Navy, then Nelson himself would clearly not have used them, since he died at Trafalgar in 1805.

Clocks

'**Thwaites & Reed,** founded in 1740 by Aynsworth Thwaites, are the oldest established clockmakers in the United Kingdom, with complete records, housed in the Guildhall Library, going back to that date. The company have exported clocks to almost every country in the world, and specialize in the production of public and special clocks.' The quotation is part of the text accompanying the photograph of a gearwheel cutting machine in Aubrey Wilson's richly illustrated book *London's Industrial Heritage* (1967).

Thwaites and Reed, whose head office and works are now at Hastings in Sussex, made the astronomical clock for the offices of the *Financial Times* in London. They also made the famous Fortnum and Mason clock, which has the figures of Mr Fortnum and Mr Mason appearing on the hour, to a tune of 17 bells (see frontispiece). This was the biggest clock to be made in this country since the great Westminster clock – of 'Big Ben' fame – in 1861. The bronze founding was executed by James Gibbons Limited, of Wolverhampton whose history goes back to 1670 (see page 77), and the bell came from the Whitechapel Bell

Tower clock made by Thwaites & Reed in 1788 and sent in for repair from Indonesia. *(Thwaites & Reed)*

Foundry, which is just a century older still (see page 67).

Coal

The company called **Charrington, Gardner, Locket and Company** was formed in 1922, when Gardner, Locket and Hinton amalgamated with Charrington Dale and Company. It was, however, back in 1719 that the history of the oldest element in the company began, when Benjamin Horne came to London from Sussex and set up as a coal factor. In the year 1969 Charrington's celebrated the 250th anniversary of this event.

At one time Charrington's dated their history from 1731, when Joseph Wright set up as a coal-merchant in Lower Thames Street. When arrangements were being made to celebrate the 200th anniversary, in 1931, it was discovered that the year 1719 was the beginning.

At the time of the 250th anniversary celebrations, eight generations of the Horne family had been connected with the business. The Charringtons first came upon the scene in 1790, when John Charrington I, 'the Gentleman Coal Merchant', started a coal business at Shadwell. John Charrington IV, who was knighted in 1949, served as Chairman of the company from 1940 to 1964, when he became its President.

One of the companies in the Charrington Group is Glover Webb and Liversidge, coachbuilders (see page 125).

Another old coal company, **Ridley's Coal and Iron Company,** of Bury St Edmunds, celebrated its 225th anniversary in 1975. In its early days the firm traded as general merchants and tanners but, with the coming of the Lark navigation and the railway, the business became primarily concerned with the sale of coal and iron. Throughout its history the business has been owned and managed by the Ridley family, in direct father to son descent, for seven generations.

Cutlery

Joseph Rodgers and Sons Limited, of Sheffield, claim to have been makers of fine cutlery since the reign of Charles II. Their trademark of a six-pointed star and Maltese Cross was granted in 1682 to William Birks. In 1724 it was let to John Rodgers, and in 1764 it was confirmed to the firm by the Cutlers' Company of Sheffield.

The firm's trade was originally confined to penknives, but other branches of cutlery were taken up after 1800. Although the firm was once described as 'the oldest cutlers in the world', an older firm of cutlers, in France, will be mentioned on page 83.

Engineering, iron and steel

Kirkstall Forge was founded as a monastic forge at the very opening of the 13th century and 'can justly claim to have been, apart from occasional short periods of depression, in continuous work for 750 years'. The engineering side of the business was created in 1841.

For 125 years the Forge was largely managed by five generations of the Spencer family, and in 1779 the Butler family took over. Mr Rodney Butler represented the fifth generation of the family to be connected with the Forge.

The company have been largely engaged on making axles since about 1919. Shortly after the First World War they decided to liquidate the iron business and, to quote Mr Butler's words as they stand in his book, 'On May 20th, 1920, iron ceased to be worked at Kirkstall Forge, after an unbroken run of more than 700 years.'

Another Yorkshire company, **Marsh Brothers and Company Limited,** of Sheffield celebrated their 250th anniversary in the year 1904. In order to commemorate their 300th anniversary, the celebration of which was planned for 1954, the firm invited Dr Sidney Pollard to write their history, which he did in *Three Centuries of Sheffield Steel; the Story of a Family Business.* Dr Pollard was able to show that the firm was older than had previously been thought, and that 'its origins can be firmly placed in the year 1631'.

In a Foreword to the book, the company's Chairman, Lieutenant-Colonel W Lockwood Marsh, said, modestly:

'It is, I think, unusual for a firm to be able to trace its continued existence in the hands of one family for more than three hundred years; and so far as the Sheffield steel trade is concerned, it is probably unique.'

In a letter to *The Times* of 10 December 1956, Lieutenant-Colonel W Lockwood Marsh, writing with reference to letters from Scott's the basket-makers (see page 86) and from Early's the blanket-weavers (see page 63) said that he could 'push back a little further the record for length of existence of a firm', as his own firm dated its foundation to 1 August 1631. He continued: 'I am the present chairman of the firm and represent the tenth generation of a family which has been engaged in the steel trade, in the direct line of succession from father to son, for 325 years' (i.e. from 1631 to 1956).

John Marsh had entered his mark with the Cutlers' Company on 1 August 1631, and the firm can be dated from then. For the first half of its existence Marsh Brothers was mainly engaged on the manufacture of 'cutlery', a term which included in the 17th century 'all trades with the exception of scissors and shearsmiths'. Steel-making was added later. Among the items made in the 19th century were piano wire and crinoline steel.

In 1907, what had hitherto been a family partnership was transformed into a limited liability company under the title of 'Marsh Brothers and Company Limited'. In 1908 it became a 'private' limited liability company. The connection of the Marsh family with the business ended in 1959, when Mr G L Willan acquired all the equity of Marsh Brothers and merged it with his own organisation, the Willan Group. Marsh Brothers are now manufacturers of engineers' cutting tools.

Family tradition was also strong in the **Butterley Company Limited,** where Mr E Fitzwalter Wright, the Chairman and Managing Director, was a direct descendant of John Wright, one of the founders of the firm, which dates from 1790. It now has works at Butterley Park, and at Ripley, near Derby.

The business was founded to operate coalworkings, and the ironworks were erected two years later. John Wright was one of the four original members. William Jessop, another of the four founders, invented the flanged railway wheel. One of the firm's productions was the roof of St Pancras Station in London.

As has already been mentioned when dealing with the cotton industry (page 60), the firm of **Dobson and Barlow,** textile machinery makers, was also established in the year 1790.

Dating from the same year of 1790 is **Whessoe Limited.** This firm traces its origin to an ironmonger's shop which was opened in 1790 in Tubwell Row, Darlington, by William Kitching, a Quaker. In 1830 a railway foundry was established, and the firm later turned its attention to the structural side of railway work. Nowadays the company is mainly concerned with the design and construction of steel-plate structures and chemical engineering. Among other products, Whessoe built the nuclear reactor vessels for Calder Hall (see 'Atomic energy', page 67).

Another historic enterprise is the **Coalbrookdale Company,** of Coalbrookdale in Shropshire, whose origins go back to 1709, when Abraham Darby became the first person successfully to smelt iron with coke, and thus made feasible the large-scale production of iron without which the Industrial Revolution would have been impossible. Among his earliest productions were domestic cooking-vessels, and in 1767 the firm pioneered the use of iron rails, having at the time a surplus of iron on their hands. In 1779 they made the Iron Bridge over the Severn, the first metal structure in the world. Today, as a subsidiary of Allied Ironfounders, the Coalbrookdale Company produces 'Raeburn cookers' and firegrates.

The modern history of Kirkstall Forge (see page 73) might be said to start in 1779. This is the date that appears on the company's notepaper beneath a portrait of Thomas Butler with the legend 'Established in Present Proprietary'. (It was presumably impossible to depict the unknown monk who began the enterprise in the year 1200.) Several other engineering firms date from the latter half of the 18th century, including:

The **Lilleshall Company** of Oakengates, Shropshire (1764);

G Gardiner and Son, of Wolsingham and Crook, County Durham, 'Agricultural and General Engineers, Blacksmiths and Farriers', who were established in 1779;

Fawcett, Preston and Company of Bromborough, Cheshire, have been 'engineering on Merseyside' since 1758.

The 'Fosset' or Fawcett story began in 1758 when George Perry, who had worked as a clerk and then as a draughtsman at the Coalbrookdale Ironworks in Shropshire (see above), was sent to Liverpool to set up and manage a branch of the company. This became known as the 'Phoenix Foundry', and produced the three-legged pots for which the Darbys were famous.

Perry died in 1771, and was succeeded by Joseph Rathbone. In 1784 a young relative, William Fawcett, who had served his apprenticeship in the foundry, joined the management, and so began a connection which was to last for 60 years and to make his name familiar to engineers in every part of the world. In 1794, Fawcett bought the foundry for £2300 and changed the name of the business to Fawcett and Company.

Early in the 19th century, Fawcett's began making sugar machinery for the West Indies. Crushing machinery, but for oil-seeds instead of sugar-cane, was also an important line of manufacture for **Rose, Downs and Thompson,** of Hull, who date their foundation from 1777 and who describe themselves as 'the oldest manufacturers of Oil Mill Machinery in the world today'.

Holman Brothers Limited, of Camborne, Cornwall, the makers of mining equipment, were already in the fifth generation of the Holman family, according to an advertisement in the *Sunday Times* of 13 June 1965.

Junior by only a year to Rose, Downs and Thompson is the **Richard Garrett Engineering Works Limited,** of Leiston, Suffolk. Richard Garrett I (1757–1839) founded the firm in 1778. He made hoes and sickles. His son, Richard Garrett II, took over in 1805 and started the manufacture of the threshing-machine invented by his father-in-law, John Balls.

The firm became famous for threshing-machines and other farm equipment. They also made portable steam-engines and steamrollers. The family connection with the works lasted until 1932, when the business was bought by Beyer Peacock and Company, of Manchester.

The **Stockton Heath Forge,** of Warrington, makers of spades and shovels, date their history from 1770, and the date appears in their trademark. It was about 1770 that the Earl of Ellesmere began work on the Bridgewater Canal, and the spades and shovels needed for the job came from the Stockton Heath Forge.

Yet another business dating from the third quarter of the 18th century is the **Carron Company** of Falkirk. The company received a Royal Charter from George III in 1773 and are said to be the only industrial firm with this distinction. There might be some argument on this score, and the firm may have a surer claim to fame in its carronades, which gave a new word to the English language, and in their 'Carron oil'. Although the firm received its Charter in 1773, its history goes back to 1759.

A 'carronade', according to the *Shorter Oxford English Dictionary*, was a short piece of ordnance, usually of large calibre, having a chamber for the powder like a mortar: chiefly used on shipboard. The word is first recorded in 1779. 'Carron oil' was a liniment of linseed oil and lime water in equal parts, which, the dictionary informs us, was much used at the Carron ironworks, but it does not say what for. This term is first recorded in 1884.

The **Wilkinson Sword Company,** of London, was established in 1772 by Henry Nock, in Ludgate Street. He made pistols and sporting guns. When he died, he left his business to James Wilkinson, his son-in-law and former apprentice. It was James Wilkinson who took up the manufacture of swords, for which the firm became famous.

Fire engineering

Merryweather and Sons Limited, of Greenwich High Road, London, are 'the oldest fire engineering company in the world'. The firm's history began in 1690, when Samuel Hadley set up in business near Long Acre in the Parish of St Martin-in-the-Fields to sell leather and make leather fire-buckets.

About 1730 the firm began to make manual fire-engines for the then newly formed fire insurance brigades. In 1799 the firm was known as 'Hadley, Simpkin and Lott'. Moses Merryweather married a niece of Lott and, about 1830, took over control of the family concern. Fire-escapes and self-propelled fire-engines were being made before the century closed.

The company now forms part of the Tecalemit Group.

Flint-knapping

Flint-knapping is 'the oldest craft in the world'. Sharp-edged tools and weapons were fashioned from stones thousands of years before the discovery of metal. Flint-knappers still pursue their ancient craft at Brandon, in Suffolk, making gun-flints for the old game guns still used in parts of Africa.

Arthur Mee's *Suffolk* calls the work of knapping flints 'the oldest industry in England, 200 generations old'.

An illustrated article in *Civil Service Motoring* of September 1974 about the pits at Grimes Graves near Brandon from which the flints were dug says that 'the cutting tool industry in this country began, not in Sheffield as one would expect, but in the heathlands of Norfolk'. It says that mining for the good-quality flints that are to be found here began 'about 2000 BC'.

An article in the *Bulletin* of the Ministry of Agriculture, Fisheries and Food of August 1963 came to the conclusion that 'it is not beyond the bounds of possibility that primitive man learnt the art of knapping flints long before he cultivated a crop or tended a flock'.

According to the *Guinness Book of Records*, there is no evidence that agriculture was practised 'before *c.* 11 000 BC'. It goes on to say: 'The oldest known industry is flint knapping, involving the production of chopping tools and hand axes, dating from *c.* 1 750 000 years ago.'

The Flint Knappers, Brandon, Suffolk. *(Studio Five, Photographers, Thetford)*

On 14 December 1967, Mr Eldon Griffiths, MP, asked the President of the Board of Trade 'on what grounds he refused an export licence to Mr Herbert Edwards of Brandon, Suffolk, the only master flint-knapper in Great Britain, who has orders for gun-flints for South African flintlock muzzle-loaders: and if he will rescind his ban on the sale to South Africa of flints for muzzle-loading flintlock guns'. The reply was that 'Mr. Edwards was told that a licence, if applied for, would be refused, and that the general ban is enforced, in conformity with the Government's announced policy on the export of arms to South Africa'. (*Hansard*, column 225.) This suggests that the industry is not dead yet.

Goldbeaters

Geo M Whiley Limited, now of Ruislip, Middlesex, were established in 1783. A brief account of the firm's history was given in a booklet entitled *Goldbeating and the Standard of Gold Leaf* that seems to have been published about 1929, when the old premises in Whitfield Street, London, had just been extended. The firm had been founded in Long Acre and moved to Whitfield Street in 1830.

The craft of goldbeating has remained unchanged since 'the days of Tutankhamun and a thousand years before'.

Ironmongers

King and Company Limited, of Kingston-upon-Hull, was founded by Henry King in 1744, who started business in Church Lane but moved to larger premises, in Market Place, in 1746. In 1877 the business was transferred to South Church Side. In 1946, the fifth generation of the King family was represented on the Board of Directors by Professor W B R King.

An Exeter ironmongery business was started by John Atken in Fore Street in 1661 and developed into the business known today as the

Exeter Foundry of **Garton and King Limited.**
Despite the recurrence of the name 'King',
there does not seem to be any link between
the business in Hull and the business in Exeter.

The old ironmongery business of **A Macintosh and Sons** that used to be found in the
Market Place at Cambridge, opposite the
Guildhall, was established in 1688. It was still
there in 1962, but the building has since been
pulled down, and the business exists no more.

Locks

James Gibbons Limited, of Wolverhampton,
was established about 1670 by Thomas
Gibbons. In 1966 the business was taken over
by Radiation Limited, and in the following year
Radiation itself was taken over by Tube
Investments. The connection with the Gibbons
family ended a few years ago.

The firm make locks, metal windows and
builders' hardware. They executed the bronze-
founding for the Fortnum and Mason clock
(see 'Clocks' and frontispiece). When the clock
was made, in 1964, the firm was still controlled
by members of the Gibbons family.

Bramah Security Equipment Limited,
of London, were established in 1784 and
describe themselves as 'The oldest Patent
lockmakers in the world'. The key word in
this context – *sit venia verbo* – seems to be
'Patent'. Joseph Bramah, who was born in
1749, patented his lock in 1784.

Bramah's first patent, for 'a Water Closet
upon a New Construction', had been granted
in 1778. This is said to have served to
introduce him to the problems of hydraulics,
the study of which was to lead to the invention
of the hydraulic press for which he obtained a
patent in 1795. The French genius Blaise Pascal
(1623–62) had expounded the secret of the
hydraulic press in a work published just after
his death, in 1663, but Bramah was the first
man to find a practical application of the principle expounded by Pascal.

Mints

The **Heaton Mint** in Birmingham was in
existence in 1794 and appears to have been
founded in that year by Ralph Heaton, who
died in 1832. The Heaton Mint is said to be
the oldest private mint in the world.

John Pinches (Medallists) Limited,
London, celebrated their 125th anniversary in
Clapham in 1965, having been established in
1840. They design and make medals of all
kinds. They make the insignia of Companions
of Honour for this country and, at the time
of the celebration, they had just produced the
Order of the Star of Sarawak in five grades.

The Royal Mint has a good claim to be
regarded as the oldest existing business in
Britain and also as our oldest Government
Department. In addition, it could be taken to be
our oldest nationalised industry.

The official *Outline History* by H G Stride,
published in 1956, contains a Foreword by
Hugh Gaitskell, who was Chancellor of the
Exchequer in 1951, when the first edition
appeared. (The Chancellor of the Exchequer
is *ex officio* the 'Master Worker and Warden'
of the Mint, the day-to-day running of
the establishment being in the hands of the
Deputy Master.) The booklet mentions the
recapture of London from the Vikings by
Alfred the Great 'a few years' after 871,
whereupon Alfred arranged 'a large issue of
pennies from the London Mint. From about
this time the story of the London Mint
becomes continuous . . .'.

About 1279 'the London Mint was situated
in the Treasury and Exchequer buildings at
Westminster but in 1300 a new mint

Coin struck by Carausius about AD 287. *(British
Museum)*

(comprising a building 400 feet (120 m) long)
was erected in the Tower of London between
the inner and outer walls'.

According to Sir John Craig's *The Mint –
A History of the London Mint from A.D. 287 to
1948*, the first London mint was set up by
Carausius, 'who proclaimed his suzerainty in
AD 287 and struck Roman coins in his own
name in the island' (see illustration above).
But the London mint, having been closed by
Constantius (292–306) and reopened by

Constantine the Great (306–37), was then closed down for about three centuries.

At the end of this period, to quote Sir John Craig again, 'London accepted a bishop and gained a mint between 600 and 604'. This mint, again, was closed for most of the 8th century. It probably reopened about the year 830, but it is only from the time of Alfred the Great (871–901) that the continuous history of the mint begins.

For many hundreds of years the Mint was situated within the precincts of the Tower of London. The exact year when it moved there is not known, but it was certainly there in the year 1299, and may have been there as early as 1248. (Thornbury, in his *Old and New London*, volume 2, goes so far as to say: 'That the Romans had a mint in London is certain, and probably on the site of the present Tower. . . . The chief Mint of England was in the Tower, at all events from the Conquest till 1811'.)

The Mint remained in the Tower until 1811. It was Edward I (1272–1307) who gave the Mint 'an organization which endured in form till the nineteenth century and a technique that was kept till the mid-seventeenth'.

The provincial mints were gradually closed down, and from 1552, 'except for the Civil Wars and the branch mints opened for the silver recoinage of 1698–9, one Mint hence-forward served England and Ireland, and after 1709 Scotland'.

In the year 1555 the Mint struck some Spanish coins – a consequence of Mary's marriage to Philip of Spain. This was 'the first foreign coin ever struck by the Mint'.

Richard (afterwards Sir Richard) Martin (1534–1617) became Warden of the Mint in 1572, an office which he held until 1599. In 1581 he was appointed Master of the Mint too. In various capacities he worked at the Mint from 1559 until he died in harness at the age of 83.

In 1680 the Master of the Mint was suspended and replaced by a Commission which included Sir Charles Duncombe, 'the richest commoner in England'. Sir Isaac Newton was appointed Master of the Mint in 1697, after being appointed Warden of the Mint in 1694, and held office until his death in 1727.

After much consideration and debate, the Mint was moved from the Tower of London to its site on Tower Hill early in the 19th century. The new buildings were finished in 1809. After the machinery had been installed, the move from the premises in the Tower began in 1811 and was completed in the following year. The keys of the old Mint were formally handed over to the Constable of the Tower in August 1812, thus ending an occupancy of more than 500 years.

One other milestone in the Mint's long history should be mentioned here. 'Gold coinage ceased in 1917, 574 years after the effective introduction of a gold currency'.

The Royal Mint can look back on 1000 years of history, and over an even longer period than this if gaps of a century or more are ignored. It has, therefore, a strong claim to be regarded as the oldest manufacturing business in these islands, and indeed as one of the oldest businesses of any kind in the world.

Motor cars (*see 'Transport', page 125*)

Oil companies

Oldest

In 1970 the 'Business Diary' of *The Times* recorded a spirited contest for the title of 'the oldest British oil company'. The claim put forward by the **Burmah Oil Company** (based on the Rangoon Oil Company, established in 1871) was disputed by **British Petroleum,** who traced their ancestry to Young's Paraffin Light and Mineral Oil Company, established in 1866.

Two other contenders for the title were **Price's Patent Candle Company,** which began making candles in 1847 but started refining lamp oil and lubricants ten years later, and the improbably named firm **Carless, Capel and Leonard,** founded in 1859. The latter claim to have been the first to introduce a motor spirit for the internal-combustion engine (for Gottfried Daimler) and to have given this the name 'petrol' when introducing it on the British market at the end of the last century.

Finally, the Leeds company called **Filtrate Limited** was mentioned. They traced their origin to a Yorkshire firm of seed-crushers and oil-refiners founded in 1807, which is said

MILESTONES IN THE HISTORY OF OIL

1847 First shale oil refinery established by Dr James Young at Alfreton, Derbyshire.

1851 First US oil lease, Pennsylvania.

1854 First oil company, Pennsylvania Rock Oil Company, incorporated on 30 December 1854, in New York City by George H Bissell of New Haven, Connecticut, with a capital stock of $250 000 (10 000 shares at $25).

1859 First discovery of oil in US at Titusville, Pennsylvania, by Colonel Drake. It produced approximately 400 gal (1818 l) a day.

1861 First shipload of oil crosses Atlantic in *Elizabeth Watts*, a 224-ton brig. The shipment was made from Philadelphia, Pennsylvania to London.

1864 First oil-tank rail-cars were introduced by Charles P Hatch of the Empire Transportation Company, Philadelphia, Pennsylvania.

1865 The first oil pipeline of importance to transport crude petroleum successfully was completed on 9 October by Samuel van Syckel of Titusville, Pennsylvania. Wrought-iron pipes measuring 2 in (5 cm) in diameter and about 5 miles (8 km) long were laid underground in 15 foot (4.5 m) sections.

1873 Oil production in Russia first commences.

1908 Oil first struck in Iran (Persia).

1914 First discovery of oil in Venezuela.

1922 First UK refinery on stream at Llandarcy.

1925 First international oil consortium formed which became known as IPC (Iraq Petroleum Company).

1926 First production of synthetic oil from coal.

1927 First Schlumberger electric log produced.*

1932 First oil discovery in Bahrein.

1933 First World Petroleum Congress in London.

1934 UK Petroleum (Products) Act passed.

1938 First nationalisation of an oil industry in Mexico.

1938 First offshore oil-field discovered off Louisiana.

1939 First oil discovered in the UK in Nottinghamshire.

*Inventor – Conrad Schlumberger, France. Used for measuring the resistivity and other properties in rock-beds particularly with reference to the poracity with a view to finding the potential for oil- or gas-bearing rock. The log is inserted into the drilled oil-well. First produced in Techelbrone, Alsace (France).

1948 First 50 : 50 profit sharing agreement made in Venezuela.

1948 First natural gas discoveries in the Netherlands.

1960 Proteins first produced from hydrocarbons in industrial conditions.

1960 OPEC (Organisation of the Petroleum Exporting Countries) formed in Baghdad, during a conference convened by the Government of Iraq. Members: Governments of eleven countries with a substantial net export of crude petroleum (Algeria, Libya, Nigeria, Venezuela, Abu Dhabi, Indonesia, Iran, Iraq, Kuwait, Qatar, Saudi Arabia).

1964 First North Sea Oil and Gas Licence is granted for the UK sector.

1965 Natural gas first discovered in the North Sea.

1967 First Arab Oil Embargo.

1967 Worst oil pollution from some 30 000 tons of Kuwait crude resulted from the largest vessel ever to be wrecked in British waters: the 965 ft (294 m) long tanker, *Torrey Canyon*, of 61 275 tons gross and 118 285 tons deadweight. It struck the Pollard Rock of the Seven Stones Reef between the Isles of Scilly and Land's End, Cornwall at 8.50 am on 18 March.

1968 Oil first struck in Alaska.

1969 The longest commercial oil pipeline in Britain was opened on 19 March at a cost of £8½ million. It is 242 miles (389 km) long, runs from the Thames to the Mersey and is owned by Chevron, Mobil, Petrofina, Shell-Mex and BP, and Texaco.

1970 Oil first discovered in the Forties Field in November.

1971 The most productive oil-field found in Brent Field in July is expected to reach 22 million tons per year by 1981.

1973 OPEC countries set posted prices for the first time.

1973 The largest oil-tank ever constructed is the Million Barrel Ekofisk Oil Tank completed in Norway and implanted in the North Sea measuring 301.8 ft square and 269 ft high (92 × 92 m; 82 m high) and containing 7873 tons (8000 metric tons) of steel and 198 809 tons (202 000 metric tons) of concrete. The capacity of 209 272 yd^3 (160 000 m^3) is equivalent to 1.42 times the amount of oil which escaped from the *Torrey Canyon*.

Continued overleaf

MILESTONES IN THE HISTORY OF OIL *continued*

1974 Man's deepest penetration into the earth's crust is under Rig No 32 gas well at No 1 Bertha Rogers Field, Washita County, Oklahoma, USA. After 503 days drilling the Loffland Brothers Drilling Co. reached 31 441 ft (9583 m) on 3 April — this is 2413 ft (735.4 m) deeper than Everest is high.

1974 The world's largest oil company is the Exxon Corporation (formerly Standard Oil Company (New Jersey)), with 135 500 employees and assets valued at $32 839 398 000 on 1 January 1976. Their turnover in 1974 was $45 821 million.

1975 The world's largest oil-refinery is Amuya Bay refinery in Venezuela, owned by Lagoven, with a capacity of 31.5 million tons (32 000 000 million t).

1975 The largest oil-refinery in the UK is the Esso Refinery at Fawley, Hampshire. Opened in 1921 and much expanded in 1951, it has a capacity of 19 500 000 tons (19 800 000 t) per year. The total investment on the 1300 acre (526 ha) site is £150 000 000.

1975 Oil production from the UK and Norwegian sectors of the North Sea commences in November.

1975 The largest fixed leg drilling platforms are the two BP Forties Field platforms. The overall height from below the mud-line to the top of the drilling rig is 686 ft (209 m). Each weighs 57 000 tons (57 900 t).

1975 The world's most massive oil platform is Shell-Esso's 230 000 ton (233 600 t) deadweight Condeep Brent B Field platform built in Stavanger, Norway and positioned in June.

1976 The world's longest crude oil pipeline is the Interprovincial Pipe Line Company's installation from Edmonton, Alberta, to Buffalo, New York State, USA, a distance of 2856 miles (1775 km). Along the length of the pipe 13 pumping stations maintain a flow of 6 900 000 gal (31 367 145 l) of oil per day.

1977 The world's most expensive pipeline is the Alaska Pipeline running 798 miles (1284 km) from Prudhoe Bay to Valdez. By completion in 1977 it will have cost at least $6000 million.

Compiled by Dr R W Ferrier, BP

---

to have supplied oil for Stephenson's *Locomotive No 1* and the famous *Rocket*.

It is obviously impossible to say which is the oldest oil company without first defining the words 'oil company'.

Largest

The list of the 300 largest industrial corporations outside the USA that appeared in *Fortune* in August 1975 showed that the Anglo-Dutch giant, the **Royal Dutch/Shell Group,** had maintained its position at the head of the table, with sales of more than $33 000 million, while **British Petroleum,** with sales of more than $18 000 million, had taken over the position No 2, which was previously occupied by the other Anglo-Dutch giant, Unilever. Unilever had in fact fallen to No 4, National Iranian Oil having moved up from No 28 to No 3.

Pewterers

The firm of **Englefields (London) Limited,** of Cheshire Street, London E2, was established in 1700 by Thomas Scattergood. They are the last of the great general manufacturing pewterers. They still manufacture in accordance with traditional methods, by casting in gun-metal moulds. Many of these moulds have been in their possession for more than 200 years.

Pewter was first used nearly 2000 years ago by the ancient Orientals and Romans.

Timber-merchants

Firms in the timber trade often show the date of their foundation in their advertisements, and in the months of May, June and July 1956, the *Timber Trades Journal* carried a number of letters about old firms in this particular line of business.

In the issue of 26 May 1956, **William Oliver and Sons Limited,** of Bow Lane, London EC4, stated that, as far as they had been able to ascertain, their business was founded in 1799. The same issue also recorded the fact that the firm of **Dobson and**

Company Limited of Leith was founded by Andrew Park in the year 1790.

Robert Melville and Company Limited, of Falkirk, started back in 1790; and **Simeon Bateman Limited,** of Stourbridge, were established in 1788.

Joseph Gardner and Sons Limited, at Liverpool, were founded in 1748 and celebrated their bicentenary in 1948. Mr Edmund Gardner claimed

'In actual fact, although the Gardner family can definitely trace the beginning of the company to 1748, there is evidence in the records of Liverpool that members of the Gardner family were trading in the town as far back as the second half of the 16th century. We believe we can justly claim, therefore, to be one of the oldest firms in the British timber trade, and perhaps what makes the firm more unique is that the same family has been in control of the firm since its inception. In fact, such is the longevity of the Gardner family that during the course of two centuries the business has been carried on by only five generations, and the board today consists of one member of the fifth generation and two members of the sixth generation.'

Mr G R Fox, of **Fox, Stanton and Company,** Penryn, Cornwall, established a claim to be the runner-up in what he called 'a competition in antiquity' with the statement that he had 'a timber ledger in front of him belonging to this firm dated 1769'.

Bradford and Sons Limited, Yeovil, were incorporated in 1893, and before that date were trading as 'Job Bradford and Sons'. They have ledgers going back to 1763. While the date of commencement of trading is unknown, there is no doubt but that they have been selling timber for over 200 years.

Mr Philip R Bradford stated that the Board of the company consisted of six members of the family, five of whom were active executives, and at no time had anyone other than a Bradford been a Director.

James Latham Limited, Leeside Wharf, Clapton, London, E5, was operating in Lancashire some 200 years ago. Edward Locks Latham, who died in 1951, spent 70 years with James Latham Limited.

Weighing-machines

The firm of **Vandome and Hart** was founded in London in 1660 by a Huguenot refugee, Richard Vandome. (He is not the only Huguenot refugee to find a place in this book.) He set up shop in Leadenhall Street. In 1785 the original David Hart set up a rival shop nearby, and in 1930 the two firms amalgamated. The present company makes weighing-machines of all kinds, from weighbridges to fine balances. Vandome's have supplied the Bank of England with weighing-machines since 1694, when the Bank was established.

Wire-manufacturers

In a letter to the *Daily Telegraph* of 18 March 1970, Mr John Ormiston, of Ealing, drew attention to the fact that his firm, **P Ormiston and Sons,** had been established by his great-grandfather as wire-manufacturers in Cheapside in London in 1793.

B. BUSINESSES IN OTHER LANDS

Arms

Friedrich Krupp (1787–1826) founded the firm that still bears his name in 1811, but it was his son Alfred (1812–87) who developed it and who, in the process, became the wealthiest man in Europe. Contrary to popular belief, it was railways that set him on the road to riches, not guns. He obtained his first major railway contract in 1849, but his first large order for guns did not come until 1859, when Prussia ordered 312 six-pounders.

Some of the famous (or infamous) guns made by Krupps include 'Big Bertha' (named after the elder daughter of Fritz Krupp, Alfred's son), the 17-inch (43 cm) mortar whose projectile weighed nearly a ton; Long Max, the gun that shelled Paris from a distance of 75 miles (120 km) in 1918, and 'Fat Gustav', said to be the biggest gun ever made. This monster was used at the siege of Sevastopol in 1942, and could fire a shell weighing 7 tons a distance of 25 miles (40 km).

Asbestos

Oldest company

The **Asbestos Corporation Limited,** of Thetford Mines, Quebec, Canada, describe themselves as 'the world's oldest and most experienced producers of quality asbestos fibres'.

Largest mine

One of the mines operated by the Canadian **Johns-Manville Company** – the Jeffrey open-pit mine in Asbestos, Cantons-de-l'Est, Southern Quebec Province – is said to be the largest asbestos-mine in the world.

Augers and bits

Job T Pugh Incorporated, of Philadelphia, USA, manufacturers of augers and bits, were established in 1774 and described in Etna M Kelley's *Business Founding Date Directory* (1954) as 'the oldest auger works in the world'. She went on to say that it was believed that the holes bored in the wood of the support of the 'Liberty Bell' (see page 70) were made with Pugh bits.

The wife and daughter of Job T Pugh III have since retired from the business, feeling that there was then little or no room for hand-made tools.

Bells

We have not come across any other bell-foundry as old as the Whitechapel Bell Foundry (page 67), but Holland has two bell-foundries with a fairly long history. The firm of **Petit and Fritsen** at Aarle-Rixtel dates from 1660, and the firm of **Van Bergen** at Heiligerlee, Groningen, dates from 1795.

Copper

Any list of the oldest firms in the world would have to include **Stora Kopparbergs Aktiebolag,** of Falun, Sweden. They are 'known internationally as STORA, Sweden's oldest industrial enterprise, in continuous operation since the 11th century. Originally concerned with the mining and processing of copper, it is today one of the country's most up-to-date forest and steel industries producing pulp and paper, steel and cemented carbides, chemical products and hydroelectric power'.

The company began as a working fellowship round an old copper-mine, which may have been known and worked 'in the 12th century or even earlier'. It is first mentioned in

historical records in the year 1288, when a Swedish Bishop bartered an eighth share in the enterprise. In 1310 the King of Sweden had a share in the undertaking, and in 1347 a later King, Magnus Eriksson, granted a great Charter of Privileges, which still exists (see illustration, page 88). In the middle of the 17th century the output of copper reached its peak of more than 3000 tons a year.

In the 18th century the output of copper declined, and its production ceased in the 19th century (apart from a brief revival in 1917). The company's activities now cover iron and steel, chemical products, woodpulp, newsprint, timber and electric power.

Another of Sweden's oldest industrial enterprises, the 500-year-old **Atvidaberg Industries,** was first a farming estate, but it began to get into industry in 1419, when it started to mine copper about 125 miles (200 km) south of Stockholm. Later, making use of its oak forests, it began to manufacture furniture. In 1921 it took over a small company that had been making calculating-machines.

A number of copper-mines were worked at Atvidaberg as early as the 13th century. In 1413, 'on the third Sunday after Easter', King Erik of Pomerania (1398–1435) granted a Royal Charter to the mine-owners and declared that all willing to make their home in Atvidaberg might freely mine there. The copper-mine 'eventually became a cartwheel factory which later went over to manufacturing office furniture and was subsequently reorganized for business machine production'.

The **Gränges Metallverken,** of Västerås, Sweden, advertise themselves as producers of semis of copper and copper alloys since 1607.

Gusums Bruk AB dates from 1653. It makes copper and copper alloy tubing.

Another very old concern that started round a copper-mine is the **Mansfeld Aktiengesellschaft für Bergbau und Hüttenbetrieb,** otherwise known as the 'Salzdetfurth Company' whose head office is now in Hanover. Its early days are hidden in a veil of saga and oblivion, but its beginning was generally put at 1199 or 1200, when two miners started to mine copper near the town of Heckstedt. In 1364 the Count of Mansfeld received a grant of the copper-workings from the Emperor Charles IV. On 12 June 1900, the copper-miners of

Mansfeld celebrated the 700th anniversary of the opening of the mines. The celebrations were held at the nearest town, Eisleben, in the Province of Saxony. The Kaiser, one of whose titles was Count Mansfeld, honoured the celebrations with his presence before rejoining his train on the way to Homburg.

In the First World War the company produced more than three-quarters of Germany's copper, but today it is concerned with many things, notably metals (not only copper) and chemicals.

The **Rio Tinto** mines in Spain are said to be the oldest still being worked, with the exception of those in Cyprus. The Rio Tinto deposits have been worked since Phoenician times, originally for precious metals and, since the rediscovery of the mines in 1556, mainly for copper, sulphur and iron-ore.

Delving further into the past, the *Sunday Times* of 8 December 1974, reported that a British-backed archaeological expedition in Israel had just excavated the oldest underground mines ever found. The old workings, near the port of Eilat, date from 1400 BC and produced copper.

Cutlery

Thiers in central France might be described as 'the Sheffield of France'. It is the home of **J Delaire et fils, Purier-Sauvade successeur,** a cutlery firm founded in the year 1664. They are makers of table cutlery, scissors, secateurs and many similar goods.

Electro-chemical engineering

The **Hanson-Van Winkle-Munning Company,** of Matawan, New Jersey, USA, was established in 1820 and is the oldest manufacturer of electro-plating and polishing equipment in the world.

Engineering

The *Neue Zürcher Zeitung* of 18 February 1968 had an article about Swiss heavy industry in which mention was made of the growing co-operation in recent years between two of Switzerland's oldest engineering firms – **Escher Wyss,** founded in 1805, and **Maschinenfabrik Oerlikon,** founded in 1876.

Salomon von Wyss was a banker who acted as legal adviser to the firm that Escher set up in Zürich.

Farm tools

The **O Ames Company,** of Parkersburg, West Virginia, was listed in the *New York Times* of 20 April 1974, as one of the American companies that predated the birth of the United States. The company had then been making shovels and farm tools for 200 years, having been founded in 1774. The plant at Parkersburg is said to be the world's largest shovel factory, turning out 50000 pieces a day.

Hardware

The **Steinman Hardware Company,** of Lancaster, Pennsylvania, USA, wholesalers and retailers, was established in 1744. It is the oldest hardware company in America and has been in the same location since its inception.

A F Brombacher and Company, once located at 29–31 Fulton Street, New York, but now at Lyndhurst, New Jersey, was described as the oldest established hardware, cutlery and mechanics' tool business in New York. It had been founded in 1760 by two brothers, Hubert and Garrett Van Wagenen, who came from Holland.

The Augustus F Brombacher who was to give his name to the company had entered the employ of Osborn and Swan, as it was then called, in 1869. Along with another employee, William H Hanna, Brombacher formed a partnership which took over the business in 1885.

In 1930, all departments were phased out with the exception of the lawn and garden equipment department. In 1950 the name of the company was changed to American Grass Equipment Corporation, the word 'Grass' later being changed to 'Lawn'.

Iron and steel

The **Schwäbische Hüttenwerke,** with headquarters in Wasseralfingen in the State of Baden-Württemberg, is now owned half by the State and half by the Gutehoffnungshütte Group. The oldest of the company's five works, at Königsbronn, was founded in 1365. The plant at Wasseralfingen is the third oldest of the five and celebrated its 300th anniversary in 1971. It was in 1671 that the blast-furnace in Wasseralfingen of the 'Princely Provost Ellwangen' (Das Fürstpröpstlich Ellwangische Hüttenwerk) began its first run off. The ruling House of Württemberg founded the **Friedrichstal Works** in the Black Forest, near Freudenstadt, in 1536 and the **Ludwigstal Works** in Tuttlingen in 1695/6.

The **Taylor-Wharton Iron and Steel Company,** of Cincinnati, Ohio, USA is the oldest company of its kind in that country. It dates from 1742.

The **Steel Company of Canada,** with headquarters at Hamilton, Ontario, is one of the few Canadian companies dating from the 18th century, having been established in 1790.

Metal-processing

The **William Prym Werke,** of Stolberg (Rheinland), Germany were established at Stolberg in 1580. The Managers in 1972, Axel and Dieter Prym, were direct descendants of the founder, and the company then employed some 4000 people. It ranks among the leading metal-processing companies in Germany. (See also chapter 11, page 176.)

Motor cars *(see 'Transport', page 128)*

Office machinery

The **Burroughs Corporation** of Detroit was established in 1886 and is described as a

The world's first successful adding machine built by William Seward Burroughs in 1895. *(Burroughs Machines)*

One of Burroughs Large-Scale computers out of the powerful '700 systems' family. *(Burroughs Machines)*

manufacturer of adding-machines.

A Burroughs advertisement in the *Financial Times* of 8 January 1975 carried a picture of a Burroughs adding-machine made in 1895 which was said to be 'the world's first adding machine'. The corporation had apparently overlooked the French genius Blaise Pascal (1623–62), who had invented an adding-machine to help his tax-collecting father in the period 1642–4. This machine is described in the latest edition of the *Encyclopaedia Britannica* as 'the first digital calculator', and seems to have the edge on the Burroughs machine in the matter of age by a quarter of a millennium. (Another example of Pascal's genius has already been mentioned on page 77.)

According to the *History of Burroughs Corporation,* William Seward Burroughs (1857–98) invented and patented 'the first workable adding and listing machine in St Louis, Missouri, in 1885'. With three other men he formed the **American Arithmometer Company** in January 1886, to produce and market his machine.

Petroleum

Petroleum products have been known and used since early Biblical times, but the modern petroleum industry can be said to have begun with Drakes Well at Oil Creek, Pennsylvania, on 27 August 1859. It produced from a depth of $69\frac{1}{2}$ ft (21 m) about 400 gal (151 l) a day. E B Bowditch and Edwin Laurentine Drake of the **Seneca Oil Company,** formed on 23 March 1858, bored through the rock at Titusville in a section known as 'Oil Creek'.

Exxon is the present name for the Standard Oil Company of New Jersey, founded by John D Rockefeller I in 1870.

The *Fortune* list of the 500 largest industrial corporations that appeared in 1975 showed that Exxon then occupied the top position. This was the first time for forty years that General Motors had not been the leader. As well as being top in sales, Exxon was also first in assets, in net income and in stockholders' equity. Exxon was still on top in the 1976 list, with sales of more than $44000 million, while the sales of General Motors were less than $36000 million.

Other oil companies that have risen in the rankings are Texaco (now No 3), Mobil Oil (No 5), Standard Oil of California (No 6) and Gulf Oil (No 7). For the different fortunes of the car companies, see pages 128–9. Imperial Oil of Canada, an Exxon subsidiary, appeared as No 47 in the 1975 list of the 300 largest industrial corporations outside the USA, whereas in the previous year it had not even managed to get into the first 300.

Springs

One of the public corporations in the USA that has a long history of family management is the **Associated Spring Corporation,** the world's largest producers of springs. In 1972 the company was being run by the fifth generation of the Barnes family.

Their great-great-grandfather had started the company in 1857 to make springs for clocks and for the hoops in ladies' skirts. Later they made springs for the automobile industry.

Several American corporations can point to more than five generations of family participation, and to a history going back well beyond 1857.

Timber

The Swedish firm **A-B Billingsfors-Långed,** of Billingsfors (Lake Vener), described as manufacturers of 'Sawn Woodgoods', was founded in 1738. It therefore appears to be slightly older than the oldest firms in the British timber trade.

The **Price Company** of Quebec City, Quebec, was established in 1816.

CHAPTER 4

OTHER INDUSTRIES

A. BUSINESSES IN THE BRITISH ISLES

Artists' materials

Reeves and Sons Limited, of Enfield, Middlesex, celebrated their 200th anniversary in 1966 with the publication of Michael Goodwin's *Artist and Colourman*. This traces the development of the business that was established about 1766 by the brothers William and Thomas Reeves. Their particular claim to fame was the invention of the water-colour cake, which 'precipitated a new vogue for water-colour painting'. At the time of the bicentenary two members of the Board of Directors of the company were direct descendants of the original Thomas. The company has since become part of the Reckitt and Colman Group.

George Rowney and Company Limited, of Percy Street, London W1, describe themselves as 'Pencil Manufacturers and Artists' Colourmen since 1789'. The brothers Richard and Thomas Rowney started a business in perfumery, to which artists' colours were added, in Broad Street, St Giles, in 1789. Like Reeves and Sons, they received the Royal Warrant of appointment to George III. George Rowney (b 1793), who gave his name to the business, was the son of Thomas.

The business of **Winsor and Newton Limited,** of Harrow, Middlesex, started in 1832, when William Winsor and Henry Charles Newton opened a shop in Rathbone Place, where Rowneys were already established.

Winsor and Newton's factory at Lowestoft, opened in 1946, is said to be 'the biggest factory in the world devoted to Artists' brushes'.

Basket-making

A firm that could trace its history back to the reign of Charles II, but which did not long survive its tercentenary, was **G W Scott and Sons Limited,** basket-makers, of Tower Street, Cambridge Circus, London WC2 which was passed from father to son till the last war. The firm began in the City of London but had to move out after the Great Fire of 1666.

The methods of manufacture were still the same as they were 300 years ago, and the workers still used the same type of willows. The firm's main products were picnic-baskets, cane furniture, hampers and all other forms of basket-ware. Among the less common articles that they produced were the wickerwork baskets that support the bearskins of the Brigade of Guards.

For a long time the firm was believed to date only from 1699, but the records of the Basketmakers' Company have shown that it was in existence in 1661.

Another old family firm of basket-makers is **J Collins and Son Limited,** of Stowmarket, Suffolk. The firm was founded in 1686 in Spitalfields, and incorporated as a private limited company in 1923. It was carried on in the original area until 1921, when it was obliged to move. It moved to Quaker Street, London E1, and in 1937 it moved again, to Shoreditch.

Boot- and Shoe-makers

Before the rebuilding of part of Duke Street, St James's, London, the premises at No 28 housed the firm of **Hoby and Company Limited,** boot- and shoe-makers, whose notepaper showed them to have been established in the year 1623.

Johnstone's *London Directory* of 1817 gives 'Hoby, George, boot maker to the Royal Family', at 48 St James's Street. It also gives 'Hoby, G, Boot and shoe maker to the Royal Family', at 163 Piccadilly.

According to the Manager Mr S G Hendy, the firm was definitely established in 1623 but it had changed hands so many times since that date that its records had been destroyed.

Buttons, badges, etc

Firmin and Sons Limited, of London and Birmingham, who hold the Royal Warrant of appointment as button-makers, are believed to have been founded some time before 1677 by Thomas Firmin, whose name appears in the London directory of 1677, with an address at 3 King's Court, Lombard Street. Mr J W Firmin, the Chairman, represents the ninth generation of the family. Nathaniel Firmin received the Royal Warrant as button-maker in the reign of George II, and Firmin and Sons Limited have been so honoured ever since.

Marlborough's soldiers wore their buttons in the days of Queen Anne. Both sides wore them in the American War of Independence and in the American Civil War. In the Second World War they were worn by at least eight of the Allied nations.

J R Gaunt and Son Limited, of Birmingham, also make buttons, badges, medals, etc, and they hold the Royal Warrant as ribbon-makers. The business was established in the 19th century, but acquired the business of Edward Thurkle, a sword cutler, in Soho, which was established over 200 years ago.

Candles

One of the oldest manufacturing businesses in the whole of the British Isles is to be found in Ireland. **John G Rathborne Limited,** of Dublin, carry on their notepaper the impressive inscription 'established 1488', and they have been making candles since then.

One of the firm's main claims to fame is that in 1932 it made the biggest candle ever manufactured in the British Isles; the candle was 8 ft 6 in in height (2.59 m) and weighed 144 lb (65 kg). The firm is said to have been in the hands of the Rathborne family for 424 years, from the date of its foundation until 1912, when it was taken over by the present company.

Most of the firm's records were lost when the factory was transferred to its present site in the year 1925. The firm is generally believed to date from 1488, but recent researches indicate that its origin may be even earlier and that its history may have started in Chester as early as 1265.

By a curious coincidence, one of the earliest common-price arrangements in England was concerned with candles (see page 171).

Chemicals

Whiffen and Sons Limited, of Fulham, became a member of the Fisons Group of companies in 1947.

Thomas Whiffen (b 1819) did not come upon the scene until 1854, when he joined Edward Herring and Jacob Hulle at a chemical works in the Borough (i.e. in Southwark). They later moved to Battersea, where they began to make quinine and strychnine in a building at the bottom of Whiffen's garden.

Whiffen was in business on his own from 1868, and in 1887 he acquired the firm of George Atkinson and Company. This firm had a long-established reputation as drug-grinders, oil-pressers and saltpetre-refiners. They traced their history back, through many changes of title, to the year 1654, in the time of Oliver Cromwell.

Imperial Chemical Industries is the largest chemical firm in the UK. In *The Times 1000 (1975–6)* it ranked No 4 in the list of the largest UK industrial companies, with sales in 1974 of nearly £3000 million.

Chemists (manufacturing)

Allen and Hanburys Limited, of Bethnal Green, London E2, describe themselves as

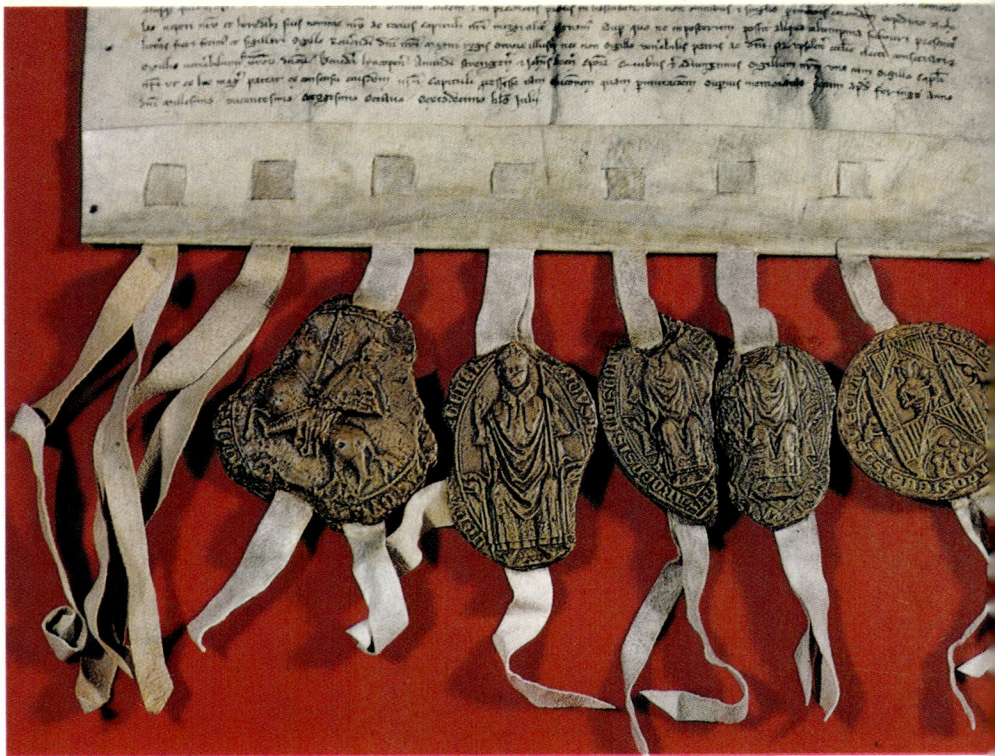

Stora Kopparberg's Royal Charter of 1347. *(Stora Kopparberg)*

Eleutherian Mills – the black powder manufactory of E I du Pont, *c* 1806. *(Hagley Museum, Wilmington, Delaware)*

'manufacturing chemists and makers of surgical instruments'. The business dates from 1715, when Silvanus Bevan, apothecary, established the Old Plough Court Pharmacy.

After a while, Silvanus took his brother Timothy into partnership. In 1735, Timothy married Elizabeth Barclay. Their second son, another Silvanus, became a partner in Barclays Bank and Barclays Brewery (see page 16)

Timothy's two eldest sons, Timothy and Silvanus, were taken into partnership in 1766, but Silvanus retired in 1767 to become a partner in Barclays Bank. Timothy the son died in 1773 but his father carried on until 1775, when he retired in favour of his third son, Joseph. In 1792, Joseph engaged William Allen as his confidential clerk. In 1808, Daniel Bell Hanbury entered the firm, then being carried on by Allen and by John Thomas Barry, who became a partner in 1818.

There were a number of changes of name until Allen and Hanburys in 1856. Allen, who died in 1843, was one of the founders of the Pharmaceutical Society, in 1841, and was elected its first President.

Allen and Hanburys Limited now forms part of the Glaxo Group. Its notepaper carried a picture of the old pharmacy in Plough Court as it appeared in the early part of the 18th century, and also a portrait of William Allen, with the dates 1770–1843.

Chemists (retail)

In 1798 **Savory and Moore** opened their chemist's shop at 136 New Bond Street. The business has been on the same site ever since. Mr D A Savory, the Chairman of the company, is the great-great-great-grandson of Thomas Field Savory, who joined the firm early in the 19th century. Savory and Moore are particularly proud of their record of being 'chemists to the Royal Family since the Reign of George III'.

Horner and Company, of Mitre Square, chemists and druggists, were said to have been established in Bucklersbury before 1666 the year of the Great Fire. **Corbyn, Stacey and Company** 'were, it appears, in business before the Great Fire'. **William Sutton and Company,** of Chiswell Street, were at the 'Sign of the Golden Ball' in 1669.

Christmas cards

An article in the London *Evening Standard* of 21 December 1956 described a visit to the premises of 'the nation's largest and oldest Christmas card firm'. The staircase was said to be 'bristling with royal warrants'.

The firm of **Raphael Tuck and Sons Limited,** of Raphael House, Stanhope Gate, Park Lane, London W1, was founded by Raphael Tuck in 1866. In that year he opened a small picture-framing shop in City Road, London. His wife helped him in the business, and in 1871 he was joined by his three sons. In the same year, 1871, the firm published its first Christmas card. After a number of moves in the City of London, the firm moved to Raphael House in 1899. The foundation-stone of this building was laid by Raphael Tuck in 1896.

The building, along with all the firm's records, was completely destroyed by bombing during the last war, but they survived this blow and have recovered their old position.

Fireworks

Brock's Fireworks Limited, formerly known as Brock's Crystal Palace Fireworks, were 'established before 1720'. John Brock, who laid the foundations of the present business, was the son of a fireworker-maker who died, 'no doubt as the result of an accident, on November 5, 1720'.

The firm has moved a number of times in the course of its long history. It started in Clerkenwell, left London in 1866, moved to Hemel Hempstead in Hertfordshire in 1933, and is now to be found at Gateside Works, Sanquhar, Dumfries, Scotland.

The expression 'Brock's Benefit' is said to date from 1826. According to a poster of that year, an explosion nearly ruined Brock's business, and a sympathiser gave him 'the gratuitous use of his commodious Ground (in the City Road) to display an exhibition of FIREWORKS for his BENEFIT'.

From 1865 or 1868 to 1910, and again from 1920 to 1936, the firm was responsible for the great firework displays at the Crystal Palace, which explains the name given to the firm's products.

On 8 June 1946, Brock's arranged the firework display for the London Victory Celebrations, which is said to have been 'the most elaborate show of aerial pyrotechny ever fired'. The firm have held the Royal Warrant of Appointment as Pyrotechnists to King George VI and to Queen Elizabeth II. (Pyrotechnists sounds much grander than firework-makers.)

Glass-making

The glassworks of **James Powell and Sons (Whitefriars) Limited,** Wealdstone, Middlesex, was originally situated, as its name indicates, in the City of London. For more than 200 years it occupied a site between Fleet Street and the River Thames, with its main entrance in Tudor Street.

This glassworks occupied part of the land formerly belonging to the White Friars, and the picture of a White Friar is still used as the firm's sign, together with the words 'established 1680'. The significance of the date is not clear. According to the account given in L M Angus Butterworth's article *Two Hundred and Seventy Years of Glassmaking* in *Pottery and Glass*, the glassworks was probably built soon after 1697, when an Act of Parliament abolished the right of sanctuary previously attaching to the precincts of the old monastery. The chief products of the glassworks were table-ware, including decanters for the port wine that was then coming into fashion.

James Powell and Sons appeared as owners of the works in 1835, after a number of previous owners. James Powell himself was born in 1774 and died in 1840. The family had previously had some experience of glass-making in Bristol.

In 1923 the old premises were abandoned, and production was transferred to the present works at Wealdstone, near Harrow. In accordance with an old tradition of the industry, the fires at Whitefriars had always been kept burning, and on the final day a brazier mounted on a cart carried the fire to the new works to light the furnaces there.

In 1750 Lady Frances Erskine erected a glassworks on the foreshore at Alloa, in Clackmannanshire, which 'has grown into the leading establishment of its kind in Scotland today', the **Alloa Glass Works.** There have been frequent changes of ownership during the firm's 200 years of existence.

Just a year junior to the Alloa undertaking is the firm of **Beatson, Clark and Company Limited,** of Rotherham. The Rotherham firm, 'whose roots go back to 1751, claim to be the oldest glass container maker in the country'. The family connection with the business dates from 1783, when the great-great-grandfather of Dr A W Clark (the firm's Chairman in 1967), William Beatson, bought the business.

William Beatson's daughter married J G Clark, who was Dr Clark's great-grandfather, and the business has since been managed by members of the family bearing this name. In the early years a very wide range of articles was manufactured, but for the past 100 years the output has been concentrated on glass bottles and jars.

Pilkington's of St Helens have been making glass since 1826.

Golf clubs

Ben Sayers, of North Berwick, Scotland, claim to be the oldest firm of golf-club makers in the world, having been established in 1874.

Gramophone records

A Voice to Remember – The sounds of 75 years on EMI records 1898–1973 was issued in 1973. This unusual form of business history came in four parts. It consisted of two records and two booklets, all neatly contained in a box displaying the famous picture of a dog gazing into the horn of an old-fashioned gramophone and listening to 'His Master's Voice'.

The two records contain 53 items selected from the various record companies now within the **EMI Group.** The earliest item, recorded in August 1898, is a spirited rendering of 'Comin' Through the Rye' by Syria Lamonte, a barmaid at Rules' Restaurant. The final item is a rendering of the same song by Janet Baker in 1973, which well illustrates the improvement in recording and reproduction in the course of 75 years. A spoken commentary by Alistair Cooke links the items together.

The booklet entitled *A Voice to Remember* tells the story of the business that started life in 1898 under the title of The Gramophone and Typewriter Company Limited. For a few years the company sold the 'Lambert typewriter' as well as its records.

The second booklet is entitled *The story of 'Nipper' and the 'His Master's Voice' picture painted by Francis Barraud.* Perhaps the most interesting part of this little history is the disclosure that Barraud's original picture, which he had copyrighted at Stationers' Hall in 1899, had depicted the dog listening to a cylinder record on a phonograph and not to the familiar gramophone. As the author points out, the dog was more likely to have heard his master's voice on a phonograph, which could be used to make recordings at home, than on a gramophone record, unless his master happened to be a recording artist.

The EMI Group has been called the world's largest record company. It ranked No 179 in *Fortune's* list of 1976 of the 500 largest industrial companies outside the USA, with total sales of more than $1100 million.

Hatters

James Lock and Company, of 6 St James's Street, once called the most famous hat shop in the world, is one of the oldest firms in that street, but not the oldest of all. The firm's notepaper carries the date 1759, that being the year in which James Lock I came into possession of the business. Some years earlier, about the end of 1725, there was, however, a hatter's business belonging to Charles Davis on the other side of St James's Street, where No 64 now stands. James Lock married the daughter of Charles Davis, who died in 1759, and in the same year the rate-books show Lock as tenant of the shop. There is some doubt whether the occupant of the shop was this James Lock or his father, who bore the same name. For ease of reference, Davis's son-in-law is called James Lock II (1731–1806).

In 1765 the business was moved across the road to No 6, where it has since remained.

James Lock III, the son of George James, appears as the owner of No 6 in 1822. James Lock III died in 1876, aged 76. On his retirement, in 1872, the business passed to his nephew, Charles Richard Whitbourn, and James Benning, an old employee taken into partnership by James Lock III along with Whitbourn in 1865.

James Benning died in 1899 and was succeeded by his grandson, George James Steph-

enson. Two of the present Directors of the firm, which was turned into a limited liability company in 1928, are his descendants, and the third, Mr C R W Whitbourn, is a grandson of C R Whitbourn and a direct descendant of James Lock I.

On 15 January 1975 Lock's were holding their first sale, after 250 years. Bowler-hats were being worn less these days, and were on offer at £8.50.

Instruments *(see 'Musical instruments' and 'Scientific instruments, pages 91 and 95)*

Leather

There are said to be only two firms in England that still use oak-bark liquor for tanning instead of minerals. One is **J Croggon and Son Limited,** of the Manor Tannery, Grampound, Cornwall. The other is **J and F J Baker and Company Limited,** of Colyton, Devon.

The Baker firm occupy a site called 'Hamlyn's Mill', some of the buildings on which are believed to be 300 years old. There are two wooden water-wheels. One undershot wheel is still used for grinding oak bark. This is said to be the only tannery in the country that combines the functions of tanning and currying leather. Both sole and harness leather are produced, a large proportion of the sole leather going to the orthopaedic trade.

The Croggon business was founded in 1799, when John Croggon and his son Thomas established their tannery in the main street. It has been handed on from father to son through seven generations of the Croggon family.

Musical instruments

William E Hill and Sons were reported in March 1975 to have moved from their shop at 140 New Bond Street, London, to Great Missenden. They describe themselves as 'Violin Makers, Repairers and Experts'. Their notepaper carries the following quotation from Pepys's *Diary* for 17 February 1660: 'In ye morning came Mr. Hill ye Instrument Maker, and I consulted with him about ye altering my lute and my viall.' The family connection with musical instruments, therefore, extends over three centuries. Joseph Hill (1715–84) was the founder of the firm of William E Hill and Sons still being carried on by his descendants.

The firm of **John Broadwood and Sons Limited,** pianoforte-makers, is 'the oldest firm of keyboard makers in existence'. The firm's head office and its factory are now at Ealing, London W3.

Broadwood's was established in 1728, and is still run by the descendants of the founder. Among its other distinctions is a remarkable series of Royal Warrants from George II on. Today the firm holds the Royal Warrant of Appointment as Pianoforte Manufacturers to Her Majesty the Queen.

The business was founded by Burkhardt Tschudi from Glarus, Switzerland, in Dean Street, Soho. Tschudi, who was a maker of harpsichords, moved to 33 Great Pulteney Street in 1742. Here, in 1760, John Broadwood started to work for him. John Broadwood married his master's daughter, Barbara, in 1769, and took the business over when Tschudi died, in 1773.

Harpsichords were made from 1728 until 1793, but the first pianofortes were not made until after Tschudi's death.

The names of many great musicians are associated with the name of Broadwood. Mozart played on Broadwood instruments at Great Pulteney Street. Haydn lived opposite their premises and was a frequent visitor. Beethoven would allow nobody but his tuner to touch his Broadwood. In more recent times, Chopin, Liszt, Wagner and Elgar used Broadwood instruments for their compositions and recitals.

Music shops

The firm of **Chappell and Company Limited** musical instrument makers, now at 50 New Bond Street, dates from December 1810. A deed of partnership was signed between Samuel Chappell, Francis Tatton Latour and John Baptist Cramer to carry on the 'trade and business of composers of music, music and musical instrument sellers at 124 New Bond Street'.

The firm soon moved to No 50, where they have since remained. Since 1897 the business has been carried on as a limited liability company.

The shop opened in January 1811. Chappell's soon established a leading position as music-publishers. Beethoven, writing from Vienna in 1822 to a friend in London, said: 'Potter says that Chappell in Bond Street is now one of the best publishers.'

J B Cramer, one of the original partners in Chappell's, was also the founder of **Cramer's,** now at 139 New Bond Street, in 1824.

Paper-making

Portals Limited, of Laverstoke Mills, Whitchurch, Hampshire are one of the oldest firms of paper-makers in the country.

According to family tradition, the founder of the firm, Henri Portal, along with his brother Guillaume, was smuggled out of France in a wine-cask to escape the persecution of the Huguenots under Louis XIV and eventually started a paper-mill at Whitchurch in the year 1712. Six years later, he leased the property at Laverstoke. Here a new mill was built, which went into production in 1719.

In 1724, Henry Portal (as he had become) obtained the order for making the paper for the Bank of England's notes, 'a privilege which has continued from father to son to the present day'. The Chairman of the company in 1952 was Mr Francis Portal, a great-great-great-grandson of Henry Portal, making six generations in all at that point of time.

Almost as old as Portals is the **Culter Mills Paper Company,** whose origins go back to 1751. This is said to be 'the oldest paper mill in the Aberdeen area, still serving the country in all classes of paper of the finest quality, as the founder undertook to do'. The date 1751 appears in the watermark of various brands of writing-paper now made by the firm.

Perfumers

The firm of **Floris,** makers and retailers of perfume, whose present address is 89 Jermyn Street, London, was founded in the year 1730 by Juan Faminias Floris, a native of Minorca. The business is still on its original site, almost opposite the back of St James's Church, Piccadilly, a church that Sir Christopher Wren had built not long before the business began. Even in those days, Jermyn Street rivalled

The Floris Shop in Jermyn Street, London. (*Floris*)

Bond Street as a fashionable shopping thoroughfare.

Floris received their first Royal Warrant in 1820, from George IV. The business is now in the hands of the fifth generation of the founder's family. Johnstone's *London Directory* of 1817 shows the occupant of 94 Jermyn Street as Floris, 'Comb maker to the Prince Regent'. (The number is now 89.)

A little younger than Floris is **Yardley's** of Bond Street, whose name is now almost synonymous with lavender. Yardley's history began in the year 1779.

Another firm of perfumers dating from the 18th century is **J and E Atkinson Limited (Atkinson's).** This firm was founded in 1799 and moved to Bond Street in 1832. It is one of the few firms that have been carrying on business in Bond Street for more than a century.

James Atkinson, the founder of the firm, was a poor boy from Cumberland who came to London with a recipe for a special kind of pomade called 'Bear's Grease'. He started business in 1799 in Dryden's old house in Gerrard Street, and numbered Beau Brummell among his clients.

James's brother, Edward, joined him in the business, and in 1832 they moved to the firm's present address, 24 Old Bond Street, where the business has since been carried on.

Atkinson's have held the Royal Warrant for six reigns, and their 'Gold Medal Eau de Cologne' is so called after the Gold Medal awarded to the firm at the Paris Exhibition of 1878. The firm now has factories in Argentina, Brazil, Australia, Italy, Spain and Portugal. And it all began in Dryden's old house in Gerrard Street.

Pianofortes *(see 'Musical instruments', page 92)*

Pipes (for smoking)

The firm of **Charatan's** or **Charatan Pipes Limited,** makers of briar pipes, was established in 1863. They have shops at 49 Whitcomb Street and 18 Jermyn Street, London, and call themselves 'England's Oldest Pipemakers'.

Inderwick's, of Carnaby Street, London, who were established in 1797 (long before Carnaby Street achieved its present fame and appearance), also describe themselves as 'England's Oldest Pipemakers'. The explanation of the apparently contradictory claims of Charatan's and Inderwick's seems to be that Inderwick's were 'the first house in England to import and manufacture the Meerschaum pipe', whereas Charatan's were the first in England to make *briar* pipes (or 'brier': from French *bruyère* – 'heath', the White Heath, of which the root is used for tobacco pipes. The material was introduced about 1859).

Pottery

The potter's craft is 'one of the oldest in the world'. It is not, therefore, surprising to find a number of potteries among our oldest businesses.

Two of the best-known business names in these islands are Guinness and **Wedgwood.** The Guinness business (see page 13) was founded in Dublin in 1759, and it was in the same year that the firm of Wedgwood was founded by Josiah Wedgwood, FRS (1730–95).

In 1967 the Chairman and Managing Director was the Honourable Josiah Wedgwood, sixth in line from the first Josiah. His cousin, John Wedgwood, the Deputy-Chairman, was also a great-great-great-grandson of Josiah I. It was in December 1967 that the Press reported that Josiah Wedgwood was retiring from the Board and as Chairman of Josiah Wedgwood Limited and that, for the first time in its history, the company was to have someone outside the Wedgwood family as Chairman. This was Mr Arthur Bryan, then the Managing Director of the company.

The Josiah who had founded the business in 1759 himself represented the fifth generation of a potting family, being the great-great-grand-son of Gilbert Wedgwood (1588–1678), a potter who came to Burslem in 1612. The business that Josiah founded had since been carried on by five succeeding generations of potters, including Josiah I, or ten generations of Wedgwood potters in all.

Josiah's first works were at the Ivy House, Burslem. In 1764 he moved to the larger Brick House Works (or Bell Works) in Burslem, and two years later he laid the foundations of the factory and village which he called Etruria. The new works was opened on 13 June 1769, and in the same year the family moved to Etruria Hall. When Joseph died, in 1795, Etruria was the largest pottery in the world.

In 1936 the company decided to leave Etruria and move into the country, and in 1937 they bought the Barlaston Estate of about 380 acres (150 ha), 4 miles (6 km) south of Stoke. Production of Wedgwood fine earthen-ware began here in 1940, but it was not until 1949 that the new works was completed. Production at the Etruria Works ceased on 13 June 1950, exactly 181 years to the day after Josiah I had opened the factory.

Wedgwood is not the oldest pottery firm in the country. Some years ago the British Ceramic Research Association listed all the British pottery-manufacturers established before 1800 and still operating when the list was compiled. There were 15 names on the list, and Wedgwood was the eighth.

Two of the firms were operating under the old names, but there had not been complete continuity in their history. One of these, the **Coalport China Company,** of Stoke-on-Trent (now part of the Wedgwood Group) dates from 1750. The **Royal Crown Derby Porcelain Company,** of Derby, also dates from 1750. The **Worcester Royal Porcelain Company** dates from 1751, and **Clokie and Company,** of Castleford, from 1752.

The three oldest potteries all traced their origin back to the 17th century. The oldest of all, **Pountney and Company's Bristol Pottery** at Fishponds, Bristol, was established in 1652 and had been in the same family for about 100 years. The factory had been built in 1905 and was then regarded as one of the most up-to-date and best-equipped potteries in the whole of Europe.

The **Bristol Pottery** sold its Fishponds factory in 1969, severing a 317-year link with Bristol, and moved to a new factory at Camborne in Cornwall. *The Times* of 30 November 1971, reported that 'Britain's oldest pottery, Cauldron Bristol Potteries, which moved from Bristol to Cornwall two years ago, will close after 320 years of life unless a buyer can be found'.

Next in point of time comes the pottery of **William Adams and Sons (Potters) Limited,** of Tunstall, Staffordshire. The firm (which, like the Coalport China Company, is now part of the Wedgwood Group) dated its establishment from 1657. Records show that the Adams family has been in the area since 1299 and has been making pottery since 1448, the representative of each generation since that date being described in his will as a Master Potter. The date of 1657 was taken as that of the firm's foundation because it was in that year that the first pottery factory as such was built in north Staffordshire by John Adams.

Pottery retailers

Barrett and Sons, of Cambridge, announced in 1974, when a new shop was opened, that seven generations of Barretts had been supplying the citizens of Cambridge with pottery and glass since the 18th century, in fact since 1782. (See also 'Old customers', page 170.)

Radio

The **Marconi Company Limited**, formerly known as 'Marconi's Wireless Telegraph and Signal Company Limited', has been called the world's oldest radio company. It was first registered in 1900. Marchese Guglielmo Marconi, GCVO (Hon), (1874–1937), Italian physicist, was the inventor of a practical system of communication by means of electro-magnetic waves. The first patent for this system, No 12039, was granted on 2 June 1896.

Ropes

One of the oldest, and at the same time one of the oddest, manufacturing enterprises in the country was the old **Rope Walk** in the Peak Cavern at Castleton, Derbyshire. Since the 16th century, rope had been made by hand in this cavern, under the ruins of Peveril Castle, but by 1956 only one man was left who knew the secrets of the craft: Mr Herbert Marrison. He started work here at the age of twelve, about the turn of the century, when 20 people worked on the Rope Walk. Members of his family had worked here for two centuries.

Ropes are still made not far from the Loughborough Bell Foundry described on page 70. **John Pritchard (Ropes) Limited,** of Loughborough, established in 1820, made the ropes that were used when the world record for change ringing was set up, so that Loughborough provided both the bells and the ropes that were used on that occasion.

'Britain's Best Bellropes' are made by **Joseph Bryant Limited,** of Bristol, a firm with 'experience gained in 12 reigns by eight generations of a West of England family of Ropemakers'. The firm began when ropemaking for shipping was an important Bristol industry, and it now makes a variety of articles, including rope, twine, sacks, tarpaulins, tents and sunblinds. Church bellropes are still made entirely by hand, as they were when the firm began more than 200 years ago, in 1718. Eight generations of the family have been connected with the business.

Almost as old as Bryant's is the **Gourock Ropework Company,** one of the oldest businesses in Scotland, whose history goes back to 1736. Its story was told by George Blake in his last book, entitled *The Gourock*.

Scientific instruments

Until 1968, one of the oldest family businesses in the country was that of **W Ottway and Company Limited,** of Ealing. The firm had been making scientific and optical instruments since 1640, when they were established in the heart of the City, at the Royal Exchange. The concern had been handed down from father to son in unbroken succession for over 300 years and was 'the oldest firm in the British Scientific Instrument Industry'. The number of generations of the Ottway family concerned with the business is not known but 'must be quite eight or nine'.

It was not until 1899–1900 that Ottways left the City for Ealing, having previously moved from site to site in the City as the firm needed more room for expansion. The exact year in which the firm began is not known, as its early records were lost in the Great Fire of London in 1666, but it may have been earlier than 1640, which is the date generally given. It was about 1900 that the firm became a real manufacturing concern with a factory instead of a workshop, and this was due to the development of the gun-sighting telescope. They also made terrestrial and astronomical telescopes, surveying instruments and optical laboratory equipment.

Another maker of scientific instruments whose origins go back to the 17th century is the firm of **Cooke, Troughton and Simms Limited,** of Haxby Road, York, mathematical and optical instrument makers (now operating as Vickers Limited, Vickers Instruments). Their story has been told in *At The Sign of the Orrery*, by E Wilfred Taylor and J Simms Wilson.

The British National Standards of length were made by Troughton and Simms, as were also the National Standards for the Imperial Russian Government and the American National Standards of Length.

Dring and Fage Limited, makers of measuring instruments, were established in 1725. Their shop is to be found At the Sign of the Half-Moon and Dagger, at 150–152 Tooley Street, London, SE1. They hold

Fourteen-inch Altozimuth made by Cooke, Troughton and Simms Limited, c 1830. *(Vickers Ltd)*

numerous Warrants of Appointment from the Board of HM Customs and Excise and from Governments overseas.

It was in or about 1725 that John Clarke, a 'Turner and Engine Maker', invented a metal hydrometer, an instrument for measuring the strength of spirits. His mark was the half-moon and dagger, a mark still used by the firm. Clarke was followed by his son Richard, who married a sister of John Dring. This John Dring later went into partnership with William Fage.

The 'Sikes Hydrometer', an improved instrument, was produced in 1803 and legalised in 1816. The firm have been makers and repairers of hydrometers and saccharometers to HM Customs and Excise for over 150 years. The firm also supply various kinds of measuring instruments to other Government Departments in this country, and in the Commonwealth, as well as to brewers, timber-merchants, rubber-producers, and users of scientific instruments throughout the world.

Snuff *('See Tobacco')*

Stationers

George Waterston and Sons, of Edinburgh, started in 1752 as makers of sealing-wax. They now supply a wide range of stationery products, but still make and export a considerable tonnage of sealing-wax.

Tobacco

One of the largest industrial companies in the UK is the **British-American Tobacco Company.** It ranked third in *The Times 1000 (1975–76)* list, with sales of more than £3400 million. Its main activities were there described as 'Tobacco and Cosmetics'. In the *Fortune* list of 1976 of the 500 largest industrial companies outside the USA the British-American Tobacco Company ranked No 22. As well as being one of the largest companies in the UK, it is also the world's biggest tobacco company.

The development of the **Wills** tobacco business at Bristol has been traced by B W E Alford from its beginnings as a small family partnership until the end of the 19th century, by which time it had become the biggest tobacco-manufacturer in the UK. In 1901 the Wills business joined with others to form the **Imperial Tobacco Company.** At the time of its formation, this was by far the biggest company in the land.

William Day Wills (1797–1865) and Henry Overton Wills (1800–71) were the sons of another Henry Overton Wills (1761–1826). It is this first H O Wills who appears on the scene in 1786 as a partner in the tobacco business of Wills, Watkins and Company, who carried on their activities in a converted house at 73 Castle Street, Bristol.

Four of the grandsons of H O Wills I, who all died between 1909 and 1911, left fortunes of £3 million, £2.6 million, £5.2 million and £2.5 million. In the next generation, Sir George Wills, who died in 1928, left £10 million, while his brothers Harry and Melville left £2.75 and £4.3 million respectively. The business that began in that house in Castle Street had certainly come a long way in the succeeding century and a half.

The number of millionaire estates in the Wills family since 1910 has been 14. These totalled £55 million, of which death duties (introduced in 1894) took more than £27 million.

The famous 'Woodbine' cigarettes, selling at five a penny, made their first appearance in 1888, and by 1889 they represented more than half of Wills's total sales of cigarettes, by number. (At this period, cigarettes accounted for only a fraction of 1 per cent of total tobacco consumption.)

Brand-names were introduced in 1847, for two smoking tobaccos. The other well-known pioneer in this sphere was John Horniman, the Quaker tea-merchant, who began to pack his teas in sealed labelled packets as early as 1826.

It is not possible to tell with certainty which is the oldest tobacco-manufacturing firm in the country. Some of the old tobacco firms began as grocers or general trading businesses, and the exact date when they started to manufacture tobacco is not known.

Imperial's oldest branch is the firm of **Stephen Mitchell and Son,** which was established at Linlithgow in 1723. This was at first a grocer's business, selling – and perhaps manufacturing – tobacco as a sideline. They can be definitely classed as tobacco-manufacturers from 1741, when Stephen Mitchell IV, then the head of the firm, contracted for the erection of a snuff-mill at Waukmilton.

Another old firm, one of Imperial's subsidiaries, is **E and W Anstie Limited,** of Devizes. Richard Anstie, the founder of the business, was a grocer in Devizes in 1695. Snuff and tobacco probably formed part of his stock in trade, but it is not until 1740, when his son John was manufacturing snuff in partnership with William Leach at Whistley Mill, Potterne, that the Ansties can be claimed to have been tobacco-manufacturers with any certainty.

Carreras Limited, the makers of 'Craven A' and 'Black Cat' cigarettes, trace their history back to the year 1788. In that year a Spanish gentleman named José Joaquín Carreras opened a tobacconist's shop in Regent Street. The Carreras family were connected

with the business for more than 100 years. In the days when smokers blended their own mixtures, one of their customers was the third Earl of Craven, after whom 'Craven Mixture' was named.

In 1896 the business was bought by W J Yapp, who was joined in 1903 by Mr Bernhard Baron. In 1904 they opened a factory in St James Place, Aldgate, to manufacture cigarettes. Other factories were acquired, but each in turn became too small until finally in 1928 the Arcadia Works in Hampstead Road was opened.

Among the businesses that have been on their present site for more than 200 years we must include **Fribourg and Treyer,** tobacconists and cigar-merchants, of 34 Haymarket, London SW1.

The double-fronted shop with its two bow-windows has been in the Haymarket since about 1720, when the business was founded by Mr Peter Fribourg. The shop-front and the interior of the shop, as far back as the Adam screen, are still in their original state.

In 1780, Mr Fribourg sold the business to a Mr Treyer. Mr Treyer had married a Miss Martha Evans, and two of her nephews were brought into the business. It has been in the Evans family ever since, and has been handed down from father to son through six generations.

The passer-by on the west side of the Haymarket who notices the quaint old shop, with its painted Sign of the Rasp and Crown, and crosses over for a closer inspection will see a sign on the shop-front proclaiming the fact that the firm were suppliers of tobacco and snuff to His Majesty the King of Hanover. Mr Alfred Bryant, the Snuffman at No 34 Haymarket, has written an interesting little booklet entitled *Behind the Bow Windows* in which he tells how snuff is made and describes about 20 different brands or blends of snuff.

The author's attention was first drawn to the existence of another 18th-century firm of snuff-makers by an advertisement on the London Underground for **Wilsons and Company (Sharrow) Limited,** of Sharrow Mills, Sheffield. This proclaimed them to have been established in 1750 and 'famous since the reign of George the Second'. A leaflet about their 'Gold Label Snuff' gave the date of the

The Fribourg & Treyer shop in the Haymarket, London. *(Fribourg & Treyer Ltd)*

firm's origin as 1737. M H F Chaytor's book *The Wilsons of Sharrow – The Snuff-Makers of Sheffield* (1962) sheds some light on the apparent discrepancy in dates.

Joseph Wilson (1723–96) is generally regarded as the founder of the snuff-manufacturing business at Sharrow Mills. This was about 1750. His father, however, who was a shearsmith and edge-tool maker, came to Sharrow in 1737 and leased two water-wheels for his business.

Mr Chaytor is himself a descendant of

Joseph Wilson. At the time when he was writing, the partnership at Sharrow Mills comprised four persons, all of whom were great-great-great-grandchildren of Joseph Wilson. (See illustration, page 99.)

The House of **Samuel Gawith,** of Kendal, proclaim that their snuffs and tobaccos have been 'manufactured in the heart of the English Lakeland for 150 years'.

Near the famous Cheshire Cheese, at No 146 Fleet Street, London, stood the tobacconist's shop of **D and S Radford.** The firm was established in 1700 and was therefore, some 20 years older than Fribourg and Treyer. It moved to this site in the year 1739. An inscription on the wall of the passage adjoining the shop proclaimed it to be 'Ye most Antient Segar Store in ye Citye of London. Established in 1700 under Ye sign of Ye Shippe and Star'. The original sign, which could be seen inside the shop, carries the name of 'Wm. Hoare, Snuff Maker'. The present shop, one of the few wooden buildings left in the City of London, is classified as an Ancient Monument. When last seen, the shop was empty, but a notice informed potential customers that the business formerly carried on in it would shortly be reopening in temporary premises next door, at No 147.

Yet another old firm of tobacconists dating from the 18th century is the **House of Bewlay,** which was founded in 1780, at No 49 in the Strand.

The poet C S Calverley, a member of the same Cambridge college as John Milton, wrote an *Ode to Tobacco* in 1862 in which he paid tribute to a well-known Cambridge tobacconist named **Bacon.** In his *Ode*, Calverley wrote of

'Jones – (who, I'm glad to say,
Asked leave of Mrs. J.) –
Daily absorbs a clay
After his labours.'

This suggests that the typical pipe at that date was a clay rather than a briar. Bacon's business is still conducted from a shop on the Market Place, and Calverley's Ode can be seen on a tablet outside the shop.

The tobacconist's shop at 16 Market Hill, Cambridge, is known officially as Bacon Brothers but usually called Bacon's. Its history goes back to the early days of the 19th century,

Snuff-grinding mill, about 240 years old. *(Wilsons & Co. (Sharrow))*

to the year 1805, and it was, therefore, already something of an institution when Charles Stuart Calverley immortalised it, in 1862, in his *Ode to Tobacco*.

B. BUSINESSES IN OTHER LANDS

Candles and wax figures

The German firm **Wachsindustrie Fulda Adam Gies,** of Fulda, has a history going back to 1589. As its notepaper shows, the firm of today is an amalgamation of Adam Gies and of Gautsch. The firm of Joseph Gautsch was founded in January 1589, when Hans Ebersperger set up in business as a candle-maker, gingerbread-baker and mead-brewer.

In 1849, the business passed into the hands of Joseph Gautsch, who had married into the family of the previous owners. The firm was famous for its wax figures as well as for its candles.

Chemical manufacturers and wholesalers

Geigy (J R Geigy SA), of Basle, Switzerland, was founded in 1758 by J R Geigy, a merchant domiciled in Basle, who set up his business in chemicals, dye-stuffs and drugs.

Geigy is 'the oldest chemical firm in Basle, and perhaps the oldest in the world with a continuous record of progress in the chemical field'. The insecticide 'DDT', which was developed by the firm's Plant Pesticides Division, first appeared on the market in 1941.

Another famous chemical firm with its home in Basle is **CIBA,** dating from 1884. When it celebrated its 75th anniversary, in 1959, it did not produce the simple history of the company that might have been expected on such an occasion, but instead it published a handsome volume entitled *The Story of the Chemical Industry in Basle*. With a wealth of illustrations this work traced the development of science and technology from the Middle Ages on.

CIBA and Geigy, joined in 1970 in CIBA-Geigy, constitute one of the largest chemical firms in the world and one of the largest firms of any kind in Switzerland. In the *Fortune* list of 1976 of the 500 largest industrial companies outside the USA, the CIBA-Geigy company ranks No 54, with sales of more than $3400 million. The only Swiss firm that ranks above it is Nestlé (see page 53).

Two South African firms can be traced back to the 18th century, the older of the two being **Heynes Mathew Limited,** wholesale chemists, which was started by a Dr Liesching in 1791. The other is a tobacco firm, **Sturk and Company,** dating back to about 1793.

Many people know the name **E I du Pont** but not all of them could say what the initials stand for. The man to whom they relate, Eleuthère Irénée du Pont, was born in France in 1771 and, after working for a time with Lavoisier (later guillotined), emigrated to

Eleuthère Irénée du Pont (1771–1834). *(Hagley Museum, Wilmington, Delaware)*

America. He settled on the Brandywine River in Delaware and, in 1802, began the construction of a black powder manufactory which he named 'Eleutherian Mills'. The Du Pont mills operated continuously until 1921, and their powder-yards grew to be the largest in America.

It has been tentatively estimated that the combined value of the assets nominally controlled by the du Pont family of some 1600 members may be of the order of $150000 million. The family arrived penniless in the USA from France on 1 January 1800, and is now the richest family in the world.

Chemists (retail)

In Trier (Trèves), one of the oldest towns in Germany, is the **Löwenapotheke,** dating from 1241. This is said to be the oldest apothecary's shop in Germany.

According to *The Week in Spain* for 1 November 1965, Europe's most ancient chemist's shop – founded in 1400 – is to be found at Llivia (Gerona). It was open to the public right up to 46 years ago, 'though the prescriptions had altered over the centuries'. It is now a National Museum. Apart from the fact that it is no longer an active business, the shop at Llivia seems to be considerably younger than the shop at Trier (Trèves).

The **Hammerstein Apotheke** in the Rennweg in Zürich was established by Conrad Hottinger in 1677, who was in charge of it until 1706. His name, along with the names of his successors, is prominently displayed outside the shop. One wishes that other old businesses would do likewise.

The oldest chemist's shop in Switzerland is said to be the **Weinmarktapotheke** in Lucerne, with a history going back to the 16th-century. One of the earliest proprietors was Konrad Klauser (1480–1553).

Two other old chemist's shops are the **Pharmacie Brun** in Geneva – 'Maison Fondée en 1453'–and the **Winter Apotheke** in Innsbruck, founded in 1500. The latter still carries a memory of the past in its description as 'alte Hofapotheke' ('court pharmacy').

The **Caswell-Massey Company Limited,** of New York, describe themselves as 'The Oldest Chemists and Perfumers in America', having been established in 1752.

The business was started in Newport, Rhode Island. Although the firm uses the date 1752, some of the records of the Newport Historical Society indicate that the founding date extends back to 1740. The Newport shop was given up in 1906. The New York branch, which was established before the American Civil War, is now the company's headquarters. The name of the company was registered as 'Limited' instead of 'Incorporated' (in 1890) because the business was originally British.

Dr Hunter, the founder of the business, made America's first Cologne water, now sold as 'Number Six Cologne'. This is still made according to the formula that Dr Hunter brought with him from England. It contains 27 natural ingredients, which are aged in oaken casks for two years and rolled from one end of the laboratory to the other once a month to help some of the gums and resins dissolve. The customers for this product included George Washington and Lafayette.

The company's catalogue invites customers to visit their 'historic apothecary at 518 Lexington Avenue'. (See also Schieffelin, 'Winegrowers, etc', page 58.)

Druggists *(see 'Chemists')*

Films

'*The Oldest Film Company in the World*' was the title of an article in *The Times* of 29 November 1956, commemorating the 50th anniversary of the founding of **Nordisk Films,** Copenhagen. The company was founded on 6 November 1906, by Ole Andersen Olsen, who died in 1943 at the age of 80.

Glass

The great French industrial concern of **Saint-Gobain** dates its history from 1665, when Louis XIV granted Letters Patent to Nicolas du Noyer for the manufacture of glass for mirrors 'comme il s'en fait à Venise'. The mirrors for the famous Galerie des Glaces at Versailles came from the *Manufacture royale de glaces de miroirs* between 1678 and 1683. (There is reason to think that the early success of the French concern was partly due to successful industrial espionage conducted in the workshops of the Venetian glass-manufacturers

at Murano.) At the end of the 17th century a move was made of part of the works to Saint-Gobain, near La Fère in the Aisne Department.

The company of today covers a wide range of products, not only glass but also chemicals, fertilisers, plastics and atomic energy. (See Jean Choffel's *Saint-Gobain, du miroir à l'atome,* 1960.)

Leather and belting

On the demise of the Perot Malting Company in 1962 (see page 53), the title of America's oldest company passed to **J E Rhoads and Sons** of Wilmington, Delaware, manufacturers of leather and industrial belting. Etna M Kelley's *Business Founding Date Directory* (1954), gave the firm's date as 1702 and its address as Philadelphia and stated that it was the oldest firm of tanners in America and was being operated by the eighth generation of the Rhoads family.

In September 1974 a number of articles about 'the Nation's Oldest Company' appeared in the American Press, featuring both Mr Richard Rhoads, the Chairman of the company, aged 65, and his cousin, J Edgar Rhoads, the Chairman Emeritus, aged 91. Edgar set up the firm's chemistry laboratory in 1903 and estimates that he has developed between 50 and 100 different glues during his 70 years with the firm. In recent years the nature of the business has changed from being primarily concerned in producing industrial leather beltings to the making of nylon-reinforced belting, with increasing emphasis on conveyor-belts of a wide variety. The tanning activities of the firm ceased some years ago.

Joseph Rhoads started tanning leather in 1702 at Marple, in Pennsylvania, some 12 miles (20 km) from Philadelphia. Here the business was carried on until 1867 when Jonathan E Rhoads, representing the fifth generation of the family to tan leather at Marple, bought a tan-yard in Wilmington and abandoned the Marple site.

In 1881, Jonathan sold the tannery in order to devote all his time to the manufacture of leather belting. A few years later, when his three sons had been admitted to partnership, the business was renamed J E Rhoads and Sons. In 1897 the head office was established

Above: Mr Richard H Rhoads, Chairman of J E Rhoads & Sons, Wilmington, Delaware, America's oldest company, and his cousin J Edgar Rhoads, Chairman Emeritus, aged 91 (see page 101). *(J E Rhoads & Sons)*

Right: Extract from the oldest Rhoads day-book showing a transaction with an Abraham Lincon (so spelt) in 1732. *(Eleutherian Mills Historical Library, Greenville, Delaware)*

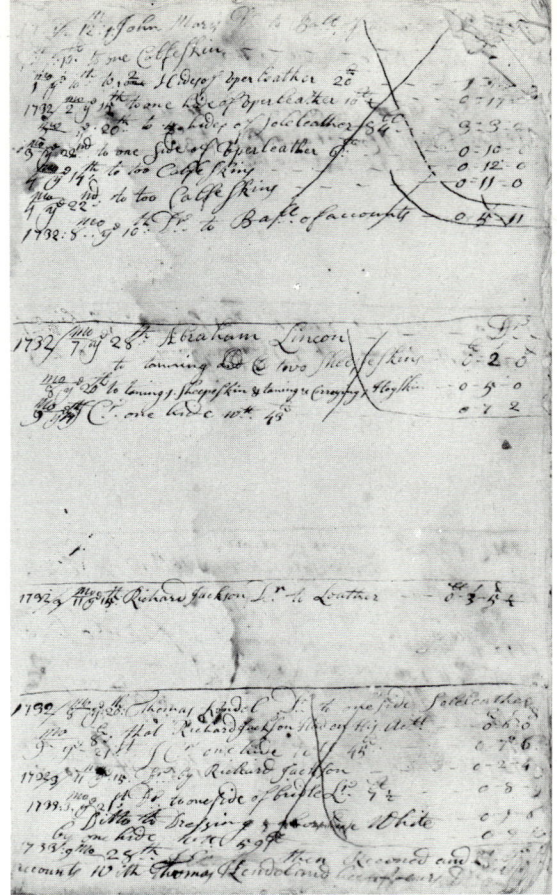

in Philadelphia, which explains the entry in Etna M Kelley's book.

In the early days, Rhoads's leather was used in the production of boots, harnesses and other necessities of colonial life. Jonathan, who took over the tannery about the time of the American Civil War, added the manufacture of industrial leather belts to the tanning operations. Nowadays, in addition to various types of belting, the firm make tapes and packings for hydraulic and pneumatic equipment.

By 1952, eight generations of the Rhoads family had been connected with the business. There is now no representative of the eighth generation. Mr Richard Rhoads and his cousin Edgar represent the seventh generation and seem likely to be the last generation of the

family to play an active role in the business.

The oldest surviving document relating to the Rhoads business is a day-book, carefully bound in leather, covering the years 1727–38. The entry for 28 May 1732 shows the charges made for tanning and currying 'sheepeskins' and hogskins for a man called Abraham Lincon (so spelt). This was the great-great-great-uncle of the man who was to achieve fame more than a century later as the President of the United States. A picture of the page from the Rhoads book is on this page. It will be seen that, in those years before the War of Independence, the accounts were kept in pounds, shillings and pence. The day-book is now among the records of the Rhoads company deposited in the Eleutherian Mills Historical Library at Wilmington.

Etna M Kelley's *Business Founding Date Directory* gives the dates 1719 and 1910 for the **Amalgamated Leather Companies** of Wilmington, Delaware, USA, with the comment that they can use either date. The oldest predecessor company was established in 1719.

Winslow Brothers and Smith, tanners, of Boston were established in 1776.

Leather goods

Etna M Kelley's *Business Founding Date Directory* contains two entries under the name Winship. The **Winship Company,** of Utica, New York State, leather goods manufacturers, dates from 1850, but the founder is said to have been originally associated with **W W Winship Incorporated,** of Boston, founded between 1773 and 1776. This is said to be Boston's oldest retail establishment, with the Winship family in control since 1842.

Paper

The paper-mill of **Richard-de-Bas** at Ambert in the Auvergne must certainly be counted among the oldest industrial enterprises in western Europe. Paper is still made here by hand in the same way as in 1326. The watermark of a heart crossed by two horizontal lines was found on a sheet of paper in the Archives of Le Puy some years ago. The paper had been used for drawing up a legal document which was dated 1326, so that the paper must have been made not later than that year. The story goes that some of the crusaders who accompanied Louis on the Crusade of 1248 were captured and made to work in a paper-mill at Damascus. After being ransomed they returned to France and set up the first paper-mills in France in the region of Ambert.

At one time there were more than 300 mills in the district, but the mill of Richard-de-Bas is the only one now left. Part of the mill has been turned into a museum. Here the visitor can see exhibits to illustrate the history of paper and of the other media that man has used through the ages for purposes of record.

Several old paper firms are mentioned in the *Swedish Export Directory* of 1966. They are **Fiskeby AB,** Norrkoping, given as 1637/1871. **Grycksbo Papersbruk AB,** Grycksbo, 1740.

Old paper-mill, Ambert, France

and **Klippans Finpappersbruk,** Klippan, 1573.

The **Dexter Corporation,** Windsor Locks, Connecticut, belongs to that small group of businesses in the USA that were established before the Declaration of Independence of 1776. The company was founded in 1767 and remained a family company for 200 years.

In its early days the firm engaged in several types of business: wool-scouring, a saw-mill, a grist-mill, purveyors of hay, grain and cattle-feed. It was not until 1835 that paper was first manufactured, in the grist-mill.

Herbert R Coffin, who entered the business in 1867, was the son-in-law of C H Dexter, who was then the head of the firm and was the grandson of the founder. It was in 1847 that the firm was organised under the name of C H Dexter and Company. In 1867, when C H Dexter took his son and his two sons-in-law into the business, the name was changed to C H Dexter and Sons. Today the company forms one of the two divisions of the Dexter Corporation.

Tileston and Hollingsworth, of Hyde Park, Boston, describe themselves as 'the original Yankee papermaker'. It was in 1801 that Mr Tileston and Mr Hollingsworth took over a paper-mill on the Neponset River. The history of paper-making on the Neponset River could be traced back to 1728, when the Provincial Government issued a Charter to Thomas Hancock (uncle of the illustrious John) and others, allowing them to set up a paper-mill there. The mill of today is the direct descendant of the mill that was established under the Charter of 1728.

Pipes

The **Zenith Pipe Company,** of Gouda, Holland, dates from 1749. They have been called 'the world's oldest pipemakers'. The founder of the business, Pieter van der Want, passed his master-test before the Deans and Headmen of the Pipemakers' Guild on 17 March 1749. The pipes they made were of clay.

Seven generations of the family have been connected with the business since 1749.

The **Missouri Meerschaum Company,** of Washington, Missouri, was established in 1872. According to Etna M Kelley's *Business*

Founding Date Directory it is the oldest manufacturer of corncob pipes.

Soap

The soap-factory of the Golden Hand **(De Vergulde Hand)** in Amsterdam is believed to be the oldest soap-factory in the world. The factory is still on its original site, not far from the main railway station in Amsterdam and not far from the old Bols Distillery, the oldest distillery in the world (see page 46). The factory celebrated its 400th anniversary in 1954, but there had been a soap-factory on the same spot even before 1554.

The author spent an interesting morning with the head of the firm (Mr Woltman Elpers), whose family has been connected with the business since 1692. He was shown some of the old books of the firm, and given details of the production of summer soap and winter soap (a term for soap using fat of animals killed either in summer or winter) hundreds of years ago, from 1595. The firm still makes soap and soap products, such as shaving-cream.

The firm's full title is 'C. A. Woltman Elpers' Koninklijke Zeepfabriek 'De Vergulde Hand' N.V.'. Its notepaper carries a picture of the Golden Hand with the date 'Anno 1554' and the words 'Oudste zeepfabriek ter wereld' ('Oldest soap factory in the world').

Tobacco

Holland has several old tobacco firms. The packets of 'Holland House aromatic pipe tobacco' inform us that the contents of the packets are made by **Theodorus Niemeyer,** successors to **Franciscus Lieftinck** of Groningen. We also learn that the tobacco business of Franciscus Lieftinck was established in 1820.

Nearly 40 years earlier, according to the packets of 'Zuiderzee superior mild cavendish tobacco', the firm now known as **De Erven de Wed: J. van Nelle NV,** of Rotterdam, was established, in 1782.

Demuth's tobacco shop at Lancaster, Pennsylvania, was established in 1770 and describes itself as 'The Oldest in America'. According to Etna M Kelley's *Business Founding Date Directory* again, it is operated on its

PAVLVS PAPA V.

Ad perpetuam rei memoriam.

PAVLVS PAPA · V.

Papal Bull of Pope Paul V (1605) establishing the Banco di Santo Spirito, Rome. *(Banco di Santo Spirito)* (see page 115) original site by descendants of the founder.

Another claim to pre-eminence in the to-bacco world is made by the **P Lorillard Company,** of New York. They were established in 1760 and describe themselves as 'America's oldest tobacco merchants'.

Umbrellas

In 1854 a man named **Johann Etscheid,** of Bonn, borrowed 164 Thalers from his cousin, Joseph Aschermann, in Paris and opened a little shop next to the University in Bonn where he sold such things as umbrellas, walking-sticks, braces and students' caps. The address of the University was Am Hof 1, and the address of the shop was Am Hof 3.

Johann's son, Franz, took over the business in 1892, and he in turn was succeeded by his daughter Gretel who, as Gretel Stucke-Etscheid, was able to celebrate the centenary of the business in 1954. It was still close to the original site, but the old premises went up in flames, along with part of the University, during an air raid in October 1944. The shop still adjoins the University, but the address is now Am Hof 5 (see illustration opposite).

Utilities

The giant **American Telephone and Telegraph Company** of New York easily heads the *Fortune* list of 1975 of the largest utility companies in the USA, with assets of more than $74 000 million and almost 1 million employees. Among the utility companies the

The old umbrella shop, Bonn, Germany. *(Stucke-Etscheid)*

next largest employer was **General Telephone and Electronics,** of Stamford, Connecticut, with nearly 200 000. (In the previous year this company was included among the industrials.)

CHAPTER 5

FINANCE AND INSURANCE

A. BUSINESSES IN THE BRITISH ISLES

Banks

Child's Bank, whose address is No 1 Fleet Street in the City of London, is one of the oldest banks in England, if not the oldest.

According to the *Bankers' Almanack*, the bank – Child and Company – was established in 1560 but its Archivist, Mr S W Shelton, maintained that its origins go back to the year 1559. The short history of the bank to be found in *The Three Banks Review* of September 1955 says, somewhat cautiously, that it is 'probably the oldest existing bank in the country'.

The origin of Child's Bank can be taken back to 1559 at least. In that year John Wheeler, a goldsmith 'of Chepe' (i.e. Cheapside) was one of the pikemen in the guard of honour furnished by the Goldsmiths' Company from their livery to escort Queen Elizabeth through the City on her way to Greenwich. As John Wheeler was a member of the livery at that time, he must have been established in business even earlier.

The Wheelers continued as goldsmiths for many years and moved to the Strand in the early part of the 17th century. Between 1664 and 1668, Francis (later Sir Francis) Child joined the business, and in 1671 he married Elizabeth Wheeler, the daughter of the owner of the business at that time. Francis Child, who was also a great-great-grandson of the original John Wheeler, inherited the business on the death of his father-in-law and began to develop the banking side of it. He has been called 'the Father of the Profession'.

The business remained in the hands of the Child family until 1924, when **Glyn, Mills and Company** bought it from the executors of George Henry Robert Child-Villiers, the eighth Earl of Jersey.

'The Banker M.P.', an article in *The Three Banks Review* of December 1956, gives an interesting account of Sir Richard Glyn and Sir Thomas Hallifax, two of the founder-partners of Glyn's, and of the steps taken by them to obtain a seat in the House of Commons. The many advantages included free postage available to Members which was worth as much as £800 a year to one firm of bankers in the 1760s.

The 'Three Banks' responsible for *The Three Banks Review* were the **Royal Bank of Scotland** (founded 1727), **Glyn, Mills** (founded 1753), and **Williams Deacon's** (founded 1771). In 1969 they came together with the National Commercial Bank of Scotland and its associate, the National and Commercial Banking Group. It was in 1771 that the banking-house of Raymond, Williams, Vere, Lowe and Fletcher had been established, at 81 Cornhill, London, a firm that was to become the oldest constituent of Williams Deacon's Bank.

Child's Bank moved to its present site in Fleet Street, at the Sign of the Marigold, about 1620. (The sign of the marigold can still be seen on the outside of the building.) **Martins Bank,** at 68 Lombard Street, has an even longer record of business on one site, although the record is a somewhat interrupted one. One of the advertisements for Martin's Bank that appeared in 1968 was headed 'Business as usual since 1563'. It said that the Golden Grasshopper first appeared in Lombard Street in Elizabethan times as the symbol of the goldsmith's business founded by Sir Thomas Gresham, which was 'one of the forerunners of Martin's Bank'.

The indisputable date when Gresham is known from the national records to have been engaged in large-scale banking transactions in Lombard Street is 1563, but Gresham's own day-book confirms that 'between 1546 and 1551 Gresham had already a claim to be considered "a father of English banking"'. (Francis Child, as we noted above, has been called 'the Father of the Profession', but Gresham would appear to have a better claim to be the progenitor.)

The grasshopper was the sign of Sir Thomas Gresham, the founder of the Royal Exchange, who lived at what is now 68 Lombard Street in the year 1560. According to tradition, a banking business had been carried on here since 1563. Sir Richard Martin, who served as Lord Mayor of London in the year 1588 and as Master of the Mint from 1572 to 1617 (see 'Mints', page 78), had frequent transactions with Gresham and thus began the connection of the Martin family with the grasshopper. The coats of arms of the two families can be seen carved over the large windows of the bank's present building in Lombard Street.

Due to loss of records in the Great Fire of 1666 and in the Royal Exchange fire of 1825, it is difficult to ascertain what business was carried on here in the early 17th century. It is known that Edward Backwell, a prominent goldsmith, carried on his business here from 1662 to 1672, and that Samuel Pepys kept his account here. Backwell's apprentice, Charles Duncombe (see page 78) succeeded him, and carried on business in partnership first with Richard Kent and later with his brother, Valentine. In 1686 the name of Richard Smythe appears as a partner with the Duncombes and Kent. Before his death in 1699, Smythe had engaged as a clerk Thomas Martin, who become a partner four years later, in 1703.

In 1890 the bank's name was changed to Martin's Bank Limited. In 1918, when the bank was amalgamated with the Bank of Liverpool, the name was changed to Bank of Liverpool and Martins. In 1928, with the incorporation of the Lancashire and Yorkshire Bank, this unwieldy title was shortened to Martins Bank Limited. The date 1831 which used to appear in the advertisements for Martins Bank ('Bankers since 1831') was the year in which the Bank of Liverpool was established. This explains the presence of the Liver Bird, along with the grasshopper, in the bank's crest. At the end of 1969, Martins was amalgamated with Barclays, and the old name gradually disappeared from the premises of the enlarged company.

Kent's *Encyclopaedia of London* (1951 edition) contains the statement that 'the oldest of this group of banks is said to be Martin's, which, as a goldsmith's business, was in Lombard Street in 1558'. This, it will be seen, makes Martins Bank a year older than Child's Bank, for which Kent gives the date 1559. However, as the booklet published by Martins Bank is content to date their business from 1563, which is also the date shown in the sign outside the premises in Lombard Street, it seems fair to follow the verdict of *The Three Banks Review* and to take Child's Bank as the oldest in the country, always provided that mergers and amalgamations can be ignored in the present context.

Number 71 Lombard Street is the head office of **Lloyds Bank,** whose prancing black horse with the date 1677 is a familiar sign. One of the bank's advertisements informs us that Pepys was a frequent visitor to Lombard Street, and that 'he entrusted his financial affairs to the good offices of Humphrey Stokes, a goldsmith and "keeper of running cashes" under the sign of "The Black Horse"'.

According to H L V Fletcher's *North Wales*, Charles Lloyd, the founder of Lloyds Bank, came of an old Meifod family in Montgomeryshire and was born in the parish in 1637. He became a Quaker while a student at Oxford and then settled in Birmingham, where he became an ironmaster and founded his bank.

Gosling's Bank at 19 Fleet Street is now Gosling's Branch of Barclay's Bank, but the cheques issued there still carry the mark of Gosling's Bank and the legend 'established 1650'. Gosling's Bank was founded in 1650 by Henry Pinckney, a goldsmith, at the 'Sign of the Three Squirrels', still to be seen over the central window.

All these family banks were established before the Bank of England. The private bank of **C Hoare and Company** was 'established before 1673 at the Sign of the Golden Bottle in Cheapside'.

In 1955 the six partners of the bank, all named Hoare, were all descendants of the founder; one of them, H P R Hoare, has recounted the bank's long history in *Hoare's Bank – A Record, 1672–1955, The Story of a Private Bank*. This dates the bank's history from the year 1672, which makes it five years older than Lloyds Bank, founded in 1677. The following account of the bank is largely based on this work.

Richard Hoare (1648–1718), the founder of the bank, was in 1665 apprenticed to a goldsmith in London, but his master died before his term was up and he was then apprenticed to another goldsmith, Robert Tempest, who carried on his business at the Sign of the Golden Bottle in Cheapside. When Tempest died, in 1673, this business was continued in a sole name of Richard Hoare. He was a goldsmith and banker, and had 'a chocolett dish of Eq. Pepypes to mend' while at Cheapside. In 1690, between 2 October and 24 December, Richard Hoare moved to Fleet Street, to the present site of the bank. He renamed the premises The Golden Bottle. Richard Hoare was Lord Mayor of London for the year 1712–13. All the partners, bar two exceptions, have been his direct descendants.

Richard's younger son Henry succeeded him and took his younger brother Benjamin (1693–1750) into partnership. This Henry died in 1725 and was succeeded by his two sons, Henry (1705–85) and Richard (later Sir Richard) (1709–54). Sir Richard was Lord Mayor in the year 1745–6. The senior branch of the family came back into the business with another Henry (1750–1828), who became a partner in 1778 and was the senior partner from 1788 to 1828.

The premises that had been occupied by the founder of the bank remained until 1828 or 1829. On 29 May 1829, 'ye anniversary of K. Ch. 2 Restoration', the first brick of the present building was laid by Henry Ainslie Hoare, then aged five, the great-great-great-great-grandson of the founder.

In the middle of the 19th century the two sole partners were Peter Richard Hoare (1803–77) and yet another Henry Hoare (1807–66). Both were deeply religious men, but Peter was a High Churchman while Henry was a Low Churchman. They took it in turns to spend six months in the bank and six months on their country estates. Owing to their different views, they rarely met except when business required it, and were never in Fleet Street together for more than a few hours at a time.

In 1929 the partnership was converted into the present unlimited liability company. In 1932 a West End branch was opened in Park Lane. Ten generations of the Hoare family have been connected with the bank.

In 1972 Hoare's Bank celebrated its 300th anniversary. It was then said to be the only independent survivor of more than 750 private banks in England and Wales. (See page 176.)

Richard Hoare moved his business to Fleet Street in 1690. The banking-house of **Coutts** dates from that period. 'The exact date of its foundation is not known, but, in 1692, the earliest date of which records are preserved in the bank, the proprietor was John Campbell, who was goldsmith as well as banker.' Both banks are, therefore, older than the Bank of England.

John Campbell carried on business 'At the Three Crowns in the Strand next door to the Globe Tavern'. These words appear today on the bank's cheques and in some of their advertisements, together with a reproduction of the sign, the date 1692 and Campbell's initials.

The connection with the Coutts family dates from 1755, when James Coutts was taken into partnership on his marriage to Mary Peagrim, the niece of George Campbell (John Campbell's son). In 1760, when George Campbell died, James Coutts invited his younger brother Thomas to join him. It is to Thomas Coutts (1735–1822) that the bank owes its rise to the high position that it came to occupy in the banking world. Coutts is now a subsidiary of the National Westminster Bank.

Junior by a few years to Coutts and Company is the **Bank of England,** which was founded in 1694. It was 'started and founded on a plan the entire credit of which was due to William Paterson'. Paterson, however, withdrew in 1695 and turned his attention to Scotland.

The **Bank of Scotland** was founded a year later than the Bank of England, in 1695. Like the Bank of England it consists legally of the 'Governor and Company' of the bank. David Spence held office as Secretary of the bank from 1696 to 1746. His son, after helping him for a time, became Secretary in 1746 and went on till 1790, a remarkable record of family continuity.

The Scottish Parliament passed the Bill 'For the Erection of a Publick Bank' on 17 July 1695, but the first meeting of the 'Adventurers' (i.e. shareholders) was not held until 14 February 1696, so that it was only in 1696 that its modest capital of 1 200 000 pounds Scots (£100 000) was secured and business began. The bank describes itself as 'Scotland's First Bank', and it is sometimes referred to as 'The Old Bank', in order to distinguish it from the **Royal Bank of Scotland.**

The latter is the oldest *private* bank in Scotland and came into existence in 1727, by virtue of a Charter passed under the Great Seal of Scotland on 31 May in that year. It was not until 1828 that it moved to its present headquarters in St Andrew Square.

On 25 April 1968, *The Times* reported that the Royal Bank of Scotland was to merge with the National Commercial Bank of Scotland to form the National and Commercial Banking Group.

Another old Scottish bank, the **British Linen Bank,** of Edinburgh, was incorporated by Royal Charter in 1746 as the British Linen Company.

The **Chartered Bank of India, Australia and China,** to give this bank its full title, received its Charter on 29 December 1853, not without opposition from the East India Company.

According to Neil Munro, the Royal Bank of Scotland is 'older than any joint-stock bank in England except the mother of all British banking' but there are a number of banks in England that are older than the Royal Bank of Scotland. Another such bank is **Drummond's Bank** in London, founded by Andrew Drummond in 1717 and taken over by the Royal Bank of Scotland in 1923.

Andrew Drummond had his first business premises close to the site, near Admiralty Arch, where Drummonds Branch of the Royal Bank of Scotland now stands. Throughout its independent existence the bank was continuously owned and administered by successive generations of the Drummond family. The bank still has the ledger that Andrew Drummond opened in 1715, two years before the founding of the bank, which is given over to his business as goldsmith and silversmith.

Although Drummond's Bank was taken over by the Royal Bank of Scotland in 1924, the family connection was maintained by Mr Angus Drummond, who 'still sits at the tall sloping ledger-table in the "Partners' Room"'. A financial journal of the time commented that 'one of the oldest private firms of banks in London had been acquired by one of the oldest established institutions in Scotland'.

Spencer Perceval, the only British Prime Minister to be assassinated (in 1812), was a customer of the bank, as his descendants still are. He was the brother-in-law of Andrew Berkeley Drummond, a great-nephew of the founder of the bank.

The **National Provincial Bank** (now part of the National Westminster) was established comparatively recently, in 1833, but it claimed to be 'the first bank to be formed in London for the express purpose of providing a banking service throughout the length and breadth of England and Wales'. Part of the bank, however, could look back on a much longer history than this.

The bank of **Samuel Smith and Company,** Nottingham, once said to date from 1688, merged in the Union of London and Smith's Bank in 1902. This bank in turn merged in the National Provincial Bank in 1918. There is, however, much more to the story than that.

This, the oldest provincial or 'country' bank in England, was in fact founded in 1658 (not 1688) by Thomas Smith (1631–99), a mercer and Alderman of Nottingham. Banks were founded by other members of the Smith family at London, Lincoln and Hull in the latter half of the 18th century, and at Derby and elsewhere in the 19th century. The Smith family's banks carried on business as partnerships until 1902, when they were amalgamated with the Union Bank of London. At No 1 Lombard Street, in the City of London, the words 'Smith's Bank' still stand over the entrance to the building that is now occupied by the National Westminster Bank.

The year 1688 was for long taken as the date of foundation of the Nottingham bank, but Mr Leighton-Boyce states that there is 'sound evidence' to suggest an earlier origin; it 'is certain that in 1658 Thomas Smith I completed the purchase of the premises which became known as the old bank-house at Nottingham, and there he set up business as a mercer'. (According to Aytoun Ellis's *The Penny Universities*, Nottingham 'can boast of having the first – and for many years the only – bank outside London', namely Smith's Bank.) Very little is known of the operations of the bank until the middle of the 18th century, the records being few and far between. There is reason to believe that an account was opened 'at least by 1709' for Abell Collin's Hospital, an account later held by the Nottingham branch of the National Provincial Bank housed in the building formerly occupied by Samuel Smith and Company. 'An unbroken history of some 250 years surely qualifies Abell Collin's Hospital as the oldest surviving account in a provincial bank in England', wrote Mr Leighton-Boyce in 1958.

The league table of the clearing banks that forms part of *The Times 1000 (1975–76)* list shows that Barclay's had moved ahead of the National Westminster, their gross deposits being £12 463 million and £12 308 million respectively. (For 'Savings banks' see page 113.)

Building societies

According to the *Guinness Book of Records*, the **Chelmsford and Essex Society,** which was established in July 1845, is the oldest building society in the world.

The **Alliance Perpetual Building Society** of London, which was established in 1854, is described as 'One of the Oldest Building Societies'. It is, however, some nine years younger than the society at Chelmsford.

Companies (general) (See pages 165–6)

Friendly Societies

According to *Whitaker's Almanack* of 1951, the Voluntary Register of Friendly Societies at that time included 'eleven societies which have been in existence for upwards of 200 years, the four earliest all operating in Scotland, the oldest being the "Incorporation of Carters in Leith", established as long ago as 1555'. The four oldest in England were all formed in London, early in the 18th century; the two oldest, the Norman Society and the Society for the Mutual Help of Swiss in London, were both established in 1703.

Three of these four English societies were still mentioned in the edition of 1957 but, according to *Whitaker's Almanack* of 1968, the oldest English society on the Register then was the Bottesford Friendly Society, which was established in Leicestershire in 1747.

The 1976 edition of the same work shows that the **Carters of Leith** still hold their place as the oldest society. The five *largest* societies, according to the same authority, were the **National Deposit Friendly Society,** established in 1868, with a membership of 331 000 and total funds of £25 301 000; the **Hearts of Oak Benefit Society** (1842); the **Independent Order of Odd Fellows, Manchester Unity** (1810); the **Ancient Order of Foresters** (1834), and the **Independent Order of Rechabites, Salford Unity** (1835).

Those friendly societies that are known as collecting societies because they collect members' premiums for life assurance by house-to-house visits are bigger institutions than the friendly societies proper. The three largest collecting societies are the **Liverpool Victoria Friendly Society** (1843), with total funds of £283 666 000, 8 616 000 premium-paying industrial assurances and 4 169 000 free paid-up industrial assurances; the **Royal Liver Friendly Society** (1850), with total funds of £121 284 000 and the **Scottish Legal Life Assurance Society** (1852), with total funds of £30 198 000.

Hire purchase

North Central Finance Limited used to describe itself as 'the oldest hire purchase company in the world'. It was formerly known as North Central Wagon and Finance Company Limited and now, under the title Lombard North Central Limited, is a subsidiary of the National Westminster Bank.

The company was formed at Rotherham in 1861 as The North Central Wagon Company, Rotherham and its original purpose, as the name indicates, was 'purchasing, hiring, and manufacturing railway wagons to Railway Companies, Coal Proprietors and other persons'. The North Central has, therefore, been hire-purchasing and leasing industrial plant and machinery for more than a century.

The Wagon Finance Companies played an important part in the development of the British coalfields in the latter part of the 19th century, when practically all coal had to be moved from the collieries in railway wagons, and when there were no ready facilities at the pithead for handling accumulating stocks of coal.

Insurance

Not far from Drummond's Bank (see page 110), in Trafalgar Square, stood the West End branch of the **Sun Insurance Office,** proclaiming it to be the oldest insurance company in the world, having been founded in 1710. A little farther on, in Lower Regent Street, was the London office of the **Caledonian Insurance Company,** which was founded in 1805 and described itself as 'Scotland's oldest insurance company'. (The Caledonian is now part of the Guardian Royal Exchange Company.) England, however, has several insurance companies older than the Caledonian, including the **London Assurance Company** and the **Royal Exchange Assurance Company,** both of which date from 1720. The Royal Exchange Assurance, like the Caledonian, is now part of the Guardian Royal Exchange Company, which was formed in 1968.

There were earlier insurance companies. Thornbury writes (Volume I, page 378):

'In 1698, hoping to clear off their debts, the **Mercers' Company** engaged in a ruinous insurance scheme, suggested by Dr Assheton, a Kentish rector. It was proposed to grant annuities of £30 per cent to clergymen's widows according to certain sums paid by their husbands.'

(There is an interesting parallel to the oldest American life insurance company – see page 121).

In 1745 the Mercers' Company had to stop, and petitioned Parliament for relief. An Act of George III allowed them to issue new bonds and to pay them off by a lottery.

Both the London Assurance Company and the Royal Exchange Assurance Company were incorporated in 1720. The Royal Exchange Assurance Company is proud of the fact that its head office has been in the Royal Exchange building for more than 200 years.

The Royal Exchange Assurance Company was first organised in 1717, at meetings in Mercers' Hall. They began business under the title of the Mining, Royal Mineral, and Batteries Works, and the Royal Charter was granted on 22 June 1720. The London Assurance Company obtained its Charter on the same day. Both companies, like the Hudson's Bay Company, described their Annual General Meeting as the 'Annual General Court'.

The Sun Fire Office still has its original minute-books dating from its beginning in April 1710. The original company evolved from a scheme of one Charles Povey, but in March 1710, Povey sold his interest to the Company of London Insurers, and on 7 April 1710, the deed of the company's co-partnership was executed. At first each policy covered a loss by fire not exceeding £500, but this limitation was removed in 1721. In 1711, the Sun Fire Office transferred from Paul's Coffee House to Garraway's, taking with them 'the carved sign of the Sun, their house-mark, for which they had paid 16 shillings'.

The company's original premises were in Hatton Garden, but a Westminster branch was opened in Craig's Court, Charing Cross, in 1726. This was the office that moved to the site in Trafalgar Square in 1867.

As early as 1710 the company had its own 'thirty lusty able-bodied firemen who are clothed in blue Liveries and having Silver Badges with the Sun Mark upon their arms', as well as 20 porters for putting out fires and carrying goods to safety. The London Assurance and the Sun Insurance Office now both form part of the Sun Alliance and London Insurance Limited.

Lloyd's is not a business in our sense of

the term, but it should be mentioned here. According to Paul Bareau's *The City*, 'Lloyd's is a corporation but it has no corporate liability for the transaction [*sic*] of its members'. The origins of Lloyd's 'go back to 1688, to the famous coffee house of Edward Lloyd in Tower Street, later moved to Lombard Street, where today a plaque shows where once it stood'. The passer-by in Lombard Street will find the plaque on Coutts's Bank at 15 Lombard Street, facing Martins Bank. The plaque records that this was the site of Lloyd's Coffee House from 1691 to 1785.

Almost contemporary with Lloyd's was the old **Hand-in-Hand Fire and Life Insurance Society,** instituted in 1696. Until 1905, when it was merged with the Commercial Union Assurance Company, this was the oldest fire office in the country, and probably in the world. The old head office of the Hand-in-Hand was at 26 New Bridge Street in the City of London. The building has been demolished but, until a few years ago, the Hand-in-Hand still operated, as a branch of Commercial Union, with its own branch Board of Directors; its notepaper still carried the old sign of the clasped hands with crown, and the heading 'Commercial Union Assurance Company Limited in which is merged the Hand-in-Hand Fire and Life Insurance Society-Inst. 1696' (i.e. instituted in 1696).

In his book on the coffee-houses (*The Penny Universities*), Aytoun Ellis says that Tom's Coffee House, on the site of the London Coliseum,

'was the coffee-house in which Britain's oldest fire insurance company – the Hand-in-Hand – was formed. The initiative was taken by the three Tooley Steet wharfingers, Hay, Chamberlain and Beale, all of whom owned property in Westminster.

(For the Tooley Street wharfingers, see page 127.)

Aytoun Ellis also says that the name was suggested by an alley called Hand-in-Hand Alley almost opposite to the entrance to Stoney Lane. He adds that Tom Nye's coffee-house was among the first to be insured by the Sun, on 7 May 1710.

Ellis does not quote the source of his information, but it is not entirely consistent with the information given to the author by

the Hand-in-Hand office. The original office was certainly constituted at a meeting in Tom's Coffee House, on 12 November 1696, and John Chamberlin was one of the founders. But there was no Beale and no Hay (although there was a Joseph Hayes). The name of James Paterson also appears on the original deed.

As early as 1707 the society had its own fire-engine and its own water-men, possibly so called because they supplied water for the pumps. The society's water-men, distinguished by their coats and badges, were free from being impressed for service in the Royal Navy.

The bicentenary notice of 1896 says that the name 'Hand-in-Hand' was given to the society by its customers and the public from its fire-mark, a couple of hands clasped in each other, as a symbol of friendship and good faith. A house was not deemed to be properly insured until the fire-mark had been affixed to it.

In 1714, the **Union, or Double Hand-in-Hand, Fire Office** was formed for insuring goods and merchandise. Like the older society, its operations were at first confined to London and Westminster. In 1717 the **Westminster Fire Office** was formed as a result of the Hand-in-Hand moving its office from St Martin's Lane (in Westminster) to the City of London.

The **Equitable Life Assurance Society,** was established in 1762 as 'The Society for Equitable Assurances on Lives and Survivorships'. It describes itself in advertisements as 'the oldest mutual life office in the world'.

Before the merger leading to the formation of the Sun Alliance and London Insurance Group the Sun used to describe itself as the oldest insurance company. This was true if the field was confined to offices that were still operating independently, although the Hand-in-Hand branch of Commercial Union antedated it by 14 years.

The **Railway Passengers Assurance Company,** founded in 1848, was described as the oldest accident office in the world in the centenary history by F H Cox. It now forms part of the Commercial Union Group.

Savings banks

The Henry Duncan Museum in the village of Ruthwell, Dumfriesshire, was opened on 8

October 1974, the 200th anniversary of the birth of **Henry Duncan,** described as 'the Father of World Savings Banks'. He founded the first savings bank, in Ruthwell, in 1810. (See also page 122.)

Stockbrokers

The stockbroking firm of **R Edwards, Chandler, Wagstaffe** celebrated its 150th anniversary on 7 December 1967. It was founded by Thomas Chandler in 1817. R Edwards amalgamated with Chandler and Company shortly before the Second World War. **Foster and Braithwaite,** another stockbroking firm, was established in 1825.

The oldest stockbroking firm in the City is **Mullens,** which received its broker's licence in 1767. Sir William Mullens, who died in February 1975, was the senior Government Broker from 1950 to 1962. It was recorded in his obituary that his firm, Mullens and Company, had provided the Government Broker since the office was instituted in 1786.

Stock Exchange, London

The official booklet entitled *The Stock Exchange*, published by the Council of the Stock Exchange, contains a brief history of the institution since the days of the coffee-houses. To quote one paragraph from the booklet:

'In 1773, two years before the American War of Independence, a meeting of stockbrokers decided to take over a building at the corner of Threadneedle Street and Sweetings Alley, and over its door inscribed a new title: "The Stock Exchange"'.

Thornbury tells us that there were many dealers in Jonathan's Coffee House in 1698 and that on 14 July 1773, according to an old paper:

'The brokers and others at "New Jonathan's" came to a resolution, that instead of its being called "New Jonathan's" it should be called "The Stock Exchange".'

An echo of the days of the coffee-houses is to be found in the fact that the attendants are still called 'waiters'.

Unit trusts

The **M and G Group** advertise themselves as 'the Founders of Britain's Unit Trusts'. The

Part of the Egibi archives, Babylon. *(British Museum)*

first such trust was formed in 1931. At the beginning of 1975, M and G were involved in the management of over £300 million. (See also page 227.)

B. BUSINESSES IN OTHER LANDS

Banks

Bankers in Babylon

The house of **Egibi and Son,** of Babylon, was described by F G Hilton Price in his history of Child's Bank (*The Marygold by Temple Bar*) as the oldest known banking firm in the world. Egibi, the founder of the firm, probably lived in the latter part of the reign of Sennacherib (705–681 BC).

Several hundred cuneiform tablets relating to the bank's activities are now in the British

Museum – cheques, receipts and other banking documents. Translations of the two tablets shown in the illustration are given in R H Sack's *Amel-Marduk 562–560 BC.* (Neukirchen-Vluyn 1972), where they appear as Nos 8 and 6.

The first tablet, BM 30232, concerns a loan and is dated the 14th day of the month of Du'uzu in the second year of Amel-Marduk, King of Babylon. The second tablet, BM 30492, concerns a loan of eleven *minas* of silver charged against a house and was dated at Babylon on the 20th day of the month of Tebetu in the first year of Amel-Marduk.

Futher information about the banking activities of the Egibi family is given by A Ungnad in *Archiv für Orient-Forschung*, 14 (1944), pages 58–64. Ungnad lists six generations of the family, starting with the founder whose dates, given as 690–610 BC, are described as 'nur approximativ'. His great-great-great grandson lived from 550 to 480 BC.

O blessed serendipity! F A Mumby's classic work on the book trade (see page 149) opens with the words:

'The secret of the philosopher's stone is not more difficult to discover than the name of the Father of the Book Trade. We should look for it in vain among the records of the baked clay tablets of Babylonia and Assyria'.

Banking is more fortunate in this respect.

Bankers in modern times

Banks in this country generally display the date of their foundation, and banks in other countries often do the same. A number of them also draw attention to the fact that they are the oldest bank in their own country.

The Bank of Naples **(Il Banco di Napoli),** which was founded in 1539, used to describe itself as the oldest bank in the world. Its origin can be traced to a *monte di pietà*, a pawnshop or bank, which was founded in 1539 by a few philanthropists.

The only possible challenger to the Bank of Naples seemed to be another Italian bank, the **Monte dei Paschi di Siena.** Although generally dated from 1624, the bank has a connection with an early *monte di pietà* established in 1472 and renewed in 1568. The bank's office in Siena described the bank as

'Fondata nel 1472'. It was, however, the year 1624 that saw the opening of the institution whose full title is the 'Monte non vacabile dei Paschi della Città e Stato di Siena'.

It would seem that the Bank of Naples has now ceded the title of the world's oldest bank to the Siena bank, which celebrated its 500th anniversary in 1972.

Yet another Italian bank dating from the 16th century is the **Istituto Bancario San Paolo di Torino** (Turin). It was established in 1563.

Early in the 17th century the **Banco di Santo Spirito** (the Bank of the Holy Ghost) at Rome was established by a Bull of Pope Paul V dated 13 December 1605. (See illustration, page 105.) The bank 'came into being under the aegis of the oldest and most memorable hospital institution in Rome, the Hospital of Santo Spirito'. Until 1607 it occupied an apartment in the hospital. (For 'Savings banks', see page 122.)

The bank of **Joh Berenberg, Gossler and Company,** of Hamburg, Germany, was founded in the year 1590.

The *Economist* of 27 July 1957 reported that 'Sweden's **Riksbank** – reputedly the world's most venerable central banking institution – has marked the tercentenary of its foundation in 1657'. It was not, however, until 1968 that the Riksbank celebrated its tercentenary.

The Riksbank's explanation of this apparent contradiction is that the first Swedish bank, **Stockholms Banco,** was founded by Johan Palmstruch and seems to have started its business activities in July 1657. The bank, however, collapsed, and an entirely new bank, the **Rikets Ständers Bank** (Bank of the Estates of the Realm), now called the 'Sveriges Riksbank', was founded in 1668. The latter date, therefore, seems to be the appropriate one to take in this case, but it still leaves the Riksbank with the title of 'the oldest *central* bank in the world'.

Just one year older than the Riksbank is the French banking-house of **de Neuflize, Schlumberger et Compagnie,** of Paris. This firm of private bankers was established in 1667.

The year 1786, saw the formation of the firm of **Rougemont, Hottinguer et Compagnie,** in Paris.

Holland's oldest bank, **Vlaer en Kol,** at

Johann Jakob Leu (1689–1768). *(Leu & Co)*

Utrecht, dates from 1691. Eight generations of the family of the founder have been represented in the bank. Another Dutch firm, **R Mees en Zoonen,** bankers and insurance brokers, of Rotterdam, was founded in 1720. The bank of **Hope en Compagnie,** of Amsterdam, whose office is in one of the gracious old houses situated on the Keizersgracht, celebrated its 200th anniversary in 1962.

Leu & Compagnie was established in Zürich in 1755. The bank is today 'the oldest financial institution of Switzerland and superior in age to most banks on the continent of Europe north of the Alps'. Unusually, it started as a State-owned enterprise (of the City of Zürich) but developed into a private one. The name of the bank commemorates J J Leu, the City Treasurer of Zürich, who was born in 1689 and died in 1768. (See illustration, above.)

The **Swiss Volksbank,** or Volksbank in Berne as it was first called, opened on 1 July 1869. Its purpose was 'to make available to craftsmen and workers the necessary funds to operate their own business'. In 1881, in order to facilitate the establishment of offices outside Berne, the bank's name was changed to Schweizerische Volksbank, while French and Italian versions of the name were adopted at the same time.

The book entitled *Swiss Volksbank 1869–1969* that was published at the time of the bank's centenary contains an interesting discussion on the changing value of money through the centuries. It shows that some of the problems of today were also the problems of yesterday and of even earlier times. The French franc had a gold content of 3.877 grams in 1360 but two centuries later it was down to 1.07 grams.

The bank known as **von der Heydt-Kersten und Söhne** of Elberfeld in Germany dates from 1754.

Conrad Kersten left his native town of Spangenberg for Elberfeld in the early part of the 18th century. He soon made his mark as a yarn- and cloth-merchant, and became a Member of the Town Council. He also dealt in *Kolonialwaren* – sugar, coffee, currants, ginger and so on. In 1754 he handed over his business to his two sons Abraham and Caspar. The banking side of the business developed naturally out of Conrad's dealings with suppliers and customers in other countries. Indeed, apart from Cologne, Elberfeld was for many years the only place in western Germany of major importance as a banking centre.

The son of Abraham Kersten died young, but Abraham's daughter, Wilhelmine, helped her mother to carry on the business during the last years of her father's life and married Daniel Heinrich von der Heydt in 1794. Abraham died in 1796 and Daniel became a partner in the firm in 1798, taking then the name von der Heydt-Kersten.

The balance-sheets of the bank have been preserved from 1803 on. More than 70 different currencies were circulating in the Rhineland in those days, which must have made bookkeeping difficult. The letter-books of the bank go back to 1836.

Junior by more than a century to the Elberfeld bank is the **Deutsche Bank,** which was established by virtue of a decree of King William I of Prussia in March 1870 and opened its doors for business on 9 April 1870. In March 1914, after its amalgamation with the

Bergisch-Märkische Bank of Elberfeld, it was described by the *Frankfurter Zeitung* as the biggest bank in the world. It was true that the Société Générale had a bigger issued capital and that some English banks, such as Lloyds, had bigger foreign deposits, but none of these other banks covered such a wide field of interests as the Deutsche Bank.

The bank played a prominent part in the development of the railways in Anatolia and of the Berlin–Baghdad Railway. It was concerned with the development of the oil industry in Romania (Steaua Romana) and with the reorganisation of the Northern Pacific Railroad in America. It was also among the first to see the possibilities inherent in electricity, as a source of both light and power.

Another German bank dating from 1870 is the **Commerzbank.** The Commerz- und Disconto-Bank, as it was originally called, was established in Hamburg early in 1870 and opened its doors for business on 25 April. The centenary history tells the story of the bank itself and of two of the other banks that now form part of it, the **Mitteldeutsche Privat-Bank** (1856–1920) and the **Barmer Bank-Verein** (1867–1932).

The founders of the bank were mostly Hamburg merchants and bankers. During the first 50 years or so of the bank's existence, the centre of gravity of its activities shifted from Hamburg to Berlin, but Hamburg remained its headquarters. After the Second World War, by edicts of the Military Governments, the bank was split up into nine units, one for each *Land* in the American, British and French zones. Its buildings and businesses in the Russian Zone were confiscated without compensation. In 1958, the various elements in the West were reunited and the Commerzbank was reborn, but this time with its headquarters in Düsseldorf.

Because of the amalgamations that have taken place over the years, the Commerzbank of today incorporates several banks whose history goes back much further than its own. In 1920, for instance, the Commerzbank took over the Breslau Bank of **G von Pachaly's Enkel,** dating from 1679.

The **Mitteldeutsche Kreditbank,** in 1915, took over the old Frankfurt banking-house of Johann Goll und Söhne, then 250 years old.

In 1917 the Mitteldeutsche Kreditbank took over the business of the oldest Frankfurt banking-house **Johann Mertens,** founded in 1605. From 1911 on, the Barmer Bank-Verein was linked with the banking-house of von der Heydt-Kersten und Söhne.

The banking-house of **B Metzler seel. Sohn and Company,** in Frankfurt, was established by Benjamin Metzler in 1674. The bank is still in the hands of his direct descendants.

The **Société Générale de Belgique,** mentioned above, started life in 1822 as the 'Société Générale des Pays-Bas pour favoriser l'Industrie nationale'. It was William I, King of the Netherlands, who set up the society, Belgium at that time being linked to Holland, and the first Governor, Repelaer van Driel, was of Dutch origin.

The society played an important part in the industrial development of Belgium and also of the Congo. The Société Générale, the name of which is said to indicate its manifold purpose, is described as 'the world's first development company', coming some time in advance of the Crédit Mobilier of the Pereire Brothers and before a German bank, unnamed, which is sometimes regarded as the forerunner.

Let us now cross to the other side of the Atlantic, where the **First National Bank of Boston,** established in 1784, describes itself as 'the oldest bank in America' and also as 'the oldest Chartered Bank in the USA'. According to a report in *The Independent Ledger* of 5 July 1784, the Massachusetts Bank, as it was then called, opened that day, but its Charter had been signed by the Governor, John Hancock, on 7 February 1784, and it was said to be 'the first independent joint-stock bank in America'.

The **Bank of New York,** 'New York's First Bank', was also founded in 1784, by Alexander Hamilton.

According to the *Financial Times* of 27 March 1968, an office had just then been opened in London by the **First Pennsylvania Banking and Trust Company,** 'which was set up, though not under its present name, in 1782, and claims to be the oldest bank, and the 20th largest, in the United States'. The bank's advertisement in the *Economist* of 13 April 1968, however, described it as 'Banking since 1792'.

The table of American commercial banking companies that was published in *Fortune* of July 1975 was headed by the **Bank America Corporation of San Francisco** with assets of more than $60 000 million and deposits exceeding $50 000 million.

'Bermuda's Oldest Bank' is the title claimed by the bank of **N T Butterfield and Son Limited,** of Hamilton, Bermuda, which was established in the year 1858.

The **Banco de Londres y México,** which was founded in 1864, describes itself as 'The Oldest Bank in Mexico'.

The **Banco de Crédito del Perú,** with its head office at Lima, was established in 1889. It describes itself as 'Peru's Oldest National Commercial Bank'.

The **Wells Fargo Bank International Corporation,** with its head office in San Francisco, claims to be 'the oldest bank in the West'. In the *Fortune* list of 1975 of American commercial banking companies, Wells Fargo was placed No 12, with assets of well over $12 000 million. The bank's history goes back to 1852, when Wells Fargo and Company,

Poster issued by Wells Fargo. *(Wells Fargo)*

Express and Banking, opened an office in Montgomery Street.

Still journeying westward, the **Dai-Ichi Bank** at Tokyo, Japan, established in 1873, describes itself as 'Oldest in Years, Modern in Service'. The **Mitsui Bank** at Tokyo, however, boasts of being 'older than the Bank of England', having been established in 1683.

An even longer history is claimed by the **Sanwa Bank** of Osaka. The present bank was established in 1933 as a result of the amalgamation of three commercial banking institutions in Osaka, but the history of one of the constituents of the bank of today goes back to a *ryogae* (money-changing) business opened in Osaka in 1656.

The **Bank of New South Wales,** Sydney, Australia, was celebrating its 150th anniversary in 1967. The bank was granted a Charter by Governor Macquarie on 12 February 1817; the original charter is preserved in the bank's archives.

The 'Wales' claims to be 'the first bank and first public corporation in the whole South West Pacific area'. It also boasts of being 'older by far than any government in Australia or New Zealand'. The bank still has its first ledger, dating from 1817.

The part played by the 'Wales' in the development of Australia and neighbouring countries recalls the similar role played by the Standard Bank in South Africa (see page 119). In each case the discovery of gold played an important part. The 'Wales' was associated with the Colonial Sugar Refining Company since the formation of the company in 1855, and in the 1860s it became interested in the pioneering efforts of growing sugar under the stimulus of land made available by the Queensland Sugar and Coffee Regulations of 1864.

The bank's first office was in Mary Reibey's house in Macquarie Place, very different from the bank's modern offices of today. (See illustration, page 119.)

The **Bank of Montreal** celebrated the 150th anniversary of 'Canada's First Bank' in 1967. The Montreal Bank, as it was originally called, first opened its doors on 3 November 1817, and was granted a Charter as the 'Bank of Montreal' in 1822. The 'Wales', therefore, has the edge on the Bank of Montreal

Mrs Mary Reibey's house, Sydney, the first home of the Bank of New South Wales. *(The Bank of New South Wales)*

in the matter of age by nearly nine months, but the Bank of Montreal can still boast of being Canada's oldest bank.

The **Bank of Nova Scotia,** founded in 1832, in an advertisement in *The Times* of 30 June 1967, congratulated Canada on being 100 on 1 July and proudly pointed out that it was older than the nation, as it was notching up its 135th year.

The **Standard Bank** of Johannesburg, South Africa, calls itself 'the oldest bank in Africa south of the Sahara'. The history of the bank may be said to begin with a public meeting that was held in Port Elizabeth on 3 June 1857 to discuss the formation of a bank. It was not, however, until October 1862 that the bank was incorporated, as the Standard Bank of British South Africa Limited. In January

1863 it began business at Port Elizabeth. The history of the bank is closely intertwined with the history of South Africa, particularly with the development of the diamond-fields and the gold-fields.

As though challenging the claim of the Standard Bank, the **Mauritius Commercial Bank** described itself as the 'oldest banking institution south of the Sahara'. The bank was established in 1838 and is, therefore, older than the Standard Bank. But it seems to have overlooked the Bank of New South Wales (see page 118), which is even older and which also lies south of the Sahara.

Finally, to complete our banking tour of the world, we must mention the **National Bank of Egypt** and the bank **Leumi Le-Israel BM.** The National Bank of Egypt was founded

Banking in the Goldfields, Australia, in 1894. *(The Bank of New South Wales)*

in 1898. It describes itself as 'the oldest and largest Egyptian Bank' and 'not quite as old as the Pyramids'. The bank **Leumi Le-Israel** similarly claims to be 'the oldest and largest bank in Israel'. It was formerly known as the 'Anglo-Palestine Bank'. 'Established in 1902, it opened its first office in Palestine in 1903 at a time when the country was still in a most primitive stage and modern banking was practically unknown.'

Fraternal benefit societies

The **Independent Order of Foresters,** whose headquarters are at Don Mills, Ontario, on the outskirts of Toronto, celebrated its 100th birthday on 17 June 1974. It claims to be the largest non-sectarian fraternal benefit society in the world. In June 1974 the Order boasted a membership of more than 1 million, $6000 million of insurance in force and assets totalling more than $434 million.

Although the Order was founded by Alonzo B Caldwell in 1874, an American Indian, Dr

Oronhyatekha, who had been a student at Oxford and who was elected Supreme Chief Ranger of the Order in 1881, is known as 'the builder of the Order'. He held the office of Supreme Chief Ranger until his death, in 1907.

In 1898 the Order moved into new offices known as the 'Temple Building' at the corner of Bay and Richmond streets in Toronto's business and financial centre. This building, twelve storeys high and 200 ft (60 m) tall, was said to be the highest building erected in Canada till then.

The **Aid Association for Lutherans,** New York, is said to be the largest fraternal benefit society in the world, but dealing only with people of their own sect.

Insurance

In 1752, the **Philadelphia Contribution-ship for the Insurance of Houses from Loss by Fire** was founded in America on the scheme of the Hand-in-Hand (see page 113), and adopted the sign of the four clasped hands used by the Union Office. Benjamin Franklin was an early Director of the Philadelphia business, which is now the oldest American fire insurance company. In 1924 it claimed to be 'the strongest active fire insurance company in the world'.

When the Contributionship was founded, Philadelphia was not only the principal city in the North American colonies but also the most populous community in the realm of George II after London. Although the company describes itself as the nation's oldest insurance company, it admits that it was not quite the first in the field. A Friendly Society for the Mutual Insuring of Houses against Fire had been founded in Charleston, South Carolina, in 1735, but it failed because of the disastrous Charleston fire of 1740.

The **Presbyterian Ministers' Fund,** of Philadelphia, has been called the oldest life insurance company in America and the oldest business corporation in America. The Fund was established in 1717 as The Fund for Pious Uses. It developed into The Widows' Fund, in 1754. Five years later, in 1759, it was incorporated and received its Charter from Thomas Penn and Richard Penn. It was then known as 'The Corporation for the Relief of Presbyterian Ministers and Their Widows and Children', and began to issue life insurance policies.

After other changes of name it assumed its present designation in 1888 or 1889. The Fund's relation with the Presbyterian Church is 'historic and sentimental, but not corporate', as the Fund insures Protestant clergymen, and their families, of all denominations.

The **Insurance Company of North America** was founded in 1792, in the same room in Independence Hall in Philadelphia in which the Declaration of Independence had been signed 16 years earlier. The company was a marine company in the beginning, but in 1794 it inaugurated the underwriting of fire risks.

The Hundred Year Association of New York, which comprises businesses and organisations more than 100 years old which are 'New York City based', provided a list of members with founding dates earlier than 1783. The oldest was the Collegiate School (1638), followed by

the **Sun Insurance Office,** although the latter is primarily an English concern (see page 112). The list includes the impressively named **Corporation for the Relief of Widows and Children of Clergymen of the Protestant Episcopal Church in the State of New York.** Although this appears to be a charitable organisation rather than an insurance company, it seems a fit companion for the Presbyterian Ministers' Fund.

The largest life insurance company in the United States, according to the *Fortune* list of July 1975, is the **Prudential** of Newark, with assets of nearly $36000 million.

The **Hartford Fire Insurance Company** achieved a different kind of distinction when it was taken over in 1970 by the International Telephone and Telegraph Corporation in 1970 in the largest merger in American corporate history.

The **Halifax Insurance Company,** of Halifax, Nova Scotia, is Canada's oldest in-

Head Office, Bank of Montreal. *(Bank of Montreal)*

surance company, having been established in 1809. The **Canada Life Assurance Company,** of Toronto, was established in 1847 and describes itself as 'the oldest Canadian Life Company'.

The **Triton Insurance Company Limited,** whose head office is in Calcutta, was established in 1850. It describes itself as 'the oldest Indian Insurance Company'.

The **Rentenanstalt,** of Zürich, founded in 1857, is 'la plus ancienne et la plus importante des sociétés suisses d'assurances sur la vie'.

One of the sights of Sydney is the new building of the **Australian Mutual Provident Society (AMP),** which rises to a height of 383 ft (116.7 m) above Circular Quay. The building stands on the site of the old Mort's wool store, which was built more than a century ago by Thomas Sutcliffe Mort, a founder of AMP. The society is said to be the largest life office founded on the mutual principle in the British Commonwealth.

The oldest reinsurance company in the world is to be found in Cologne – the **Kölnische Rückversicherungsgesellschaft,** dating from 1846.

The Belgian **A G Group** celebrated the 150th anniversary of its formation in 1974. The original company – Compagnie d'Assurances Générales sur la Vie – was incorporated with limited liability on 14 July 1824. This was during the reign of King William I of the Netherlands, Belgium being joined to Holland at that time.

Savings banks

The **Cassa di Risparmio delle Provincie Lombarde,** whose head office is in Milan, describes itself as the first savings bank in the world. It was founded in 1823. (See also page 113.)

The basis of the Italian claim is not clear. The Cassa di Risparmio of the City of Zürich (also known as the **Sparkasse** and the **Caisse d'Epargne**) was founded some years earlier, in 1805. Zürich is also the home of the **Sparkasse Zinstragender Sparhafen,** which was founded in 1850.

Stock exchanges

In November 1958 Dr Erhard, the German Minister of Economics, took part in the celebrations of the 400th anniversary of the **Hamburg Stock Exchange,** which dates its beginnings from the year 1558.

The Buttonwood Agreement of 17 May 1792 laid the foundation of the **New York Stock Exchange.** The agreement was signed under a buttonwood (sycamore tree), by 21 partners and three brokers.

CHAPTER 6

TRANSPORT

A. BUSINESSES IN THE BRITISH ISLES

Aircraft

Handley Page Limited, of Cricklewood, London, 'the first company to be constituted exclusively for the design and construction of aeroplanes', had been in existence for half a century in 1959.

Short Brothers and Harland Limited, of the Seaplane Works, Queens Island, Belfast, described themselves as 'The First Manufacturers of Aircraft in the World'. The firm was, however, established in the first place for making balloons, not aeroplanes. As early as 1898, the brothers Oswald and Eustace Short had gained an Indian Government contract for balloons, and in 1901 they were appointed official balloon-makers to the Aero Club.

Some years later their elder brother Horace joined them, and in 1908 they made their first powered aircraft. This machine was ordered by Frank McClean, of the Aero Club, and first flew in July 1909.

About this time the firm moved from Battersea to the Isle of Sheppey. Here their second machine was built, for Mr J T C Moore-Brabazon (who later became better known as Lord Brabazon). It was in this machine that Mr Moore-Brabazon won the prize of £1000 offered by Lord Northcliffe for the first circular flight of a mile (1.6 km) by a British aircraft.

In 1920, Short's produced the *Silver Streak*, the first British aircraft to be constructed entirely of metal. In 1921 they made their first flying-boat. The first 'Sunderland' appeared in 1937, a year after the formation of the combined firm of Short Brothers and Harland. The move to Belfast was completed in 1948.

Among the many aircraft produced during the Second World War was the 'Shetland' flying-boat of 1944. With an all-up weight of 130 000 lb (60 000 kg), this was the biggest British aircraft built up to that date.

Coachbuilders

One of the old firms that has survived from an earlier age by changing the nature of its activities is **Hooper and Company (Coachbuilders) Limited,** of Acton and, until 1959, of 54 St James's Street, London.

George Adams and George Hooper founded the business in 1807, as coachbuilders. They obtained their first Royal Warrant, as coachbuilders, in 1830. The firm's current Warrant, however, is as 'coachbuilders and motor body builders'. In 1901 they were given the task of renovating the old State Coach, built in 1761, which had last been used by Queen Victoria at the opening of Parliament in 1861.

An even older firm, which also holds the Royal Warrant of Appointment to HM the Queen as coachbuilders, is **Offord and Sons Limited,** of 154 Gloucester Road, London SW7. They were established before 1800. Mr Norman Offord's great-grandfather, George Offord, set up as a wheelwright at Boston, Lincolnshire, in 1791.

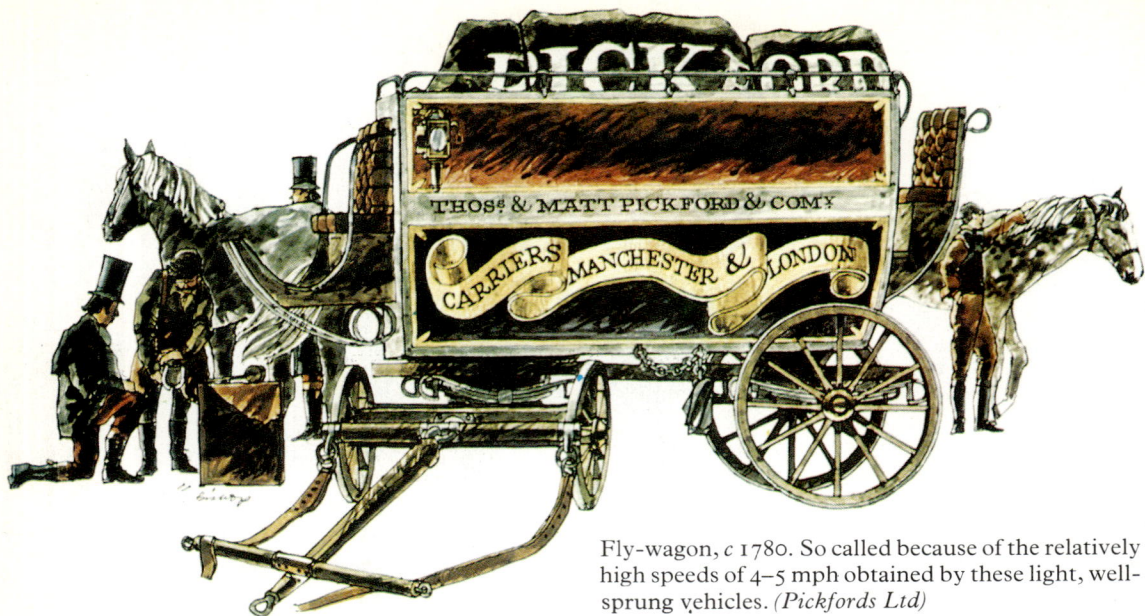

Fly-wagon, c 1780. So called because of the relatively high speeds of 4–5 mph obtained by these light, well-sprung vehicles. *(Pickfords Ltd)*

Daimler-Motorkutsche 1886. *(Daimler-Benz AG Bildarchiv)*

The firm of **Glover Webb and Liversidge** in the Old Kent Road, London, dates from 1720. They started their existence as carriage-builders and wheelwrights, and have since made many kinds of vehicles. At one time it was phaetons, gigs and broughams. Then came Royal Mail coaches and brewers' drays. More recently they have made security vehicles and various types of vehicles for refuse collection. The firm is now part of the Charringtons Group of Companies.

Coracles

One of our oldest industries, and one that seems to be on the point of dying out, is the making of coracles. These primitive wicker boats have been made in these islands for thousands of years, but may not be made here for much longer.

In his book *South Wales*, published in 1956, H L V Fletcher described Cenarth in Cardiganshire, where a number of coracles could be seen hanging up outside the houses.

Country Life of 8 February 1968 contained a letter from Miss M Wight, of Hereford, with a photo of Ironbridge showing one of the **Rogers** family with his coracle. Miss Wight wrote:

'I believe they were the last makers of coracles there, if not on the Severn as a whole, and have now stopped making them. If so, that means the end of a craft that has probably been followed on the river since prehistoric times.'

Motor cars *(see also 'Coachbuilders', page 123)*

Rolls-Royce is neither the oldest nor the biggest maker of cars. One of their modest claims to fame is that their 'Camargue', launched in March 1975 at a price of £29 500, was the world's most expensive car ever to go into series production.

It was in 1904 that the Honourable Charles Stewart Rolls (1877–1910) and Frederick Henry (later Sir Henry) Royce (1863–1933) formed Rolls-Royce Limited. It is curious that their names, like those of Daimler and Benz, should be linked by a hyphen rather than by an ampersand.

The **Leyland Motor Corporation,** later to become part of the British Leyland Motor Corporation, evolved from the Lancashire Steam Motor Company that was established in the Lancashire village of Leyland in 1896 by James Sumner and Henry Spurrier. Their business was 'based upon the manufacture of steam lawn-mowers', but soon switched to the building of steam-powered road wagons. Their first export was a steam mail-van shipped to Ceylon (Sri Lanka) in 1901.

In *The Times 1000 (1975–76)* list the British Leyland Motor Corporation was No 8 among the largest industrial companies in the United Kingdom, but had more employees – 207 770 – than any other industrial company. Speaking in the House of Commons on 24 April 1975, however, the Prime Minister said that British Layland at that time was employing 'over 170 000 people directly in this country'.

The **Aston Martin Company** at Newport Pagnell, which ran into difficulties at the end of 1974, traced its history back to 1820, but it then made carriages, not cars. Four generations of the Petts family had been with the firm ever since its early days in a cobbled farmyard. The founder of the business was Joseph Salmons.

Motor-car dealers and hirers

Wimbush and Company Limited, of Headfort Place, Halkin Street, Hyde Park Corner, London SW1, have been described in their advertisements as 'Britain's Oldest Car Organization'. The firm was established in 1760 – perhaps even before – long before the days of motor cars. In its early days, the business was that of jobmasters (a jobmaster being defined in the *Shorter Oxford English Dictionary* as a man who keeps a livery stable and lets out horses and carriages by the job). With the passing of the years the firm's activities have changed from horses to cars, and they now deal with the car trade in all its aspects, selling and hiring cars, arranging car tours and so on.

Road transport

Pickfords Limited, the carriers, sometimes advertise with the slogan '300 Years' Experience at Your Service'. An advertisement of 1962 stated that the present Pickfords organisation had grown from 'Thomas Pickford and his packhorses of 300 years ago'. No

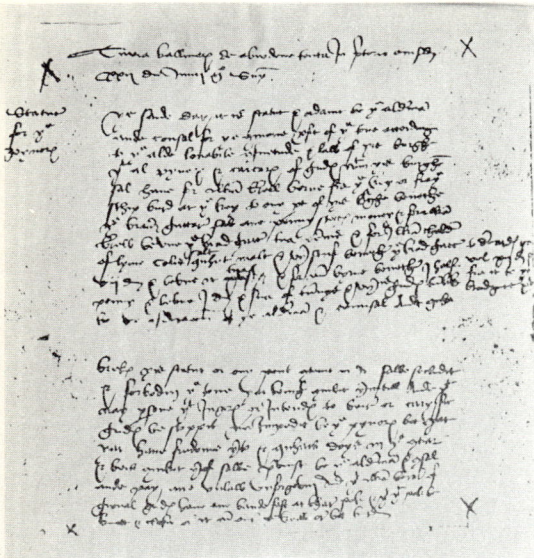

Above: Extract from the minutes of the Aberdeen Town Council, 1948. *(Shore Porters' Society)*

Below: Modern vehicles of the Shore Porters' Society. *(Shore Porters' Society)*

precise date, however, is given for the start of the firm.

The vans and lorries of the **Shore Porters' Society** of Aberdeen carry the inscription 'Established 1498'. Their vans can sometimes be seen in London.

It was in 1498 that the Town Council of Aberdeen decided that the 'pynours' (as the shore porters were then called) should have one penny Scots for every barrel they carried from the ships at the quay to any part of the burgh 'benethe the Braid Gutter', and twopence for journeys beyond that. During the 18th century the porters were in demand as chairmen to carry sedan-chairs. The Society is still a partnership, with a transport fleet, a furniture store and a bonded warehouse.

Ships and shipping

The **Bristol City Line of Steamships Limited** has been said to be the oldest shipping company in the world, having been in continual existence for over 250 years. Its history can be

traced back to the year 1704, when James Hilhouse was admitted to the liberties of the City of Bristol. He turned his attention to shipowning and became head of the Merchant Venturers' Society in 1730. His son succeeded him but died young, in 1761, and the son's son, James Martin Hilhouse (1748–1822), following on, turned his attention to shipbuilding, about 1772. His first ship built for the Admiralty, during the American War of Independence, was launched in April 1778.

In October 1810, a young man named Charles Hill joined the business. He was made a partner in 1825, and in 1827 he married a niece of the brother-in-law of George Hilhouse. George was the elder son of J M Hilhouse and a great-grandson of the founder of the firm.

In 1879 the Bristol City line was formed to run a service of steamships between Bristol and New York, particularly for freight and cattle. Its first ships were the *Bristol City* and the *New York City*. In 1897 the last three sailing-ships were sold, as they could no longer be run profitably in an age of mechanically propelled ships.

It was only during the last war that the firm adopted its present motto 'Shipshape and Bristol Fashion', which appears, with a picture of the Clifton Suspension Bridge, on the badge affixed to new ships built at the Albion Dockyard. Four generations of the Hilhouse family and five generations of the Hill family span the 250 years or so of the firm's history. The **General Steam Navigation Company Limited,** the oldest member of the P and O Group, dates from 1824. It is thus 13 years older than the Peninsular and Oriental Steam Navigation Company itself.

Scott's shipyard at Greenock has been called the oldest in the world.

John Scott, who founded the firm in 1711, built herring busses and small craft. It was under his grandson, John Scott II (1752–1837), that the firm first undertook shipbuilding work for the Royal Navy. Their first warship, a sloop, was built in 1803.

Hillhouse (see above), was a shipowner, and it was his grandson who turned from privateering and shipowning to ship*building* in the latter half of the 18th century. The fact that the Bristol City line is believed to be the oldest shipping

company in the world does not, therefore, prevent us from taking Scott's to be the oldest shipyard in the world.

Wharfingers

Hay's Wharf, the oldest and largest wharf in the Port of London, 'began in Cromwell's day, in April 1651, when Alexander Hay took over a small wharf near London Bridge and there, in an Elizabethan building formerly used as a granary, set up as a brewer and wharfinger'. Hay soon concentrated on the business of the wharf, and let the brewery. Hay joined with neighbouring wharfingers, Chamberlain and Beale, in founding the first fire office in Britain, namely the Hand-in-Hand (see page 113).

The last of the Hays died in 1838, and the business was taken over by Alderman John Humphery (Lord Mayor of London in 1842). In 1851, as the result of a series of devastating fires, Humphery had to have recourse to his bankers, and in 1862 a partnership was formed under the name 'The Proprietors of Hay's Wharf'. One of the partners was Hugh Colin Smith of the banking-house of Smith at 1 Lombard Street, now incorporated in the National Westminster Bank (see page 110).

The company used to handle over 2 million tons of foodstuffs a year, at wharves stretching almost all the way from London Bridge to Tower Bridge.

B. BUSINESSES IN OTHER LANDS

Aircraft

Boeing, of Seattle, was No 39 in the *Fortune* list of 1975 of the 500 largest industrial companies in the USA. Its sales exceeded $3700 million. It was the largest aircraft company to appear in the list.

Lockheed Aircraft, of Burbank, California, was No 49, with sales of $3200 million. The decision of Lockheed Aircraft, in 1974, to write off $800 million of 'Tristar' aircraft development costs represented the largest such reduction in assets in American corporate history. It easily surpassed the previous record, which was held by the RCA Corporation with its decision of 1972 to write off its computer business at a cost of $490 million.

Lockheed was also in the news in August 1975, when Senator William Proxmire, the Chairman of the US Senate's Banking Committee, was reported in the English press as saying that Lockheed had made a £3.7 million pay-off to one foreign Government official in return for export business. This could well be a record payment of its kind, but it appeared that neither the name of the recipient nor the country involved was known to the Committee.

Airlines

The oldest existing commercial airline is **Koninklijke - Luchtvaart - Maatschappij NV (KLM)** of the Netherlands, which opened its first scheduled service (Amsterdam–London) on 17 May 1920, having been established in 1919. One of the original constituents of BOAC, Aircraft Transport and Travel Limited, was founded in 1918 and merged into Imperial Airways in 1924. **Delag** (Deutsche Luftschiffahrt AG) was founded at Frankfurt-am-Main on 16 November 1909 and started a scheduled airship service in June 1910.

Qantas, originally Queensland and Northern Territory Aerial Service Limited, was formed on 16 November 1920, at Winton, Western Queensland.

The Brazilian airline **Varig** was established in 1927.

With airlines, as with banks, the age of the institution may help to create a comforting feeling of safety and reliability.

In the *Fortune* list of 1975 of transportation companies No 1 was **Trans World Airlines,** with an operating revenue of $2515 million. Trans World had moved up from No 3 to No 1 in the list, while **United Air Lines (UAL),** with $2365 million, had fallen from No 1 to No 2.

Whatever the relative size of the companies might be, United Air Lines certainly has a claim to be regarded as one of the oldest. William E Boeing and Edward Hubbard were the first civilian mail-carriers in the USA. On 3 March 1919, in a home-built seaplane, they carried mail on the 80-mile (130 km) run from Seattle to Victoria. They later were the

inspiration behind Boeing Air Transport, which became part of the United Air Lines organisation in 1931.

Motor cars

Mercedes-Benz of Stuttgart advertise themselves as 'the oldest manufacturers of motor cars in the world'.

The name of the Daimler-Benz company recalls two pioneers of the motor industry. On 16 December 1883, Gottlieb Daimler (1834–1900) received his patent for the first light petrol-engine in the world. Two months before, in October 1883, the firm of Benz and Company had been founded in Mannheim to make power-driven vehicles designed by Karl Benz (1844–1929). In August 1885, Daimler patented his first vehicle.

The first successful petrol-driven car, the 'Motor-wagen', built by Benz, ran at Mannheim, Germany, in late 1885. It was patented on 29 January 1886. These patents laid the foundation for the world's motor industry.

Daimler's engine was first installed in a motor cycle, and in November 1885 his eldest son covered the 'colossal distance' of 2 miles (3 km) on it. In the same year, Daimler made the first motor-boat, which was tried out on the River Neckar. In 1886, Daimler produced his first motor carriage, the first practical petrol-driven motor car.

In 1894, the first car-race in the world was won by a Daimler car. In 1890 Daimler-Motoren-Gesellschaft was founded at Cannstatt and in 1899 the firm built the first Mercedes car. In 1911, a world speed record of 228 km/h (141.6 miles/h) was set up at Daytona, a record that stood for nine years.

As early as 1887, Daimler's thoughts turned to the air, and in 1888, with the help of the Leipzig balloonist Wölfert, he produced a balloon driven by a Daimler engine.

The two firms became associated in 1924, and were finally joined in 1926 as the Daimler-Benz Company, thus uniting the two oldest motor-car firms in the world.

Just as the oil companies rose in the *Fortune* list of 1975, so the car firms generally had to be content with lower places than they had previously occupied. **General Motors** (see page 85) lost the top place to Exxon. Ford

Mercedes-Benz S-Klasse. *(Daimler-Benz AG Bildarchiv)*

Motors, of Dearborn, managed to hold on at No 3, but Chrysler fell from No 4 to No 11. Despite their relative changes, the top eleven places in the list were occupied by the same eleven companies as in the previous year.

This pattern was repeated elsewhere. In the list of the 300 largest industrial companies outside the United States, Volkswagenwerk fell from No 6 to 14, Daimler-Benz from No 9 to No 16, Toyota from No 10 to No 19, Renault from No 17 to No 23 and British Leyland from No 29 to No 48.

General Motors remained the largest employer among the industrial companies in the USA with 734 000 employees. Ford Motor was next, with more than 464 000, whereas Exxon, top of the list in other respects, had only 133 000 employees.

Salvage

The oldest salvage company in the world is the Danish undertaking of **Emil Z Svitser**, founded in 1833.

Ships

The Vierwaldstätterseedampfschiffgesellschaft has sometimes been quoted as a splendid example of the capacity of the German language to string words together in order to form compound nouns. There is in fact a company operating steamships on the Lake of the Four Forest Cantons, otherwise known as the Lake of Lucerne, and it celebrated its centenary in 1970.

The **Schiffahrtsgesellschaft des Vierwaldstättersees** (SGV for short) was formed by the merger of two rival concerns and began its career on 1 January 1870. The older of the two concerns had been founded by C F Knörr as early as 1836, and the other in 1847. Both had their headquarters in Lucerne.

The *Rigi*, in service on the Lake of Lucerne 1848–1952; Mount Rigi in background. *(Archiv, J Gwerder, Meggen, Switzerland)*

Two of the earliest vessels to be put into service on the lake, the *Waldstätter* and the *Rigi*, were built by **Ditchborn and Mare,** of London, in 1847 and 1847–8. The *Wald-stätter* was in service until 1918 but the *Rigi* was not withdrawn until 1952, by which time it had covered nearly 1.3 million km (800 000 miles).

CHAPTER 7

PERSONAL AND PROFESSIONAL SERVICES

A. BUSINESSES IN THE BRITISH ISLES

Accountants

Mann Judd Gordon and Company, a Glasgow firm of chartered accountants, celebrated their 150th anniversary in 1967. The exact year in which the firm began is not known, but it was between 1815 and 1819.

One of the partners, R W Begg, gave a brief history of the firm in *Interim Account of a Going Concern*. According to Begg, 'there are perhaps less than half a dozen older accounting firms in the world – all of which are probably in Scotland . . .'. The oldest of all seem to be:

D and A Cuthbertson Provan and Strong – Glasgow (1787).
Scott Moncrieff, Thomson and Shiells – Edinburgh (1800).
Kerr MacLeod and Macfarlan – Glasgow (1804).
Wm Home Cook – Edinburgh (?).
Mann Judd Gordon and Company – Glasgow (1817).

(The continuity of some of the very old firms is not always easy to establish.)

The Institute of Chartered Accountants of Scotland 'is believed to be the oldest existing accountancy body in the world'. The Institute celebrated its centenary in 1954. (The Society of Accountants in Edinburgh was in fact formed in January 1853, and received its Royal Charter in October 1854.)

Deloitte and Company, of London, were established in 1845 (see page 165).

Advertising agencies

The Times of 5 December 1964 reported that **Samuel Deacon and Company** had been acquired by Graham Cooke Advertising, with headquarters at 72 Fleet Street, London. Samuel Deacon and Company, according to the report, claimed to be the oldest advertising agency in the world. It was founded in 1773 and was accredited agent to newspapers by 1812.

Auctioneers and estate agents
(*See also 'Art dealers', page 135*)

The rivalry between the famous firms of **Christie's** and **Sotheby's** was well illustrated by two advertisements that appeared side by side in *The Times* of 14 June 1966. Christie's proclaimed themselves to be 'The Oldest Fine Art Auctioneers in the World', while Sotheby's were described as 'Fine Art Auctioneers since 1744'. Sotheby's also describe themselves as the largest firm of art auctioneers in the world.

Christie's celebrated their 200th anniversary in 1966, and in January of that year they held an exhibition of works from museums and collectors all over the world.

James Christie (1730–1803) opened his rooms at 125 Pall Mall in 1766. The firm moved to its present premises, at 8 King Street, in 1823. James Christie's first sale, held on 5 December 1766, brought in £174 16s 6d.

But what of Sotheby's? According to an article by Goronwy Rees in the *Sunday Times* of 14 May 1961, the firm was founded in 1744 by Samuel Baker, the bookseller; the first Sotheby joined the firm in 1778 when John

Sotheby, Baker's nephew, became a partner. The last of the Sotheby family to be actively engaged in the business was Samuel Sotheby, who died in 1861. According to Goronwy Rees, Sotheby's were known almost exclusively as booksellers throughout the 19th century, and indeed until much later.

Phillips, 'the Auction People since 1796', announced on Monday 21 October 1974 that they would be holding their 20 000th sale in the course of that week. The firm's headquarters are in Blenheim Street, off New Bond Street.

Messrs Clutton, of London, the well-known firm of chartered surveyors, were established in 1765. It was in that year that William Clutton 'began rendering accounts to clients in his own name', but the history of the firm can be traced further back than this.

William Clutton, born in 1740, was apprenticed to Robert Chatfield, who practised as a surveyor at Cuckfield in Sussex. 'No books of his have survived from before 1744 but it seems reasonable to suppose that he was in business by some considerably earlier date.' William Clutton married his master's daughter, and gradually took over the business from his father-in-law.

Counting Robert Chatfield as a direct ancestor, the representatives of the Clutton family in the firm at the time of the bicentenary were the seventh generation to practise as surveyors. This was 'a record believed to be shared only by the Jonas family of the firm of **Drivers, Jonas & Co.,** which was founded in 1725'.

Dreweatt, Watson and Barton, of Newbury, celebrated their bicentenary in 1959. **Baxter, Payne and Lepper,** of Beckenham, were established a year later, in 1760. **Sparrow, Son and Bagley** of Nottingham were established in 1765; as was the firm of **Morley Hewitt,** of Fordingbridge, Hampshire.

The year 1973 witnessed the bicentenary of two other firms, **Richard Ellis,** of London, and **Herring, Daw and Manners,** also of London.

Scotland, however, is the home of 'the oldest mart in the British Isles'. The firm of **Andrew Oliver and Son Limited,** of the Auction Mart, Hawick, was established in 1817 and is still in the hands of the Oliver family.

Bookmakers

The London *Evening Standard* of 25 October 1957 reported that 'the oldest firm of bookmakers in the country, **Ould and Company,** are to be taken over by the second-oldest firm, **Ladbroke's**'. Ould and Company were said to have been founded in 1869, but no date was given for Ladbroke's.

In March 1975 the papers reported that Ladbroke's was to take over Vernon's, the second largest football-pool operator in Britain, for about £17.1 million, and that this would make Ladbroke's the largest betting concern in the country. In April it was reported that the proposed deal had been called off.

Dyers and cleaners

Davis and Sons Dyers London Limited, of the Westbourne Cleanery, London W10, who hold the Royal Warrant as dyers and cleaners to Her Majesty the Queen, have been 'dyers and cleaners since 1790', according to the heading of their notepaper. The business was established in or before 1790 by a man named Guy, who was a relative of the Davis family.

Hairdressers

The firm of **Truefitt and Hill,** court hairdressers and perfumers, at 23 Old Bond Street, was founded by Francis Truefitt at 40 Old Bond Street in 1805. It later moved to 1 New Bond Street and then to 2 Burlington Gardens. In 1819, Peter Truefitt started business in Burlington Arcade and later moved to Old Bond Street. He traded under the name of H P Truefitt.

The business of **E S Hill,** who was then at 23 Old Bond Street, was bought by H P Truefitt in 1935, and the name was changed to Truefitt and Hill. The business started by Francis Truefitt was merged into the present firm in 1941. Truefitt's held royal appointments as Wig-makers to George IV and as Hairdressers and Perfumers to Queen Victoria.

Literary agents

The Times of 6 August 1965 reported the death of Peter Watt, 'the seventh and last member of the family to engage in the business of

A P Watt and Son, founded as the first literary agency by his grandfather in 1875'.

News Bureau

Paul Julius Reuter, born in 1816, worked for Charles Havas, founder of what was probably the world's first news bureau, before establishing his own office, in Aachen (Aix-la-Chapelle), in 1849. In 1851, Reuter moved to London and started his 'telegraphic office' in rented rooms at Royal Exchange Buildings. In 1857 he became a British subject.

Opticians

Dollond and Aitchison, the opticians, of London, date their business from 1750.

Pawnbrokers

Pawnbroking has a long history. According to the *Economist* of 2 March 1957, the three brass balls 'have a long tradition, going back to the Lombard merchants with whom, in 1338, Edward III pawned his jewels to raise money for a war on France'.

We have not been able to discover which is the oldest pawnbroker's shop in the country. In the early part of 1957 a number of shops in the Strand near Charing Cross Station were pulled down in order that the road could be widened. Among them was the shop at No 39 – **Vaughan,** gunsmith and pawnbroker, established in 1782.

Pest control

One of the most unexpected of the old family businesses is that of **William Dalton and Sons Limited,** 'vermin control specialists', of 295 Kennington Road, London SE11. The business was established as long ago as 1710, and is still in the hands of the founder's family. An associated company of the same address, W H J Dalton Limited, describe themselves as 'Expert Ratcatchers and Pest Exterminators, Suppliers of Insect Spray and Powders, Etc.'.

An even older firm in the same line of business is **H Tiffin and Son Limited,** George Street, London W1, described as 'Timber Decay Consultants and Contractors'. This pest-control business was established as long ago as 1695 by a Mr Tiffin, an ancestor

of two of the present Directors. The firm boasts 'over 200 years' experience in pest control'.

Shorthand-writers

The firm of **W B Gurney and Son** was founded in 1707 by Thomas Gurney, the inventor of a system of shorthand called 'Brachygraphy'. His grandson, William Brodie Gurney, was appointed the Official Shorthand Writer in the Houses of Parliament in 1813. Since 1813, the senior partner of the firm has always been appointed as the Official Shorthand Writer.

Sugar-brokers

Woodhouse, Carey and Browne, of 51 Eastcheap, London EC3, is 'one of the oldest if not quite the oldest firm of sugar brokers in existence'. It was started by Mark Woodhouse, who was apprenticed to a sugar cooper on 5 February 1750.

Thatching

In the village of North Walsham, Norfolk, is the firm of **W R Farman Limited,** 'Norfolk Reed Thatchers, basket manufacturers and fencing contractors'. According to the firm's bill-head, they have been 'thatchers for many centuries'. White's *History and Directory of Norfolk* of 1845 shows that in that year there was a William Farman, patten-maker, at North Walsham and a John Farman, basket-maker, at Coltishall, about 10 miles (16 km) away. The edition of 1883 shows Robert Farman, basket-maker and thatcher, at North Walsham. At one time the firm's bill-heads used to read 'Thatchers, established 1106', but the basis of this claim is not clear.

Theatrical agencies

Foster's Agency, of London, has been called 'the oldest theatrical agency in the world'.

B. BUSINESSES IN OTHER LANDS

Funeral directors

Kirk and Nice, of Philadelphia, describe themselves as 'The First Funeral Directors in the U.S.A.', having been established in 1761. They had been in business for 15 years when the Declaration of Independence was signed and, like the Rhoads firm (see page 102), their early accounts are in pounds, shillings and pence.

Jacob Knorr, the founder of the business, was a joiner or cabinet-maker in the village of Germantown. In 1761 he erected a shop where he made coffins and also fine furniture.

In 1830 the business was bought by a farmer named John Nice for his twin sons, one of whom married a grand-niece of Jacob Knorr. In 1849 the firm acquired an apprentice whose name was B Frank Kirk. When he finished his apprenticeship he married his master's daughter.

Kirk ran his own business for some years but in 1869 he and William Nice, the youngest son of Kirk's old master, bought the firm. Henceforth it was known as Kirk and Nice.

Kirk and Nice are the fourth oldest firm in the City of Philadelphia, preceded only by the Presbyterian Ministers' Fund (1717), the Franklin Printing Company (1728) and the Philadelphia Contributionship (1752).

Investments and real estate

Biddle, Whelen and Company of Philadelphia were established in 1764. In 1954 Etna M Kelley gave the company's activity as 'Investments', and the senior partner as a lineal descendant of the founder.

Minot, De Blois and Maddison, of Boston, Massachusetts, trace their history back to 1782, 'six years before the Constitution of the United States was adopted'. In that year, George Richards Minot opened an office on Court Street in Boston, where he was engaged in real estate management.

Following a number of mergers and changes of partners, the firm of Minot, DeBlois and Maddison was formed in 1950. Their activities are now described as 'managing real estate and investments as trustees and agents for trustees and others'.

CHAPTER 8

MERCHANTING AND DISTRIBUTION

A. BUSINESSES IN THE BRITISH ISLES

Agricultural merchants *(see 'Seedsmen', page 145)*

Art-dealers *(for Auctioneers and estate agents, see 'Auctioneers' page 131)*

At the end of 1967, **Agnew's** celebrated their 150th anniversary with a splendid exhibition of paintings and watercolours by Turner in their Bond Street gallery in London. They also published a history of the firm entitled *Agnew's 1817–1967* by Geoffrey Agnew, with a foreword by Hugh (Tim) Agnew.

The business began in Manchester in 1817, when Thomas Agnew (1794–1871) was taken into partnership by Vittore Zanetti, to whom he had been apprenticed in 1810. In 1860 he started business in London at 5 Waterloo Place.

The origin of the house of **P and D Colnaghi and Company Limited,** of 14 Old Bond Street, 'dates back to the middle of the 18th-century, when Paul Colnaghi (1751–1833) came to London from North Milan'.

The **Parker Gallery** is described as 'the oldest firm of picture and print dealers in the world'. Henry Parker founded the business in 1750, in Cornhill in the City of London.

The Parker Gallery is now at 2 Albemarle Street. A small painting displayed in the window of the present shop depicts the original premises in Cornhill.

Another business in the same line of country also dating from 1750 is that of **Arthur**

Reader at 71 Charing Cross Road, London. Paintings, prints and books are dealt in. The firm was established in 1750 at Cranbrook, in Kent, where the old shop still stands. The firm moved from Kent to Booksellers' Row in London, which was pulled down to make room for the present Law Courts, but the year of the move to London is not known.

For many years **Spink and Son Limited,** of St James's, London, dated their origin from the year 1772. The late Aytoun Ellis, however, who was commissioned to write the history of the firm, no doubt with an eye to the celebration of its bicentenary in 1972, traced its beginnings back to a member of the Spink family who was a goldsmith in the year 1666. Aytoun Ellis unfortunately died before his work was finished. Spinks are now particularly well known as numismatists and medallists, but the wide range of their artistic interests was shown by the exhibition that they held in their showrooms in King Street as part of their tercentenary celebrations.

Chain stores

John Boot (1816–60) inherited from his mother a great knowledge of herbs and folk-medicines. In 1850 he opened a little shop in Goosegate, Nottingham which he called 'British and American Botanic Establishment', advertised 'vegetable remedies' both wholesale and retail and announced that he could be 'consulted at his residence, 6 Goosegate, on Mondays, Wednesdays, and Saturdays' (the other days he presumably reserved for

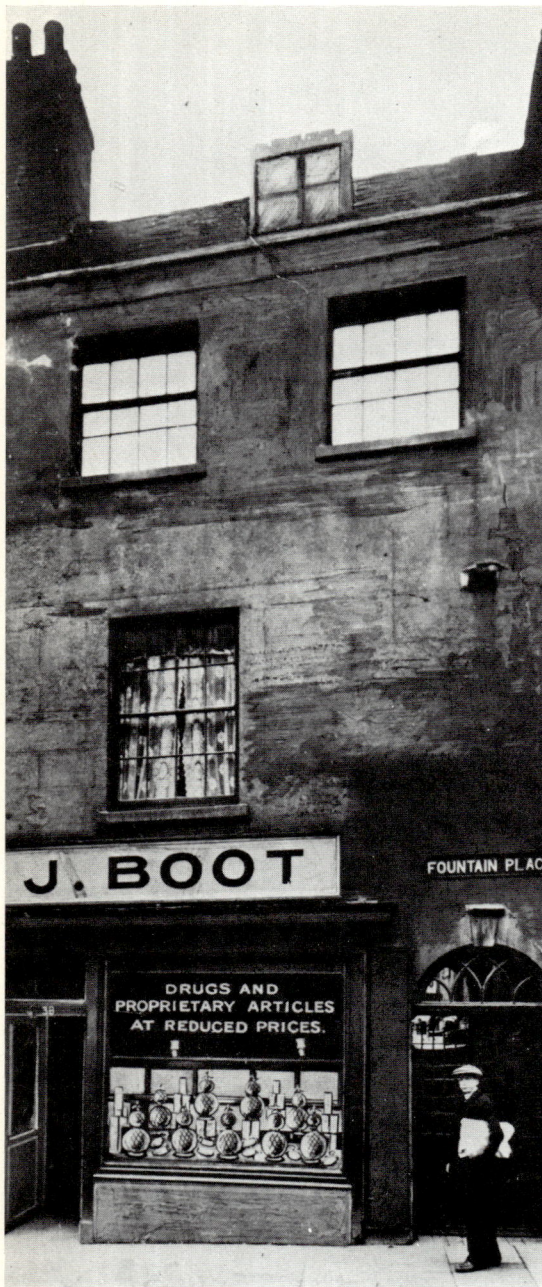

Jesse Boot's first shop, Goosegate, Nottingham. (Boots)

collecting wild herbs). John Boot claimed that within a space of five years he had 'successfully treated almost every kind of disease' and could 'confidently assert that the vegetable kingdom affords a remedy for all'. When he died at the age of 44, he left a widow, 34, and two children, a daughter Jane and a son Jesse (1850–1931).

At the age of 13 **Jesse Boot** left school to help his mother run the little shop, and began to take over the management. To the herbal remedies on which the business was founded he added a wide range of household goods, offering them at cut prices. About 1873 Boot opened a branch at 60 Alfreton Road, Nottingham, which did not last long.

In 1874 Jesse Boot decided to enter the proprietary medicine business. He found that everywhere articles, especially drugs, were being sold at ridiculously high prices, and without any regard to packaging and attractiveness. His novel idea was simply to buy tons where others bought hundredweights or less, thus buying more cheaply, and cutting the buying price.

Jesse Boot launched a major advertising campaign in 1877 in which he offered 128 separate proprietaries at cut prices, arranged alphabetically from 'Allen's Hair Restorer' to 'Woodhouse's Rheumatic Elixir'. He offered £10 to anyone who could prove that any patent medicines sold by him at his 'reduced prices' were not equal to those sold anywhere else at higher prices.

Boot's 1877 advertising campaign had also offered to supply cut-price patent medicines by post and, by 1881, a mail-order service had been established. Wholesale sales continued to grow through the 1880s. Jesse Boot directed all his enormous energy into his business, working a 16-hour day every week day.

From 1878 onwards the next few years showed a steady growth in his business and he established several new branches in Nottingham; Luton; St Albans; Leeds; Bradford; Halifax; Princes Street, Edinburgh and Regent Street, London. In 1888 Boots Pure Drug Company Limited was founded. Its phenomenal rate of growth was only maintained by the most aggressive salesmanship. Boot introduced sensational and high-pressure selling techniques, catching the public eye with constantly changing cut-price offers and gimmicks. In 1901 Boots Cash Chemists (Southern) Limited was established. By 1907 Boots had branches in all the principal towns

Jesse Boot's first large shop, opened in Goosegate, Nottingham, in 1884. *(Boots)*

and were the 'largest gift sellers in the country'. Jesse Boot's motto 'Boots, Largest, Cheapest, and Best' now gave way to a call to win the 'Classes' as well as the 'Masses'.

Toiletries and fancy goods were managed by Mrs Boot and her influence could also be recognised in two other developments: the book departments and the tastefully furnished cafés.

Jesse Boot had started with one small shop in Nottingham in the 1870s. When he retired in 1920 he had no fewer than 618. In 1933 the number reached 1000 and by the end of March 1976 the total amounted to 1276 shops with a selling area of 3 682 000 ft² (342 069 m²): and they trade in 50 000 different lines. Boots also own 14 shops in New Zealand.

Jesse received a knighthood in November 1909 and a baronetcy in December 1916, when

he became Lord Trent. John Campbell Boot (1888–1956) – who also became Lord Trent on the death of his father – was chairman from 1931 to 1954. He was followed as Chairman from 1954 to 1961 by John Savage. In 1961 Willoughby R Norman, John Campbell Boot's son-in-law, became the 'Third Mister Boot' when he succeeded John Savage.

Another remarkable development in the field of retail distribution is that of the **Marks & Spencer** chain of shops. It was about 1882 that Michael Marks (1863–1907), a 19-year-old refugee from Bialystok, Russian Poland, arrived in London, penniless, untrained to any trade; he knew no English. In 1884 he moved to Leeds, which already had a Jewish community of about 7000 people, and there set up in business as a pedlar. He carried on his back a stock of buttons,

Marks & Spencer – Marble Arch branch No 1 store. *(Marks & Spencer)*

mending wools, pins, needles, tapes, table-cloths, woollen socks and stockings. One of his first suppliers was the firm of I J Dewhirst Limited of 32 Kirkgate, wholesale merchants, who still supply Marks and Spencer to this day. It is said that Isaac Dewhirst lent Michael Marks £5, which he used to buy goods from the warehouse, and as he paid off the debt in instalments, Dewhirst allowed him to make further purchases to the same amount.

When Michael Marks gave up peddling later in 1884 he opened a stall in the open market at Kirkgate, Leeds, selling the same kind of merchandise as he had carried on his back round the Yorkshire villages. From the open market he then moved to a permanent stall in the covered market hall which was open throughout the week. By displaying his goods in open baskets, with the price clearly marked, he introduced the idea of self-selection, and

self-service (this was known already in the USA, see 'Woolworths', page 140). He arranged his merchandise according to price, placing all those costing a penny in one section of his stall and hung a board above that section saying 'Don't ask the price, it's a penny.' Thus was created the famous and immediately successful Marks' Penny Bazaar (see illustration on dust-jacket).

Michael Marks' success was partly due to his extremely hard work and integrity, and also to his idea of a fixed price limit – at the same time offering the best possible quality and the widest possible choice of goods.

In 1886 Michael Marks married Hannah Cohen and in 1888 their son, Simon, was born.

Their small business prospered and on 28 September 1894 Michael Marks took into partnership Thomas Spencer (1852–1905),

Marks & Spencer – Food area without customers, Croydon store. *(Marks & Spencer)*

Dewhirst's first-class book-keeper. By 1903 the firm of Marks and Spencer Limited was registered. Simon Marks joined the business in 1907, became Chairman in 1916 and died in 1964 as Lord Marks. Working with his brother-in-law, the late Lord Sieff, a unique partnership was formed, from which Marks and Spencer, as we know it, evolved. By the middle of 1914 Marks and Spencer was a fully developed variety chain store, organised on a national basis, the typical unit being the fixed shop, out of which the Marks and Spencer store of the future evolved. The company became a public company in 1926, when there were about 120 stores throughout the UK. 'St Michael', their brand-name, was first registered in 1928 when Simon Marks chose the name, this being his father's first name; moreover, the Archangel Michael was the guardian angel and patron of the Jews.

Independent suppliers provide 'St Michael' merchandise to the company's specifications at over £14.5 million each week.

The department store with the fastest-moving stock in the world is their premier branch, known as 'Marble Arch' at 458 Oxford Street, City of Westminster, Greater London. The figure of £250 worth of goods per square foot of selling space per year is believed to have become an understatement when the selling area was raised to 72000 ft² (6690 m²) in October 1970.

The company has 252 branches in the UK, from which over 13 million customers make purchases every week. It operates on over 5870000 ft² (506000 m²) of selling space and now has stores on the Continent and in Canada. Turnover (less VAT) for the year to 31 March 1976 was £840 million (UK sales), made up of £584 million on clothing, accessories and home furnishings, and £256 million on foods, with £25 million on exports.

F W (Franklin Winfield) Woolworth

(1852–1919) was a merchant who developed a chain of more than 1000 5- and 10-cent general merchandise stores throughout the USA. He opened his first '5-cent' store in Utica, New York in 1879 and later in the same year an even more successful '5- and 10-cent' store in Lancaster, Pennsylvania. He pioneered the walk-around open-display type of store from which retailers have developed the self-service, supermarket, hyper-market and now cash/wrap operation.

Woolworth's collaborators started their own chains of stores; in 1912, however, the chains were merged into the F W Woolworth Company, incorporated in 1911. The company then expanded to Canada, Cuba, Great Britain, Germany, the West Indies, Rhodesia, Cyprus and Jamaica. Woolworth's estate was estimated to be $27 000 000 at his death.

In 1900 Frank Winfield Woolworth paid his first visit to Europe and on Friday, 5 November 1909 the first store opened in Church Street, Liverpool. People were shy at first of strolling among the well-stocked counters, but by the end of the second-day's trading 60 000 people had visited the store. (When Woolworth first arrived in this country he was clean-shaven; however, he decided that he needed a moustache to give him the same look of authority as his hairier British counterparts. So a moustache was grown – and each time Frank sailed for America, off came his moustache only to be regrown on each return passage to England!)

The same trading methods that had worked so well in the USA were adopted in Britain. In the shops the same efforts were made to display, as accessibly as possible, the greatest possible variety of merchandise. Everything carried a plain price-tag. Supplies were bought directly from manufacturers.

A young man named William L Stephenson was mainly responsible for the British expansion of Woolworth's 3d and 6d stores. He became Managing Director in 1923 and Chairman in 1931. An important change he made was to buy freehold properties for his stores instead of taking leases. Under his dynamic management Woolworth's were soon opening stores in Britain at the rate of one every 18 days and this extraordinary rate of growth was maintained for a number of years. The operating total in April 1976 in Great Britain stood at 988 stores, including 11 Woolco hypermarkets.

The sales area of all stores has now reached over 9 million ft² (over 800 000 m²) – one-third of the size of the City of London, and they trade in over 40 000 different lines. The largest store is in Wolverhampton, with an area of 64 000 ft² (6000 m²) and $1\frac{1}{4}$ miles (2 km) of counter. The first Woolco opened at Oadby, Leicester, in 1967; by the end of 1976 there will be 13 Woolco stores.

In the *Fortune* list of 1975 of the 50 largest retailing companies, the Woolworth business ranked No 8 in the world, with sales of nearly $4200 million.

F W Woolworth and Company now also operate the largest restaurant chain in the world with 2074 restaurants throughout six countries.

Department stores

The business founded by **William Whiteley** in Bayswater was the first store to be opened as a departmental store in this country, although some shops that have since developed into department stores have a longer history. William Whiteley, known in his day as 'The Universal Provider', was born near Leeds in 1831 and died in 1907, murdered by a man who claimed to be his son. The business remained in the control of Whiteley's descendants until 1927, when it was bought by Gordon Selfridge.

Whiteley opened his first shop, in Westbourne Grove, in 1856. By 1875 he had an unbroken row of shops in Westbourne Park and had overflowed into what was then Queen's Road. He met with strong opposition from the local tradesmen, and on more than one occasion he suffered heavy losses from fires believed to have been started by unscrupulous competitors.

A much older business than Whiteley's is that of **Fortnum and Mason's** in Piccadilly. Its history goes back to the year 1707, when William Fortnum first met Hugh Mason. This Mason had a small shop in St James's Market, where Fortnum lodged. Fortnum himself

Boeing aircraft
under
construction.
(Boeing)

Hudson's Bay
Company's
Charter, 1670.
*(Hudson's Bay
Company)*
(see page 144)

became a footman in the Royal Household of Queen Anne, 'thereby establishing a connection with the Royal Family which has continued without a break to the present day'. He became a grocer in his spare time, selling to the ladies of the Household the used candles which he received as the perquisite of his office. When he retired, he opened a grocer's shop with his friend Mason close to the present site of Fortnum and Mason's shop in Piccadilly.

Under Charles Fortnum, William's grandson, the business began to get a grip on the luxury trade in foodstuffs. Later, during the Crimean War, many a case of foodstuffs from Fortnum and Mason's was dispatched to the troops abroad, including 250 lb (113 kg) of 'Concentrated Beef Tea' sent to Florence Nightingale by Queen Victoria. In 1886 'an alert-looking young man called Mr. Heinz' called at the shop in Piccadilly and obtained an order for five cases of his canned foods.

It was only after the First World War that the activities of the shop were extended to women's and children's clothes, kitchenware and other goods apart from food. As a department store, therefore, Fortnum and Mason's is a comparatively new business, but as a grocer's shop we must count it among the oldest businesses of its kind in the country. (See frontispiece illustration).

The great store of **Harrods** at Knightsbridge celebrated its centenary in 1949. Henry Charles Harrod, a wholesale merchant of Eastcheap, took over a small grocer's shop from a friend, P H Burden, in Knightsbridge Village in 1849. At the time of the centenary, a replica of this original shop was erected in a small corner of the vast store that now stands there.

Harrod was a tea-merchant before becoming a grocer. His son, Charles Digby Harrod, joined him in the business and later took it over. The business gradually expanded, and by 1880 employed nearly 100 people. Shortly before Christmas 1883, the entire premises were destroyed by fire, but new premises were opened in September 1884. The store then occupied Nos 101, 103 and 105 Brompton Road.

In 1889 the business was turned into a limited liability company, and C D Harrod received £120000 from the company for it. He retired from the business but was soon brought back to run it, retiring finally in 1891.

It was not until 1911 that Harrods were able to obtain the whole of the island site on which the building now stands, and not until 1939 were the final touches put to the present building.

Harrods is now part of the House of Fraser. It is the largest department store in the UK with a total selling floor space of 23 acres (9.3 ha).

Arthur Walter **Gamage** was born in 1858 and opened a little shop in Holborn in 1878. The shop had a frontage of 5 ft (1.5 m), but was to grow into a vast emporium unlike any other.

Gamage's *Christmas Catalogue* of the year 1913 has recently been reissued by Book Club Associates. It runs to 472 pages, and the publishers have added some pages from the general catalogue of 1911 that cover subjects not fully represented in the Christmas catalogue.

Gamage's premises gradually extended along Holborn, and by 1904 already had more than 2 acres (8000 m²) of floor space for the display of goods. There was also a large mail-order business. The mail-order catalogue of 1911 ran to no less than 900 pages. One of the illustrations in the 1911 catalogue shows a stream of Gamage's vans, one of which carries the words: 'Largest sports outfitters in the world'.

Eric Gamage succeeded his father, but in 1970 the Sterling Guarantee Trust acquired the property for a redevelopment scheme of shops and offices. During the rebuilding, Gamage's business moved to Oxford Street, but the old atmosphere had gone.

The story of the **Army and Navy Stores,** Victoria Street, London, begins in 1871, when a group of Army and Navy officers clubbed together to buy their port and other wines at cheaper rates than those then current. The Army and Navy Co-operative Society Limited was incorporated in September 1871, with a capital of £15000. It was designed to be a closed shop dealing only with members of the co-operative, and so it remained for many years.

Whereas the Army and Navy Stores was thus, so to speak, floated on wine, the **Civil Service Stores** sprang, as one might expect, from tea. To quote from an article by Julia Hood and

Old premises of Skilbeck Brothers Limited, 203–5 Upper Thames Street, London. *(Skilbeck Holdings Ltd)*

B S Yamey 'The Middle-class Co-operative Retailing Societies in London, 1864–1900.' (*Oxford Economic Papers*, 1957, pages 309–22): 'The first of the middle-class societies had very humble origins. In the winter of 1864 a few clerks in the General Post Office clubbed together to buy half a chest of tea, which they divided amongst themselves, allegedly saving 9d. a lb. and being assured of its quality.' The Post Office Supply Association was formed in January 1865, but membership was soon thrown open to all civil servants, and in April 1865 the name was changed to the Civil Service Supply Association.

When Macintosh's business closed down (see page 77), **Eaden Lilley and Company,** dating from 1750, probably became the second oldest retail business in Cambridge. The founder of the business, John Purchas, was in fact well established by 1750. His Bill-heading described him as 'Haberdasher and Mercer' and 'Oil-man'.

Drysalters

Until a few years ago, the most striking building in Upper Thames Street, London, not far from the site of the old City of London Brewery (see page 15), was occupied by **Skilbecks Limited.** Built in the semi-ecclesiastical style of the mid-19th century, and with two great hoists that swung out over the street, the building seemed to typify all that was solid and trustworthy and respectable in mid-Victorian commerce. There was, however, nothing to indicate to the casual passer-by that the business carried on in the building was more than 300 years old. In 1962 the business was moved to Glengall Road, London SE15.

Skilbeck Brothers Limited, wholesale dry-salters, celebrated their tercentenary in 1950. It was in 1650, 'as near as can be judged', that Richard Bagnall set up business in Bread Street, less than a quarter of a mile (0.4 km) away. The precise date cannot be established with certainty, but 1650 is the traditional date for the firm's foundation. This makes it coeval with **Davison, Newman and Company,** whose business is also said to date from that year (see page 34).

The Skilbeck family came into the business in 1796, and five generations of the same family have since guided its destinies. For some years previous to that date, since 1768, the business had been in the hands of the Gouthit family. The Gouthits were related to the Skilbecks, and Mr Donovan Dawe, who has recounted the firm's history in *Skilbecks: Drysalters 1650–1950*, could, therefore, claim that, at the time of the tercentenary celebrations, 'the firm has been in the same family for nearly two hundred years'. A drysalter, we should perhaps add, is a merchant of dye-stuffs and allied commodities.

The crane used to haul goods up outside Skilbeck's old premises, on the north side of Upper Thames Street, once stood out prominently against the skyline. Now, alas, it has gone – (see illustration page 143).

Furs

The **Hudson's Bay Company** held its 307th Annual General Meeting at Winnipeg, Manitoba, on 21 May 1976. There are very few companies with such a record.

The Hudson's Bay Company was incorporated by Royal Charter of Charles II on 2 May 1670, and has traded with Canada continuously since that time. In 1970, its headquarters were transferred from London to Winnipeg, Canada. It is sometimes regarded as the oldest Canadian company, but one should perhaps regard it, for most of its existence as least, as a British company operating in Canada rather than as a native Canadian company. (See chapter 10, page 165.)

In its early days the company had many fierce struggles with the French. In later times there was great rivalry between the Hudson's Bay Company and the North West Company, a rivalry which was finally ended by the union of the two companies in 1821. This united company, under an Act of Parliament of 1821, was given a monopoly of what were called the 'North West Territories', and for nearly half a century the company held administrative as well as trading powers over an area covering all modern Canada except the Great Lakes basin and the Maritime Provinces.

The administration of this vast area was relinquished under a Deed of Surrender of 1869, which was given Royal Assent in 1870. The company, while giving up some of its trading privileges, still kept its Royal Charter. Supplemental Charters were issued in 1884, 1892, 1912 and 1920. The company is now entitled to carry on trade and commerce and to establish agencies in all parts of the world.

One of the most remarkable men connected with the company in its long history was Donald A Smith (1820–1914). Starting as a fur-trader on the Labrador, he rose to become Governor of the Company, Baron Strathcona and Mount Royal, Chancellor of McGill University, and Canadian High Commissioner to Great Britain. He was Governor for 25 years, and presided over the General Court in 1913, at the age of 93. He died in January 1914.

The fur trade is still carried on, but the company is best known today, at any rate in Canada, by its department stores, a number of which have evolved from old trading-posts. Their title is simply 'The Bay'. But the company is still said to be 'the world's largest single dealer in furs', with offices and agents all over the world.

Along with its Royal Charter the company still has 'the unique right to fly its own flag – the red ensign with HBC in white on the red field'.

Ivory

The delightfully named firm of **Puddefoot, Bowers and Simonett Limited,** London, started life as ivory-traders and then graduated to making articles in ivory. In the course of time they acquired the firm of G Betjeman and Sons, who were fine wood makers. In 1966 the business was taken over by Englefields (London) Limited, who are the oldest real pewterers in the business (see page 80).

Thomas Bowers was making ivory scurf combs in 1685. There is a legend that a Bowers was cutting combs on Old London Bridge before the Great Fire of London of 1666 but this seems to be only a legend.

Bailey's *Directory* of 1783 showed **Nathaniel Bowers,** comb-maker, at 44 Cannon Street, London.

Roses

Alex Dickson and Sons Limited, of Hawlmark, County Down, Northern Ireland, are 'the oldest established Rose breeding firm in the world and the recipients of more Gold Medals than any other world grower', to quote the catalogue of the Gardening Centre, Syon Park. The firm was established in 1836 and is now managed by the fifth generation of the Dickson family. Their first series of new roses was introduced in 1887.

Benjamin R Cant and Sons Limited, of The Old Rose Gardens, Mile End, Colchester, claim to be the 'Top Name for Roses for over two hundred years'. According to the firm's catalogue, it began in 1765 and has been in continuous family control up to the present day.

Another firm of rose-growers is **James Cocker and Sons,** of Aberdeenshire. In January 1975 they received the Royal Warrant of Appointment. This was said to be the first time that it had been conferred on rose-growers.

Seedsmen, nurserymen and agricultural merchants

One of the old Scottish businesses mentioned by George Blake in *The Gourock* was **Austin and McAslan Limited,** agricultural seedsmen, of Glasgow, established in 1717. They were taken over by Clan Seeds Limited some years ago, but the whole group has since gone into liquidation. This seems to leave **Finneys** of Newcastle as the oldest seed-merchants. They date from 1749, and in 1955 they took over Toogoods of Southampton, founded in 1815.

The 'Seed and Nursery Establishment' of **W Drummond and Sons Limited** at Stirling was established in 1760, but most of the firm's records were destroyed in two fires, in 1898 and 1950. Their earliest surviving record is a catalogue of 1815.

Other firms of seedsmen and nurserymen can trace their origins back to the reign of George III. **Geo Bunyard and Company Limited,** of Maidstone, have grown and supplied seeds since 1796. **R and G. Cuthbert** of Goff's Oak, Hertfordshire, describe themselves as 'The Nation's Nurserymen since 1797'.

Toogood and Sons Limited, mentioned above, now hold the Royal Warrant of Appointment as Seedsmen to Her Majesty Queen Elizabeth II. They have been 'holders of royal appointments to successive sovereigns since 1884'.

Finally, mention should be made of the firm of **Hurst Gunson Cooper Taber Limited,** of Witham, Essex, which was formed in 1961 by the merger of five wholesale seed-houses. The new business was said to 'trace its beginnings back to a business started in 1560'. The background material issued by a public relations firm at the time of the merger said that the new company 'has direct links with the business of Mr. Child and Mr. Field, established in 1560', but the family tree attached to the Press release jumps from J Field in 1560 to J and J Field in 1771, and from Child in 1560 to Field and Child in 1810. Both Mr Child's and Mr Field's successors are said to have suffered loss in the Great Fire of London of 1666, having had premises in Pudding Lane, where the Great Fire began.

Thompson and Morgan, of Ipswich, were established in 1855. (See also page 167.) They issue what is described as 'the World's largest and most famous Seed Catalogue'.

Stamp-dealers

The 'Lincoln' stamp albums formerly published by **William S Lincoln,** of 2 Holles Street, London, described the publisher as 'The Oldest-Established Stamp Dealer in the World', but there was nothing in the album to show when the firm began.

William Simpson Lincoln, according to *The Postage Stamp* by L N and M Williams (1956), was a notable London dealer who for many years had a shop in Holborn and later in Holles Street, near Oxford Circus. His stock of stamps was sold to **Stanley Gibbons** in 1931.

According to *Postage and Philately*, published by PEP (Political and Economic Planning) in August 1957, the business of Stanley Gibbons Limited, founded at Plymouth in 1856, was the first stamp firm to celebrate its centenary. If W S Lincoln's claim was correct, his firm must, therefore, have been founded before 1856 but not have survived to celebrate its centenary.

The firm of Stanley Gibbons celebrated its centenary in 1956 with an exhibition at the Waldorf Hotel in London. There must have been some rivalry between Lincoln and Gibbons, as the eighth edition of the Gibbons catalogue, published in 1891, described Stanley Gibbons Limited as 'The Largest and Oldest Stamp Dealers in the World'. Stanley Gibbons started his business in Plymouth, but moved to London in 1874.

Ticket agencies

Austin Brereton's booklet *A Walk Down Bond Street,* published in 1920, has for its sub-title 'The Centenary Souvenir of the House of Ashton and Mitchell 1820–1920'.

Bond Street takes its name from Sir Thomas Bond, who died in 1685, although the street named after him was not built until 1686. It soon became 'the most select and fashionable of all the shopping streets in London'.

The 'libraries' for which Bond Street was long famous did not only sell books and engravings. They were also publishing houses and agents for theatre tickets. The most famous of these old librarians was **John Mitchell I** (1806–74), who started his business at 33 Old Bond Street in the year 1834. He had previously been employed in a similar business belonging to William Sams, in which he had acquired an interest. **George Ashton** came to Bond Street in the early 1870s, and early in his career had to receive the Prince of Wales (afterwards Edward VII) at the Court Theatre. For nearly 50 years, Ashton was 'in personal attendance upon the Sovereign at every theatre or place of entertainment during that period', as well as arranging the Command Performances at Windsor, Sandringham and theatres in London.

John Mitchell was succeeded by his nephew, upon whose death Ashton set up his own business at No 38, but a few years later he took over the business at No 33 and moved back there. In 1901, King Edward allowed Ashton and Mitchell to use the word 'Royal' in describing their theatre and concert ticket agency. The agency is now at 4 Woodstock Street, but the connection of the Ashton family with the business ended with George Ashton's death.

It will be seen from this brief account of the business that its centenary might have been more appropriately celebrated in the year 1934 than in 1920.

Older as a firm, though not as a ticket agency, is the well-known firm of **Keith Prowse Limited** – 'You want the best seats, we have them'. This firm traces its origins back to 1780. In that year 'Robert W. Keith was manufacturing musical instruments in Rathbone Place, Oxford Street. He specialised in flutes and clarinets.'

Keith moved his business to Cheapside about the turn of the century, and soon afterwards took William Prowse into partnership. At that time the business was devoted to the manufacture of musical instruments and to music-publishing.

An advertisement in Halstead's book showing a gentleman in 18th-century costume booking a theatre seat by telephone is accompanied by the comment: 'This could not have happened in 1780 when Keith Prowse were founded, as the telephone had not yet been invented. But patrons of the theatre were well served by Keith Prowse in those early days.' According to Halstead's account of the firm's development, however, it was only when Queen Victoria had been on the throne for ten years, i.e. in 1847, that 'the house of Keith Prowse established the theatre ticket side of its business almost accidentally'. Thus, although the firm of Keith Prowse is about half a century older than the firm of Ashton and Mitchell, the latter firm has a good claim to be regarded as the older ticket agency.

Travel agencies

Thomas Cook and Son Limited is the world's oldest travel agency.

Thomas Cook (1808–92) was the innovator of the conducted tour and founder of Thomas Cook and Son. In 1841 he persuaded the Midland Counties Railway Company to run a special train between Leicester and Loughborough for a Temperance gala. This was the first publicly advertised excursion train in England. In 1844 the railway agreed to make the arrangement permanent if Cook would provide passengers for the excursion trains. During the Paris Exhibition of 1855 Cook conducted excursions from Leicester to Calais, France. In 1856 he led the first grand tour of Europe. In the 1860s he became an agent for the sale of domestic and overseas travel tickets. On Thomas Cook's death the business passed to his son John Mason Cook.

B. BUSINESSES IN OTHER LANDS

Department stores

The story of **Eaton's** of Toronto could be said to begin in 1860, although the centenary was celebrated in 1969.

Timothy Eaton was born at Ballymena in County Antrim, Ireland, in 1834 and went to Canada in 1854. In 1860, with his brother James, he opened a dry-goods establishment in St Mary's, Ontario. In 1869 he moved to 178 Yonge Street, Toronto, and in 1870 introduced what was then regarded as the daring innovation of 'Goods Satisfactory or Money Refunded'.

In 1883 he moved from 178 to 190 Yonge Street and, six months later, sold the premises at No 178 to Robert Simpson (see page opposite). The year 1884 saw the introduction of the mail-order catalogue, which became known as 'The Homesteader's Bible' or simply as 'The Book'.

The centenary history puts forward a number of claims to pre-eminence on behalf of Eaton's. It is described as 'the world's oldest and largest family retail chain'. It is still a private firm owned and run by a direct descendant of the founder and, 'of all the great mercantile empires established in the last century, only one in all the world is still in the hands of the family who founded it. That one is Eaton's'. Further, 'Eaton's remains the largest merchandising enterprise in Canada, and vies with the Canadian Pacific Railway for the position of the largest private employer in Canada. Its average payroll covers 55 000, peaking to perhaps 70 000 on rush days.'

Timothy Eaton revolutionised the methods and ethics of retail selling; his insistence on sales for cash and no haggling was unprecedented in 1869.

Simpson's, also of Toronto, celebrated their centenary in 1972. Robert Simpson, the founder of the business, was born in Morayshire, Scotland, in 1834 and sailed for Canada when he was 22 years old. In 1872 he took over a dry-goods business at 184 Yonge Street, only a few doors away from young Timothy Eaton, and in 1881 he moved to 174 Yonge Street. In 1883, as noted above, he acquired the premises at 178 Yonge Street vacated by Timothy Eaton.

Simpson died in 1897 but, unlike Timothy Eaton, he had no son to follow him in the business, and for a time there were fears that the store might drift into American hands. It was, however, a Toronto wholesaler, Harris Henry Fudger, who became President of the company in 1898. In their centennial year Simpson's described themselves as 'Canada's second largest department store chain', with large department stores in six cities in Canada. The company is also associated with Sears, Roebuck and Company in Simpson-Sears Limited.

The supplement issued by the *Boston Sunday Advertiser* in 1963 to mark its 15th anniversary contained an advertisement for **Jordan's,** 'New England's Largest Store', which was established in 1851, some 38 years after the *Advertiser*.

Macy's, New York, America's first department store, was opened in 1877. R H Macy, the founder of the business, had opened a dry-goods store in 1868, just about the time, as it happened, when young Timothy Eaton was opening a dry-goods store in Toronto (see above).

The *Fortune* list of 1975 showed that Sears, Roebuck, of Chicago, had retained its position as the nation's largest retailer, with sales of more than $13 000 million. **Safeway Stores** (Oakland) was still No 2, with sales of more than $8000 million. **Great Atlantic and**

Pacific Tea (Montvale, New Jersey), however, with sales of $6875 million, had fallen to No 4, having been overtaken by **J C Penney,** of New York, with sales of $6936 million. Macy's was No 27, with sales of $1242 million.

Merchants

One of the oldest of all Canadian companies, **Robin, Jones and Whitman,** of Halifax, Nova Scotia, was established in 1766, and was, therefore, exceeded in age only by the *Chronicle-Telegraph* of Quebec (1764) and by Wm Stairs, Son and Morrow (1758) (see opposite) – if we regard the Hudson's Bay Company, for our purposes, as an English company operating in Canada for most of its history (see page 144).

Charles Robin was born in Jersey in 1743, and in 1766 he sailed across the Atlantic to examine the possibilities for trade along the Canadian coast. A trading voyage was made the following year. Robin settled in Canada, in the Gaspé Province, after the American War of Independence, and founded the firm of Charles Robin and Company. His diaries for the years from 1766 onwards were discovered in Jersey and were used by A C Saunders, the Librarian of the Jersey Historical Society, as the basis for an article in *The Maritime Merchant* of 6 March 1930.

It appears that the firm ceased operations in Halifax in the late 1960s, although some of the branches are said to be still operating in the Gaspereau area in Quebec Province.

Retail stores

Wm Stairs, Son and Morrow, of Halifax, Nova Scotia, traces its history back to 1758, when Brook Watson, a merchant, opened a small retail general store in downtown Halifax, described as 'the second oldest business in Canada'. The word 'second' appears to have been used in deference to the Hudson's Bay Company (see pages 144 and 165). Although the 'Bay' was indeed established some time before the Halifax store opened for business, it would seem fairer to regard it throughout most of its career as an English company operating in Canada rather than as an indigenous Canadian company, in which case Wm Stairs, Son and Morrow could properly be regarded as Canada's oldest business.

William Stairs entered the business as an apprentice in 1803, and bought it in 1810. The Robert Morrow who contributed his name to the business married the daughter of William Stairs. The President of the company in 1960, Arthur D Stairs, was the sixth Stairs and of the fifth generation to head the company.

Seedsmen

The American seedsmen **Comstock, Ferre and Company** were established in 1820 and celebrated 150 years in the seed business in 1970. James L Belden started the business, at Wethersfield, Connecticut. He was succeeded by William and Franklin Comstock. Henry Ferre became a partner in 1853.

CHAPTER 9

PRINTING, PUBLISHING AND BOOKSELLING

A. BUSINESSES IN THE BRITISH ISLES

Almanacs

One of the oldest of the publications that appear annually is the **Oxford University Almanack,** which has been printed each year since 1674 (according to one authority) or since 1676 (according to *Willing's Press Guide*).

Foulsham's Original Old Moore's Almanack, published by W Foulsham and Company Limited of Yeovil Road, Slough, Berkshire, is 'published under the original copyright dating back to 1697'. Dr Francis Moore, the astronomer, astrologer and physician who founded the *Almanack*, was born in 1657. **Raphael's Almanac,** also published by W Foulsham and Company, is a comparative youngster, dating back only to 1819, when Edwin Raphael published his first *Raphael's Almanac or The Prophetic Messenger and Weather Guide.*

Booksellers (retail)

One of the oldest retail businesses of any kind in the country is the bookshop of Bowes and Bowes at 1 Trinity Street, Cambridge. An advertisement for Bowes and Bowes in *The Year's Work in Modern Language Studies* of 1931 described it as 'the oldest bookshop in England'. The history of this bookshop has been told by G J Gray in *Cambridge Bookselling* (1925).

The premises at 1 Trinity Street were certainly used as a bookshop as early as the year 1581. John Deighton, who later started a shop farther along Trinity Street, was here in 1780. In 1845 the shop was bought by Daniel and Alexander Macmillan, who moved from 17 Trinity Street. Mr Bowes did not appear on the scene until later.

The evidence about the age of **Deighton and Bell's** bookshop is not entirely consistent. Gray says: 'Messrs. Deighton Bell's was established 1700 at 13 Trinity Street. John Deighton became proprietor in 1778.' F A Mumby in his *Publishing and Bookselling* says that the business dates from about 1777. Roberts, in *The Cambridge University Press 1521–1921*, puts the matter rather differently. He says that John Deighton 'had begun business in Cambridge about 1777 and removed to London in 1786; in 1795 he appears to have returned to Cambridge, where he established the bookselling firm that has since become Deighton, Bell and Company.'

Hatchard's dates from 1797, when John Hatchard started his bookshop in Piccadilly, London. **John Bumpus,** according to F A Mumby, 'set up as a bookseller-publisher in Clerkenwell about 1790'.

Unlike the static bookshop at 1 Trinity Street, **Heffer's** bookshop at Cambridge has had three homes in exactly 100 years. William Heffer (1843–1928), the founder of the business, who is now commemorated by a medallion outside the present premises, opened his first shop, in Fitzroy Street, in 1876. In 1896 the bookseller's business was transferred to Petty Cury, and it was not long after the transfer that the firm's stationery began to

Bookshop of Bowes & Bowes, Cambridge. *(Bowes & Bowes)*

carry the slogan 'The bookshop known all over the World'.

The shop in Petty Cury, along with the old Red Lion and the rest of the south side of the street, was knocked down to make a new shopping precinct and car park. The business then moved again, in 1970, to spacious new premises in Trinity Street, opposite the main entrance of Trinity College.

The history of **Ellis's Bookshop,** at 29 New Bond Street, began in 1728. Its story was told by George Smith and Frank Benger in *The Oldest London Bookshop – A History of Two Hundred Years,* which was published in the year 1928 on the occasion of the firm's bicentenary.

The world's largest bookshop is that of **W and G Foyle Limited,** City of Westminster, Greater London. First established in 1904 in a small shop in Islington, the company is now at 119–25 Charing Cross Road. The area of one site is 75 825 ft² (7044 m²). The largest single display of books in one room in the world is in the Norrington Room at **Blackwell's Bookshop,** Broad Street, Ox-

ford. This subterranean adjunct was opened on 16 June 1966 and contains 160 000 volumes on 2½ miles (4 km) of shelving in 10 000 ft² (929 m²) of selling space.

Booksellers (wholesale)

Simpkin, Marshall Limited, the famous wholesale book firm, started business in 1779. In May 1955 the firm was compulsorily wound up, and bought by Hatchard's of Piccadilly. In 1956 the business was sold to Wyman and Sons Limited.

Diaries

Charles Letts and Company was founded in 1796 by John Letts. In 1966 the company celebrated the 150th anniversary of the first commercial diary ever printed, which was issued by John Letts in 1816.

Directories

The firm now known as **Kelly's Directories Limited** was established in 1799. They describe themselves as 'the oldest and largest directory publishers in the world'.

Libraries

The largest library in the UK is that in the **British Museum,** London. It contains more than 9 000 000 books, about 115 000 manuscripts and 101 000 charters on 158 miles (254 km) of shelf. There are spaces for 370 readers in the domed Reading Room, built in 1854. The largest public library in the UK will be the extended **Mitchell Library,** North Street, Glasgow with a floor area of 510 000 ft² (47 380 m²) or 11.7 acres (4.7 ha) and an ultimate shelving capacity for 4 000 000 volumes.

The **London Library,** founded in 1841, is said to be the largest private subscription library in the world.

The oldest public library in Scotland is in **Kirkwall,** Orkney, founded in 1683.

Newspapers, magazines and periodicals

There are a number of difficulties in settling arguments about the relative age of newspapers. Often the early issues are missing and the date of the first issue has, therefore, to be estimated by reckoning back from the dating and numbering of the earliest surviving issues. Also, one has to decide whether a paper that amalgamates with another can, so to speak, assume the age of the older paper. The tables which follow are a simplification of the older issues in the UK and overseas.

Foyles Bookshop, London. *(McMaster Christie Studios Ltd)*

Newspapers, magazines and periodicals (Some of these have ceased to exist)

Newspapers

Name	Established	Comments
The London Gazette	1665	Oldest in UK – neither daily nor weekly.
Berrow's Worcester Journal	1690	Oldest weekly, since 1709.
Stamford Mercury	1695	
Bristol Post Boy	1702	
Daily Courant	1702	
Norwich Postman	1708	
Nottingham Guardian (Journal)	1710 or 1711	
North Mail	1711	
Newcastle Journal	1711	
Norwich Gazette	1712	
Liverpool Courant	1712	
Exeter Mercury	1714	

Continued overleaf

Newspapers, magazines and periodicals *continued*

Newspapers *continued*

Name	Established	Comments
Northampton Mercury	1720	Published for 250 years without a single interruption.
Lloyd's List	1726 weekly	
	1734 daily	Oldest daily in the UK still existing.
Belfast Newsletter	1737	
Coventry Standard	1741	Formerly the *Coventry Mercury*.
Birmingham Gazette	1741	
Press and Journal	1748	Aberdeen.
Yorkshire Post	1754	
Public Ledger	1759	'London's Oldest Daily Newspaper'.
The Kilkenny Journal	1767	Formerly the *Leinster Journal*.
Morning Post	1772	
Glasgow Herald	1783	
The Times	1785	First appeared as the *Universal Register*. Changed on 1 January 1788.
The Observer	1791	Oldest Sunday paper.
North Wales Chronicle	1808	Oldest continuously produced newspaper in Wales.
London Illustrated News	1842	First illustrated newspaper in the world.
Amserau Cymru	1843	Oldest national newspaper in Wales. Absorbed by *Y Faner* in 1859.
Y Faner	1857	
City Press	1857	
Daily Telegraph	1885	Incorporated *Morning Post* (established 1772) in 1937.
Financial Times	1888	Incorporated *Financial News* (established 1884).

Magazines

Name	Established	Comments
The Scots Magazine	1739	Publication ceased after about 90 years, not resumed until 1880s.
Methodist Magazine	1778	'The oldest magazine in the World'.
Blackwood's Magazine	1817	Oldest monthly.
The Child's Magazine	1824	Oldest children's magazine in the world.
Spectator	1828	Oldest weekly review.
Chambers's Journal	1832	
Punch	1841	
Jewish Chronicle	1841	
The Economist	1843	
The Kiddies' Magazine	1846	Formerly *The Child's Magazine*.
Twentieth Century	1877	
Flight	1909	Oldest aviation weekly in the world.

Journals

Name	Established	Comments
New Law Journal	1822	Originally *Law Journal*.
The Lancet	1823	
Mining Journal	1835	
Building	1843	Originally *The Builder*.
Ironmonger, Builder's Merchant and Metal Trades Advertiser	1859	Oldest trade journal in the UK.

Periodicals

Name	Established	Comments
Philosophical Transactions of the Royal Society	1665 (March)	Oldest continuously produced periodical in the world after *Journal des Scavans* (January 1665).

The University presses at Oxford and Cambridge

Printing and publishing, like brewing, have a long connection with the Universities of Oxford and Cambridge. It is difficult to say exactly when the **Oxford University Press** and the **Cambridge University Press** began, but they must both be counted among our oldest businesses.

In 1921 the Cambridge University Press published *A History of the Cambridge University Press 1521–1921* by S C Roberts, who was then the Secretary to the Press and who later became Master of Pembroke College and Sir Sydney Roberts. In 1922, possibly inspired by the Cambridge publication, the Oxford University Press published, anonymously, *Some Account of the Oxford University Press 1468–1921*. The situation is, however, more complicated than the titles of the two books just mentioned would suggest.

Despite the title of his book, the anonymous Oxford author concedes that 1468 must be a misprint for 1478; his statement that the Press of 1517 to 1520 'was really the University Press' carries the implication that there is doubt whether the Press of 1478 can properly be so described; and there is 'a gap in the history' of about 65 years, from 1520–85.

Turning now to the Cambridge Press, Roberts tells us at the outset that his book was written 'to mark the four hundredth anniversary of Cambridge printing' (and not, it will be noted, of the Cambridge University Press). He refers to the efforts that had been made to establish that Oxford printing was older than Caxton's and quotes Maitland's remark: 'The oldest of all inter-university sports was a lying match.' Roberts states that Cambridge printing was formally established by royal charter on 20 July 1534.

Before attempting to form a judgment on the rival claims of the two Presses, one might consider the evidence of F A Mumby in his *Publishing and Bookselling* (1954):

Printing was not permanently established at either University until towards the end of Elizabeth's reign. To Oxford, however, belongs the unique distinction of being able to produce a list of practically all its publications for over 340 years.

This statement appears to derive from the

Henry Bullock's *Oratio* of 1521, the first book printed in Cambridge. *(Curators of the Bodleian Library, Oxford)*

first edition of the book, published in 1930. It was in 1585 that the first issue of the new Press at Oxford celebrated the Earl of Leicester as its founder. From 1585 to 1930 is 345 years. Mumby apparently overlooked the fact that the Cambridge University Press can produce an unbroken list of publications longer than Oxford's by one year, starting in 1584, so that Oxford's distinction cannot rightly be called 'unique'.

Which, then, of all the possible dates are we to take for the beginning of the University Presses? Should it be the year in which printing was first carried on, the first year in which the University can be shown to have had some interest in the printing that was being done, or the year from which publication has been continuous? On the whole, the last choice would seem to be the fairest. Books were admittedly printed in Oxford as early as 1478 whereas Cambridge cannot claim any publication earlier than 1521, but Cambridge can show a list of works published in every year from 1584 without a break, whereas Oxford's list begins only in 1585. Moreover, the printers in Cambridge between 1574 and 1690 (from which year, according to Johnson and Gibson, 'may be dated the continuous history of the Learned Press administered directly by a Delegacy of the University in Oxford') appear to have been much more closely integrated with the University than were their contemporaries at Oxford. (See also 'Price Stability', page 171.)

Printing

One of the oldest firms of printers in the country is **Burrup, Mathieson and Company,** now at Crane House, Lavington Street, London SE1. The firm was established in the City of London in 1628, but unfortunately little is known of their history as few records have survived. The paucity of records can be readily understood if one looks at one of their old letter-headings. At the top of the page, almost like battle honours, is printed:

Destroyed in Great Fire of London 1666
Destroyed by Fire in First Royal Exchange
Destroyed by Fire in Second Royal Exchange
Destroyed by Fire in the Attack on London
                              December 29th, 1940

(The fires in the Royal Exchange occurred in 1666 – the Great Fire of London – and in 1838.) It was in 1628 that Stephens and Meredith started business at the Sign of the Crane in St Paul's Churchyard, which explains the name of the company's present works, built to replace the premises that were bombed in 1940.

In Great Smith Street, Westminster, not far from Caxton Hall, used to stand the deserted premises that bore the name of **Vacher and Son Limited,** established in 1751. Some years ago, the firm moved to Clerkenwell Road, and the old premises were demolished in 1959. The firm is perhaps best known for its handy little Parliamentary guide, *Vacher's Parlia-*

mentary Companion, generally known as 'Vacher'.

Outside the old premises in Great Smith Street used to hang the firm's sign 'At the Red Pale', a white shield with a vertical red stripe. Although the firm claimed no connection with Caxton beyond the fact that he also printed in Westminster, it is interesting to recall that Caxton also carried on business under the sign of the red pale.

One year older than Vacher and Son is the firm of **Harrison and Sons Limited** of London, established in 1750, Printers by Appointment to the Queen, the Queen Mother and also to the late Queen Mary. This no doubt explains their telegraphic address: 'Reginarum'.

According to H L V Fletcher's *South Wales*, the first printing-press in Wales was set up at Adpar in Cardiganshire. 'The printer was **Isaac Carter,** and he issued his first book from here in 1719'.

Publishers

The Society for the Promotion of Christian Knowledge (*the SPCK*), was founded in 1698. The SPCK would thus appear to be older than all other publishing firms in this country except the two University Presses mentioned earlier in this chapter.

Apart from these three, the oldest publishing firm in the country now is the **House of Longman,** which was founded in 1724.

When Thomas Longman set himself up in business at the Sign of the Ship in Paternoster Row in 1724, he established the firm that his successors were to claim to be the oldest commercial publishing-house in Britain. When Thomas died, in 1755, the business passed to his nephew, another Thomas. It was two grandsons of Thomas II, Thomas Norton Longman (1849–1930) and Charles James Longman (1852–1934) who had the foresight to acquire, in 1890, the Rivington publishing firm and thereby eliminate a possible challenger for the title.

Before 1890, always excepting the University Presses and the SPCK, the oldest publishing firm in the country for many years was the **House of Rivington.** The business had been founded by Charles Rivington in 1711, when he set up his Sign of the Bible and Crown in Paternoster Row. Rivington soon became the leading theological publisher in London. The Bible and Crown, says Mumby, is the oldest publishing sign in London. The Rivingtons traded under this sign from 1711 to 1890. The sign 'is now in the possession of their successors, Longman, Green and Company'. Mumby says that Rivington's lost the title of the oldest publishing house in the trade 'when Longmans, some few years their junior, acquired their business in 1890'.

The title-page of Bishop Burnet's *History of the Reformation of the Church of England*, published in 1825, shows that it was 'Printed for C. & J. Rivington, Booksellers to the Society for Promoting Christian Knowledge'. The name of the Society is also embossed on the cover. Apart from illustrating the close link between publishing and bookselling, the title-page also brought together two bodies founded within a quarter of a century of each other, the Society in 1698 and Rivington's in 1711.

After the sale of the Rivington business to Longmans in 1890, Septimus Rivington started publishing again in partnership with John Guthrie Percival, under the style of Percival and Company. The name was changed to Rivington, Percival and Company from 1893 to 1897, when the name Percival was dropped. The Rivington family can, therefore, claim that they have probably been publishing continuously for longer than any other family in the world, although not always in the one firm.

Longmans held an exhibition, first at the National Book League and then at Longman House in Harlow, to mark the first 250 years of the House of Longman. One of the exhibits, which was featured in the catalogue of the exhibition, was the first-known dust-jacket, which was introduced by Longmans for Heath's *Keepsake* in 1833.

In 1968 Longmans, Green was merged in the Pearson organisation, where it now goes under the name of the Longman Group. With the death of Mark Longman in 1972, as Philip Wallis records, 'we come to the end of the Longman line of publishers, seven generations ranging over a quarter millennium'. Mention might be made, however, of a letter from Mr Thomas Michael Longman that appeared in *The Times* of 26 July 1974, showing that one

Dust-jacket of Heath's *Keepsake*, 1833. *(Curators of the Bodleian Library, Oxford)*

member of the Longman family was still active in the publishing world. The writer of the letter has been a partner in Longmans from 1947 to 1959, but he then left the business, along with G C Darton and John Todd, to start his own publishing business under the imprint **Darton, Longman and Todd.**

Longmans may be the oldest commercial publishers in Britain, but there are at least two older publishers on the Continent (see page 158).

Longmans and **Murrays** were the only two of the 26 houses which published the first edition of Johnson's *Lives of the Poets* (1779–81) to have remained in their original family until recent times. The House of Murray has the same impressive dynastic sequence as the House of Longman. It was founded in 1768 by a retired naval officer whose name was MacMurray. This explains his emblem of a ship in full sail, which is still used by the firm. John Murray I died in 1793 and was succeeded by John Murray II, who died in 1843, and he in turn was succeeded by John Murray III, Sir John Murray (1851–1928). It was John Murray II, 'Glorious John', the friend of Byron, who moved the business to its present address in Albemarle Street in the year 1812. John Murray IV, who was born in 1884, died in 1967, having previously been joined in the business by his son, John Murray V. His

(335)

The PENNSYLVANIA EVENING POST

Price only Two Coppers. Published every *Tuesday, Thursday,* and *Saturday* Evenings.

Vol. II.]   SATURDAY, JULY 6, 1776.   [Num. 228.

In CONGRESS, July 4, 1776.
A Declaration by the Representatives
of the United States of America,
in General Congrefs affembled.

WHEN, in the courfe of human events, it becomes necessary for one people to diffolve the political bands which have connected them with another, and to assume, among the powers of the earth, the feparate and equal ftation to which the laws of nature and of nature's God intitle them, a decent refpect to the opinions of mankind requires that they fhould declare the caufes which impel them to the feparation.

He has diffolved Representative Houfes repeatedly, for oppofing with manly firmnefs his invafions on the rights of the people.

He has refufed for a long time, after fuch diffolutions, to caufe others to be elected; whereby the legiflative powers, incapable of annihilation, have returned to the people at large for their exercife; the flate remaining in the mean time expofed to all the dangers of invafion from without, and convulfions within.

He has endeavoured to prevent the population of thefe flates; for that purpofe obftructing the laws for naturalization of foreigners; refufing to pafs others to encourage their migrations hither, and raifing the conditions of new appropriations of lands.

He has obftructed the adminiftration of juftice, by refufing

The *Pennsylvania Evening Post* of 6 July 1776

nephew, John Grey Murray, joined the firm in 1930. It became a private limited liability company in 1951.

Adam **Black,** another well-known figure in the history of publishing, 'laid the foundations of his firm in 1807'. He retired in 1870 'from the business over which he had ruled for sixty-three years', and died in 1874, in his 90th year.

According to Mumby 'The **Epworth Press and Methodist Publishing House,** founded in 1739, is one of the oldest businesses in our trade if we allow this date'. The reason for this qualification is not clear. An advertisement in the centenary issue of *The Bookseller*, dated 3 May 1958, announced that the Epworth Press was 'founded by John Wesley in 1733'.

B. BUSINESSES IN OTHER LANDS

Almanacs

A similar publication to *Old Moore's Almanack* is **Le Véritable Messager Boiteux,** published at Vevey in Switzerland. It is called an 'almanach historique'. It was founded in 1708, and the 1959 edition carried the description '252e année'.

Newspapers, magazines and periodicals
(See also page 157)

Printing

According to the *Encyclopaedia Britannica* (sv Haarlem), the printing establishment of **Joh. Enschedé en Zonen,** Haarlem, Holland, the publishers of the *Haarlem Courant* (page 157), 'has the reputation of being the oldest in the Netherlands'. It was established in 1703 by Izaak Enschedé (1681–1761), and the President of the company in 1963 was in the seventh degree a direct descendant of the founder. The Johannes Enschedé who gave the firm its name was the son of Izaak and lived from 1708 to 1780. The present style of the firm dates from 1773, when Johannes I took his sons Johannes II and Jacobus into partnership.

The first number of the *Haarlem Courant* showing part of the front and back pages. *(Enschedé)*

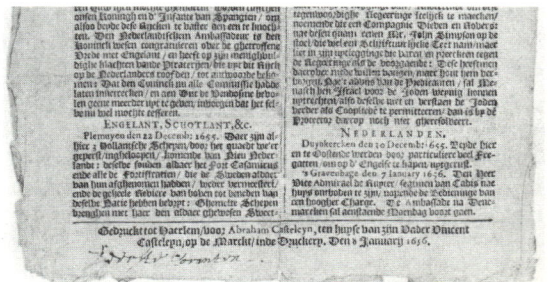

Overseas newspapers, magazines and periodicals

Name	Established	Comments
Petites Affiches (France)	1612	Date of royal *brevet*.
Post-och Inrikes Tidningar (Sweden)	1645	Oldest existing newspaper in the world.
Haarlemsche Courant (Holland)	1656	Now appears under the joint title of *Haarlems Dagblad/Oprechte Haarlemsche Courant*. See illustration (page 156).
Journal des Scavans (France)	1665 (January)	Oldest continuously produced periodical in the World.
Hildesheimer Allgemeine Zeitung (Germany)	1705	
Pfälzischer Merkur (Germany)	1723	
Hanauer Anzeiger (Germany)	c. 1725	
Feuille d'avis de Neuchâtel (Switzerland)	1738	
Darmstädter Tagblatt (Germany)	1738	
Bremer Nachrichten (Germany)	1743	
Berlingske Tidende (Denmark)	1749	
Giessener Anzeiger (Germany)	1750	
Leeuwarder Courant (Holland)	1752	
Provinciale Zeeuwse Courant (Holland)	1758	
Norrköpings Tidningar-Ostergotlands Dagblad (Sweden)	1758	
Saarbrücker Zeitung (Germany)	1761	
Feuille d'avis de Lausanne (Switzerland)	1762	
Schaumburger Zeitung (Germany)	1762	
Hersfelder Zeitung (Germany)	1763	
Offenbach Post (Germany)	1763	
Hartford Courant (USA)	1764	
Quebec Chronicle-Telegraph (Canada)	1764	
Aalborg Stiftstidende (Denmark)	1767	
Adresseavisen (Norway)	1767	
New Haven Journal Courier (USA)	1767	
Lippische Landeszeitung (Germany)	1767	
Philadelphia Inquirer (USA)	1771	
Neue Zürcher Zeitung (Switzerland)	1780	See illustration above.
Diario de Barcelona (Spain)	1792	Spain's oldest newspaper.
Boston Sunday Advertiser (USA)	1813	
Revue des Deux Mondes	1824	'France's oldest journal' (but see 1665).
Fiji Times	1869	First newspaper in the world every day – it is published just west of the International Date Line where the new day begins!
Summary (USA)	1883	Oldest penal publication.

The type-founding factory dates from 1743, and the firm claim to be 'the oldest surviving typefounders in the world'.

The **Franklin Printing Company,** Philadelphia, USA, was established by Benjamin Franklin in 1728.

Bowne and Company, of New York, established in 1775, describe themselves as 'the nation's oldest and largest financial printer'.

Robert Bowne (1744–1818) set himself up in business as a stationer in Queen Street (now Pearl Street) in February 1775. Along with writing-paper, account-books, quills and pens he also sold such things as nails, glass, pitch-pine boards and cutlery. After the American War of Independence the business

MILESTONES IN TYPESETTING

1392   Korea: first type-foundry.

1822   USA: First mechanised type-setting machine, Dr William Church.

1840   First type-composing machine: 'piano-type', patented in England by James Young and Adrien Delcambre of Lille, 13 March.

1841   First commercial use of type-composing machine 'pianotype' used to set weekly magazine *The Phalanx*, London.

1842   First book set by type-composing machine: Edward Binn's *The Anatomy of Sleep,* London. First book illustrated with photographs: two photo-mechanically reproduced daguerreotypes printed by Hippolyte Sizeau's process in Volume 2 of N P Lerebours's *Excusions Daguerriennes,* Paris.

1866   The first newspaper set by type-composing machine: *Eastern Morning News*, Hull, England, by 'Hattersley Typesetter'.

1872   The first national newspaper set by type-composing machine: *The Times*, by 'Kestenbein Typesetter'.

1884   First 'Linotype' machine: patented by Ottmar Mergenthaler, Baltimore, 26 August.

1886   First book set by 'Linotype' machine: *The Tribune book of Open Air Sport*, New York.

1887   First 'Monotype' machine patented by Tolbert Lanston, Troy, Ohio.

1889*   England: first 'Linotype' machine.

1890*   'Linotype' machine used first time in Great Britain by *Leeds Mercury* (February). USA: 'Monotype'.

1894   First 'Monotype' machine manufactured by Sellers and Company, Philadelphia.

1928   First teletypesetter installed by Rochester Times Union, Rochester, New York.

1946   First photo-setting machine (practical): 'Harris Intertype Photosetter' installed by Government Printing Office, Washington, DC.

1948   First film-setting machine in Great Britain: 'Rotofoto', devised by George Westover, London.

1960   First typesetting by computer: introduced at Imprimerie Nationale, Paris.

These dates are unconfirmed

specialised in stationery and printing. One of Robert Bowne's young associates, who turned out to have an aptitude for the fur trade, decided to strike out on his own. His name was John Jacob Astor.

After Robert's death the business was carried on by his sons Robert and John. John left in 1824 to become the first President of the United States Fire Insurance Company, but Robert retired in November 1898 after serving the company for 50 years.

Publishing

Breitkopf und Härtel, the famous music publishers of Leipzig, celebrated their 250th anniversary in 1969, five years earlier than Longmans (see page 154).

It was in 1719 that Bernhard Christoph Breitkopf married the widow of a printer whose business could be traced back to 1542. (It is a nice question whether more businesses can be said to have been founded by men who married widows than by men who married the master's daughter.)

This Breitkopf was born in 1695 and died in 1777. His son, Johann Gottlob Immanuel Breitkopf, was born in 1719, apprenticed in 1736, and took over the business in 1745. He died in 1794. His son, Christoph Gottlob Breitkopf, was born in 1750, became a partner (*Gesellschafter*) in 1793, and took Gottfried Christoph Härtel as a partner in 1795. On Christoph Gottlob's death, in 1800, Härtel inherited the business.

Even older than Breitkopf and Härtel is the **Orell Füssli Verlag,** printers and publishers of Zürich, founded by the German printer Christoph Froschauer in Zürich as long ago as 1519. With a modesty akin to that of the House of Longman, the Orell Füssli business is content to claim merely that it is the oldest business of its kind in the German-speaking world.

Type-founding *(see 'Printing', page 157)*

The Enschedé typefoundry in the 18th century. *(Enschedé)*

MILESTONES IN THE HISTORY OF PRINTING

AD **650**   Chinese practice of using lamp-black ink (invented in AD 400) for taking rubbings led to introduction of wood blocks for printing.

AD **704**   Oldest printed work: Korean scroll or *sutra*.

AD **765**   Japan: first pictorial block printing.

AD **780**   Japan: earliest printing.

AD **868**   China: Earliest printed book, unbound, *Diamond Sutra*, Buddhist scripture.

between 1040 and 1050   China: first movable type by Pi Cheng.

1392   Korea: first type-foundry.

early 15th century   Germany: First wood block.

mid 15th century   First woodblock books.

c. **1455**   Earliest mechanically printed book: 42-line Gutenberg Bible, printed in Mainz, Germany by Johann Henne zum Genzfleisch zur Laden, called 'zu Gutenberg' (*c.* 1398–*c.* 1468).

1457   Earliest exactly dated printed work: Psalter printed by Johann Fust and Peter Schoffer, Gutenberg's assistants.

1465   First printing in Italy at Subiaco.

1470   First printing in France at Scrbonne.

1471   First printing in Holland.

1473/4   Earliest printing in Britain by William Caxton (*c.* 1422–91): *History of Troy (Recuyell of the Historeys of Troye)*.

1476   Bruges, Belgium: first copper-plate engravings.

mid 15th century   Wooden hand-press.

1495   First book printed in Denmark: a rhymed history.

1508   First book printed in Scotland.

1539   Printing began in Mexico City – probably first Trans-atlantic press.

1564   *The Apostle*, first printed book in Russia: on French paper.

1638   Printing-press established at Cambridge, Massachusetts: first in North America.

1710   First English copyright came into force. Three-colour printing invented by J C Le Blon (1667–1741).

1798   German Alois Senefelder (1771–1835) invented lithography: printing from flat stone bed. Earl Stanhope: wooden printing-press replaced by metal one.

1798   First lithography.

1800   First all-iron press, Earl Stanhope.

1814   First power-driven press, two-cylinder: Frederic Koenig. It made 1100 impressions per hour.

between 1815 and 1816   First perfector: by Koenig.

1827   First four-cylinder press put in for *The Times*.

1851   First rotary press (curved printing plates).

1851   USA: first platen.

1854   First half-tone process in Vienna.

1875   Offset lithography: William Barclay.

1880   First ever half-tone in the New York *Daily Graphic*.

1904   First Offset-litho printing press (paper): rotary machine built for Eastern Lithographic Co by Ira Rubel of Nutley, JJ.

1907   First silk-screen printing process in Great Britain by Samuel Simon, Manchester.

1908   First Offset-litho printing press in Great Britain.

Fourteenth-century Chinese
Ming Blue and White bottle.
(Sotheby & Co) (see page 171)

Gold snuff-box made about 1760
and sold at Sotheby's on 10 June
1974 for £86000.
(Sotheby & Co) (see page 172)

CHAPTER 10

MISCELLANEA

Just as the Customs tariff provides for the imposition of duties on goods not elsewhere specified, just as the agenda for a meeting usually makes provision for Any Other Business, so a book of this kind needs a chapter for those aspects of the business world that cannot properly be accommodated in the other chapters. The chapter might also have been called, in the Spanish fashion, *olla podrida*. One dictionary defines this as 'any incongruous mixture or miscellaneous collection' in addition to the more usual meaning of 'a Spanish mixed stew or hash of meat and vegetables'; this, as visitors to Spain know, can be most appetising.

Agricultural shows and societies

The **Royal Dublin Society** has been called the oldest surviving agricultural institution of any kind in the British Isles.

The following table lists some of the oldest institutions in this field:

Royal Dublin Society	1731
Royal Society of Arts	1754
Brecknockshire Agricultural Society	1755
Wolsingham Show	(?) 1763
Manchester Agricultural Society	1767
Bath and West Society	1777
Royal Highland and Agricultural Society of Scotland	1784
First Board of Agriculture	1793
Smithfield Club	1798
Farmers' Club	1842
Rothamsted Experimental Station	1843

Some people may be surprised to find Manchester figuring prominently in this list.

Yet the **Manchester Agricultural Society** was founded in 1767, as the Agricultural Society for the Hundred of Salford, ten years earlier than the Bath and West Society, which has frequently been called the oldest agricultural society in England. The Manchester Agricultural Society held its first show, in St Ann's Square, Manchester, in 1768 (see illustration, page 162). As a result of a series of mergers, the Manchester Agricultural Society now forms part of the Royal Lancashire Agricultural Society, whose Bicentenary Show was held at Blackpool in 1967.

The date of the first **Wolsingham Show** is uncertain. In a show catalogue it has been described as 'England's oldest Show'. Professor W L Burn, who was Professor of History at Durham University and also Chairman of the Wolsingham and Wear Valley Agricultural Society from 1947 to 1950, wrote a pamphlet entitled *How Old is Wolsingham Show?* in which he reached the conclusion that 'there was evidence to support the theory that the Show was founded in 1763 and reorganized in or about 1806', although he admits that 'the evidence is scanty and conflicting'.

The history of the **Brecknockshire Agricultural Society** has been told at length by Henry Edmunds in *Brycheiniog* (Volume II, 1956, and Volume III, 1957).

One society at least had been founded even before the **Royal Dublin Society**. This was the splendidly named **The Honourable the Society of Improvers in the Knowledge of Agriculture in Scotland,** which was founded in Edinburgh in 1723 by certain noblemen and gentlemen. The Honourable Society of Improvers does not appear to have survived the 'deluge' of 1745.

The Royal Society of Arts (founded in 1754) inspired at least one similar society on the Continent. This was the grandiloquently named **Königlich Gross-Britannische und Kurfürstlich Braunschweigisch-Lüneburgische Landwirtschafts-Gesellschaft.** Its Charter was promulgated in Celle, in what was then the Electorate of Hanover, on 4 June 1764 the birthday of the Elector of Hanover, George Ludwig, known also as King George III of England. The interest taken by 'Farmer George' in agricultural affairs is well known. The King assured the new society of his protection, and signed the Letters Patent for it on 29 May 1764.

The **Philadelphia Society for Promoting Agriculture** was founded in 1785, four years before the Constitution of the United States was adopted. The key man in the founding of the Society was John Beale Bordley, a friend of Benjamin Franklin.

Age and size do not always go together. The **Royal Agricultural Winter Fair** held annually in Toronto is said to be 'the world's largest indoor agricultural exhibition'. The Fair was established in 1922 'to serve as the Show Window of Canadian Agriculture'. According to the account of the 1974 exhibition that appeared in the *Daily Telegraph* of 16 November 1974, the show featured 3000 exhibitors and included 17000 entries. Princess Anne and her husband, Captain Mark Phillips, opened the show, which attracted an attendance of about 300000.

Arms and armour

In 1972 a Louis XIII flintlock antique long gun was sold at Sotheby's for £125000. In 1974 a 15th-century tilting helm was sold for £22000. Both of these were world records.

St Ann's Square, Manchester – site of the Manchester Agricultural Society's first show, 1768. *(Royal Lancashire Agricultural Society)*

Bargains

In 1626 a Dutchman, Peter Minuit, bought **Manhattan Island** from the Indians for a miscellaneous collection of goods valued at 60 guilders, or about $24. It must be worth a good deal more now.

Less than two centuries later, in 1803, President Thomas Jefferson bought **Louisiana** from the Emperor Napoleon and thereby doubled the size of the United States at a stroke. The transaction involved the purchase of some 828 000 miles² (more than 2 million km²) at a cost of $27 267 622, or just over $30 a mile². The original Louisiana Purchase Treaty could be seen in the British Museum in the autumn of 1975 as one of the exhibits in the exhibition 'The World of Franklin and Jefferson' that had been arranged in connection with the bicentenary celebrations of American independence in the UK.

Later in the same century, in 1867, the Secretary of State, W H Seward, bought **Alaska** from the Tsar of Russia for a mere $7 200 000, thereby acquiring for the United States a further 586 400 miles² (just over 1½ million km²) of territory, at a cost of about $12 a mile². This transaction was much criticised at the time, and the newly-acquired territory was nicknamed 'Seward's Folly'.

Beware of imitations

A notice or *Avertissement* issued in Danzig in 1776 by the makers of **Danzig Goldwasser** and other liqueurs (see page 49) warned their customers that the products of the distillery were being imitated, not only in Danzig but also elsewhere. Customers were advised to look for the firm's sign and signature on the bottle. (See illustration opposite.)

Board of Trade

Sir Hubert Llewellyn Smith, once the Permanent Secretary of the Board of Trade, wrote a history of his Department which appeared in 1928. He pointed out that the Board of Trade differed from most other Departments in being neither responsible for certain functions of the once one and indivisible Secretary

Avertissement.

Unsere Liqueure, distillieret in der Fabrique unter dem Zeichen des Lachßes

mit einem doppelten, übereinander gelegeten Dreyecke versehen, welches die folgenden Buchstaben I.W.L. enthält, sind seit vielen Jahren in gantz Europa, ebenso in anderen Provintzen und Ländern höchlichst geschätzet. Sie sind bißher in ohngefähr alle Länder verschicket worden. Nun ward uns kund, daß sowol in der Stadt Dantzig, als ausserhalb andere itzt unsere Petschaft und Zeichen benutzen und in der Weise nicht nur viele Menschen betrügen, insonderheit dabey auch unsere Fabrique in ein schlechtes Licht setzen. Deshalb sey allen und im allgemeinen zur Beurtheilung das ächte Siegel dienlich, mit welchem wir unsere Flaschen zeichnen, wie auch unsere Schrifft mit den zwey übereinander gelegeten Dreyecken. Giebt es bey diesen etwan nur den kleinsten Unterscheid, dann soll der Innhalt als unächt und gefälscht erkannt werden und dieß nicht für unser rechtmäßiges Product.

Gedruckt in Dantzig bey Johann Emanuel Friedrich Müller 1776

'Beware of imitations' – notice issued by the makers of Danzig Goldwasser in 1776

of State, nor a statutory body such as the old Boards of Agriculture and Education. In one form or another, from 1622 on, the Board of Trade had been 'an emanation from or a committee of the King's Privy Council'.

King James I, in 1621, directed the Privy Council to 'take into their consideration the true causes of the decay of trade and scarcity of coyne within the Kingdom and to consult of the meanes for removing of these inconveniencies'.

The Council set up a committee to collect evidence, and in 1622 a new committee was set up, which became a standing body to advise the Privy Council on trade matters. Responsibility for 'the good of all Foreign Plantations and Factories belonging to this Commonwealth' was added in 1649.

In 1650 a Committee for Trade and Plantations was appointed. Charles II appointed separate Councils for Trade and for Plantations, but these were united in 1672 in a Standing Council for Trade and Plantations.

Chambers of Commerce

Whitaker's Almanack used to contain a section dealing with Chambers of Commerce in different parts of the world. According to the 1951 edition, easily the oldest Chamber of Commerce in the world was the one at **Marseille,** dating from 1650.

Next in order of foundation, according to *Whitaker*, were the Chambers of Commerce at **Glasgow** and **Dublin,** (both from 1783) then came **Edinburgh** (1785), **Belfast** (1796) and **Birmingham** (1813).

The Chamber of Commerce at Marseille, which had been said to be the first Chamber of Commerce (under such title), disappeared after the 1952 edition, and the whole section last appeared in 1955. According to the 1952

The Department of Trade and Industry, Victoria Street, London. *(Department of Trade and Industry)*

The Board of Trade, Whitehall, 1814

edition, however, the first British Chamber of Commerce was the **Jersey** Chamber, dating from 1768, followed by Glasgow, Belfast and Dublin, all dating from 1783.

It would appear, however, that *Whitaker* had overlooked the **New York Chamber of Commerce,** a somewhat unexpected holder of a Royal Charter and the oldest Chamber of Commerce in the USA. It was founded as long ago as 1768 and received its original Charter from George III in 1770. It would thus appear to rank second only to the Marseille Chamber of Commerce in the matter of age.

Cigars

The first known date at which Havana cigars were imported into Britain was 1796. The importers were **Fribourg and Treyer,** of the Haymarket, London (see page 97).

Coins

On 26 November 1974, a Queen Anne five-guinea piece was sold at Sotheby's for £26 000, a record price for an English coin.

Companies of various kinds

The **New River Company** is the oldest incorporated company in the UK, founded by Royal Charter in 1619.

The company was formed to give London its first 'laid-on' water-supply. In 1904 it sold out to the Metropolitan Water Board and in 1974 London Merchant Securities made a £4.6 million cash offer for the ordinary shares and convertible loan stock in the Company. It is one of the few companies to have a Governor instead of a Chairman.

According to the *Guinness Book of Records*, the oldest company in the world is the **Faversham Oyster Fishery Company,** referred to in the Faversham Oyster Fishing Act 1930 as existing 'from time immemorial', i.e. from before 1189.

The Act of 1930 was passed in order to enable those men of Faversham who enjoyed certain rights akin to rights of common with regard to oyster-beds in the river to come together in order to sell these rights to a London firm of fish-merchants. These rights had existed 'since time immemorial', but the company can hardly be regarded as a 'business' existing through the centuries in our sense of the term.

It is arguable that the association of the men of Faversham should be treated as a Guild, rather than as a commercial company, at any rate for the period up to 1930. It is significant that the long title of the 1930 Act begins 'An Act to incorporate and confer powers upon the Faversham Oyster Fishery Company . . .'.

Another indication of the antiquity of England's oyster-fisheries was given by a report in the *Daily Mail* of 20 November 1965. A man who had been accused of stealing oysters from the Helford River, in Cornwall, invoked Magna Carta in his defence. The oyster-fishery was leased to MacFisheries by the Duchy of Cornwall but the defending solicitor argued that the Crown's right to grant exclusive fishing rights in tidal waters at will had been lost when King John signed (*sic*) the Charter in 1215.

Another answer to the question about the oldest company was provided by the *Board of Trade Journal* of 14 November 1958. This issue carried a report of a lecture by Sir Frank Lee (then its Permanent Secretary) on the work of the Board of Trade and contained a picture in which 'an official at the Registration Branch examines the original registration of the oldest company in existence'. This relates to the Berwick Corn Exchange Limited, registered in 1856, which is No 43 on the books and the oldest existing company registered under the Companies Acts. In this context the word 'company' is clearly used in the narrow sense of a body registered under the Companies Acts of the UK.

The present series of company registration numbers started at No 1 in 1856. No 10000 was registered in 1875 and No 100000 was incorporated in 1908. There are now less than 300 live companies on the register with numbers under 10000.

The Hudson's Bay Company, otherwise known as 'The Company of Adventurers of England Trading into Hudson's Bay', was incorporated by Royal Charter of Charles II on 2 May 1670. Like the New River Company it is headed by a Governor. It held its 301st Annual General Court (the equivalent of its Annual General Meeting) at Beaver Hall in London on 28 May 1970, the year in which it celebrated its 300th anniversary. In 1970, too, the company was continued as a Canadian corporation, and its headquarters were transferred from London to Winnipeg. The old Annual General Court is now called, more prosaically, the Annual General Meeting. (See also 'Furs', page 144.)

An advertisement in *The Times* of 26 February 1968 referred to the company as 'the world's oldest chartered trading company', but this is open to challenge (see pages 82, 101 and below).

Some people may be surprised to discover how many chartered companies there are. Sir Russell Kettle, in his history of the accountants Deloittes (*Deloitte & Company 1845–1956*, published in 1958) said that his firm had, as clients, no less than six corporations still operating under Royal Charter. In addition to the Hudson's Bay Company, these were the **Russia Company** (1553), **London Assurance** (1720), the **Bank of Ireland** (1783), the **P and O** shipping line (1840), and the **Chartered Bank** (1853).

To these we might add the Bank of England (1694), the Bank of Scotland (1695), the Royal Exchange Assurance (which received its charter on 22 June 1720, the same day as the London Assurance just mentioned), the Royal Bank of Scotland (1727), the Carron Company of Falkirk (1773) and the Falkland Islands Company (1851).

The **Russia** or **Muscovy Company** was founded in 1553 (i.e. well over a century before the Hudson's Bay Company) with the splendid title of 'The Mystery and Company of Merchant Adventurers for the Discovery of Regions, Dominions and places unknown' and a Charter was granted in 1554. The first Governor was Sebastian Cabot.

Although the company's trading privileges have been in abeyance for the past two centuries, it still remains a corporation especially interested in Russia, and it devotes its income to charitable purposes.

We might, therefore, conclude that, at least before its move to Canada, the Hudson's Bay Company was the oldest chartered trading company in these islands that was still trading but that it was not the oldest chartered trading company *tout court* nor was it the 'world's' oldest chartered trading company.

Conglomerates

The **International Telephone and Telegraph Corporation** (ITT), with headquarters in New York, is America's largest conglomerate (and, presumably, the world's). Its assets exceed $10000 million.

Corkscrews

A brass corkscrew was sold at Sotheby's for £160 on 2 October 1974, a world record price for such an item.

Corporations

The **American Telephone and Telegraph Company,** with assets of more than $74 billion, has been called the largest *privately owned corporation* in the world. The word 'privately' is to be understood as meaning 'not Governmentally'.

Customs and Excise

The first Board of Customs was appointed by King Charles II on 27 September 1671.

Sir Louis Petch, the Chairman of the Board in 1971, claimed that 'the framework of organisation of an operational Department under a Board of Commissioners has not since been disturbed'. He went on to say: 'Indeed, we trace our lineage back to evidence of Customs collection in the Port of London under the Kings of Mercia, and for as long as men can remember there has been a Customs House on or near this spot in the City of London'.

The kingdom of Mercia had been formed 'by the beginning of the seventh century' (Arthur Bryant, *The Story of England*, page 62) and lasted until AD 825. While the Customs do not, therefore, appear to claim a link with the period of the Roman occupation, unlike the Royal Mint (see page 77), they certainly have a claim to rank among the oldest Government Departments.

Employment, Department of

Shortly before the Second World War, in 1939, the old Ministry of Labour became the Ministry of Labour and National Service. Its dodecasyllabic title was longer than that of any other wartime Department, but about 1960 it reverted to its old style. It was later retitled 'Department of Employment and Productivity', with its 13 syllables. If productivity means making two syllables grow where only one grew before, then there is productivity for you!

With the change in the title of the Department, Mrs Barbara Castle was transformed from Minister of Labour, with six syllables, to Secretary of State for Employment and Productivity, with 16. Subject to verification, she thereby became the longest titled Minister in the history of Parliament.

Export markets

The total number of separately administered territories in the world is 225. This would suggest that the maximum number of export markets open to manufacturers or merchants is 224, as sales in the home market would not count.

Jesse Hart Rosdail, the most travelled man in the world, has visited 220 of the 225

Hallmarking – Platinum medal awarded by the Institute of Metals to Professor Robert Hutton – first piece of platinum to be hallmarked. *(The Worshipful Company of Goldsmiths)* (see page 168)

countries or territories, the exceptions being North Korea, North Vietnam, China, Cuba and the French Antarctic Territories.

Cuba, by a curious coincidence, was also mentioned in an advertisement for **Black & White whisky** that appeared in the issue of *Vision* for January 1972. It was headed 'You can count the countries that don't drink Black & White on one hand', and went on to name Albania, Cuba and Mongolia. The whisky was said to be drunk in 168 countries, which would make 167 export markets, but it would need a multi-fingered hand to stretch from 168 to 225.

The **Molins company,** precision engineers, makers of cigarette-making and packaging machinery, advertise that they trace with 121 countries. Sixty per cent of the world's cigarettes are made or packed by Molins machines.

The contributors to the **New Encyclopaedia Britannica,** which appeared in 1974, came from 131 different countries.

Guinness is brewed in 19 countries, and sold in more than 120 others.

The elevators and other products made by the **Otis Elevator Company** are said to operate in 141 countries. The company make electric trucks, buses and automatic hospital service vehicles as well as lifts, escalators and 'Trav-O-Lators'. Every nine days, they claim, Otis move about 3 552 000 000 people, which is comparable with the entire population of this planet (4 000 000 000 in January 1976).

The credit cards of the **Diners' Club** can be used in 150 countries.

The catalogue of **Thompson and Morgan,** the seedsmen of Ipswich, is sent to 154 countries.

First factory

The *Daily Telegraph* of 2 December 1974 reported that a 1702 silk-mill on the banks of the River Derwent in Derby, 'the world's first factory', had just been opened as an industrial museum.

More about this factory can be found in Peter Mathias's book on *The First Industrial Nation,* which is sub-titled *An Economic History of Britain 1700–1914.*

Guilds or Gilds

The exact age of the **Worshipful Company of Weavers,** the oldest of all the London Livery Companies, is unknown. The earliest mention of the company or gild is to be found in a Pipe Roll of the Exchequer in 1130.

Another London company, the **Ancient Company of Longbowstringmakers** or Stringers 'seems to have come into existence as the result of a petition presented . . . to the Mayor and Aldermen on 2 August 1416'. The history of the **Worshipful Company of Fletchers,** a company by prescription, goes back to 1370 or 1371.

A comparative newcomer to this scene, the **Worshipful Company of Wheelwrights** of the City of London, received their Charter from King Charles II on 3 February 1670.

Women were admitted to the Freedom of the Wheelwrights' Company from the

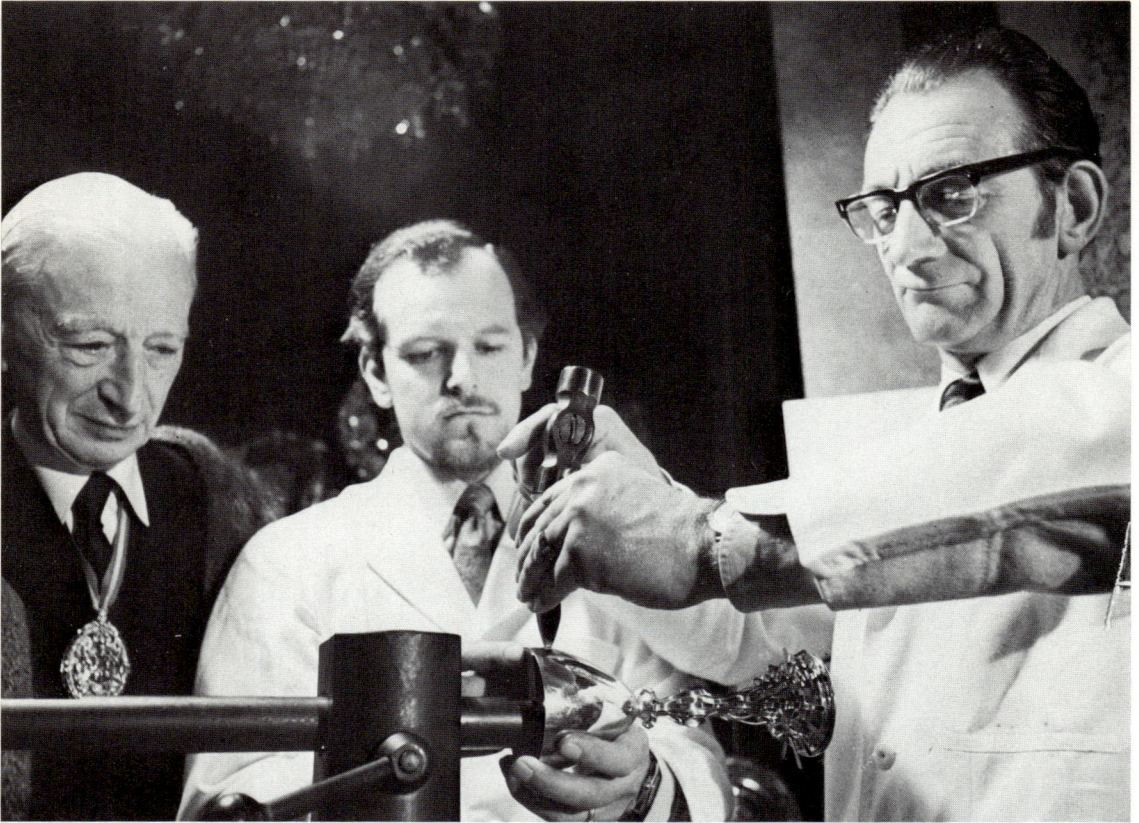

Platinum cup and cover designed and made by Miss Jocelyn Burton, the second piece of platinum to be hallmarked, 2 January 1975. *(Keystone Press Agency Ltd)*

beginning. Sad to record, the last to be admitted was Jeanette Stoffel, who was made free by patrimony in 1838.

Hallmarking

The hallmarking of gold and silver has been called the oldest form of consumer protection.

As early as the year 1238, the Mayor and Aldermen of London were to select 'six good men and true to see that no gold or silver articles were made of metal inferior to that of the coinage'. In 1300, by an Act of Edward I (28 Ed I), the Goldsmiths' Company of London was put on a sound basis and the leopard's head ('une teste de leopart') was selected as the standard mark. In 1327, during the reign of Edward III, the Goldsmiths' Company was incorporated by Charter.

The Hallmarking Act of 1973 made it

compulsory to hallmark platinum. The Act came into force on 1 January 1975, but, New Year's Day being a public holiday, the marking of the first piece of platinum did not take place until the following day. At a ceremony in Goldsmiths' Hall on 2 January 1975, the first platinum piece to be assayed was, very appropriately, the platinum medal awarded by the Institute of Metals to Professor Robert Hutton, for many years the Chairman of the Assay Office Committee of the Goldsmiths' Company. The second piece was a cup and cover designed and made by Miss Jocelyn Burton. (See illustrations, pages 167 and 168.)

Hotel sale

The hotel known as **Caesar's Palace** at Las Vegas was sold for $84 million. This was said to be the highest price ever paid for a hotel anywhere. It was at the Caesar's Palace tennis pavilion that Jimmy Connors defeated Rod Laver on 2 February 1975, in their much-publicised $100000 winner-take-all match.

Losses

The decision of the **Lockheed Aircraft Corporation** to write off $800 million of 'Tristar' aircraft development costs in 1974 represented the largest such reduction in assets in American corporate history (see page 127).

The **British Post Office** made a gallant attempt to capture what might be described as the red riband of the business world when it reported a loss of more than £307 million (about $650 million) in July 1975. A few days earlier the **electricity industry** had reported a more modest deficit of £257 million.

The Japanese were evidently determined not to be left out of the contest. In August 1975 the **Kohjin Company,** with interests in textiles and real estate, was said to be on the verge of the largest bankruptcy proceedings since Japan emerged from the Second World War. The Ministry of International Trade and Industry acknowledged that the company had unpaid total debts of about £336 million.

Mass production

Henry Ford is sometimes regarded as 'the Father of Mass Production', but its history goes much further back.

Garrett Mattingly, in *Renaissance Diplomacy*, described the printed book as 'the first standardized, mass-produced commodity'. The concept of mass production has, however, come to mean something more than production in mass.

According to Kenneth Hudson's *Industrial Archaeology of Southern England,* the first mass-production factory in the world was established at Southampton 200 years ago by a family named **Taylor** who pioneered ship's block manufacture by this method.

Another man who has been credited with the introduction or invention of mass production is **Eli Whitney** (1765–1825), who invented the cotton 'gin' for cleaning cotton about 1793. It was, however, at a later stage of his career, in his gun shop at Whitneyville, that he initiated the use of interchangeable parts in mass production. It was this use of exactly equal and, therefore, interchangeable parts that some see as the crucial element in mass production as we know it today.

In 1808 **Sir Marc Isambard Brunel** (1769–1849) perfected a method for making ship's blocks (pulleys) by mechanical means, rather than by hand. The actual construction of the machinery for the ship's block factory was effected by **Henry Maudslay** (1771–1831), the son of a workman at the Woolwich Arsenal, who was apprenticed to Joseph Bramah, the lock-manufacturer (see page 77).

In 1799 Brunel put his plans before the British Government and his machines were installed at Portsmouth Dockyard. This system of 43 machines, run by ten men, produced pulleys which were superior in quality and consistency to those previously hand-made by more than 100 men. In addition, production was much higher. This installation was one of the earliest examples of completely mechanised production.

Nationalised industries

'The history of public enterprise in the UK can be traced back to Pepys or even to King Alfred.' So writes David Peirson in his book *The Major Corporations: A Statutory Analysis,* published in 1974 by the Royal Institute of Public Administration.

The conjunction of Pepys and King Alfred suggests that the author had the building of ships in mind. The Naval Historical Library of the Ministry of Defence say that **Portsmouth** can claim to be the oldest of the **Royal Yards.** As early as 1212, King John ordered the Sheriff of Southampton to enclose his docks and storehouses at Portsmouth by a wall. In 1496, Henry VII ordered a dry-dock at Portsmouth, the first one in England. It was completed the same year, and the first ship to enter it was the 600-ton *Sovereign.*

The yard at Portsmouth was used for ship-building as well as for repairs. It remained the only royal yard until the foundation of yards at Deptford (1517), Woolwich (1518) and Chatham (1547).

(See also 'Royal Mint', page 77; 'Customs', page 166; 'Post Office', page 170.)

MILESTONES IN NATIONALISATION SINCE 1945

1946	Bank of England Act.
1946	Coal Industry Nationalisation Act.
1946	Civil Aviation Act.
1947	Electricity Act.
1947	Transport Act.
1948	Gas Act.
1949	Iron and Steel Act (repealed in 1953).
1949	Airways Corporations Act.
1953	Air Corporation Act.
1953	Iron and Steel Act (denationalisation).

1953	Transport Act.
1954	Atomic Energy Authority Act.
1957	Electricity Act.
1962	Transport Act.
1965	Airports Authority Act.
1967	Steel Act.
1968	Transport Act.
1969	Post Office Act.
1969	Transport (London) Act.
1971	Civil Aviation Act.
1972	Gas Act.

Old customers

Barrett and Son of Cambridge opened a new china and glassware shop in St Mary's Passage, in July 1974. Simon Barrett had established the business in 1782, when he began trading with Josiah Wedgwood and other leading pottery-manufacturers. On the occasion of the opening of the new shop, Josiah Wedgwood and Sons announced in the *Cambridge Evening News* that they had traded with Barrett and Son for over 175 years.

Other long-standing connections between customers and suppliers have already been mentioned (see pages 67–8 and 110 and 111).

Painting

The *Portrait of Juan de Pareja* by Velásquez was sold at Christie's on 27 November 1970 for £2310000. This is the highest price ever bid in a public auction for any painting (see illustration on jacket).

Post Office

During the past 300 years the Post Office has undergone a number of changes in organisation, and even the Government appears to have had difficulty at times in deciding how to classify it.

According to the 1973 edition of *Britain – An Official Handbook,* the Post Office, founded in 1657, 'was set up as a public authority under the Post Office Act 1969, having previously been a government department'.

The 1968 edition of the same work, which was of course issued before the passing of the 1969 Act, described the Post Office in these terms: 'Although at present a government department it is in effect a nationalised industry.' It was in 1657 that an Act of Parliament was passed under the Protectorate of Cromwell which declared that 'there shall be one general post-office and one officer, styled the Postmaster General of England and Comptroller of the Post Office'. The GPO, therefore, as it used to be called, had a run of about 300 years before it lost its 'G'.

The 1956 edition of the *Handbook* had described the Post Office as 'the oldest of Britain's nationalised undertakings' and gave its year of origin as 1649, when a Resolution of the House of Commons declared that 'the office of Postmaster is and ought to be in the sole power and disposal of Parliament'.

Whatever the status of the Post Office may be, it is difficult to see how the Post Office could maintain a claim to be senior to the Royal Mint.

The Post Office, as *The Times 1000 (1975–6)* shows, is easily the largest employer among the nationalised industries, its staff then numbering 434065. In 1975 the Post Office achieved a different kind of distinction when it announced a loss of more than £307 million, the biggest loss ever made by a British business, whether nationalised or not. (See also page 169.)

Pottery

On 24 June 1974, a 14th-century Chinese jar was sold at Christie's for 220000 guineas. The price given for the jar was said to be the second highest at auction for a work of art other than a painting. The highest price was the £420000 paid at Sotheby's in April 1974 for an early Ming blue and white bottle.

Price-rings

One of the earliest common-price arrangements or price-rings in this country was concerned with candles. In *Leet Jurisdiction in the City of Norwich during the XIIIth and XIVth Centuries* (edited by W Hudson, 1892) we may read how, in the 28th year of the reign of Edward I (1299/1300), the **chandlers of Norwich** appeared before the Leet Court, which convicted 'all the chandlers for making an agreement amongst themselves – to wit, that none of them should sell a pound of candle at less than another'. Eight persons were fined, some of them one shilling and some of them two shillings. One of them was a woman.

A slightly earlier case is to be found in the *Calendar of Early Mayor's Court Rolls of the City of London* (edited by A H Thomas, 1924). This shows that, on 22 May 1298, in the Court of the Mayor of London:

'John de Holebourne, Walter the cooper of St. Nicholas Lane, William Styward, John le Tankardmaker, and other coopers were summoned at the instance of Adam Snow, cooper, for contempt of the King and Mayor, in that they made an ordinance that no one should sell a hoop [*circulus*] formerly sold at ½d. and ¾d, for less than 1d. and so concerning other hoops, under a penalty, which ordinance was against the dignity of the Crown and to the grave damage of the Commonalty of the City'.

In August they paid fines varying from 5s to 6d 'for trespass against the King.'

Price stability

The Oxford University Press (see page 153), like other publishing-houses, has a stock of printed sheets waiting to be folded, cut and bound when required. A business as old as this seems, however, to have a different standard of time from others. As the anonymous historian of the Press (page 153 above) relates: 'From these vaults was drawn into the

The London coopers – extract from the Early Mayor's Court Rolls of the City of London, 1298 (see *Price-rings*). *(Guildhall Library, London)*

upper air, in 1907, the last copy of Wilkins's *Coptic New Testament*, published in 1716, the paper hardly dis-coloured and the impression still black and brilliant.' For nearly 200 years this work, which clearly had a limited appeal, had been continuously on sale, always at the price of 12s 6d a copy. The Oxford University Press still had, in 1921, about a dozen copies of a Gothic Gospel published in 1750, but this was a more expensive work, selling at 30s a copy.

Public-house name

Mention should be made of one of the most curiously and yet most splendidly named of all public houses, the **Never Turn Back.**

The Lacon public house at Caister in Norfolk that was opened in June 1957 was given the name *Never Turn Back* as a tribute to the lifeboatmen of Caister who, during a century of service, had saved more lives than any other lifeboat station in the country.

The origin of the name is to be found in a disaster. On 13 November 1901, the Caister lifeboat had been launched, in appalling conditions of gale, rain and heavy seas, to go to the aid of a vessel in distress on the Barber Sands. An hour later the lifeboat was seen, bottom up, near the shore. Nine of the crew lost their lives.

One of the witnesses at the inquest on the victims was James Haylett, aged 78, a former Assistant Coxswain, who had lost several members of his family in the disaster. It was suggested to him that the lifeboatmen had given up their errand as a bad job and turned back. The old man replied, in words that became world-famous overnight: 'Caister lifeboatmen never turn back.'

Research establishments

The **Royal Observatory** at Greenwich, founded by Charles II in 1675, has been called Britain's oldest and most famous scientific research establishment. The first Astronomer Royal was the Reverend John Flamsteed (1646–1719), who was under 30 years of age when appointed.

A Royal Warrant of 4 March 1675 appointed Flamsteed 'Astronomical observator'. A new observatory, in Greenwich Park, was hastily run up from a design of Sir Christopher Wren at a cost of £520, 'realised by the sale of spoilt gunpowder'.

Snuff-bottles

A Chinese enamelled glass snuff-bottle was sold at Sotheby's on 24 June 1975 for £4600, which was a world record price for a snuff-bottle.

Snuff-boxes

On 10 June 1974, a gold snuff-box encrusted with diamonds and semi-precious hardstones, which had been made about 1760 for Frederick the Great, King of Prussia, was sold at Sotheby's for £86000.

Less than three weeks after the sale of Frederick the Great's snuff-box at Sotheby's a Louis XV chased gold and lapis-lazuli snuff-box made by Justin-Aurèle Meissonier was sold at Christie's for 85000 guineas (£89250).

On 2 December 1974, a gold-mounted

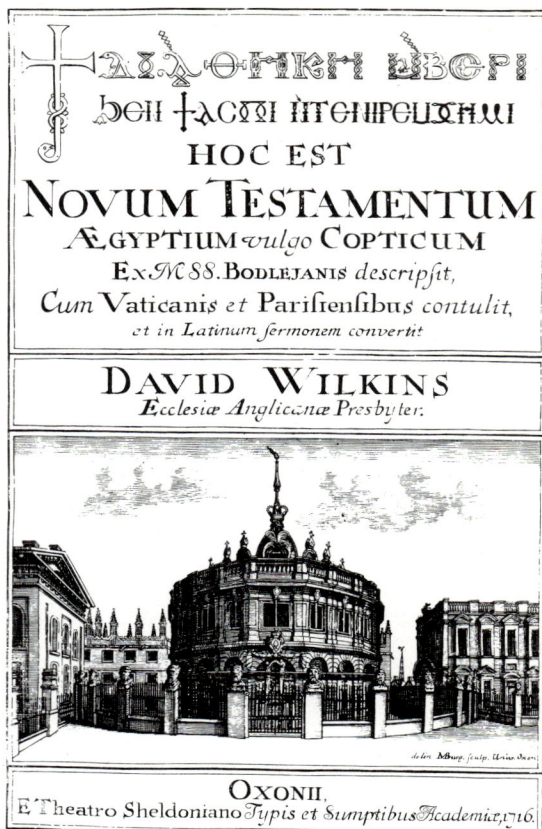

Wilkin's *Coptic New Testament*, 1716 (see *Price stability*). *(Curators of the Bodleian Library, Oxford)*

Meissen snuff-box was sold at Christie's for £15225, a record for a Meissen snuff-box. The box is dated 1741 and may have been given by Frederick the Great, King of Prussia, to the British Ambassador.

Teashops

The first **Lyons'** teashop was opened on 20 September 1894, in Piccadilly. The shop is now a Jolyon restaurant.

Trade Unions

At the time of the Trades Union Congress's Annual Meeting in September 1974, 109 unions were affiliated to the TUC, and they had a total membership of 10022224. At that time the unions with the largest affiliated membership were the Transport and General Workers'

Union, with 1 785 496 members, and the Amalgamated Union of Engineering Workers, with 1 374 866 members. The smallest affiliated unions were the Sheffield Wool Shear Workers' Trade Union, with 19 members, and the Spring Trapmakers' Society, with 90 members.

The National Society of Brushmakers and General Workers claims, apparently without challenge, to have had a longer continuous existence than any other union. It dates from 1747, but the words 'and General Workers' in the title are a recent addition.

Wartime controls

During the Second World War, the Government exercised a rigorous and detailed control over the economic activities of the country. A good idea of the nature of the controls is provided by the *Control of Tins Cans Kegs Drums and Packaging Pails (No 10) Order, 1943*, which was made by the Minister of Supply on 19 August 1943. The text of the Order ran as follows:

1. The Control of Tins Cans Kegs Drums and Packaging Pails (No. 5) Order, 1942, as varied by the Control of Tins Cans Kegs Drums and Packaging Pails (No. 6) Order, 1942, the Control of Tins Cans Kegs Drums and Packaging Pails (No. 7) Order, 1942, the Control of Tins Cans Kegs Drums and Packaging Pails (No. 8) Order, 1942, and the Control of Tins Cans Kegs Drums and Packaging Pails (No. 9) Order, 1942, is hereby further varied in the Third Schedule thereto (which is printed at p. 2 of the printed (No. 6) Order), in 'Part II. Commodities other than Food' by substituting for the reference '2A' therein, the reference '2A(1)', and by deleting therefrom the reference '2B'.

2. This Order shall come into force on the 25th day of August, 1943; and may be cited as the Control of Tins Cans Kegs Drums and Packaging Pails (No. 10) Order, 1943, and this Order and the Control of Tins Cans Kegs Drums and Packaging Pails (Nos. 5–9) Orders, 1942, may be cited together as the Control of Tins Cans Kegs Drums and Packaging Pails (Nos. 5–10) Orders, 1942–3.

For those readers who did not immediately grasp the purport of the Order, an Explanatory Note appended to it contained the information that the Order enabled tinplate to be used for tobacco- and snuff-tins other than cutter-lid tobacco-tins. (There had evidently been a slight easing in the supply of tinplate to justify this modest relaxation, but the time had not yet come to allow tinplate to be used for such frivolities as cutter-lid tobacco-tins.)

The cost of the Order, including the Explanatory Note, was 1d net.

Oldest Watch

A Saxon 10th-century pocket sundial found at Canterbury in 1938 when the Cloister Garth was lowered has been called the oldest watch in the world, at least in the English-speaking world (see illustration below).

The oldest portable clockwork time-keeper is one made of iron by Peter Henlein (or Hele) in Nürnberg (Nuremberg), Bavaria, Germany, in about 1504 and now in the Memorial Hall, Philadelphia, Pennsylvania, USA. The earliest

Oldest watch in the world. *(Painting by Nowell Edwards)*

Jack Sales of Hill Farm. Limpenhoe, Norfolk, aged 90, on the farm where he worked for 83 years (see *Working lives*)

wrist-watches were those of Jacquet-Droz and Leschot of Geneva, Switzerland, dating from 1790.

Working lives

In 1950, the De La Rue Company gave a luncheon in honour of their storeman, Mr H Adkins, who had then completed 75 years of unbroken service with them. On that occasion they challenged the National Association of Manufacturers in the United States to find a workman with a better record, and the Americans managed to find a textile worker in South Carolina with 77 years of service to his credit.

Both these records had in fact been surpassed a few years previously by Mr J Wyatt, who entered the service of a Bristol solicitor in 1865 and remained in the same office until 1947. But even Mr Wyatt, with his 82 years of service, must apparently yield the palm to Mr Jack Sales, of Limpenhoe, Norfolk. This veteran died in 1950, at the age of 91, after working on the same farm for no fewer than 83 years. (See illustration above.)

But what about the ladies? Mrs Bland, of Kettering, completed 74 years in the employ of Wallis and Linnell Limited in 1952. And Miss Polly Gadsby, as readers of the *Guinness Book of Records* will recall, has been credited with the longest recorded working career in one job in Britain. This remarkable lady started work with Archibald Turner and Company, of Leicester, at the age of nine. In 1932, after 86 years' service, and aged 95, she was still at her bench wrapping elastic.

Work in the textile industry appears to be conducive to longevity. Mr Theodore C Taylor, who died in 1952 at the age of 102, spent 86 years with the firm of J T and J Taylor Limited, woollen manufacturers, of Batley, Yorkshire, including 56 years as Chairman and Managing Director.

Service of a different kind was given by a gentleman named Matthew Lakin. A memorial tablet in the parish church of Tetney, near Grimsby, records that he was born on 18 October 1801, died on 15 January 1899, and was 'one of the regular bell-ringers of Tetney for 84 years'.

For sheer continuity in some kind of employment the record of Admiral of the Fleet Sir Provo W P Wallis would be hard to beat. This remarkable character was born in April 1791, 'entered in the books of the Royal Navy on 1st May, 1795', went to sea in 1804 and died in February 1892. He had, therefore, been 'in the books' (if not always in the ships) of the Royal Navy for nearly 97 years. The only comparable achievement so far brought to notice, which might well stand as a record for a *non*-working life, is that of Miss Millicent Barclay. As the *Guinness Book of Records* informs us, this lady became eligible for a pension from the Madras Military Fund from the day she was born until she married. When she died, unmarried, on 26 October 1969, she had drawn her pension for 97 years and 3 months.

CHAPTER 11

THE TERCENTENARIANS

In 1967, when **Hedges and Butler,** the wine-merchants of Regent Street, London, were celebrating their 300th anniversary (see page 39) they gave a luncheon on 18 October at which no fewer than 22 businesses with a history or tradition going back beyond 1667 were represented.

The luncheon took place in the 17th-century cellars below the shop, and there might have been more than twice as many businesses represented among the guests if the cellars had been large enough to accommodate them.

Hedges and Butler now forms part of Charrington Vintners Limited, which in turn is controlled by Bass Charrington Limited. The assembly, therefore, included representatives of the Bass and Charrington breweries, although they were comparative youngsters in such a company, mustering only 400 years between them. It was estimated that the assembly in that small cellar represented about 8000 years of business history. A full list of the participants in this remarkable and, as far as is known, unprecedented, gathering is given on page 177.

The Prime Minister, Mr Harold Wilson, was the guest of honour. He occupied, very appropriately, the chair that bore a plaque recording that Mr Gladstone sat in the same chair when he called at the shop to place his orders for wine. A second plaque now records that it was also occupied by Mr Wilson, and there was space for a further plaque on which to record the name of the distinguished guest who would occupy the chair on the occasion of the 400th anniversary. It has in fact been allocated to Mr Edward Heath (see illustration, page 59).

On the last day of the following year, 1968, Mr Richard Early, the Chairman of **Charles Early and Marriott (Witney) Limited,** of Witney, Oxfordshire, issued a challenge in the PHS diary of *The Times.* The Early family would be commemorating 300 years of blanket-weaving in Witney in 1969, and Mr Early offered to entertain in Witney the heads of any other firms that had been in the control of a single family for 300 years or more.

The heads of three family businesses with a history going back beyond 1669 took up the invitation, and in October 1969, Mr Early entertained them to lunch at the Old Swan Hotel, Minster Lovell. His three guests were Mr James C Kenyon, Mr Jack Tissiman and Mr Geoffrey D Durtnell.

Mr James Kenyon was the head of **James Kenyon and Son Limited,** industrial textile manufacturers of Bury, Lancashire, who celebrated their own tercentenary in 1964 (see page 63). Mr Kenyon represented the ninth generation of the family to be associated with the business.

Mr Tissiman, of **Tissiman and Sons Limited,** tailors and outfitters, of Bishop's Stortford, Hertfordshire, represented the eleventh generation of the family to be associated with the business that had been carried on in the High Street since 1601 (see page 62).

Mr Durtnell, the Chairman of **R Durtnell and Sons Limited,** of Brasted, near Westerham, in Kent, was the head of a firm that had been 'Builders since 1591' and represented the eleventh generation of his family, still working from the same place as his forebears (see page 71).

As part of the tercentenary celebrations in 1969, the Early firm decided to make an attack on the old speed record for producing a blanket. On 11 June, starting at 4 am, the blanket-makers of Witney clipped 2 hours 16 minutes off the record of 10 hours 27 minutes that had stood for 63 years.

At the end of the luncheon in 1969, Mr Durtnell invited the company to be his guests at Brasted in 1970. Mr Tissiman unfortunately died in September 1970, but Mr Early and Mr Kenyon duly presented themselves in Mr Durtnell's office on 26 October 1970. Mr Durtnell had also invited an old friend, the present writer, to join the party and to act as the Honorary Secretary of what became known as the 'Tercentenarians Club'.

In October 1971 the Club met in Bury as the guests of Mr and Mrs James Kenyon. A new member of the Club was Mr Richard Hoare, of **Hoare's Bank** (see page 109). The bank was due to celebrate its 300th anniversary in 1972 but the Richard Hoare who founded the bank had been apprenticed to a goldsmith in 1665, which was four years before Thomas Early had been apprenticed to a blanket-weaver.

The 1972 meeting of the Club was held at Hoare's Bank in Fleet Street, when Mr Richard Hoare and his wife, the Honourable Frances Hoare, were the hosts.

For the 1973 meeting the Club returned to Witney, and in 1974 the meeting was again held at Brasted. Mr and Mrs Kenyon were the hosts in 1975, when the Club paid its second visit to Lancashire.

In the course of the past few years, the Club has established what might be described as fraternal links with similar tercentenarian businesses in other countries. A list of these businesses is shown below, along with the names of businesses that are, or have been, members of the Club in England. (No potential members have yet appeared in other parts of the UK.)

As far as is known, the next business that might qualify for membership under the 300-year rule is **Firmin and Sons Limited,** dating from 1677 (see page 87). By a slight modification of Mr Richard Early's original stipulation that the *head* of the business today must be a direct descendant of the founder, Bridport-Gundry, the net-makers of Bridport, Dorset, become eligible for membership, as the Gundry branch of the business dates from 1665 and the Gundry family is still represented on the Board (see page 61).

Members of the Tercentenarians' Club and their associates in other lands

John Brooke and Sons Limited, Armitage Bridge Mills, Huddersfield.

R Durtnell and Sons Limited, Brasted, near Westerham, Kent.

Charles Early and Marriott Limited, Witney, Oxfordshire.

Hoare's Bank, Fleet Street, London.

James Kenyon and Son Limited, Bury, Lancashire.

Tissiman and Sons Limited, Bishop's Stortford, Hertfordshire.

Associates in other lands

Pasquier-Desvignes, Saint-Lager en Beaujolais, France – 1420.

William Prym, Stolberg, Germany – 1580.

Kikkoman Shoyu Company Limited, Tokyo, Japan – 1630.

Henri Maire, Arbois, France – 1632.

Hugel et fils, Riquewihr, France – 1639.

Calwer Decken- und Tuchfabriken, Calw, Germany – 1650.

Kronenbourg Brewery, Strasbourg – 1664.

B Metzler seel. Sohn and Company, Frankfurt-am-Main.

The Beretta gun firm, of Gardone, in northern Italy, has the date 1680 on its notepaper, but the family connection probably goes back to a much earlier date.

J E Rhoads and Sons, of Wilmington, Delaware, dates only from the year 1702 but, being a family business and also the oldest business in the USA, is regarded as an honorary tercentenarian.

Tercentenary Luncheon at Hedges and Butler Limited, 18 October 1967

GUESTS:

The Right Honourable Harold Wilson, OBE, MP.

Trevor Lloyd-Hughes, Press Secretary to the Prime Minister.

William Adams and Sons
(Potters) Limited,
Tunstall, Staffs.
Kenneth Cooper,
Managing Director.

John Brooke and Sons Limited,
Huddersfield, Yorks.
E H Brooke,
Chairman.

Cambridge University Press,
London E1.
R W David,
Chief Executive Officer.

Richard Durtnell and Sons,
Brasted, Kent.
G D Durtnell,
Chairman.

John Haig and Company Limited,
London SW1.
J R Cater, MA
Managing Director.

Hay's Wharf Limited,
London SE1.
Sir David H Burnett, Bt, MBE, TD,
Chairman and Managing Director.

James Kenyon and Son Limited,
Bury, Lancs.
C D Kenyon,
Chairman.

Kirkstall Forge Engineering Limited,
Leeds, Yorks.
R F Butler,
Chairman.

Marsh Brothers and
Company Limited,
Rotherham, Yorks.
D C Hill, CBE,
Deputy Managing Director.

Martins Bank Limited,
London EC3.
Sir Cuthbert B Clegg,
Chairman.

W Ottway and Company Limited,
London W13.
G C Ottway,
Chairman.

Oxford University Press,
London W1.
Colin H Roberts,
Secretary to the Delegates.

Pickfords Limited,
London WC1.
H W Elliott, CBE,
Chairman and Managing Director.

Puddefoot, Bowers and
Simonett Limited,
London SE11.
M Carr-Archer,
Chairman

The Royal Mint,
London EC3.
J H James, CB,
Deputy Master and Comptroller.

G W Scott and Sons Limited,
London E14.
J G Giddins,
Director.

Skilbeck Brothers Limited,
London SE15.
R S Skilbeck,
Chairman.

Spink and Son Limited,
London SW1.
Adrian Maynard,
Director.

George Tabor Limited,
London EC3.
Brian A H Tabor,
Joint Managing Director.

Vandome and Hart Limited,
London N1.
W M Priest,
Chairman.

Whitechapel Bell Foundry,
London E1.
William A Hughes,
Joint Managing Director.

Wilton Royal Carpet Factory,
Wilton, Wiltshire.
S H R Clarke,
Chairman.

———

The author of this book

HOSTS:

S R H Williams,
Chairman – Hedges and Butler Limited,
Managing Director – Charrington Vintners Limited.

The Lord Fraser of Lonsdale, CH,
Chairman – Charrington Vintners Limited,
Director – Bass Charrington Limited.

John V Baker,
Managing Director – Hedges and Butler Limited.

H Alan Walker,
Chairman – Bass Charrington Limited.

J B Ll Hill,
Director – Hedges and Butler Limited.

J A P Charrington,
President – Bass Charrington Limited.

Lieutenant-Colonel P L Bradfer-Lawrence, MC,
Director – Bass Charrington Limited.

APPENDIX

CHRONOLOGICAL LISTS

A. British Isles

AD 287	Carausius struck coins in England	*Mint*

ALFRED (871–900)

Continuous history of the Mint begins	*Mint*

HENRY I (1100–1135)

1130	Earliest mention of the Weavers' Company, London	*Guilds*

JOHN (1199–1216)

1200	Kirkstall Forge, Leeds	*Engineering*

EDWARD I (1272–1307)

1298	Minimum-price agreement among London coppers	*Price-rings*
1299/1300	Minimum-price agreement among Norwich chandlers	*Price-rings*
1300	Act of Edward I (28 Ed I) makes Goldsmiths' Company, London, responsible for hallmarking	*Hallmarks*

EDWARD III (1327–77)

1327	Charter of Goldsmiths' Company, London	*Guilds*
1370c.	Fletchers' Company, London	*Guilds*

HENRY V (1413–22)

1416	Longbowstringmakers' Company, London	*Guilds*

HENRY VI (1422–61)

1431	City of London Brewery	*Brewing*

EDWARD IV (1461–83)

1476	Caxton began printing in Westminster	*Printing, etc*

1477	Caxton's first book	
1478	First book printed at Oxford	

HENRY VII (1485–1509)

1488	John G Rathborne and Company, Dublin	*Candles*
1498	Shore Porters' Society of Aberdeen	*Transport*

HENRY VIII (1509–47)

1521	First book printed in Cambridge	*Printing, etc*
1523	Gayner and Son, Thornbury, near Bristol	*Drapers*
1532	Cam Mills, Dursley, Gloucestershire – see also 1887	*Wool*
1534	Royal Charter for Cambridge University Press	*Printing, etc*
1541	'New Mill' in Wooldale, Holme, Yorkshire, leased by Homfray Brooke	*Wool*

MARY I (1553–58)

1553	Russia Company, London	*Companies*
1555	Incorporation of Carters in Leith, Scotland	*Friendly Societies*

ELIZABETH I (1558–1603)

1559	Child's Bank, London	*Banks*
1560	Hurst Gunson Cooper Taber, Witham, Essex	*Seedsmen*
1563	Martins Bank, London	*Banks*
1570	Whitechapel Bell Foundry, London	*Bell-founding*
1580	B Smiths (Thirsk), Thirsk	*Drapers*
1581	Bowes and Bowes, Cambridge	*Booksellers*
1584	Beginning of continuous publication at Cambridge	*Printing, etc*
1585	Beginning of continuous publication at Oxford	*Printing, etc*
1591	R Durtnell and Sons, Brasted, Kent	*Builders*
1600	C Edwards and Son, London	*Sausage casings*
1601	Tissiman and Sons, Bishop's Stortford	*Tailors*

JAMES I (1603–25)

1616	Barclay, Perkins and Company's Anchor Brewery, Southwark	*Brewing*
1619	New River Company, London	*Companies*

1622	Committee of the Privy Council for Trade and (since the Commonwealth) for Foreign Plantations	*Board of Trade*
1623	Hoby and Company, London	*Boot and Shoe-makers*

CHARLES I (1625–49)

1627	John Haig, Windygates, Fifeshire	*Whisky*
1628	Burrup, Mathieson and Company, London	*Printing, etc*
1631	Marsh Brothers and Company, Sheffield	*Engineering*
1634	Tomson and Wotton, Ramsgate, Kent	*Brewing*
1638	C N Kopke and Company, London	*Wine-merchants*
1640	E Lacon and Company, Great Yarmouth	*Brewing*
1640	W Ottway and Company, Ealing	*Scientific instruments*
1642	Lion Brewery, Chester	*Brewing*
1642	Josiah Stallard and Sons, Worcester	*Wine-merchants*

COMMONWEALTH (1649–60)

1650	Davison, Newman and Company, London	*Tea-merchants*
1650	Gosling's Bank, London	*Banks*
1650	Skilbeck Brothers, London	*Drysalters*
1650	Upward and Rich, Newport, Isle of Wight	*Grocers*
1651	Hay's Wharf, London	*Wharfingers*
1652	Pountney and Company, Bristol	*Pottery*
1654	Whiffen and Sons, London	*Chemicals*
1655	Wilton Royal Carpet Factory, Wilton, Wiltshire	*Carpets*
1657	W Adams and Sons, Tunstall	*Pottery*
1657	General Post Office	*Post Office*
1658	Smith's Bank, Nottingham	*Banks*

CHARLES II (1660–85)

1660	Samuel Pepys consults with Mr Hill the 'Instrument Maker'	*Musical instruments*
1660	Vandome and Hart, London	*Weighing-machines*
1661	Garton and King, Exeter	*Ironmongers*
1661	G W Scott and Sons, London	*Basket-making*
1662	Charter of Royal Society, London	
1664	James Kenyon and Son, Bury, Lancashire	*Wool*
1664	J and G Oldfield, York	*Wine-merchants*
1665	Joseph Gundry and Company, Bridport, Dorset	*Nets*
1665	(March) *Philosophical Transactions of the Royal Society*	*Newspapers*
1665	(November) *London Gazette*	*Newspapers*
1666	Christopher and Company, London	*Wine-merchants*
1666	Spink and Son, London	*Art-dealers*
1666	Truman, Hanbury, Buxton and Company	*Brewing*
1667	Hedges and Butler, London	*Wine-merchants*
1669	Charles Early and Marriott, Witney, Oxfordshire	*Wool*
1669	William Sutton and Company, London	*Chemists, retail*
1670	Hudson's Bay Company, London	*Furs*

1670	Wheelwrights' Company, London	*Guilds*
1671	Appointment of first Board of Customs	*Customs*
1672c.	Ballantyne, Peebles, Scotland	*Wool*
1672	Hoare's Bank, London	*Banks*
1674	*Oxford University Almanack*	*Almanacs*
1675	Royal Observatory, Greenwich	*Research establishments*
1677	Firmin and Sons, London	*Buttons*
1677	Lloyds Bank	*Banks*
1680	James Powell and Sons, Wealdstone, Middlesex	*Glass*
1682	Joseph Rodgers and Sons, Sheffield	*Cutlery*

JAMES II (1685–88)

1685	Puddefoot, Bowers and Simonett, London	*Ivory*
1686	James Kent, Longton, Staffordshire	*Pottery*
1686	Old Bond Street opened	
1687	Green's Stores, Stansted, Essex	*Drapers*
1688	Cooke, Troughton and Simms, London – see also 1718	*Scientific instruments*
1688	Lloyd's, London	*Insurance*
1688	A Mackintosh, Cambridge	*Ironmongers*

WILLIAM III (1689–1702) and MARY II (1689–94)

1690	*Berrow's Worcester Journal*, Worcester	*Newspapers*
1690	Merryweather and Sons, London	*Fire-engineering*
1692	Coutts' Bank, London	*Banks*
1694	Bank of England, London	*Banks*
1695	Richard Anstie in Devizes – see also 1740	*Tobacco*
1695	Bank of Scotland, Edinburgh	*Banks*
1695	Henekeys, London	*Wine-merchants*
1695	*Stamford Mercury*, Stamford, Lincolnshire	*Newspapers*
1695	H Tiffin and Son, London	*Pest Control*
1696	Hand-in-Hand Fire Office, London	*Insurance*
1696	*Lloyd's News* first appeared – see also 1734	*Newspapers*
1697	*Old Moore's Almanack*	*Almanacs*
1698	Society for the Promotion of Christian Knowledge	*Printing, etc*
1699	Berry Brothers and Rudd, London	*Wine-merchants*
1700	Englefields, London	*Pewterers*
1700	D and S Radford, London	*Tobacco*
1700	Chalié Richards and Company, London	*Wine-merchants*

ANNE (1702–14)

1702	*Bristol Post Boy*, Bristol	*Newspapers*
1702	*Daily Courant*, London	*Newspapers*
1702	Silk Mill, Derby	*First factory*
1703	Norman Society, London	*Friendly Societies*
1703	Society for the Mutual Help of Swiss in London	*Friendly Societies*

1704	Bristol City Line of Steamships	*Ships*
1706	Crosse and Blackwell, London	
		Food-manufacturers
1706	R Twining and Company, London and Andover	
		Tea-merchants
1707	Fortnum and Mason, London	*Department stores*
1707	W B Gurney and Son	*Shorthand-writers*
1708	*Norwich Postman*, Norwich	*Newspapers*
1709	Coalbrookdale Company, Coalbrookdale, Shropshire	*Engineering*
1710	William Dalton and Sons, London	*Pest control*
1710	*Nottingham Guardian-Journal*, Nottingham	*Newspapers*
1710	Perrotts (Nicol and Peyton), London	*Textiles*
1710	Sun Insurance Company, London	*Insurance*
1711	*Newcastle Journal*	*Newspapers*
1711	*Nottingham Journal*	*Newspapers*
1711	C and J Rivington, London	*Printing, etc*
1711	Scotts' Shipbuilding and Engineering Company, Greenock, Scotland	*Ships*
1712	*Liverpool Courant*, Liverpool	*Newspapers*
1712	*Norwich Gazette*, Norwich	*Newspapers*
1712	Portals, Laverstoke, Hampshire	*Paper-making*

GEORGE I (1714–27)

1714	*Exeter Mercury*, Exeter	*Newspapers*
1714	Union, or Double Hand-in-Hand, Fire Office	*Insurance*
1715	Allen and Hanburys, London	*Chemists, manufacturing*
1717	Austin and McAslan, Glasgow	*Seedsmen*
1717	Drummonds Bank, London	*Banks*
1717	Westminster Fire Office, London	*Insurance*
1718	Joseph Bryant, Bristol	*Ropes*
1718	Cooke, Troughton and Simms, York – see also 1688	*Scientific instruments*
1719	Pike, Spicer and Company's Brewery, Portsmouth	*Brewing*
1719	*York Mercury*	*Newspapers*
1719	First printing-press in Wales	*Printing, etc*
1720	Brock's Fireworks, Sanquhar, Scotland	*Fireworks*
1720	Fribourg and Treyer, London	*Tobacco*
1720	London Assurance	*Insurance*
1720	*Northampton Mercury*	*Newspapers*
1720	Royal Exchange Assurance	*Insurance*
1721	New Bond Street opened	
1722	Thomas Andrews, Comber, Northern Ireland	*Flour-millers*
1723	Tollemache and Cobbold, Ipswich	*Brewing*
1723	Stephen Mitchell and Son, Linlithgow, Scotland	*Tobacco*
1724	Longmans, Green and Company, London	*Printing, etc*
1725	Charles Davis, predecessor of James Lock – see 1759	*Hatters*
1725	Dring and Fage, London	*Scientific instruments*
1725	Drivers Jonas, London	*Auctioneers, etc*
1725	Mary Tuke, York, forerunner of Rowntrees – see 1862	*Cocoa*
1727	(31 May) Royal Bank of Scotland	*Banks*

GEORGE II (1727–60)

1728	John Broadwood and Sons, London	*Musical instruments*
1728	Ellis's Bookshop, London	*Booksellers*
1728	J S Fry and Sons, Bristol	*Cocoa*
1730	Floris, London	*Perfumers*
1730	Taylor, Walker and Company, London	*Brewing*
1731	Royal Dublin Society, Dublin	*Agricultural shows*
1733 or 1739	Epworth Press, London	*Printing, etc*
1734	*Lloyd's List*, London, as a daily	*Newspapers*
1736	Gourock Ropework Company, Glasgow	*Ropes*
1737	*Belfast News Letter*	*Newspapers*
1737	Wilsons and Company (Sharrow), Sheffield	*Tobacco*
1739 or 1733	Epworth Press, London	*Printing, etc*
1739	J R Phillips and Company, Bristol	*Wine-merchants*
1739	*Scots Magazine* first published	*Newspapers*
1740	E and W Anstie, Devizes	*Tobacco*
1740	Booth's Distilleries, London	*Gin*
1740	Thwaites and Reed, London	*Clocks*
1741	*Birmingham Gazette*, Birmingham	*Newspapers*
1741	*Coventry Standard*, Coventry	*Newspapers*
1741	Stephen Mitchell's snuff-mill, Waukmilton, Scotland	*Tobacco*
1742	Lagavulin Distillery, Islay, Scotland	*Whisky*
1742	Whitbread's Brewery, London	*Brewing*
1743 also 1784	Bushmills Distillery, Bushmills, Northern Ireland	*Whisky*
1744	Cluttons, London	*Auctioneers, etc*
1744	King and Company, Kingston-upon-Hull	*Ironmongers*
1744	Sotheby's, London	*Auctioneers, etc*
1744	Worthington, Burton-on-Trent	*Brewing*
1746	British Linen Bank, Edinburgh	*Banks*
1746	Drambuie – see also 1892 – Bonnie Prince Charlie gave the formula of his personal liqueur to Mackinnon of Strathaird	*Liqueurs*
1746	Glenochil Distillery, near Stirling, Scotland	*Whisky*
1747	Bottesford Friendly Society, Leicestershire	*Friendly Societies*
1747	National Society of Brushmakers and General Workers	*Trade Unions*
1747	J and N Phillips and Company, Manchester	*Cotton*
1748	Joseph Gardner and Sons, Liverpool	*Timber*
1748	*Press and Journal*, Aberdeen	*Newspapers*
1749	Finneys, Newcastle	*Seedsmen*
1749	Justerini and Brooks, London	*Wine-merchants*
1749	William Younger and Company, Edinburgh	*Brewing*
1750	Alloa Glass Works, Alloa, Scotland	*Glass-making*
1750	Benskins' Cannon Brewery, Watford	*Brewing*
1750	Bouchard Aîné, London	*Wine-merchants*
1750	Brusna Distillery, Kilbeggan, Ireland	*Whisky*
1750	Coalport China Company, Stoke-on-Trent	*Pottery*
1750	Crosses and Heatons, Bolton	*Cotton*
1750	Dollond and Aitchison, London	*Opticians*

1750	Eaden Lilley, Cambridge	Department stores
1750	Harrison and Sons, London	Printing, etc
1750	Parker Gallery, London	Art-dealers
1750	Arthur Reader, London	Art-dealers
1750	Royal Crown Derby Porcelain Company, Derby	Pottery
1750	C Shippam, Chichester	Food-manufacturers
1750	Woodhouse, Carey and Browne, London	Sugar-brokers
1751	Beatson, Clark and Company, Rotherham	Glass-making
1751	Culter Mills Paper Company, Aberdeenshire	Paper-making
1751	Vacher and Son, London	Printing
1751	Worcester Royal Porcelain Company, Worcester	Pottery
1752	Clokie and Company, Castleford	Pottery
1752	George Waterston and Sons, Edinburgh	Stationers
1753	Glyn Mills, London	Banks
1754	Royal Society of Arts, London	Agricultural shows, etc
1754	Yorkshire Post, Leeds	Newspapers
1755	Brecknockshire Agricultural Society	Agricultural shows, etc
1756c.	Bradford and Sons, Yeovil	Timber
1756c.	James Latham, London	Timber
1757	Charrington's Anchor Brewery, London	Brewing
1757	Thomas Street Distillery, Dublin	Whisky
1758	Fawcett Preston and Company, Liverpool	Engineering
1758c.	Showerings, Shepton Mallet, Somerset	Cider
1759	Carron Company, Falkirk, Scotland	Engineering
1759	Dreweatt, Watson and Barton, Newbury, Berkshire	Auctioneers
1759	Guinness Brewery, Dublin	Brewing
1759	James Lock and Company, London	Hatters
1759	William Playne and Company, Minchinhampton, Gloucestershire	Wool
1759	Public Ledger, London	Newspapers
1759	Wedgwood, Barlaston, Staffordshire	Pottery

GEORGE III (1760–1820)

1760	Baxter, Payne and Lepper, Beckenham, Kent	Auctioneers
1760	John Burgess and Son, London	Food-manufacturers
1760	W Drummond and Sons, Stirling	Seedsmen
1760	Wimbush and Company, London	Motor-car dealers
1760	Zachary and Company, Cirencester	Wine-merchants
1762	Equitable Life Assurance Society, London	Insurance
1763	Wolsingham Show, Wolsingham, County Durham	Agricultural shows
1764	Lilleshall Company, Oakengates, Shropshire	Engineering
1765	Benjamin R Cant and Sons, Colchester	Roses
1765	Langholm Distillery, Langholm, Scotland	Whisky

1765	Morley Hewitt, Fordingbridge, Hampshire	Auctioneers, etc
1765	Sparrow, Son and Bagley, Nottingham	Auctioneers, etc
1766	Christie's, London	Auctioneers, etc
1766	Reeves and Sons, Enfield, Middlesex	Artists' materials
1767	Kilkenny Journal, Kilkenny, Ireland	Newspapers
1767	Manchester Agricultural Society	Agricultural shows
1767	Mullens, London	Stockbrokers
1767	Joseph Terry and Sons, York	Cocoa
1768	Encyclopaedia Britannica	
1768	John Murray, London	Printing, etc
1769	Curtis Distillery, London	Gin
1769	Fox, Stanton and Company, Penryn, Cornwall	Timber
1769	Hampton Court Vine	Vines, etc
1770	Dundashill Distillery, Glasgow	Whisky
1770	Flights, London	Tailors
1770	John and Robert Harvey, Glasgow	Whisky
1770	Stockton Heath Forge, Warrington	Engineering
1770	Yoker Distillery, near Glasgow	Whisky
1771	Hawkes of Savile Row, London	Tailors
1771	Williams Deacons Bank, Manchester	Banks
1772	Fox Brothers and Company, Wellington, Somerset	Wool
1772	A Laverton and Company, Westbury, Wiltshire	Wool
1772	Morning Post, London	Newspapers
1772	Wilkinson Sword Company, London	Swords
1773	Samuel Deacon and Company, London	Advertising
1773	Richard Ellis, London	Auctioneers, etc
1773	Herring, Daw and Manners, London	Auctioneers, etc
1773	Stock Exchange, London	Stock Exchanges
1775	Glenturret Distillery, near Crieff	Whisky
1777	Bass, Burton-on-Trent	Brewing
1777	Bath and West Society, Bath	Agricultural shows
1777	Deighton and Bell, Cambridge	Booksellers
1777	E F Langdale, Croydon, Surrey	Essences
1777	Rose, Downs and Thompson, Hull	Engineering
1778	Richard Garrett Engineering Works, Leiston, Suffolk	Engineering
1778	Methodist Magazine, London	Newspapers, etc
1779	G Gardiner and Son, Wolsingham and Crook, County Durham	Engineering
1779	Butler family at Kirkstall Forge – see 1200	Engineering
1779	Marrowbone Lane Distillery, Dublin (Wm Jameson and Company)	Whiskey
1779	North Mall Distillery, Cork	Whiskey
1779	Simpkin Marshall, London	Booksellers
1779	Yardley's, London	Perfumers
1780	Bewlay, London	Tobacco
1780	Bow Street Distillery, Dublin (John Jameson and Company)	Whiskey
1780	Keith Prowse, London	Ticket agencies
1781	Vauxhall Distillery, Liverpool	Whisky
1782	Barretts, Cambridge	Old customers
1782	Vaughan, London	Pawnbrokers

1783	Dublin Chamber of Commerce	
		Chambers of Commerce
1783	Glasgow Chamber of Commerce	
		Chambers of Commerce
1783	*Glasgow Herald*	*Newspapers*
1783	Bank of Ireland, Dublin	*Banks*
1783	Geo M Whiley, London	*Goldbeaters*
1784	Bramahs, London	*Locks*
1784	Bushmills Distillery, Bushmills,	
	Northern Ireland – see also 1743	*Whisky*
1784	Fitch Lovell, London	*Grocers*
1784	Wm Hollins, Nottingham	*Textiles*
1784	Royal Highland and Agricultural	
	Society of Scotland, Edinburgh	*Agricultural shows*
1785	Edinburgh Chamber of Commerce	
		Chambers of Commerce
1785	Gieves, London	*Tailors*
1785	*Universal Register* – name changed to	
	The Times on 1 January 1788	*Newspapers*
1786	Grange Distillery, Burntisland, Scotland	*Whisky*
1786	T Wall and Sons, London	*Food-manufacturers*
1786	W D and H O Wills, Bristol	*Tobacco*
1787	John Courage, London	*Brewing*
1787	D and A Cuthbertson, Glasgow	*Accountants*
1788	Simeon Bateman, Stourbridge, Worcestershire	
		Timber
1788	Bristol Brewery	*Brewing*
1788	Carreras, London	*Tobacco*
1788	C F Taylor and Company, Shipley, Yorkshire	
		Wool
1789	Jeremiah Ambler, Bradford	*Wool*
1789	George Rowney and Company, London	
		Artists' materials
1790	Bumpus, London	*Booksellers*
1790	Butterley Company, Butterley, Derbyshire	
		Engineering
1790	Davis and Son, London	*Dyers, etc*
1790	Dobson and Barlow, Bolton	*Engineering*
1790	Robert Melville and Company, Falkirk	*Timber*
1790	Park, Dobson and Company, Leith	*Timber*
1790	George G Sandeman, Sons and Company,	
	London	*Wine-merchants*
1790	Whessoe, Darlington	*Engineering*
1791	Horrockses, Preston	*Cotton*
1791	*Observer*, London	*Newspapers*
1791	Offords, London	*Coachbuilders*
1793	Avery and Company, Bristol	*Wine-merchants*
1793	Board of Agriculture	*Agricultural shows, etc*
1793	Coates and Company,	
	Black Friars Distillery, Plymouth	*Gin*
1793	P Ormiston and Sons, Ealing, London	
		Wire-manufacture
1794	Deinhard and Company, London	
		Wine-merchants
1794	Heaton Mint, Birmingham	*Mints*
1794	Oban Distillery, Oban	*Whisky*
1796	Belfast Chamber of Commerce	
		Chambers of Commerce
1796	Geo Bunyard and Company, Maidstone	
		Seedsmen
1796	John Harvey and Sons, Bristol	*Wine-merchants*
1796	Charles Letts and Company, London	*Diaries*
1796	Phillips, London	*Auctioneers*

1797	R and G Cuthbert, Goff's Oak, Hertfordshire	
		Seedsmen
1797	Hatchards, London	*Booksellers*
1797	I and R Morley, Leicester	*Drapers*
1797	Inderwicks, London	*Pipes*
1797	Paxton and Whitfield, London	*Grocers*
1798	Alfred Button and Sons, Uxbridge,	
	Middlesex	*Grocers*
1798	Savory and Moore, London	*Chemists, retail*
1798	Smithfield Club	*Agricultural shows, etc*
1799	J and E Atkinson, London	*Perfumers*
1799	J Croggon and Son, Grampound, Cornwall	
		Tanners
1799	Kelly's Directories, London	*Directories*
1799	William Oliver and Sons, London	*Timber*
1800	Scott Moncrieff, Thomson and Shiells,	
	Edinburgh	*Accountants*
1804	Kerr MacLeod and Macfarlan, Glasgow	
		Accountants
1804	Lemon Hart and Son, London	– see under *Sugar*
1805	Bacon Brothers, Cambridge	*Tobacco*
1805	Truefitt and Hill, London	*Hairdressers*
1805	Caledonian Insurance Company,	
	Edinburgh	*Insurance*
1807	A and C Black, London	*Printing, etc*
1807	Hooper and Company, London	*Coachbuilders*
1808	*North Wales Chronicle*, Bangor	*Newspapers*
1810	Chappell and Company, London	*Music shops*
1810	Henry Duncan's Savings Bank,	
	Ruthwell, Scotland	*Savings banks*
1810	Independent Order of Odd Fellows,	
	Manchester Unity	*Friendly Societies*
1812	Brown, Lennox and Company, London and	
	Pontypridd	*Chains*
1813	Birmingham Chamber of Commerce	
		Chambers of Commerce
1814	Colmans, Norwich – see also 1823	*Mustard*
1815	Toogood and Sons, Southampton	*Seedsmen*
1817	Agnew's, London	*Art-dealers*
1817	*Blackwood's Magazine*, Edinburgh	*Newspapers, etc*
1817	R Edwards, Chandler, Wagstaffe, London	
		Stockbrokers
1817	Mann Judd Gordon and Company, Glasgow	
		Accountants
1817	Andrew Oliver and Son, Hawick, Scotland	
		Auctioneers
1817	S Parkinson and Son, Doncaster	*Sweets*
1817	Vye and Son, Ramsgate	*Grocers*
1818	B Young & Co, London	*Gelatine*
1819	Maypole, Birmingham	*Grocers*
1819	*Raphael's Almanac*, London	*Almanacs*

GEORGE IV (1820–30)

1820	Aston Martin, Newport Pagnell,	
	Buckinghamshire	*Motor cars*
1820	John Pritchard, Loughborough, Leicestershire	
		Ropes
1820	John Walker, Kilmarnock	*Whisky*
1822	*New Law Journal*, London	*Newspapers, etc*
1823	J and J Colman, Norwich – see also 1814	
		Mustard
1823	*The Lancet*, London	*Newspapers, etc*

1824	P J Carroll, Dublin	Tobacco
1824	Cramer's, London	Music shops
1824	General Steam Navigation Company, London	
		Ships
1824	The Child's Magazine, London	
	– see also 1846	Newspapers, etc
1824	Marriage and Sons, Chelmsford	Flour-millers
1824	Milton Duff Distillery, Elgin	Whisky
1824	Rieclachan Distillery, Campbelltown	Whisky
1825	Arthur Bell and Sons, Perth	Whisky
1825	Foster and Braithwaite, London	Stockbrokers
1826	Pilkingtons, St Helens	Glass
1828	Beale and Inman, London	Shirt-makers
1828	Lea and Perrins, Worcester	Food-manufacturers
1828	The Spectator, London	Newspapers, etc
1829	Vickers, Sheffield – see also 1867	Arms

WILLIAM IV (1830–37)

1831	Bank of Liverpool	Banks
1832	Chambers's Journal	Newspapers, etc
1832	Winsor and Newton, Harrow, Middlesex and Lowestoft, Suffolk	Artists' materials
1833	National Provincial Bank, London	Banks
1834	Ancient Order of Foresters	Friendly Societies
1834	Ashton and Mitchell, London	Ticket agencies
1835	Independent Order of Rechabites, Salford Unity	Friendly Societies
1835	A and J Macnaughton, Pitlochry	Wool
1835	Mining Journal, London	Newspapers, etc
1836	Alex Dickson and Sons, Newtownards, County Down, Northern Ireland	Roses

VICTORIA (1837–1901)

1837	Peninsular and Oriental Steam Navigation Company, London	Ships
1840	Loughborough Bell Foundry, Loughborough, Leicestershire	Bell-founding
1840	John Pinches (Medallists), London	Mints
1841	Thomas Cook and Son, London	Travel agencies
1841	Jewish Chronicle, London	Newspapers, etc
1841	London Library, London	Libraries
1841	Punch, London	Newspapers, etc
1842	Farmers' Club, London	Agricultural shows, etc
1842	Hearts of Oak Benefit Society	Friendly Societies
1842	Illustrated London News, London	Newspapers, etc
1843	Amserau Cymru – see also 1857	Newspapers
1843	The Builder (now called Building), London	Newspapers, etc
1843	Economist, London	Newspapers, etc
1843	Liverpool Victoria Friendly Society, Liverpool	Friendly Societies
1843	Rothamsted Experimental Station	Agricultural shows, etc
1845	Chelmsford and Essex Building Society, Chelmsford	Building Societies
1845	Deloittes, London	Accountants
1846	Kiddies' Magazine – see 1824	Newspapers, etc
1848	Railway Passengers Assurance Company	Insurance
1849	Harrods, London	Department stores
1849	Reuters, Aachen and London	News bureau

1850	Royal Liver Friendly Society, Liverpool	
		Friendly Societies
1851	Falkland Islands Company	Companies
1852	Scottish Legal Life Assurance Society	
		Friendly Societies
1853	Chartered Bank of India, Australia and China	
		Banks
1854	Alliance Perpetual Building Society, London	
		Building Societies
1854	Charter of Society of Accountants in Edinburgh	
		Accountants
1855	Caledonian Distillery, Edinburgh	Whisky
1855	Daily Telegraph, London	Newspapers, etc
1856	Berwick Corn Exchange	Companies
1856	Stanley Gibbons, London	Stamp-dealers
1856	Whiteley's, London	Departmental stores
1857	City Press, London	Newspapers, etc
1857	Y Faner, Denbigh – see also 1843	Newspapers, etc
1857	W and A Gilbey, London	Wine-merchants
1859	Ironmonger, Builder's Merchant and Metal Trades Advertiser, London	Newspapers, etc
1861	North Central Finance	Hire purchase
1862	H I Rowntree starts own business, York	Cocoa
1863	Charatan Pipes, London	Pipes
1865	Civil Service Stores, London	Department stores
1865	Liebig's Extract of Meat Company, London (with Brooke Bond)	Tea-merchants
1865	Malin's, London	Fish and chips
1865	Strachan and Company, Stroud, Gloucestershire	Wool
1866	Raphael Tuck and Sons, London	
		Christmas cards
1867	Vickers – see also 1829	Arms
1868	National Deposit Friendly Society, London	
		Friendly Societies
1869	Brooke Bond, London	Tea-merchants
1869	Ould and Company, London	Bookmakers
1869	Sainsbury's, London	Grocers
1871	Army and Navy Stores, London	
		Department stores
1871	Lipton's	Grocers
1874	Ben Sayers, North Berwick, Scotland	
		Golf clubs
1875	Ranks Hovis McDougall, London	
		Flour-millers
1875	A P Watt and Son, London	Literary agents
1876	Heffers, Cambridge	Booksellers
1877	Twentieth Century Magazine, London	
		Newspapers, etc
1878	Gamage's, London	Department stores
1878	Henry Tate's Silvertown refinery	Sugar
1882	Abram Lyle's Plaistow refinery	Sugar
1886	W H Whittard, London	Tea-merchants
1887	Hunt and Winterbotham, Cam Mills, Dursley, Gloucestershire – see also 1532	Wool
1892	Name 'Drambuie' registered	Liqueurs
1894	First Lyons' teashop, London	Teashops
1898	His Master's Voice (Gramophone and Typewriter Limited), London	
		Gramophone records
1898	Short Brothers, Belfast	Aircraft
1900	Marconi Company, Chelmsford	Radio

EDWARD VII (1901–10)

1902   Bask Leumi-Le-Israel (established as
       the Anglo-Palestine Bank), London   *Banks*
1909   *Flight*, London   *Newspapers, etc*
1909   Handley Page, London   *Aircraft*

GEORGE V (1910–36)

1920   DD Ballantyne Brothers and Company, Peebles
                                                Wool

1921   Formation of Tate and Lyle   *Sugar*
1931   M and G Unit trusts   *Unit trusts*

ELIZABETH II (1952–   )

1956   Calder Hall Atomic Power Station
                                       Atomic energy
1957   The Never Turn Back, Caister-on-Sea,
       Norfolk   *Public Houses*
1975   (2 January) First hallmarking of
       platinum, Goldsmiths' Hall, London   *Hallmarks*

B. Other Lands

BC
700   Egibi and Son, Assyria   *Banks*
AD
1040   Bayerische Staatsbrauerei
       Weihenstephan, Freising, near Munich   *Brewing*
1119   Klosterbrauerei Scheyern, Bavaria, Germany
                                              Brewing
1200   Mansfeld company, Germany   *Copper, etc*
1241   Löwenapotheke, Trier (Trèves), Germany
                                             Chemists
1270   Clerget-Buffet et fils, Beaune, France
                                       Wine-growers, etc
1270   Raoul Clerget et fils, Beaune, France
                                       Wine-growers, etc
1288   Stora Kopparberg, Sweden   *Copper, etc*
1295   Urquell Brewery, Pilsen, Czechoslovakia
                                              Brewing
1319   Bürgerspital zum Heiligen Geist,
       Würzburg, Germany   *Wine-growers, etc*
1326   Moulin à Papier Richard-de-Bas,
       Ambert, France   *Paper*
1328   Augustiner-Bräu, Munich, Germany   *Brewing*
1347   King of Sweden's Charter of Privileges
       for Stora Kopparberg – see 1288 above   *Copper*
1365   Schwäbische Hüttenwerke, Württemberg, Germany
                                                Iron
1377   Reichsgraf von Kesselstatt, Trier, Germany
                                        Wine-growers
1383   Löwenbräu, Munich, Germany   *Brewing*
1385   Antinori, Florence, Italy   *Wine-growers, etc*
1397   Spatenbräu, Munich   *Brewing*
1400   Chemist's shop, Llivia (Gerona), Spain *Chemists*
1417   Hackerbräu, Munich   *Brewing*
1419   Atvidaberg Industries, Sweden   *Copper, etc*
1420   Pasquier-Desvignes, Saint-Lager (Rhône),
       France   *Wine-growers, etc*
1433   The Key Brewery (De Sleutel), Dordrecht,
       Holland   *Brewing*
1436   Grenzquell-Brauerei, Germany   *Brewing*
1453   Pharmacie Brun, Geneva, Switzerland   *Chemists*
1465   Von Simmern vineyards, Eltville, Germany
                                        Wine-growers
1472   Monte dei Paschi di Siena, Siena, Italy *Banks*
1500   Winter Apotheke, Innsbruck, Germany   *Chemists*
1513   Alphonse Mellot, Sancerre, France
                                       Wine-growers, etc

1519   Orell Füssli Verlag, Zürich, Switzerland
                                            Publishing
1520   Josef Milz, Piesport, Germany   *Wine-growers, etc*
1539   Banco di Napoli (Bank of Naples), Italy *Banks*
1554   De Vergulde Hand (The Golden Hand),
       Amsterdam, Holland   *Soap*
1558   Hamburg Stock Exchange,
       Germany   *Stock Exchanges*
1573   Klippans Finpappersbruk, Klippan, Sweden
                                                Paper
1575   Bols, Nieuw-Vennep, Netherlands   *Distilling*
1580   William Prym-Werke, Stolberg (Rheinland),
       Germany   *Metal-processing*
1590   Joh Berenberg, Gossler and Company,
       Hamburg   *Banks*
1589   Joseph Gautsch, Fulda, Germany   *Candles, etc*
1589   Hofbräuhaus, Munich   *Brewing*
1593   Jb Bussink's Koninklijke Koekfabrieken,
       Deventer, Holland   *Biscuits, etc*
1598   Isaac Wed-Ling Wwe and Eydam
       Dirck Hekker, formerly of Danzig, now at
       Nörten-Hardenberg, Germany   *Distilling*
1605   Johann Mertens, Frankfurt-am-Main, Germany
                                                Banks
1605   Banco di Santo Spirito, Rome   *Banks*
1607   Gränges, Sweden   *Iron and steel*
1612   Beginning of *Les Petites Affiches*, Paris
       – see also 1631   *Newspapers, etc*
1616   Warninks, Amsterdam, Holland   *Distilling*
1618   Gustav Adolf Schmitt'sches Weingut,
       Nierstein-am-Rhein, Germany   *Wine-growers, etc*
1620   Richard Langguth, Traben-Trarbach,
       Germany   *Wine-growers, etc*
1624   Monte dei Paschi di Siena, Italy – see 1472
                                                Banks
1628   Three Horseshoes Brewery, Breda, Holland
                                              Brewing
1630   Kikkoman Shoyu Company, Tokyo, Japan
                                            Soy sauce
1631   *Les Petites Affiches*, Paris – see 1612
                                     Newspapers, etc
1632   Henri Maire, Arbois, France   *Wine-growers, etc*
1638   C N Kopke, London   *Wine-growers, etc*
1639   F E Hugel et fils, Riquewihr, France
                                        Wine-growers
1645   *Post-och Inrikes Tidningar*, Stockholm, Sweden
                                     Newspapers, etc
1650   Marseille Chamber of Commerce
                                  Chambers of Commerce

1653	Gusums Bruk AB, Sweden	*Copper, etc*
1656	*De Oprechte Haarlemsche Courant,*	
	Haarlem, Holland	*Newspapers, etc*
1656	Sanwa Bank, Osaka, Japan	*Banks*
1657	Riksbank, Sweden – see also 1668	*Banks*
1660	Petit and Fritsen, Aarle-Rixtel, Holland	*Bells*
1664	J Delaire et fils, Purier-Sauvade	
	Successeur, Thiers, France	*Cutlery*
1664	Kronenbourg Brewery, Strasbourg, France	
		Brewing
1665	Saint-Gobain, France	*Glass*
1665	Johann Goll und Söhne,	
	Frankfurt-am-Main, Germany	*Banks*
1667	de Neuflize, Schlumberger et Compagnie, Paris	
		Banks
1668	Riksbank, Sweden – see also 1657	*Banks*
1670	Hudson's Bay Company, now at Winnipeg	*Furs*
1670	Warre and Company, Oporto, Portugal	
		Wine-growers, etc
1671	Oranjeboom (Orange-tree) Brewery, Holland	
		Brewing
1674	B Metzler seel Sohn and Company,	
	Frankfurt-am-Main, Germany	*Banks*
1677	Hammerstein Apotheke, Zürich, Switzerland	
		Chemists
1678	Croft's, Oporto, Portugal	*Wine-growers, etc*
1679	Roope, Hunt and Company, London and Oporto	
		Wine-growers, etc
1679	G von Pachaly's Enkel, Breslau, Silesia	*Banks*
1683	Mitsui Bank, Tokyo, Japan	*Banks*
1686	Café Procope, Paris	*Cafés*
1687	Perot Malting Company, Philadelphia, USA	
		Maltsters
1688	Henry Lambertz, Aachen, Germany	*Biscuits, etc*
1690	Weingut Ferd Pieroth, Burg Layen	
	bei Bingen-am-Rhein, Germany	*Wine-growers, etc*
1690	Weingut Friedrich Priesteroth,	
	Braubach-am-Rhein, Germany	*Wine-growers*
1691	Vlaer and Kol, Utrecht, Holland	*Banks*
1692	Taylor's, Oporto, Portugal	*Wine-growers*
1695	Johannes de Kuyper en Zoon, Schiedam,	
	Holland	*Distilling*
1697	Adolph Huesgen, Traben-Trarbach, Germany	
		Wine-growers, etc
1700	Gräflich von Hardenberg'sche Kornbrennerei	
	Vertriebe, Nörten-Hardenberg, Germany	*Distilling*
1701	Rouyer, Cognac, France	*Distilling*
1702	J E Rhoads and Sons, Wilmington,	
	Delaware, United States	*Leather and belting*
1703	Joh Enschedé en Zonen, Haarlem, Holland	
		Printing
1705	Fürstenberg Bräu, Germany	*Brewing*
1705	*Hildesheimer Allgemeine Zeitung*, Germany	
		Newspapers, etc
1705	Melini, Italy	*Wine-growers, etc*
1705	Rocher Frères, Côte Saint-André, France	
		Distilling
1708	*Le Véritable Messager Boiteux*, Vevey,	
	Switzerland	*Almanacs*
1713	*Pfälzischer Merkur*, Germany	*Newspapers, etc*
1715	Martell, Cognac, France	*Distilling*
1717	Presbyterian Ministers' Fund, Philadelphia, USA	
		Insurance

1717	O C Balle, Flensburg, Germany	*Distilling*
1719	Amalgamated Leather Companies,	
	Wilmington, Delaware, USA	*Leather*
1719	Breitkopf und Härtel, Leipzig, East Germany	
		Publishing
1719	Simonius, Vischer and Company, Basle,	
	Switzerland	*Wool*
1720	R Mees en Zoonen, Rotterdam	*Banks*
1724	Remy Martin, Cognac, France	*Distilling*
1725	*Hanauer Anzeiger*, Germany	*Newspapers, etc*
1728	Franklin Printing Company, Philadelphia,	
	USA	*Printing*
1728	Thomas Hancock's paper mill on the	
	Neponset River, Massachusetts, USA –	
	see 1801	*Paper*
1729	Ruinart père et fils, Reims, France	
		Wine-growers, etc
1730	Chanoine, Epernay, France	*Wine-growers, etc*
1730	Pedro Domecq, Jerez de la Frontera, Spain	
		Wine-growers, etc
1731	Bouchard père et fils, Beaune, France	
		Wine-growers, etc
1734	D and L Slade, Boston, USA	*Spices*
1734	Taittinger, Reims, France	*Wine-growers, etc*
1738	*Darmstädter Tagblatt*, Germany	*Newspapers*
1738	*Feuille d'avis de Neuchâtel*, Switzerland	
		Newspapers, etc
1738	A-B Billingsfors-Långed, Billingsfors, Sweden	
		Timber
1740	Friendly Society for the Mutual Insuring	
	of Houses against Fire, Charleston, USA	
		Insurance
1740	James E Pepper and Co, Lexington, Kentucky	
		Distilling
1742	Rückforth, Siegburg, Germany	*Distilling*
1742	Taylor-Wharton Iron and Steel	
	Company, Cincinnati, Ohio, USA	*Iron and steel*
1743	*Bremer Nachrichten*, Germany	*Newspapers, etc*
1743	Joh Enschedé en Zonen, Haarlem,	
	Holland – see 1703	*Type-founding*
1743	Moët et Chandon, Epernay, France	
		Wine-growers, etc
1743	Skillman Express, Storage and	
	Furniture Exchange, Princeton, New Jersey, USA	
		Carriers
1744	Steinman Hardware Company,	
	Lancaster, Pennsylvania, USA	*Hardware*
1745	Cossart, Gordon and Company, Madeira	
		Wine-growers, etc
1747	Poulet père et fils, Beaune, France	
		Wine-growers, etc
1749	*Berlingske Tidende*, Denmark	*Newspapers, etc*
1749	Zenith Pipes, Gouda, Holland	*Pipes*
1750	Bouchard Aîné et fils, Beaune, France	
		Wine-growers, etc
1750	*Giessener Anzeiger*, Germany	*Newspapers, etc*
1752	Caswell-Massey, New York, USA	*Chemists*
1752	Philadelphia Contributionship, Philadelphia,	
	USA	*Insurance*
1752	*Leeuwarder Courant*, Holland	*Newspapers, etc*
1753	Karl Jakob, Basle	*Biscuits, etc*
1754	von der Heydt-Kersten und Söhne,	
	Elberfeld, Germany	*Banks*

Year	Entry	Category
1755	Marie Brizard, Bordeaux, France	*Distilling*
1755	Leu & Compagnie, Zürich, Switzerland	*Banks*
1756	Real Cia Velha, Real Companhia dos Vinos do Porto, Oporto, Portugal	*Wine-growers, etc*
1757	Cinzano, Turin, Italy	*Vermouth*
1758	Geigy, Basle, Switzerland	*Chemicals*
1758	Wm Stairs, Son and Morrow, Halifax, NS, Canada	*Retail store*
1758	*Norrköpings Tidningar-Ostergotlands Dagblad*, Sweden	*Newspapers, etc*
1758	*Provinciale Zeeuwse Courant*, Holland	*Newspapers, etc*
1760	American Lawn Equipment Corporation, Lyndhurst, New Jersey, USA	*Ironmongers*
1760	Herm G Dethleffsen, Flensburg, Germany	*Distilling*
1760	Lanson père et fils, Reims, France	*Wine-growers, etc*
1760	P Lorillard, New York, USA	*Tobacco*
1761	Kirk and Nice, Philadelphia, USA	*Funeral directors*
1761	*Saarbrücker Zeitung*, Germany	*Newspapers, etc*
1762	*Feuille d'avis de Lausanne*, Switzerland	*Newspapers, etc*
1762	Hope and Company, Amsterdam, Holland	*Banks*
1762	*Schaumburger Zeitung*, Germany	*Newspapers, etc*
1762	Tassinari et Chatel, Lyon, France	*Silk*
1763	*Hersfelder Zeitung*, Germany	*Newspapers, etc*
1763	*Offenbach Post*, Germany	*Newspapers, etc*
1764	Celle Agricultural Society, Germany	*Agricultural shows, etc*
1764	Biddle Whelen and Company, Philadelphia, USA	*Investments*
1764	*Hartford Courant*, USA	*Newspapers, etc*
1764	*Quebec Chronicle – Telegraph*, Canada	*Newspapers, etc*
1766	Walter Baker's first chocolate-mill, Dorchester, Massachusetts, USA	*Cocoa*
1766	Gladding's, Providence, Rhode Island, USA	*Department stores*
1766	Walter Baker's first chocolate-mill, Dorchester, Massachusetts, USA	*Cocoa*
1766	Robin, Jones and Whitman, Halifax, Nova Scotia, Canada	*Merchants*
1767	*Aalborg Stiftstidende*, Denmark	*Newspapers, etc*
1767	*Adresseavisen*, Norway	*Newspapers, etc*
1767	C H Dexter and Sons, Windsor Locks, Connecticut, USA	*Paper*
1767	*New Haven Journal Courier*, USA	*Newspapers, etc*
1768	New York Chamber of Commerce, USA	*Chambers of Commerce*
1769	Mission San Diego, California, USA	*Vines*
1769	Corporation for the Relief of Widows and Children of the Protestant Episcopal Church in the State of New York, New York, USA	*Insurance*
1770	Demuth's Tobacco Shop, Lancaster, Pennsylvania, USA	*Tobacco*
1771	*Philadelphia Inquirer*, USA	*Newspapers*
1772	Osborne, Spain	*Distilling*
1773	Woodhouse and Company, Marsala, Sicily	*Wine-growers, etc*
1774	O Ames Company, Parkersburg, West Virginia, USA	*Farm tools*
1774	Job T Pugh, Philadelphia, USA	*Augers*
1775	Bowne and Company, New York, USA	*Printing*
1776	Heinrich Stobbe, Oldenburg, Germany	*Distilling*
1780	Garveys, Spain	*Wine-growers, etc*
1780	Baine, Johnston and Company, St John's, Newfoundland	*Fishing*
1780	*Neue Zürcher Zeitung*, Switzerland	*Newspapers, etc*
1781	Schieffelin and Company, New York, USA	*Wine-growers, etc*
1782	De Erven de Wed: J van Nelle Rotterdam, Holland	*Tobacco*
1782	First Pennsylvania Banking and Trust Company, Philadelphia, USA – see also 1792	*Banks*
1782	Minot, De Blois and Maddison, Boston, USA	*Real estate*
1784	First National Bank of Boston, USA	*Banks*
1784	Bank of New York, USA	*Banks*
1785	Hennessy, Cognac, France	*Distilling*
1785	Hellmers und Söhne, Reil-an-der-Mosel, Germany	*Wine-growers, etc*
1785	Philadelphia Agricultural Society, USA	*Agricultural shows, etc*
1786	Carpano, Turin, Italy	*Vermouth*
1786	Hottinguer Bank, Paris	*Banks*
1786	Molson's Brewery, Montreal, Canada	*Brewing*
c. 1789	Joseph Drouhin, Beaune, France	*Wine-growers, etc*
1789	Zwicker and Company, Lunenburg, Nova Scotia, Canada	*Fishing*
1790	Don Brewery, Montreal, Canada	*Brewing*
1790	Pernod, Pontarlier, France	*Distilling*
1790	Steel Company of Canada, Hamilton, Ontario	*Iron and steel*
1791	Heynes Mathew, South Africa	*Chemical manufacturers, etc*
1792	Diario de Barcelona, Spain	*Newspapers*
1792	Insurance Company of North America, Philadelphia, USA	*Insurance*
1792	New York Stock Exchange, USA	*Stock Exchanges*
1792	First Pennsylvania Banking and Trust Company, USA	*Banks*
1793	Sturk and Company, South Africa	*Tobacco, but see Chemical manufacturers, etc*
c. 1793	Eli Whitney's cotton gin	*Mass production*
1794	Schieffelin and Company, New York, USA – see also 1781	*Wine-growers, etc*
1795	Van Bergen, Heiligerlee, Holland	*Bells*
1795	James B Beam Distilling Company, Clermont Beam, Kentucky, USA	*Distilling*
1798	*Allgemeine Musikalische Zeitung*, Leipzig, East Germany	*Publishing*
1801	Ogilvie Flour Mills Company, Montreal, Canada	*Flour-millers*
1801	Tileston and Hollingsworth, Boston, USA – see 1728	*Paper*
1802	E I du Pont, Wilmington, Delaware, USA	*Chemicals*
1805	Cassa di Risparmio, Zürich, Switzerland	*Savings banks*

1805	Escher Wyss, Switzerland	*Engineering*
1805	Veuve Clicquot-Ponsardin took over on the death of her husband, Reims, France	*Wine-growers, etc*
1807	Scholtz Hermanos, Málaga, Spain	*Wine-growers, etc*
1809	Halifax Insurance Company, Halifax, Nova Scotia, Canada	*Insurance*
1811	Krupp, Essen, Germany	*Arms*
1813	*Boston Sunday Advertiser*, Boston, USA	*Newspapers, etc*
1813	Noilly Prat, Lyon and Marseille, France	*Vermouth*
1814	Rutherford and Company, Madeira, Portugal	*Wine-growers, etc*
1815	Cockburn's, Portugal and London	*Wine-growers, etc*
1815	Van Houten, Amsterdam, Holland	*Cocoa*
1816	The Price Company, Quebec, Canada	*Timber*
1817	(February) Bank of New South Wales, Sydney, Australia	*Banks*
1817	(November) Bank of Montreal, Canada	*Banks*
1818	Peter F Heering, Denmark	*Distilling*
1818	First Smirnoff Distillery, Moscow	*Distilling*
1820	Hanson-Van Winkle-Munning Company, Matawan, New Jersey, USA	*Electro-chemical engineering*
1820	Comstock, Ferre and Company, Wethersfield, Connecticut, USA	*Seedsmen*
1820	Theodorus Niemeyer, Groningen, Holland	*Tobacco*
1822	Société Générale de Belgique, Brussels, Belgium	*Banks*
1823	Cassa di Risparmio, Milan, Italy	*Savings bank*
1824	Belgian A G Group, Brussels, Belgium	*Insurance*
1824	*Revue des Deux Mondes*, Paris, France	*Newspapers, etc*
1824	Angostura Aromatic Bitters, Trinidad	*Distilling*
1826	G C Kessler, Esslingen, Germany	*Wine-growers, etc*
1828	John Labatt, London, Ontario, Canada	*Brewing*
1831	Mampe, Berlin, Germany	*Distilling*
1832	Bank of Nova Scotia, Canada	*Banks*
1832	Gooderham and Worts, Toronto, Canada	*Distilling*
1833	Emil Z Svitser, Denmark	*Salvage*
1836	J A Gilka, Hamburg, Germany	*Distilling*
1838	Mauritius Commercial Bank, Mauritius	*Banks*
1839	Brotherhood Corporation, Washingtonville, New York, USA	*Wine-growers, etc*
1846	Kölnische Rückversicherungsgesellschaft, Cologne, Germany	*Insurance*
1846	Underberg, Rheinberg, Germany	*Distilling*
1847	Canada Life Assurance Company, Toronto, Canada	*Insurance*
1850	Sparkasse Zinstragender Sparhafen, Zürich, Switzerland	*Savings banks*
1850	Triton Insurance Company, Calcutta	*Insurance*
1851	Jordan's, Boston, USA	*Department stores*
1851	B Seppelt and Sons, South Australia and Victoria	*Wine-growers, etc*
1852	Paul Masson Vineyards, Saratoga, California, USA	*Wine-growers, etc*
1852	Wells Fargo, San Francisco, USA	*Banks*
1854	Etscheid, Bonn, Germany	*Umbrellas*
1855	Henry Creed, Paris	*Haute couture*
1857	Sonoma Vineyards, California, USA	*Wine-growers, etc*
1857	Rentenanstalt, Zürich, Switzerland	*Insurance*
1857	Associated Spring Corporation, Bristol, Connecticut, USA	*Springs*
1858	Hiram Walker, Walkerville, Canada	*Distilling*
1858	N T Butterfield and Son, Hamilton, Bermuda	*Banks*
1858	Worth, Paris	*Haute couture*
1859	Drake's Well, Oil Creek, Pennsylvania, USA	*Petroleum*
1859	Great Atlantic and Pacific, USA	*Food retailers*
1860	Pleasant Valley Wine Company, Hammondsport, New York USA	*Wine-growers, etc*
1862	First Bacardi Distillery, Santiago de Cuba	*Distilling*
1862	Standard Bank, Johannesburg, South Africa	*Banks*
1864	Banco de Londres y Mexico, Mexico	*Banks*
1866	Jack Daniel Distillery, Lynchburg, Tennessee, USA	*Distilling*
1869	Eaton's, Toronto, Canada	*Department stores*
1869	Swiss Volksbank, Berne	*Banks*
1870	Brown-Forman Distillers Corporation, Louisville, Kentucky, USA	*Distilling*
1870	Commerzbank, Düsseldorf, Germany	*Banks*
1870	Deutsche Bank, Frankfurt-am-Main, Germany	*Banks*
1872	Missouri Meerschaum Company, Washington, Missouri, USA	*Pipes*
1872	Simpsons, Toronto, Canada	*Department stores*
1873	Dai-Ichi Bank, Tokyo, Japan	*Banks*
1874	Independent Order of Foresters, Don Mills, Canada	*Fraternal Benefit Societies*
1876	Maschinenfabrik Oerlikon, Zürich, Switzerland	*Engineering*
1877	Macy's, New York, United States	*Department stores*
1879	F W Woolworth Company, New York, USA	– see under *Chain stores*
1882	Christian Brothers' vineyards, Napa Valley, California	*Wine-growers, etc*
1883	Daimler-Benz, Stuttgart, Germany	*Motor cars*
1883	*Summary*, Ilmira Reformatory, USA	*Newspapers, etc*
1895	First sales of C W Post's 'Postum'	*Food manufacturers*
1897	C W Post's 'Grape-Nuts'	*Food manufacturers*
1898	National Bank of Egypt	*Banks*
1902	Bank Leumi-Le-Israel BM, Israel	*Banks*
1906	Nordisk Films, Copenhagen, Denmark	*Films*
1919	Koninklijke Luchtvaart-Maatschappij (KLM), Holland	*Airlines*
1920	Queensland and Northern Territory Aerial Service (QANTAS), Sydney, Australia	*Airlines*
1922	Toronto Winter Fair, Canada	*Agricultural shows, etc*
1927	Varig, Brazil	*Airlines*

SELECTED BIBLIOGRAPHY

SECTION I

In order to avoid repetitions, publications already mentioned under Acknowledgements (page 7) are not listed again here. Also excluded are numerous works of various kinds relating to individual businesses that have been mentioned in the text.

A number of publications not attributed to a particular author are listed in the second part of the Bibliography. They have been arranged alphabetically in accordance with the businesses or institutions to which they relate.

Alford, B W E: *W. D. & H. O. Wills and the development of the U.K. tobacco industry 1786–1968* (1973)

Allen, Herbert Warner: *Number Three Saint James's Street* (1950)

Arlott, John: *The Snuff Shop* (1974)

Atton, A and Holland, H H: *The King's Customs* (1908)

Bareau, Paul: *The City* (1951)

Barnard, Alfred: *The Whisky Distilleries of the United Kingdom* (1887)

Barnard, Alfred: *The Noted Breweries of Great Britain and Ireland* (4 vols 1889–91)

Baumer, Edward: *The Early Days of the Sun Fire Office* (1910)

Bäumler, Ernst: *A Century of Chemistry (Farbwerke Hoechst)* (Frankfurt-am-Main, 1968)

Briggs, Asa (General Editor): *Essays in the History of Publishing* (250th anniversary of Longmans) (1974)

Büll, Reinhard: *Zur Geschichte des Wachshandels* (1960)

—*Zur Phänomenologie und Technologie der Kerze* (1965)

—*Zur Phänomenologie und Technologie der Kerze – Die Kerze heute* (1967)

—*Wachs und Kerzen im Brauch, Recht und Kult – Zur Typologie der Kerzen* (1970)

(All these are published by Farbwerke Hoechst, Frankfurt-am-Main, in the series 'Vom Wachs')

Butler, Rodney: *The History of Kirkstall Forge through Seven Centuries 1200–1954 A.D.* (2nd edition, 1954)

Button, Henry G: 'Old Businesses' (*English-speaking World*, March 1962)

—'Old Chartered Companies' (*Glasgow Herald*, 7/9/63)

—'Some old Dutch Businesses' (Talk broadcast from Radio Hilversum in November 1963 and printed in the *Civil Service Author* of September and October 1964)

—'Old Family Firms' (*Glasgow Herald*, 14/11/64)

—'The Royal Dublin Society' (*Agriculture*, April 1966)

—'Repeat Orders!' (*Competitors Journal*, 8/7/67)

—'The Button Collection of Business Histories' (*Business Archives*, December 1969)

—'The World's Oldest Bell-foundry' (*Country Life*, 5/3/70)

—'Bellfounders for 400 years' (*Foundry Trade Journal*, 10/9/70)

—'America's Oldest Business' (*Business Archives*, December 1973)

—*Letters about old businesses* in various journals:
Accountant, 14/10/67

Cambridge Evening News, 1/9/73

Country Life, 8/2/62, 12/5/66, 4/8/66, 19/1/67, 1/2/68, 30/10/69, 4/12/69

Daily Telegraph, 30/3/61, 6/1/64, 8/6/67, 22/6/67, 9/9/67, 10/10/67, 11/8/70, 11/6/76

Economist, 19/1/63, 20/4/68

Field, 30/3/61, 21/5/64, 18/6/64, 2/7/64

Financial Times, 5/6/61, 27/5/63, 5/3/64, 21/4/67, 4/6/68, 31/12/68, 6/5/70, 31/8/71, 8/9/72

Foundry Trade Journal, 24/10/63

Manchester Guardian, 13/6/58

New York Herald Tribune (Paris), 16/5/58, 20/11/61

Northampton Mercury, 22/5/69

Radio Times, 22/5/69

Sunday Times, 22/5/60, 30/10/66, 21/5/67

The Times, 14/7/62, 2/5/63, 3/3/65, 1C/2/66, 7/4/73

Camrose, Viscount: *British Newspapers and their Controllers* (1947)

Chandler, George: *Four Centuries of Banking* (Martins Bank) (2 vols, 1964 and 1968)

Clapham, Sir John: *The Bank of England* (2 vols, 1944)

Clunn, Harold P: *The Face of London* (no date)

Cobb, Gerald: *Oporto Older and Newer* (no date, possibly 1966)

Cormack, Alexander A: *Our Ancient and Honourable Craft* (1953)

Cox, G V: *Recollections of Oxford* (1868)

Craig, Sir John: *The Mint – A History of the London Mint from A.D. 287 to 1948* (1953)

Croft-Cooke, Rupert: *Port* (1957)

Croft-Cooke, Rupert: *Madeira* (1961)

Daniel, Glyn: *Lascaux and Carnac* (1955)

Ellis, Aytoun: *The Penny Universities* (1956)

Elphick, George P: *Sussex Bells and Belfries* (1970)

Féraud, Francis V: *Les Grands Événements et la Vie Quotidienne (Les Petites-Affiches)* (Paris, 1968)

Fletcher, H L V: *North Wales* (1955)

Fletcher, H L V: *South Wales* (1956)

Fulford, Roger: *Glyn's 1753–1953* (1953)

Gérard, Max: *Messieurs Hottinguer – Banquiers à Paris* (Paris, 1968)

Gordon, George: *The Shore Porters' Society of Aberdeen 1498–1969* (Aberdeen, no date)

Gott, Philip P: *All About Candy And Chocolate* (Chicago, 1958)

Gray, G J: *Cambridge Bookselling and the oldest bookshop in the United Kingdom* (1925)

Halstead, Ivor: *Bond Street* (1952)

Handover, P M: *A History of the London Gazette 1665–1965* (1965)

Harper, C G: *Queer Things about London* (1923)

Heer, Jean: *World Events 1866–1966 – The First Hundred Years of Nestlé* (Switzerland, 1966)

Henry, J A: *The First Hundred Years of the Standard Bank* (1963)

Hoare, H P R: *Hoare's Bank, A Record 1673–1932* (1932)

Hoare, H P R: *Hoare's Bank, A Record 1672–1955* (1955)

Holder, R F: *Bank of New South Wales – Vol. I, 1817–1893* (1970), *Vol. II 1894–1970* (1970)

Hudson, Kenneth: *Industrial Archaeology of Southern England* (1965, second edition 1968)

Hudson, W: *Leet Jurisdiction in the City of Norwich during the XIIIth and XIVth Centuries* (1892)

Janes, Hurford: *The Red Barrel – A History of Watney Mann* (1963)

Jeffs, Julian: *Sherry* (1961)

Johnson, J and Strickland Gibson: *Print and Privilege at Oxford to the year 1700* (1946)

Johnstone: *London Commercial Guide and Street Directory* (1817)

Landmann, Julius: *Leu & Co, 1775–1905* (Zürich, 1905)

Leighton-Boyce, J A S L: *Smiths the Bankers 1658–1958* (1958)

Lipson, E: *Economic History of England* (several editions)

Machlup, F: *The Political Economy of Monopoly* (1952)

Mathias, Peter: *The Brewing Industry in England 1700–1830* (1959)

Mathias, Peter: *Retailing Revolution* (Allied Suppliers) (1967)

Mathias, Peter: *The First Industrial Nation* (1969)

McKechnie, Samuel: *The Romance of the Civil Service*

McNeil, Ian: *Joseph Bramah – A Century of Invention 1749–1851* (1968)

Mears and Stainbank: *Church Bell – illustrated catalogue of about 1919* (the Whitechapel Bell Foundry)

Mumby, F A: *Publishing and Bookselling* (first edition 1930, fifth edition, partly by Ian Norrie, 1974)

National Benzole: *Our National Heritage* (series of booklets, undated)

Niemann, Albert: *Die Landwirtschaft Niedersachsens 1914–1964* (Celle, 1964)

Plummer, Alfred: *The Witney Blanket Industry* (1934)

Plummer, Alfred, and Early, Richard E: *The Blanket Makers (History of Charles Early & Marriott (Witney) Ltd.)* (1969)

Plummer, Alfred: *The London Weavers' Company 1600–1970* (1972)

Ponti, Ermanno: *Il Banco di Santo Spirito* (Rome, 1951)

Ray, Cyril: *The House of Warre 1670–1970* (Portugal, 1970)

Ray, Cyril: *Bollinger* (1971)

Ray, Cyril: *Cognac* (1973)

Rees, Goronwy: *St. Michael – A History of Marks & Spencer* (1973)

Robertson, Patrick: *The Shell Book of Firsts* (1974)

Rottenbach, Bruno: *650 Jahre Bürgerspital zum Heiligen Geist* (Würzburg, 1969)

Russell, Sir E John: *A History of Agricultural Science in Great Britain* (1966)

Samuelsson, Kurt: *From Great Power to Welfare State* (300th anniversary of National Bank of Sweden) (1968)

Saunders, Edith: *The Age of Worth*

Scott, J D: *Vickers – A History* (1962)

Smith, George, and Benger, Frank: *The Oldest London Bookshop 1728–1928* (1928)

Stow, John: *A Survey of London* (1603)

Thier, Manfred: *Geschichte der schwäbischen Hüttenwerke 1365–1802* (Aalen and Stuttgart, 1965)

Thomas, A H: *Calendar of Early Mayor's Court Rolls of the City of London* (1924)

Thornbury, Walter and Walford, Edward: *Old and New London* (6 vols, 1879–85)

Tussenbroek, Otto van: *Gedenkboek samengesteld bij het 150 jarig bestaan van de N.V. J. P. Wyers' industrie- en handelsonderneming* (Amsterdam, 1947)

Underwood, Reginald: *Pageant of Finedon* (1942)

Universal British Directory (1798)

Wadsworth, A P, and Mann, J de L: *The Cotton Industry* (1931)

Wallis, Philip: *At the Sign of the Ship, 1724–1974* (1974)

Whitbourn, Frank: *Mr. Lock of St. James's Street – His continuing Life and Changing Times* (1971)

Williams, L N, and Williams, M: *The Postage Stamp* (1956)

Willems, Franz: *Prym – Geschichte und Genealogie* (Wiesbaden 1968)

Wilshire, Lewis: *The Vale of Berkeley* (1954)

Wilson, Aubrey: *London's Industrial Heritage* (1967)

The Banco di Napoli (Naples, 1955)

CIBA – The Story of Chemical Industry in Basle (Olten and Lausanne, 1959)

Du Pont – The Autobiography of an American Enterprise (Wilmington, Delaware, 1952)

La Maison Enschedé 1703–1953 (Haarlem, 1953)

Löwenbräu München-Vom Werden und Wirken einer der ältesten bürgerlichen Braustätten in Bayern (Munich, 1969)

Monte dei Paschi di Siena – Bank founded in 1472 (Siena, 1965)

Monte dei Paschi di Siena – Note Economiche, Anno V-n. 5–6 (1972)

Pasticcio auf das 250-jährige Bestehen des Verlages Breitkopf & Härtel (1969)

Société Générale de Belgique 1822–1972 (Brussels, 1972)

Weihenstephan – älteste Brauerei der Welt (editions of 1963, 1966 and 1970, Munich)

Wine Institute, San Francisco – booklets on The Wine Industry and on Wine Growing and Wine Types

SECTION II
REFERENCE

Fortune

Times 1000

Economist

Financial Times

Sunday Times

Observer

Sunday Telegraph

Investors' Chronicle

Economic Progress Report

The Royal Commission on the Distribution of Income and Wealth

Capital International

Guinness Book of Records

Section 2

THE FINANCIAL WORLD

Andrew P Lampert, BSc

THE FINANCIAL WORLD

U K FINANCIAL SYSTEM AND THE ECONOMY

Economic activity is determined by the decisions of individuals, companies and Government. However, the British Government must now take account of the external factors (e.g. size of balance of payments deficit) in its determining how far it can achieve its domestic objectives (e.g. higher welfare benefits, nationalised industry subsidies, etc). The magnitude of the external borrowings required to achieve such objectives has resulted in the Government having recourse to International Monetary Fund (IMF) loans, which limit the scope for carrying on the expansion of Government spending. If the international credibility of the British Government's economic policy is in question, the IMF may be the only source of help. This support would, in the circumstances, only be granted on terms which imposed stringent conditions on the Government's management of the economy.

The Government implements its internal policy in three ways. Firstly, it regulates the amount of credit available in the economy through Bank of England operations (e.g. level of interest rates and guidance to the commercial banks on their lending) and the exchange value of sterling. Secondly, it sets the level of taxes on companies and individuals and on its own spending (e.g. defence, welfare and Government employee wages and salaries). Through its revenue the Government influences the level of economic activity and effects a redistribution of the national income. Moreover, its expenditure not only reflects its general social and economic objectives, but also may be directed towards specific areas (e.g. regional development, food subsidies and support for British Leyland). Thirdly, the Government may intervene directly to control the level of wages and prices. Since 1961 different Governments have attempted to curb inflation by this means with varying degrees of success.

Business requires finance to carry stock, pay labour and buy plant and equipment to ensure future viability and growth. To meet this demand for finance to produce goods and services for consumers, savings from individuals and companies are channelled through the banks and the Stock Exchange. The financial institutions (e.g. pension funds, insurance companies, unit trusts, investment trusts and building societies) are important intermediaries in this process.

One of the main problems that has faced Britain is her propensity to consume more than she produces which is continually reflected in her balance of payments deficits.

The above summary is represented in the diagram on page 193.

COMPANY FORMATION

Companies registered in the UK

The first time the number of companies registered in a year exceeded 5000 in a year was

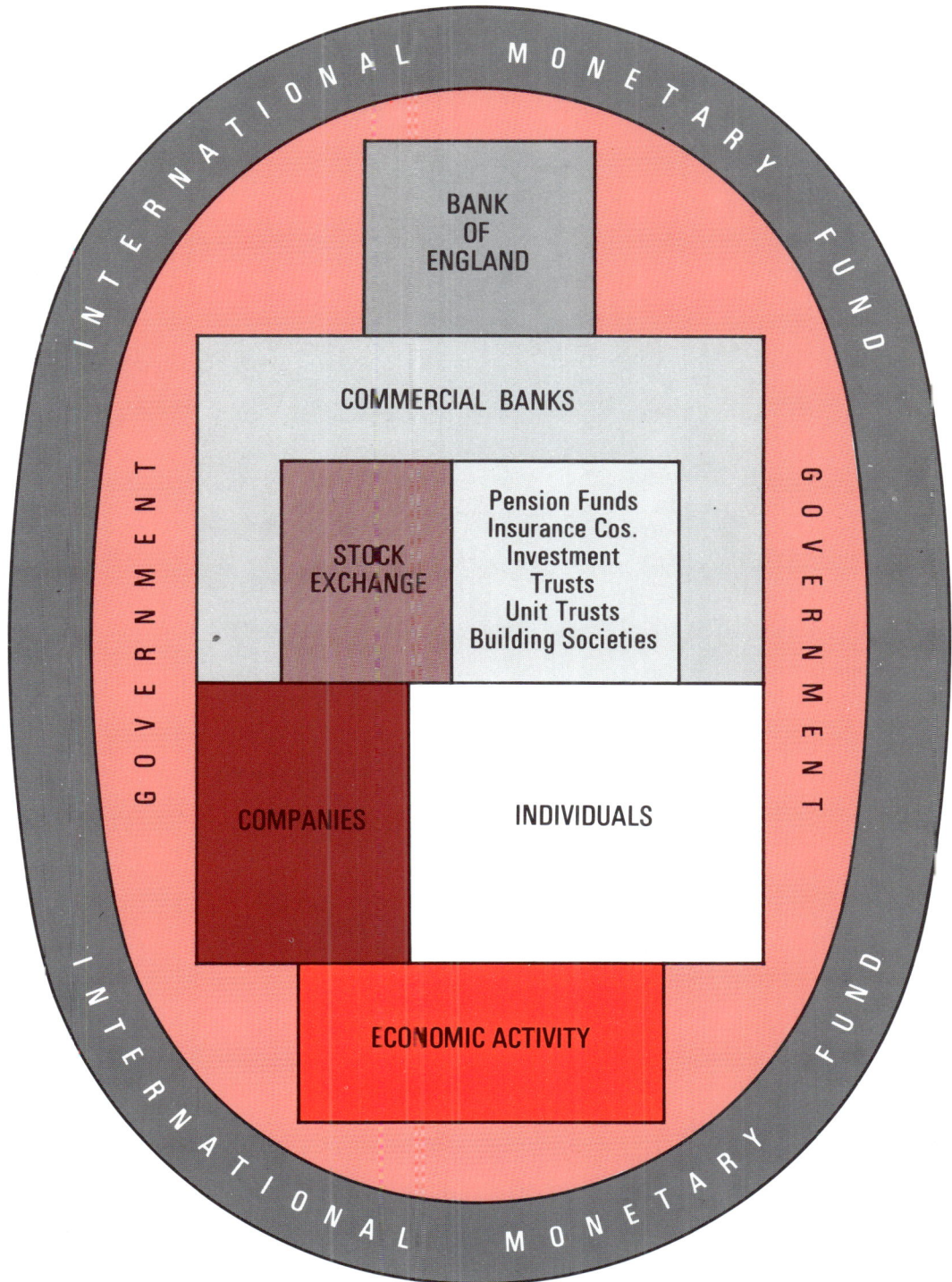

Model of UK Financial System

in 1882, and it was not until after the First World War, in 1919, that company registrations exceeded 10000. During the Second World War registrations remained at a lowly 700 a year, but in 1946 exceeded 25000 for the first time.

Greatest number in a year

Company registrations reached a peak of 67349 in 1973 compared with 1234 a century earlier.

The 1973 total can be split up as follows:

Companies with share capital

	limited	66608
	unlimited	151

Companies without share capital

	limited	569
	unlimited	21

Total of companies registered   67349

Nominal share capital

The peak total nominal share capital registered reached a record £440300000 in 1974 implying an average of £1030 per company – also a record.

The amount of share capital for England and Wales for 1974 was as follows:

Total	Not Exceeding £100	£101 to £1000	£1001 to £5000	£5001 to £10000
39884	25134	827	8034	2025

£10001 to £20000	£20001 to £50000	£50001 to £100000	Exceeding £100000
2282	740	373	469

Note that the large majority of all companies have nominal capital not exceeding £100.

Current number of companies

On 1 March 1976 the 1246577th company – Eurocastle Investments Limited – was registered at Companies House.

PATENTS

Earliest English patent

The earliest of all known English patents was that granted by Henry VI in 1449 to Flemish-born **John of Utynam** for making the coloured glass required for the windows of Eton College.

Shortest/Longest

The shortest, concerning a harrow attachment, of 48 words, was filed on 14 May 1956 while the longest, comprising 2318 pages of text and 495 pages of drawings, was filed on 31 March 1965 by **IBM** to cover a computer.

Number of patents

The peak number of patents filed in the United Kingdom in any one year was 63614 in 1969, of which 37127 were sealed, i.e. accepted and formally endorsed after the end of a three-month opposition period when the public can indicate any objections to the patent.

The highest number of patents sealed was 43038 out of total applications of 61995 in 1968. The lowest number of patents sealed since 1884 was 7465 in 1945.

Patent infringement

The greatest settlement ever made in a patent infringement suit $9250000 (then £3303000) paid in April 1952 by the **Ford Motor Company** to the Ferguson Tractor Company for a claim filed in January 1948.

Most Profitable

Probably the most profitable patent ever filed was US Patent No 174465 issued to 29-year-old **Alexander Graham Bell** on 7 March 1876 for his invention, the telephone.

BANKRUPTCIES AND LIQUIDATIONS

Bankruptcy is an often misused word – only individuals or partnerships can go bankrupt, which involves the seizure of all the bankrupt's assets, e.g. his house, car and sporting gear.

All he can rightfully hold back are bedding for his family, and the tools of his trade. However, limited companies are liquidated and then the only amounts available for the creditors are the share capital and the sale of any of the company's assets.

The only time an individual can be badly caught when a company collapses is when he has guaranteed loans or mortages made to the company. This has been one of the main features of the spectacular property company collapses of the last couple of years.

Bankruptcy figures

The old record of 5048 bankruptcies in 1923 was unsurpassed until 1974, when 5608 cases were reported. Continuing tough business conditions led to an all-time record figure of 7143 in 1975. The table below shows the breakdown of UK bankruptcies in 1975.

Type of Bankruptcy	% of 1975 total
Employees of no occupation or unemployed	22.6
Construction	22.1
Retailing	16.0
Road Haulage	6.7
Directors and Promoters of companies	5.9
Garages	4.5
Finance and Professional services	4.5
Hotels and Restaurants	4.3
Others	13.4
TOTAL	100.0

Highest bankruptcy rate

The County Court involved in the greatest number of bankruptcies (in the UK) in 1975 was that of Croydon, with 189 cases.

Largest bankruptcy in the UK

If the bankruptcy petitions against **Mr William Stern,** whose international property empire collapsed in May 1974, are successful, it will be the largest-ever bankruptcy in the UK. At 31 July 1975 his debts, from giving personal guarantees during the property boom, were shown to be a staggering £110246692 against assets of only £4462.

Company liquidations

The number of companies liquidated in England and Wales was a record 5398 in 1975

up from 3720 a year earlier. In 1975 there were 3111 voluntary and 2287 compulsory liquidations. The table below gives an industrial analysis of companies liquidated in 1975 in England and Wales.

Type of Company	% of 1975 total
Manufacturing	23.5
Construction	17.7
Financial and professional services	16.7
Retailing	10.4
Wholesaling	8.6
Road haulage	5.6
Other	17.5
TOTAL	100.0

Largest retailing liquidation.

On 10 February 1975 the creditors' lawyers declared that the 70-year-old American retailing business, **W T Grant** (1100 stores and 75000 employees), should be liquidated. It was the final chapter in the largest bankruptcy proceeding in the history of retailing, with the company's debt totalling more than $800 million.

Rolls-Royce collapse

The staggering increase in the research and development costs of the RB211 engine for the Lockheed 'Tristar' aircraft was the background to the collapse of Rolls-Royce. On 4 February 1971 the Directors requested the appointment of a Receiver for the Debenture holders, and estimates (later proved to be wildly exaggerated) of the cash shortfall reached £127 million – the highest in British corporate history. On 4 October 1971 the members and creditors of Rolls-Royce resolved that the company be put into voluntary liquidation as debts totalled £120.8 million and only £59.9 million was available for unsecured creditors, leaving a deficiency of £60.9 million, for the ordinary shareholders. However, with further realisation of assets including receipt for £50 million from the Government for the Aero-engine section, £17 million from the successful floatation of Rolls-Royce Motors and a massive £76 million from debtors, there was a surplus of £38.2 million for the ordinary shareholders by 7 November 1975. Payments to the ordinary shareholders were as follows:

21 February 1974	25.0p
25 July 1974	10.0p
17 February 1975	15.0p
4 October 1975	8.1p
	58.1p

The Rolls-Royce collapse and subsequent

realisation of assets probably led to the most successful outcome for ordinary shareholders ever. Those who bought the shares at a half pence about the time of Rolls-Royce's suspension on the London Stock Exchange made one of the most profitable investments this century – a 116-fold increase in under five years.

Auditors of companies quoted on New York Stock Exchange

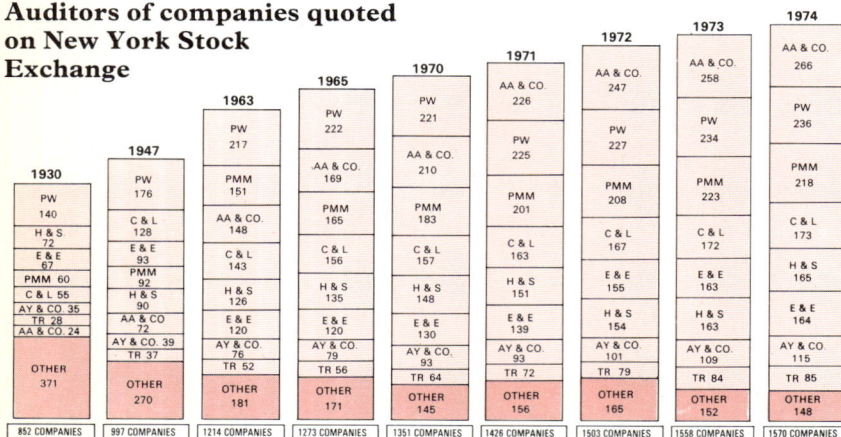

1930 — 852 COMPANIES
- PW 140
- H & S 72
- E & E 67
- PMM 60
- C & L 55
- AY & CO. 35
- TR 28
- AA & CO. 24
- OTHER 371

1947 — 997 COMPANIES
- PW 176
- C & L 128
- E & E 93
- PMM 92
- H & S 90
- AA & CO 72
- AY & CO. 39
- TR 37
- OTHER 270

1963 — 1214 COMPANIES
- PW 217
- PMM 151
- AA & CO. 148
- C & L 143
- H & S 126
- E & E 120
- AY & CO. 76
- TR 52
- OTHER 181

1965 — 1273 COMPANIES
- PW 222
- AA & CO. 169
- PMM 165
- C & L 156
- H & S 135
- E & E 120
- AY & CO. 79
- TR 56
- OTHER 171

1970 — 1351 COMPANIES
- PW 221
- AA & CO. 210
- PMM 183
- C & L 157
- H & S 148
- E & E 130
- AY & CO. 93
- TR 64
- OTHER 145

1971 — 1426 COMPANIES
- AA & CO. 226
- PW 225
- PMM 201
- C & L 163
- H & S 151
- E & E 139
- AY & CO. 93
- TR 72
- OTHER 156

1972 — 1503 COMPANIES
- AA & CO. 247
- PW 227
- PMM 208
- C & L 167
- E & E 155
- H & S 154
- AY & CO. 101
- TR 79
- OTHER 165

1973 — 1558 COMPANIES
- AA & CO. 258
- PW 234
- PMM 223
- C & L 172
- E & E 163
- H & S 163
- AY & CO. 109
- TR 84
- OTHER 152

1974 — 1570 COMPANIES
- AA & CO. 266
- PW 236
- PMM 218
- C & L 173
- H & S 165
- E & E 164
- AY & CO. 115
- TR 85
- OTHER 148

KEY

AA & Co.	Arthur Anderson
AY & Co.	Arthur Young & Co.
C & L	Coopers & Lybrand
E & E	Ernst & Ernst
H & S	Haskins & Sells
PMM	Peat, Marwick, Mitchell
PW	Price Waterhouse
TR	Touche Ross & Co.

ACCOUNTANCY

The Auditors of Britain's top 1000 companies:

Rank	Firm	First 100	Next 900	Total
1	Peat, Marwick, Mitchell	9	89	98
2	Price Waterhouse	11	61	72
3	Deloittes	11	54	65
4	Coopers and Lybrand	9	50	59
5	Thomson McLintock	4	26	30

The table above ranks the top UK accountancy firms according to their audits of Britain's top 1000 companies but does not reflect fees from management consulting, taxation services, liquidations and receivership investigations.

Turnover

Accountancy firms are very sensitive about their fees, expenses and profits and are reluctant to disclose figures. However, in 1973 the estimated world turnover of **Peat, Marwick,**

Mitchell was $350 million and of **Arthur Anderson** $300 million.

International Accountancy Firms

Rank	Firm	No of world-wide partners and staff	No of countries of operation	Year founded [*]
1	Peat, Marwick, Mitchell	17500	60	1866
2	Coopers and Lybrand	15000	73	1854
3	Price Waterhouse	14800	40	1848
4	Deloitte, Haskins and Sells	12350	42	1845
5	Arthur Anderson	12000	40	1913
6	Whinney, Murray, Ernst and Ernst	12000	77	1848
7	Touche Ross	11000	40	1898
8	Arthur Young	10000	60	1894

[*] The year in which the firms or the oldest of its predecessors or constituent firms first practised as public accountants.

Thus, **Peat, Marwick, Mitchell** heads the table in number of world-wide partners and employees; **Whinney, Murray, Ernst and Ernst** could be called the most international firm operating in 77 different countries and **Deloitte, Haskins and Sells** the oldest of the major firms.

UK accounting firms

	Clients' net tangible assets £m	Clients' sales £m	League Position by clients assets 1975	sales 1975
Deloitte	17 298	15 984	1	1
Price Waterhouse	16 813	13 170	2	2
Coopers and Lybrand	9 358	11 714	3	3
Whinney Murray	7 552	9 464	4	4
Peat, Marwick, Mitchell	7 251	6 392	5	6
Turquands, Barton, Mayhew	6 304	7 078	6	5
Touche Ross	6 008	5 118	7	7
Thomson McLintock	4 811	4 767	8	8
Arthur Young, McClelland Moores	2 241	2 240	9	9
Spicer and Pegler	1 347	1 422	10	10

Analysis by Offices and Partners in the UK

Rank	Firm	UK offices	Rank	Firm	UK partners
1	Thornton Baker	46	1	Thornton Baker	254
2	Peat, Marwick, Mitchell	35	2	Deloitte	192
3	Deloitte	28	3	Peat, Marwick Mitchell	133
4	Coopers and Lybrand	27	4	Coopers and Lybrand	110
5	Kidsons	25	5	Thomson McLintock	95
6	Armitage and Norton	20	6	Kidsons	90
7	Pannell Fitzpatrick	19	7	Binder Hamlyn Singleton Fabian	87
8	Turquands, Barton, Mayhew	17	8	Pannell Fitzpatrick	85
8	Spicer and Pegler	17	9	Tomsley Witt	84
8	Thomson McLintock	17	10	Josolyne Layton-Bennett	83
			10	Spicer and Pegler	83

Auditors of the Fortune list of 1974 companies (excluding life insurance companies)

Name	First 500 indus corp	Commercial banking	Merchandising	Transportation	Utilities	Diversified financial corps	Total	Sec. 500 indus corp	Grand Total
Price Waterhouse	97	4	5	10	10	4	130	63	193
Peat, Marwick, Mitchell	69	12	11	8	3	15	118	48	166
Arthur Anderson	80	7	6	7	14	1	115	77	192
Haskins and Sells*	51	7	4	12	14	7	95	39	134
Ernst and Ernst	57	13	3	6	—	5	84	87	171
Coopers and Lybrand	46	3	5	1	7	5	67	56	123
Arthur Young and Company	48	1	2	2	1	6	60	43	103
Touche Ross and Company	21	3	10	2	—	7	43	27	70
Others	31	—	4	2	1	—	38	60	98
TOTALS	500	50	50	50	50	50	750	500	1250

* Haskins and Sells is the US branch of Deloittes.

Thus, Price Waterhouse, which comes second in *The Times 1000*, just beats Arthur Anderson in the *Fortune* list and Peat, Marwick, Mitchell is fourth.

When one considers the auditors of companies quoted on the New York Stock Exchange (see diagram, page 196) one notices that in the past 45 years **Arthur Anderson** has shown the fastest growth and has moved from No 8 to No 1.

The largest proportion of companies, quoted on the New York Stock Exchange, audited by the biggest of the top eight firms was **Price Waterhouse** with 21.1 per cent (i.e. 140 of the total 481) in 1930.

ADVERTISING AGENCIES

Agency Billings

The largest single international advertising agency in the world is **J Walter Thompson Company** which in 1975 had total world-wide billings of $900.1 million. A higher figure of $945.8 million in 1975 was reported for Dentsu of Japan but is not believed to be comparable since revenues are not wholly derived from agency work. The largest agency group is the **Interpublic Group of Companies** consisting of mainly McCann Erickson and Wassey, which had billings of $1126 million in 1975. The group, which operated in 51 countries with 6600 employees spent a total of $102356000 on salaries (57.5 per cent of total income).

The largest wholly British firm is **Saachi Saachi and Compton** which had billings of £30.5 million in 1975.

James Walter Thompson – biggest advertising agency

Total annual advertising expenditure

A record $10200 million of billings was reported by 738 advertising agencies in 68 countries in 1975.

UK Top 20 products in rank order in 1975 by Press and TV expenditures

	COMBINED PRESS & TELEVISION			*PRESS ONLY*			*TELEVISION ONLY*	
Rank	Brand	Total expenditure £000	Rank	Brand	Press expenditure £000	Rank	Brand	TV expenditure £000
1	COI Energy Crisis	3558	1	Co-op (Local Branches)	2392	1	COI Energy Crisis	2362
2	Boots (Retail Stores)	3332	2	Boots (Retail Stores)	2115	2	Woolworth's (National)	1825
3	Co-op (Local Branches)	3026	3	C and A (Press)	1822	3	K Tel Records	1408
4	Woolworth's (National)	2167	4	Co-op (National)	1436	4	Kellogg Corn Flakes	1350
5	Brentford Nylons (Mail Order)	2115	5	Currys Limited	1421	5	Brentford Nylons (Mail Order)	1296
6	Co-op (National)	1973	6	COI Energy Crisis	1196	6	Allied Carpet and Bedding Stores	1258
7	C and A (Press)	1822	7	B and H Special Filter	1195	7	Boots (Retail Stores)	1217
8	Fine Fare and Associated Stores	1746	8	Players No 6 Filter	1184	8	Guinness (Bottled)	1116
9	Allied Carpet and Bedding Stores	1728	9	MFI	1070	9	The Sun	1094
10	Currys Limited	1490	10	Dixons Hi-Fi Photographic Centre	1062	10	Oxo Red Stock Cubes	1069
11	Martini	1461	11	Comet Discount Warehouse	1044	11	Drive Washing Powder	1024
12	Kellogg Corn Flakes	1455	12	Tesco Stores Limited	974	12	Burton Tailoring	1010
13	K Tel Records	1408	13	Plumbs Mail Order	917	13	C and A (Television)	979
14	British Airways	1385	14	Fine Fare and Associated Stores	898	14	Williams Furniture Store	970
15	Guinness (Bottled)	1326	15	Austin Morris Range	875	15	Martini	927
16	MFI	1325	16	Shopertunities	821	16	Coca-Cola	874
17	Solid Fuel Advisory Service	1286	17	Brentford Nylons (Mail Order)	819	17	Warwick Records	874
18	Williams Furniture Store	1272	18	British Airways	757	18	Kodak Cameras	865
19	Oxo Red Stock Cubes	1242	19	Debenham Local Stores	734	19	Heinz Soups	856
20	B & H Special Filter	1195	20	House of Holland	726	20	Stork SB Soft Margarine	852

Employees

The largest ever total number of employees in one agency was 7225 for J Walter Thompson in 1970.

World's biggest advertiser

The world's biggest advertiser is **Sears Roebuck,** America's largest retail chain, with $378 266 000 (£180 million) in 1975. Proctor and Gamble takes second place with $325 million in 1974.

    Carter-Wallace Incorporated, the drug and toiletry products company has the distinction of having spent 31.3 per cent of its sales revenue on advertising, the highest percentage of the top 100 advertising expenditures in 1974.

UK Advertisers

The table below lists the top 15 advertisers in the UK in 1975 by combined Press and TV expenditure.

Rank	Advertiser Holding Company	Expenditure (£m) (Press and TV)
1	Unilever	19.9
2	Imperial Group	14.1
3	HM Government	13.5
4	Cadbury Schweppes	11.5
5	Beecham	8.1
6	Mars	8.0
7	Reed	6.5
8	Gallaher	6.0
9	Co-op Wholesale	5.8
10	Allied Breweries	5.8
11	British Leyland	5.6
12	Rowntree Mackintosh	5.4
13	Boots	4.8
14	Ranks Hovis McDougall	4.7
15	Heinz	4.5

BANKING

Oldest surviving bank

The oldest surviving commercial bank in the world is believed to be the **Monte Dei Paschi di Siena** which was founded on 14 March 1472 by the General Council of the Republic of Siena (now part of Italy). The headquarters were established in the ancient castle of the Salimbeni – home of an aristocratic banking family. The castle continues to be the bank's head office. Today the bank has assets of $9862 million and 370 branches. (See also page 115.)

Oldest merchant bank

Baring Brothers and Company Limited is the oldest merchant bank in London. It was founded by John and Francis Baring in 1763, and the name was changed to its present form in 1806.

Largest bank

The **International Bank for Reconstruction and Development** (founded 27 December 1945), the United Nations 'World Bank' at 1818 H Street NW, Washington, DC, USA, has an authorised share capital of $27 000 million. There were 127 members with a subscribed capital of $30 859 965 000 at 31 March 1976.

    The **International Monetary Fund** in Washington, DC, USA has 128 members with total quotas of SDR (Special Drawing Right) 29 211 400 000 ($33 885 million) at 31 March 1976.

Largest private bank

The private bank with the greatest deposits is the **Bank of America National Trust and Savings Association,** of San Francisco, California, USA with $56 544 789 000 at 31 December 1975. Its total resources were $66 763 054 000 (then £33 000 million).

    Barclays Bank (with Barclays Bank International and other subsidiary companies) had

Bank of England

Top 20 commercial banks in the world by deposits in 1975

(Figures converted to $ by exchange rates at balance sheet date.)

Rank	Bank	Head office	G = group B = bank	Deposits $ million
1	Bank America Corporation	San Francisco	G	56 545
2	Citicorp	New York	G	44 976
3	Groupe BNP	Paris	G	37 880
4	Chase Manhattan Corporation	New York	G	33 928
5	Deutsche Bank	Frankfurt	G	32 369
6	Credit Lyonnais	Paris	G	29 422
7	Barclays Bank	London	G	29 338
8	Société Générale	Paris	G	27 145
9	National Westminster Bank	London	G	26 799
10	Dai-Ichi Kangyo Bank	Tokyo	B	23 739
11	Caisse Nationale de Crédit Agricole	Avignon	G	23 632
12	Westdeutsche Landesbank Girozentrale	Düsseldorf	B	23 484
13	Manufacturers Hanover Corporation	New York	G	23 471
14	Royal Bank of Canada	Montreal	G	22 422
15	Sumitomo Bank	Osaka	G	21 501
16	Fuji Bank	Tokyo	G	21 148
17	Banca Nazionale del Lavoro	Rome	B	21 019
18	Dresdner Bank	Frankfurt	G	20 182
19	J P Morgan & Company	New York	G	19 938
20	Mitsubishi Bank	Tokyo	G	19 762

5090 branches in 70 countries (3300 in the UK) at 31 December 1975. Deposits totalled a record £14 493 545 000 and assets £16 323 520 000. Employees totalled 94 500 world-wide, with 63 000 in the UK.

BANK OF ENGLAND

The prototype of modern central banks is the **Bank of England,** founded in 1694, which acts as a lender of last resort to the money market, i.e. it is willing to lend in times of crisis when no other lender can be found. The principal duty of the Bank of England is to act as intermediary between the Government and the financial system. Thus, the Bank manages the country's foreign exchange reserves and the exchange rate for sterling. At the same time, it seeks to regulate conditions in the UK financial markets, with a view to carrying out the Government's monetary policy and to covering the Government's borrowing needs. To achieve these aims, the Bank operates on a day-to-day basis, in the foreign exchange market, buying and selling foreign currencies against sterling, and in the money market, relieving credit shortages and selling Government securities.

If the commercial banks are short of funds, they do not borrow directly from the Bank of England but call in their short-term loans from the discount houses who get money either by re-discounting bills at the Bank or by borrowing from the Bank at 'Minimum Lending Rate' or MLR. Although the Bank of England always supplies the discount houses' needs through these two channels it reserves for itself the decision as to which channel should be used. Since MLR is usually higher than the rate at which the Bank re-discounts bills, a Bank of England decision to lend at MLR, i.e. to put the discount houses 'into the Bank', is sometimes an indication of a move towards a tighter credit policy.

The Bank of England with 6975 full-time and 900 part-time employees made an operating profit of £13 040 000 in 1975, after a special provision for losses of £9 780 000. There are also branches at Birmingham, Bristol, Leeds, Liverpool, Newcastle, Southampton and Glasgow.

Minimum Lending Rate

The highest-ever figure for the British Bank Rate (since 13 October 1972 the Minimum

Lending Rate, MLR) was 13 per cent from 13 November 1973 to 4 January 1974. The largest one day rise in MLR was 2½ per cent from 9 per cent to 11½ per cent on 27 July 1973. The longest period without a change was 12 years 13 days from 26 October 1939 to 7 November 1951, during which time the rate stayed at 2 per cent. This record low rate was first attained on 22 April 1852.

Accepting Houses Committee

The Accepting Houses Committee constitutes the inner élite of the London merchant-banking community. It was formed in 1914 and represents 17 merchant banks. The chief qualification for membership of the Committee are that a substantial part of the business of each house shall consist of accepting bills to finance the trade of others. The bill, when accepted, can command the finest rates on the discount market and the acceptances are freely taken by the Bank of England. The two banks most recently to join are **Rea Brothers** (1969) and **Singer and Friedlander** in 1973. In the summer of 1975 **Brandts,** a founder-member of the Committee, resigned from the Committee after it had announced a massive £14 million provision against losses on its loan to property companies.

The largest accepting house in London is **Hambros Bank Limited.** At its last balance-sheet date it had total assets of £1 261 423 000 and net profit after tax of £3 154 000. The smallest is **Rea Brothers Limited** which had total assets (including acceptances) of £66 908 000 at the end of 1975.

MAJOR BANKING FAILURES

Bank failures are caused when people who have deposited money in a bank get frightened that the bank will not be able to pay back their deposits. A 'run' on a bank is an attempt by large numbers of the bank's customers to withdraw all their deposits in cash at the same time, or change the bank's own notes for gold.

In the 18th century the South Sea Bubble brought down several small banks, but banking then was not as widely spread over the country as it was later on, and the first real crisis in Britain did not develop until 1793, when the collapse of a big London banking-house

started a general panic, first in Newcastle and then all over the country. Out of about 400 country bankers then in business, 100 closed completely, and others were badly shaken.

Between 1780 and 1820 nearly 1000 banks closed their doors causing obvious hardship to those with life savings in the local banks. The worst year of all for the country bankers was 1825, when 93 banks failed following the collapse of two big London banking companies.

The **North and South Wales Bank** closed its doors in 1847 as a result of a newspaper report, completely unfounded when it appeared, that the bank was about to close its doors: a prophecy that was self-fulfilled in two days, and thus a good example of the effect of a 'run'.

In 1866 **Overend, Gurney and Company** in London suspended payment on what became a legendary Black Friday, and the crisis saw not only the expected domino effect but also some of the newer foundations gravely at risk as a result of speculation in their shares.

In 1890 the big London merchant-banking house of **Barings** was in serious trouble – heavy speculative commitments in South America left them dangerously illiquid. Expec-

Barings. *(Crown Copyright)*

tation that Barings would have to suspend payments – leading to a crisis of unknown proportions – caused the City, guided by the Bank of England, to mount its first major rescue operation costing £17 million.

By the turn of the century the new joint-stock banks in Britain had grown big, and were unlikely to be disturbed by a 'run'. But smaller private banks were not so fortunate; nor were foreign countries which had not followed the British example of the powerful bank with many branches.

The world crisis of 1931 was ushered in by the failure of the **Kreditanstalt** of Vienna in May. The **Darmstädter Bank** in Germany (as large as one of the British 'Big Four' banks) followed and brought down the German banking system in July – thousands of banks all over the world failed.

Biggest bank failure

The world's largest bank collapse occurred on 8 October 1974, when the US Government declared **Franklin National Bank** insolvent. It had been the 20th largest bank in the USA. At the time of its insolvency the bank had borrowed $1700 million from the Federal Reserve Bank of New York. The bulk of Franklin National's business was subsequently taken over by the European American Banking Corporation, which is jointly owned by Deutsche Bank, Societé Générale, Societé générale de Banque, Midland Bank, Amsterdam Rotterdam Bank and Kredit Anstalt Bankverein.

Franklin National's financial difficulties stemmed mainly from the very heavy losses it made on the foreign exchange markets in the spring of 1974. In the first eight months of 1974 its total losses amounted to $89 million. In August 1975, eight former executives of the bank were indicted by a New York Federal Grand Jury on criminal charges involving the misappropriation of over $38 million of the bank's money, unauthorised foreign exchange dealing and conspiring to defraud.

Fringe banking crisis

Britain's fringe banking crisis was precipitated by the collapse of **London and County Securities** in December 1973. The bank under

the direction of Gerald Caplan had grown rapidly in the preceding three years mainly through lending money in Britain's booming property market. It pioneered the siting of banks inside stores and built up a large number of small depositors. This affair was one more prominent on the front pages than on the financial news.

The bank's future began to look progressively more precarious with the decline in property prices on which much of London and County's lending was secured. On 27 November 1973 Donald Bardsley resigned – he had been brought in from Hill Samuel in May 1973 to head the banking operations. The shares were sold heavily and on 30 November the quote was suspended. A consortium of banks headed by National Westminster stepped in to take control. It was subsequently disclosed that London and County had lost £16 million in its loan portfolio.

After the collapse of London and County, confidence in other small banks was thrown into question. Many had built up sizeable property loan portfolios with funds bought in the volatile money-markets. These funds were now withdrawn as the big clearing banks became suspicious about their continued viability. It was a classic crisis of confidence. Money was withdrawn indiscriminately from institutions which were both well and badly managed.

On 18 December 1973 **Moorgate Mercantile,** which financed car purchases, had its share quote suspended and two days later **Cedar Holdings** had to be rescued. **Cornhill Consolidated, Western Credit, J H Vavasseur and Company, Triumph Investment Trust, Cannon Street Investments** and other secondary banks were all subsequently supported or liquidated.

At the same time the Government had to mount its own rescue operation with a loan of £85 million to the **Crown Agents,** the semi-official finance and purchasing agency, which acts for Overseas Governments and public authorities, to boost its capital base and to replenish its liquid resources. The Crown Agents had been intimately caught up in the secondary banking crisis, having placed deposits with a number of the fringe banks which subsequently got into trouble. Its problems were compounded by the falling value of its long-term investments, including substantial sums tied up in the property market.

Heaviest banking loss

The **First National Finance Corporation** is believed to have incurred the heaviest losses ever of any British bank. During the early 1970s the bank lent very substantial sums to finance UK property development. Since mid 1973 property prices have plummeted. As a result the First National Finance Corporation has had to write off a total of £124 million since 1972. In the first ten months of 1975 it made a record pre-tax loss of £83.2 million. The Bank of England and the clearing bank 'lifeboat' launched to save those hit by the secondary banking crisis had up to £350 million on loan to the First National Finance Corporation at one point – to support it when depositors withdrew their funds. The share price, once high at 140p, is now languishing at about 2p.

INSURANCE

INSURANCE COMPANIES

World

The company with the highest volume of insurance in force in the world is the **Pruden-**

tial Insurance Company of America of Newark, New Jersey with $236200 million (£117000 million) at 31 December 1975, which is more than double the UK National Debt figure. Assets totalled a record $39.3 billion (then £19·4 billion).

UK Life

The largest life insurance company in the UK is the **Prudential Assurance Company Limited.** At 1 January 1976 the tangible assets were £3907000000 and the total insurance in force was £21866358000.

UK Non-life

The largest non-life insurance company is the **Commercial Union Assurance Company Limited.** Premium income in 1975 reached a record £922.6 million and gross investment income was £101.7 million.

IMPORTANCE OF BRITISH INSURANCE COMPANIES

The UK, with 781 companies authorised by the Department of Trade to write insurance policies, is the insurance capital of the world. In 1974 British companies collected a record £7155 million in premiums with more than 60 per cent coming from abroad, producing invisible earnings of £372 million.

The Top 10 UK Insurance Companies in 1974

Group	Grand total				General insurance				Ordinary life	
	World-wide premiums (£m)	Share of take (%)	UK premiums (£m)	UK share of world business (%)	Total (£m)	Share of take (%)	Fire, motor & accident (£m)	Marine (£m)	Total (£m)	Share of take (%)
Commercial Union	954	13.3	153	5·4	766	19.4	713	54	188	6.7
Royal	728	10.2	139	4.9	659	16·6	625	34	69	2.4
Prudential	597	8.3	58	2.0	181	4.6	167	14	304	10.8
Guardian Royal Exchange	509	7.1	124	4.4	362	9.2	323	40	147	5.2
General Accident	431	6.0	151	5.4	373	9.4	360	13	59	2.1
Sun Alliance and London	335	4.7	128	4.6	296	7.5	259	259	39	1·4
Legal and General	297	4.1	32	1.1	66	1.7	62	4	230	8.2
Norwich Union	273	3.8	31	2.9	151	3.8	136	15	122	4.3
Eagle Star	250	3.5	104	3.7	176	4.4	160	17	74	2.6
Phoenix	247	3.5	58	2.1	210	5.3	182	28	37	1.3
Total	4621	64.5	1028	36.5	3240	81.9	2987	256	1269	45.0
Other 789 offices	2534	35.5	1790	70.5	715	18.1	559	154	1549	55.0
GRAND TOTAL	7155	100.0	2818	39.2	3955	100.0	3545	410	2818	100.0

Alec B Stewart

LIFE POLICIES

Largest

The largest life assurance policy ever written was one of £10 000 000 (then $25 million) for **James Derrick Slater** (b. 13 March 1929), ex-Chairman of Slater, Walker Securities, the City of London investment bankers. The existence of the policy was made known on 3 June 1971.

HIGHEST PAY-OUT

The highest pay-out on a single life has been some $14 million (then £5.6 million) to **Mrs Linda Mullendore,** wife of an Oklahoma rancher, reported on 14 November 1970. Her murdered husband had paid $300 000 in premiums in 1969.

LLOYD'S OF LONDON

The latest closed year of the underwriting account at Lloyd's is 1973, when premium income reached £1191 million and profits attained a record level of £109.7 million. Membership of Lloyd's is very popular with a record number of underwriters (7666) and applicants (1288) in 1975, which seems a little surprising considering the rewards.

Profitability

The most profitable year overall for Lloyd's underwriters (since returns have been required by the Department of Trade) was 15 per cent of premiums of £126 million in 1948. The least profitable year was in 1965 when a loss of 8 per cent was made on premiums of £461 million.

Oldest member

These figures certainly have not deterred Mr **Alec B Stewart,** aged 85, who is currently the oldest working underwriter.

Foreigners were first admitted to Lloyd's in 1968 (having proved assets of at least £100 000) and women members were elected in 1969.

Record shipping lost

The largest amount of shipping lost was 802 502 tons in 1975 worth a record £122 million.

Largest insured tankers

The two tankers *Globtik Tokyo* and *Globtik London* are insured for $90 million each. Some of the largest liquified natural gas container vessels may attract even higher valuations.

Claims settled by Lloyd's

Marine

A cargo of gold and silver carried by HMS *Lutine* was lost in 1799 and, although no records survive, the loss has been variously estimated between £500 000 and £1.5 million. 'Seawise University' (ex-HMS '*Queen Elizabeth*') was sunk in Hong Kong Harbour in 1972 and claims upwards of £10 million were settled.

Lloyd's are preparing to write off the new Onassis oil-tanker *Olympic Bravery* as a total loss after salvage experts failed to rescue the ship stranded on the rocks (27 January 1976) off the Channel coast of France. With more than $50 million of the 275 000 deadweight ton tanker's insurance placed in London the *Olympic Bravery* would be the most expensive loss ever.

The record previously belonged to the Greek tanker *Kriti Sun* of 123 000 deadweight tons (i.e. the ship plus cargo, fuel oil and necessary stores) which was struck by lightning on 29 October 1975. After an explosion the ship broke in three and sank in the Far East. Its hull was insured for $30 million, some 70 per cent of which was in London.

The *Berge Istra,* a Norwegian-owned super-tanker of 223 913 deadweight tons (the *Titanic* was 46 000 deadweight tons) is the biggest ship ever to vanish. She was last reported 100 miles (160 kilometres) south-west of the Philippines on 29 December 1975. The loss of the ship will involve a pay-out of £9 520 000 by Lloyd's where the ship was insured for 70 per cent of its value.

Non-marine

Although no records survive it has been esti-mated that between £6 million and £25 million was paid out in fire claims following the 1906 earthquake in San Francisco.

Hurricane 'Betsey' which devastated New Orleans port area and the Mississippi Delta in 1966 cost about £37 million mostly in rein-surance claims.

Aviation

The highjacked airliners blown up at Dawson's Field, Transjordan in 1970 resulted in £12½ million paid out in claims.

The largest aviation loss ever, when all liability claims are finally settled, is likely to be the Turkish DC 10 airliner (hull insured for £10 million) which crashed near Paris in 1974.

GREATEST INSURANCE SALESMAN

Benjamin Feldman, aged 63, of New York Life Insurance Company is the world's most successful insurance salesman. In the 33 years he has been with New York Life he has placed over 2000 life policies with a face value of $641 million, averaging $19 million per year and $120 000 per policy. Recently his average has been $50 million a year and in 1975 he placed a total of $83 000 000. His annual com-mission, which now exceeds $1 million per year, is somewhat better than his starting wage of $35 per week at the Equitable Life of Washington when he was 26 years old.

He is challenged by **Mr Joseph Candello,** aged 40, an independent agent in Lakeland, Florida, who claims to have placed $252 million of term insurance in 1973 and $700 million in 15 years. However, he only topped $1 million in commissions in his last year.

Benjamin Feldman *(Cardell Photo)*

GREATEST ASSETS

World

The business with the greatest amount in physical assets is the **Bell System,** which comprises the American Telephone and Tele-graph Company, with headquarters at 195 Broadway, New York City, NY, USA, and its subsidiaries. The group's total assets on the consolidated balance sheet at 31 December 1975 were valued at $80 156 232 000 (then £39.6 billion), which is approximately 5 per cent of all physical assets in the USA.

The plant involved included 118 464 000 telephones. The number of employees was 939 100 at the end of 1975. A total of 20 109 shareholders attended the Annual General Meeting in April 1961, thereby setting a world record.

The first company to have assets in excess of $1 billion was the **United States Steel Corporation** with $1400 million (then £287.73 million) at the time of its creation by merger in 1900.

United Kingdom

The enterprise in the UK, excluding banks, with the greatest capital employed is the **Electricity Council** and the **Electricity Boards** in England and Wales with (at 31 March 1975) £5 890 900 000. This ranks eighth in the Western World.

The British private enterprise company with the greatest assets employed is **Imperial Chemical Industries Limited** with £2748 million, as at 31 December 1975. Its employees averaged 195000 during the year. The company, which has 509 UK and overseas subsidiaries, was formed on 7 December 1926 by the merger of four concerns – British Dyestuffs Corporation Limited; Brunner, Mond and Company Limited; Nobel Industries Limited and United Alkali Company Limited. The first Chairman was Sir Alfred Moritz Mond (1868–1930), later the first Lord Melchett.

The net assets of The **'Shell' Transport and Trading Company Limited,** at 31 December 1975 were £2366615491 comprising mainly its 40 per cent share in the net assets of the Royal Dutch/Shell Group of Companies. Group companies employ 164000. 'Shell' Transport was formed in 1897 by Marcus Samuel (1853–1927), later the first Viscount Bearsted.

GREATEST SALES

The first company to surpass the $1 billion mark in annual sales was the **United States Steel Corporation** in 1917. By the end of 1975 there were around 500 companies with annual sales exceeding $1 billion. However, only 16 companies can claim membership of the exclusive $10 billion annual sales club. The list is headed by **Exxon** of New York with sales of $44864824000.

The *Fortune* list of the 500 largest US industrial corporations had sales totalling a record $865.2 billion in the year to end 1975 which represents two thirds of the sales of all US industrials against 50 per cent in 1954.

Turnover of the top 500 UK companies in 1974–5 totalled £113366538000 giving net profits before interest and tax of £12424679000. Approximately half the total turnover was accounted for by the largest 50 companies but they made 62 per cent of the total profit.

Sales of the 50 largest industrial and commercial groups in the world (excluding financials and utilities) reached a record $553 billion in the year to end 1974.

British Petroleum is the biggest industrial concern in the UK, ninth largest by sales in the world, and operating in 70 countries through 650 subsidiaries and associated companies this multi-national oil company had 78000 employees in January 1976.

US sales per employee

In 1975 **American Beef Packers** topped the list of the highest sales per employee at $1740383 which compares with an industry average of $50273.

US sales growth

Occidental Petroleum, over the period 1954–75, has multiplied its sales at a staggering average annual rate of 178 per cent – a barely calculable total of 99 million per cent – from sales of only $3000 in 1954 to $5333919000 in 1975, thus ranking No 25 in the *Fortune* list of the top 500 US Industrial Companies.

In the same period **Gulf and Western Industries** powered its sales growth of 38 per cent per annum with a record 123 mergers and takeovers.

In the past 21 years, the total annual sales of the *Fortune* list of the largest 500 US Corporations leaped from $136.8 billion to $865.2 billion – an average annual growth rate of 9.1 per cent. After taking account of inflation real sales of the 500 have grown at an average annual rate of 6.1 per cent.

Most efficient UK company

The highest return for a UK company in The *Times 1000* (1975–76) list is the 674.8 per cent recorded by **Export Advisory Services** (No 290 in sales) on a capital employed of £469000. This is equivalent to a profit of £674.80 on every £100 invested in the company. For the first time in the last five years Tampimex Oil Products (No 60 in sales) fell out of the top two in the table, despite its highest return over the period of 165.1 per cent.

Lowest return UK company

The lowest return on capital employed in 1975–6 other than a loss was announced by **Chevron Oil (UK)** (No 407 in sales) whose

The thirty largest industrial and commercial groups in the world
(excluding financials and utilities)

Rank	Company	Country	Main activity	1975† Sales ($ million)	1975† Net income ($ million)
1	Exxon	USA	Petroleum products, gas, chemicals	44865	2502
2	General Motors	USA	Automobiles	35725	1253
3	Royal Dutch/Shell Group	UK/NETH	Petroleum products, gas, chemicals	30750	1523
4	Texaco	USA	Petroleum products, gas, chemicals	24508	831
5	Ford Motor	USA	Automobiles	24009	228
6	Mobil Oil	USA	Petroleum products, gas	20620	810
7	Standard Oil of California	USA	Petroleum products, gas, chemicals	16822	773
8	National Iranian Oil	IRAN	Petroleum products, gas, chemicals	16802*	N.A.
9	British Petroleum	UK	Petroleum products, gas, chemicals	15753	336
10	International Business Machines	USA	Office equipment, computers	14437	1590
11	Gulf Oil	USA	Petroleum products, gas, chemicals	14268	700
12	Unilever	UK	Food, detergents	13686	334
13	Sears Roebuck	USA	Retailing	13640	523
14	General Electric	USA	Heavy electrical, aero engines	13399	580
15	Chrysler	USA	Automobiles	11699	(259)
16	International Tel and Tel	USA	Communications	11368	398
17	Philips' Gloeilampenfabrieken	NETH	Electronic and electrical equipment, chemicals	10095	95
18	Standard Oil (Indiana)	USA	Petroleum products, gas, chemicals	9955	787
19	Safeway	USA	Food retailing and manufacturing	9717	149
20	Cie Française des Pétroles	FRANCE	Petroleum products	8743	161
21	US Steel	USA	Iron and steel	8167	560
22	Shell Oil	USA	Petroleum products, gas, chemicals	8143	515
23	August Thyssen-Hütte	GER	Iron and steel	8079	92
24	Daimler-Benz	GER	Motor vehicles	7936	N.A.
25	Hoechst	GER	Chemicals	7783	129
26	J C Penney	USA	Retailing	7679	190
27	BASF	GER	Chemicals, petroleum production, potash, salt	7631	143
28	Renault	FRANCE	Automobiles, tractors and machine tools	7486	(123)
29	Atlantic Richfield	USA	Petroleum products, gas, chemicals	7308	350
30	E I du Pont de Nemours	USA	Chemicals	7270	272

* 1974 figures   † Conversion to dollars at balance sheet date

profit of £9000 represents a return of 0.1 per cent or only 10p on every £100 of assets.

For comparison, the average return on capital for the 1000 largest UK companies is approximately 25 per cent. The highest return on capital employed relates to companies falling in the range 251–300 with a return of 34.7 per cent. The worst, at 5.2 per cent, is that of companies falling in the bracket 501–551 (mainly due to the Harland and Wolff loss).

UK exporters

British Leyland narrowly beat Imperial Chemical Industries as the UK's largest exporter with £589 million in 1975.

GREATEST PROFIT AND LOSSES

PROFITS

The greatest net profit ever made by a business in a year was $3169946000 (then £1348913000) by the **American Telephone and Telegraph Company** in 1974.

The top gross profits ever achieved in the UK were **British Petroleum's** in 1974 with £2271.9 million which after all charges, including £1747.8 million in overseas tax, resulted in a net profit of £487.4 million.

Profits Growth

Kane-Miller, an American company which grows and processes food, increased profits at an unsurpassable annual rate of 48.3 per cent between 1954 to 1975.

This compares with the *Fortune* list of 500 (unadjusted for inflation) average rate of 7.6 per cent.

LOSSES

World's greatest loss

The greatest loss ever sustained by a commercial concern in a year is $431.2 million by **Penn Central Transportation Company** in 1970 – a rate of $13.67 per second.

Largest UK industrial loss

For the year ending September 1975, **British Leyland** declared the largest ever UK industrial pre-tax loss of £76.1 million on turnover of £1.87 billion. The after-tax figure, including extraordinary items, was £123.5 million.

Among the nationalised industries, the **National Coal Board** made a record £110 million loss on turnover of £1589.6 million in 1974.

Government support

A record £506.6 million of Government support was given to **British Rail** in 1975 despite the three fare rises that year. Grants made to BR comprised £324.1 million towards passenger services, £66.3 million for the deficit on freight, £10.2 million for research and infrastructure, £9.0 million for level crossings and £97.0 million towards funding railmen's pensions. This was £113 million more than the 1974 grant.

Biggest write-off

The largest reduction of assets in corporate history was the $800 million (then £344 million) write-off of **'Tristar' aircraft** development costs announced on 23 November 1974.

Singer, which abandoned and wrote-off its unprofitable business-machines division, suffered the biggest ever loss of the top 500 US companies – a huge $451.9 million in 1975.

Biggest paper loss

The biggest recorded paper loss in one day was $24 768 630 (then £10 552 416) by Arthur Decio, President of **Skyline Corporation** of Elkhart, Indiana on 26 December 1972, due to share depreciation.

BIGGEST WORK FORCE

The world's largest employers

Rank	Employer	Country	Employees
1	USSR National Railway★	USSR	1 996 600
2	Indian Railways★	India	1 370 000
3	American Telephone and Telegraph Company	USA	999 796
4	General Motors	USA	734 000
5	KGB★	USSR	700 000
6	Ford Motor	USA	464 731
7	Post Office★	UK	434 065
8	Philips Gloeilampen-fabrieken	Neth.	412 000
9	International Tel and Tel	USA	409 000
10	Sears Roebuck	USA	405 524
11	General Electric	USA	404 000
12	Unilever	UK/Neth.	357 000
13	Steel Authority of India★	India	336 821
14	National Coal Board★	UK	321 000
15	Siemens	Ger	309 000
16	CIA★	USA	300 000
17	International Business Machines	USA	291 250
18	Chrysler	USA	255 929
19	British Rail★	UK	255 902
20	British Steel★	UK	223 000
21	F W Woolworth	USA	210 000
22	British Leyland	UK	207 770
23	Renault	France	206 000
24	Volkswagenwerk	Ger	203 730
25	General Electric Company	UK	202 000
26	Imperial Chemical Industries	UK	201 000
27	Westinghouse Electric	USA	199 248
28	Western Electric	USA	189 972

★Government owned.

The greatest pay-roll of any single civilian organisation in the world is that of the **USSR National Railway** system with a total work force of 1 996 600.

In the UK the nationalised industries continue to be the country's major employers with the **Post Office** by far and away the largest with 434 065 in 1975.

A Postman who is 0·0023038 per cent of the UK's largest public employer. *(Popperfoto)*

Wall Street. *(Popperfoto)*

WORLD STOCK MARKETS

STOCK EXCHANGE

The functions of a Stock Exchange are twofold:

(1) to raise capital for businesses or money for government and other public authorities in exchange for securities,

(2) to act as a secondary market, i.e. where holders of the existing securities can sell to those who want to invest their savings.

Stock Exchanges as they are known today have evolved over close on 300 years. In its early days stockbroking was almost entirely concerned with government debt or with water supply – the earliest public utility. Joint stock companies were known but existed mainly for foreign trading (e.g. the Hudson's Bay Company formed in 1670). Industry in general was in the hands of family firms who financed their growth by their own earnings or from other members of the family and friends.

It was the need to finance the development of the railways and relatively big business after 1825 that led to a significant increase in dealings in company securities. To be able to raise funds outside family and friends, business required first the extension of limited liability and secondly the development of organised stock exchanges in company securities. Limited liability means that if the business becomes insolvent the most its shareholders can lose is what they have paid for their share plus any unpaid amounts on such shares. Thus, their maximum loss is limited to a *known* amount, in contrast to a partnership where insolvency involves each and every partner in a liability to contribute up to the whole of his personal capital, if necessary, to meet the firm's debts.

Until comparatively recently the typical company was still run by directors or their families who were themselves the largest shareholders. Thus, in effect the company was still a family business which had attracted a good deal of outside equity capital. This position is still found in some small quoted companies, particularly ones which have recently 'gone public'. In most of the larger companies family holdings have been eroded by steeply increased taxation so that directors' holdings often represent only a small fraction of the total equity capital. The joint stock system, limited liability and the efficiency of the stock markets have resulted in the divorce of management from capital ownership.

WORLD STOCKMARKET STATISTICS

Stocks quoted on the principal exchanges in the world reached an all-time aggregate peak capitalisation of $1439.7 billion at the end of March 1973 and had an average price/earnings ratio of 18.1 and yield 2.8 per cent. In the 1973–4 bear market, the world equity capital-isation fell to a low of $856 billion by the end of September 1974 with a price/earnings ratio of 7.2 and yield of 5.7 per cent.

A breakdown of the statistics of the major Stock Exchanges at 31 January 1976 as calculated by *Capital International*, are given below:

	Market* capi- talisation $ bn	P/BV	P/CE	P/E	Yield %
USA	764	1.59	7.6	13.6	3.5
Japan	143	1.87	7.1	23.1	2.5
UK	85	1.10	6.2	12.2	4.9
Canada	54	1.33	5.8	10.1	4.3
Germany	53	1.64	4.4	15.8	3.1
France	35	0.91	3.9	16.4	5.5
Spain	25	1.47	9.3	—	4.1
Australia	23	1.12	6.4	11.5	5.0
Switzerland	19	1.11	—	10.9	2.5
Netherlands	16.8	0.77	4.3	15.8	5.6
Italy	11.0	1.06	2.3	—	4.1
Hong Kong	11.0	1.92	15.2	24.1	3.1
Sweden	9.9	0.83	3.3	6.5	4.2
Belgium	9.7	1.11	4.5	20.2	9.2
Singapore	6.0	2.27	12.3	18.6	2.5
Denmark	3.0	0.79	3.7	9.7	4.5
Norway	1.7	1.33	4.7	10.2	3.3
Austria	1.4	1.64	4.8	—	2.9
World	1271.5	1.46	6.7	13.7	3.7

P/BV = Price to book value and is the sum of the market value to the aggregate book value.

P/E   = Price/earnings ratio and is based on net earnings (after tax, minority interests preference dividends) to ordinary shareholders.

P/CE = Price/cash earnings based on above earnings + reported depreciation on fixed assets.

Yields are gross before withholding taxes and take into account special tax credits when applicable.

* The market capitalisation for each country is an estimate of the aggregate market value of all ordinary shares listed, excluding foreign securities and investment trusts.

The 18 countries represent between 90 and 95 per cent of all ordinary shares quoted in the world.

NEW YORK STOCK EXCHANGE

US LISTED COMPANIES' FINANCIAL DATA

Of the approximately 1 800 000 publicly and privately owned corporations filing reports with the US Treasury, 2500 have their shares quoted over the counter; about 11 000 have sufficiently wide ownership to be considered publicly owned, and 3200 are listed or traded on stock exchanges.

The New York Stock Exchange at the end of 1973 listed the common stock of 1536 corporations. These relatively few companies had assets of $1491 billion ($1.5 trillion) about 40 per cent of all US corporations; sales of $1072 billion again about 40 per cent of the total and net income of $63 billion about 85 per cent of all companies.

MEMBERSHIP OF THE NEW YORK STOCK EXCHANGE

The Exchange Community's work force – members and allied members of the Exchange, registered representatives and other personnel of member firms; and employees of the Exchange and its subsidiaries – reached a peak of 165 000 persons in 1969.

On 28 December 1967 the first woman member was admitted – Muriel F Siebert.

A member of the Exchange may combine with other individuals to form a partnership or a corporation as a member organisation and do business with the public. **Woodcock Hess and Company** became the first member corporation on 4 June 1953. The number of member organisations declined from a peak of 681 in 1961 to 508 at the end of 1974, the lowest year-end total this century.

'Seats' owned by members of the New York Stock Exchange may be transferred – by sale or otherwise – the record price being $625 000 (then £128 600) in February 1929. Attached to this price, however, was the privilege to sell a quarter interest in a new membership. Thus, the actual price for a single seat in this transaction was $500 000. This price was surpassed several times in late 1968 and early 1969 by the present record of $515 000. At the other extreme, seats changed hands for only $4000 in 1876 and 1878. The lowest price this century occurred in 1942 at $17 000.

Gross income of New York Stock Exchange member firms reached a record $6008 million in 1972 and net profits after taxes topped $676 million the same year.

The largest investment company in the world, and also once the world's largest partnership (124 partners, 61 200 stockholders at 31 December 1971) is **Merrill, Lynch, Pierce, Fenner and Smith Incorporated** (founded 6 January 1914 and was the first member organisation to be listed on 27 July 1971) of New York City, USA. It has 19 000 employees, 285 offices and 1 400 000 separate accounts and was responsible for 11.4 per cent of all the business (by volume) on the New York Stock Exchange in 1975. The firm is referred to in US Stock Exchange circles as 'We' or 'We, the people' or 'The Thundering Herd'. The company's assets totalled $4 879 012 000 at the end of December 1975.

DOW JONES INDEX

The Dow Jones Index (instituted on 8 October 1896) is a continuously updated arithmetic average of 30 leading industrial stocks. The current constituents are listed below:

Allied Chemical Corporation
Aluminium Company
American Brands
American Can Company
American Telephone and Telegraph Corporation
Anaconda Company
Bethlehem Steel Corporation
Chrysler Corporation
E I du Pont de Nemours
Eastman Kodak Company
Esmark
Exxon
General Electric Company
General Foods Company
General Motors Corporation
Goodyear Tire and Rubber Company
International Harvester Company
International Nickel Company of Canada Limited
International Paper Company
Johns Manville Corporation
Owens-Illinois Company
Procter and Gamble Company
Sears Roebuck and Company
Standard Oil of California
Texaco Incorporated
Union Carbide Corporation
United Aircraft Corporation
US Steel Corporation
Westinghouse Electric Company
F W Woolworth and Company

All-time high

The Dow Jones Index closed at an all-time high of 1051.70 on 11 January 1973 after reaching its highest-ever recorded level of 1067.20 during the day. During the subsequent bear market the greatest paper loss in security values was $209 957 million in 1974.

The great crash

The Dow Jones Industrial average, which had reached 381.17 on 3 September 1929 plunged a record 38.33 points on Monday, 28 October 1929. Tuesday, 29 October 1929, was the most devastating day in the history of the New York Stock Exchange and combined all the bad features of huge volume, collapsing prices, uncertainty and alarm. The Dow Jones Index dropped 48.31 points in the panic but rallied 27.64 points to close the day at 230.07.

Thereafter, with the exception of a substantial rally in January, February and March 1930, the market dropped week by week, month by month, and year by year until its Depression low point of 41.22 on 8 July 1932. General Motors was a bargain at $8 that day, down from $73 on 3 September 1929. The total lost in security values was $125 000 million.

Customers' accounts

The member firms of 29 exchanges in 1929 reported themselves as having accounts with a total of 1 548 707 customers. Of these 1 371 920 were customers of member firms of the New York Stock Exchange. Thus, only 1½ million people, out of a population of about 120 million, had an active association of any sort with the stockmarket. About 600 000 of the above accounts were for margin trading, i.e. speculation, as compared with roughly 950 000 in which trading was for cash. Thus, allowing for duplication of accounts it seems fair to say that at the peak in 1929 the number of active speculators was less – and probably much less – than a million (i.e. 0.5 per cent of persons over 21). Thus, the cliché that by 1929 everyone 'was in the market' is far from the literal truth.

Daily increase

The record daily increase of 28.40 on 30 October 1929 was beaten on 16 August 1971 when the Dow Jones Index increased 32.93 points to 888.95.

Monthly increase

In January 1976 the Dow Jones Index rose 122.87 points to 975.28, the biggest-ever jump in a single month; and over 635 million shares were traded, also a record.

Magic 1000 level

The Dow Jones industrial average first approached the 1000 mark in early 1966 when it climbed as high as 995 before slipping sharply back to 744 in the autumn of that year. It had two further attempts – in December 1968 and in April 1971 but both failed.

The first move through 1000 on an intra-day basis was on 10 November 1972 and two days later the Dow Jones Index closed above that level for the first time.

VOLUME

The quietest day in the history of the New York Stock Exchange Board was 16 March 1830 when only 31 shares traded. Since 1900 the lowest volume recorded was 50000 on 30 December 1914. The first million share day – 1200000 was on 15 December 1886.

The old record trading volume in a day on the New York Stock Exchange of 16410030 shares on 29 October 1929 the 'Black Tuesday' of the famous 'crash' was unsurpassed until 10 April 1968. In the former case the 'ticker' recording the transactions lagged by two and a half hours at the close.

Most of the long-standing volume records have been surpassed since the start of the world bull market at the end of 1974. Reported share volume records for a day's trading are shown below:

44510000	20 February 1976
39210000	19 February 1976
38510000	30 January 1976
38450000	15 January 1976
38270000	3 February 1976
36690000	20 January 1976
35158320	13 February 1975
34530000	13 January 1976

On 20 February 1976 the new high-speed 'ticker' ran up to 30 minutes late during frantic early trading when a record 13 million shares were traded in the first hour. Trading hours are 10 am to 4 pm.

The highest annual stock volume (round lots only, i.e. multiples of 100 shares) was 4693400000 in 1975 valued at a record $185110000000. The daily average volume was a record 18551000 shares.

The lowest annual figure was 47.4 million in 1914 averaging only 270000 shares a day although the Exchange was closed several months at the outbreak of World War I.

Volume on the New York Stock Exchange hit the 1 billion mark on 19 February 1976, the 34th trading day of the year – a record.

Small investor interest

Participation by the small investor in the form of odd-lot transactions (i.e. less than 100 shares) reached a volume peak of 301.8 million and a value record of $15625.4 million in 1967. An all-time low figure of 31.6 million shares with value $1017.5 million was reached in 1942.

The turnover rate (i.e. round-lot volume divided by shares listed) reached a record high of 319 per cent in 1901 and a low of 9 per cent in 1942 and is currently standing at 16 per cent.

Institutional interest

Large block transactions (those in which 10000 shares or more are traded on the New York Stock Exchange floor) is an indicator of institutional participation in the stockmarket. In 1972 a peak figure of 31207 transactions totalling 766406000 shares (18.5 per cent of reported volume) and worth $26.3 billion was attained.

The largest transaction on record 'share-wise' was on 14 March 1972 for 5245000 shares of **American Motors** at $7¼ each.

The record for one block was $76135026 for 730312 shares of **American Standard Class A Preferred shares** at $104¼ a share on 13 June 1968.

The 'largest deal' value-wise was for two 2000000 block of **Greyhound Corporation** shares at $20 each sold to Goldman Sachs and Saloman Brothers on 9 February 1971.

Bond volume

The par value of reported bond volume totalled a record $6 563.8 million in 1971 up from a century low of $461.7 million in 1914, which was depressed by the closure of the Exchange due to the outbreak of the First World War.

The lowest reported daily volume was $0.5 million on 13 August 1900 and the highest of $83.1 million on 6 September 1939.

EXTREME YIELDS

Yields on common stocks reached a record high of 9.3 per cent in 1941 and low of 2.5 per cent in 1968 while the estimated aggregate cash dividends on common stocks was a record $25 662 million in 1974.

SHORT SALES AND SHORT INTEREST

A short sale is one made by an investor when he sells stock he does not own. He borrows the stock to make delivery and expects that the price of the stock will be lower when he buys (or covers) later to return the borrowed stock.

In 1974 about 50 per cent of the total short sales were effected by specialists in their function of maintaining orderly markets. Other Exchange members accounted for another 25 per cent and the public the remainder.

Public short sales increased to 82 906 000 shares in 1974, the highest total on record, but as a proportion of all sales 1974's figure was below the 1970 ratio.

The short interest, or position, is the total of all shares sold short and not covered or bought back as of a given date. The public accounts for the bulk of the short interest. The short interest reached a peak of 27 142 204 on 9 January 1976 and a low of only 349 000 on 31 December 1941.

CORNERING IN THE STOCK MARKET

Corners are of historic interest only, since their occurrence under modern conditions is very improbable. Corners in the stockmarket may be of two kinds: natural and manipulated. In a natural corner a group of persons, through the regular course of investing and trading, find themselves in control of the stock of a given corporation. Without planning or intention, the regular chain of circumstances puts control in their hands. But once conscious of holding control such persons begin to utilise it and force a corner. The manipulated corner is, as its name implies, one that is deliberately, maliciously planned and executed with all the ingenuity at the command of the manipulators. The method of procedure in carrying through a manipulated corner involves three stages: (1) the accumulation of the floating supply of stock; (2) the stimulation of a large short interest; and (3) managing the lending of stocks to the short interest.

One of the most notable natural corners in the history of the New York Stock Exchange occurred 9 May 1901, when the Hill-Morgan interests on the one hand and the Harriman interests on the other were attempting to get control of the **Northern Pacific Railroad.** The Hill-Morgan interests represented the Northern Pacific and Great Northern railroads and the so-called Harriman-Kuhn, Loeb syndicate represented the Union Pacific. Each group wanted a controlling interest in the Chicago, Burlington, and Quincy Railway in order to get an outlet into Chicago for their own systems. The Hill-Morgan interests won out by buying practically all the Burlington stock and refusing to allow the Union Pacific people participation in stock ownership.

The next move on the part of the Harriman group was to buy control in the Northern Pacific which owned half of the stock of the Burlington. Here the fireworks began. The two most powerful financial groups in the country were pitted against each other. As the price advanced, a large short interest was built up. Since there were no reasons with respect to fundamentals for an advance in the price of Northern Pacific, many traders sold the stock heavily, thinking that the bubble must soon burst. During the latter part of January 1901 the stock was selling at about $78; 2 April, at somewhat above $100; 3 May, at $115; 6 May, high $133; 7 May, high $150 and low $127; 8 May, high $180, low $145; and 9 May, high $700 and low $160.

Without any intention on the part of the contending interests to manipulate a corner, one had actually come into existence as the result of the chain of circumstances arising out of the contest between the two powerful groups. When the extended short interest realised their situation and began to cover, they found that the two groups had all the stock and also the contracts calling for delivery. Out of a total of 800 000 shares of common stock outstanding, about 636 000 shares were sold during the week of the corner; and on the day of the corner, 9 May, at a quotation of $700 few shares were to be had. The story runs that the shorts were offered settlement at $1000 per share.

The effect of the corner was to demoralise completely the prices of stocks. The short interests were compelled to liquidate large blocks of their long stocks in order to buy Northern Pacific. Such stocks as Pennsylvania Railroad dropped from $147 to $137; New York Central, $153 to $140; Delaware and Hudson, $165 to $105; US Steel, $47 to $24. Total sales for the day of the corner amounted to over 3 281 000 shares, a record that stood for 25 years. Support came into the market on 10 May. While on 9 May the average high price of eight leading rails was 134.75 and low 108.63, a decline of over 26 points, on the next day the highs for the same rails averaged 133.70.

NEW ISSUES

A record total of $15 242 million in new issues of stocks by corporations was raised in 1972, although the peak value of new issues of bonds totalled $31 917 million a year earlier.

New debt securities issued by State and Local Governments rose to a new record in 1974, when a total of $51 865 million of new municipal bonds were issued.

Private placement of corporate securities, which bypass open market investment channels, peaked at $10 183 million in 1973.

The **American Telephone and Telegraph Company** offered a record $1375 million's worth of shares in a rights offer of 27 500 000 shares of convertible preferred stock on the New York market on 2 June 1971.

Largest single equity offering

On 16 June 1976 **American Telephone and Telegraph** completed its public sale of 12 million new Common shares, raising $658.5 million (then £371 m) before undisclosed underwriting fees which could collectively exceed $25 million (then £14 m).

The offering exceeds in size the previous public record of $640 million, when the Ford Foundation sold its **Ford Motor** shares and the $530 million raised by Howard Hughes when he unloaded his 75 per cent stake in **Trans World Airways** in 1966. It also beats AT and T's own previous record of $531 million when it sold 12 million Ordinary shares to the public in October 1975.

SECURITIES INDUSTRY CREDIT

'Margin', in popular usage, is the amount put up by the investor using credit to buy securities. It is currently at 50 per cent having ranged from 45 per cent on 15 October 1934 to 100 per cent (= no margin) on 21 January 1946.

The number of margin accounts reached a peak of just under a million at the end of 1968 and compares with a total of about 600 000 in 1929.

The largest monthly increase in brokers' loans for margin trading was in September 1929 with nearly $670 million.

Stock margin debt (i.e. money owed New York Stock Exchange member firms by customers through margin accounts) reached a record $7900 million in December 1972.

OPTIONS

In April 1973, organised trading in call options of 16 New York Stock Exchange securities began on the Chicago Board Options Exchange (CBOE). A call option gives the holder the right to buy 100 shares of a stock at a stipulated price, called the striking price, with a specified expiration date, usually three, six or nine months. The option buyer pays the option writer a sum known as the 'premium' for this right. Options are rapidly growing in popularity (see statistics on page 215) as a small cash outlay can bring handsome rewards during periods of rising security prices. By 31 March 1976 the CBOE had expanded its coverage to include call options in 83 securities and a further 99 stocks were optionable on other exchanges in the USA and Canada.

Options

	Chicago Board Options Exchange	American Options Exchange	Philadelphia Baltimore Washington Exchange	Montreal Options Clearing Corporation
	CBOE	AMEX	PBW †	MOCC‡
	13 January 1976	30 January 1976	4 February 1976	19 February 1976
Peak day				
Volume (contracts)	168 555	52 298	7 839	631
Value ($000s)	$72 523	n/a	n/a	$165
Peak month	January 1976	January 1976	February 1976	February 1976
Volume (contracts)	2 587 506	847 642	109 717	5 780
Value ($000s)	$1 269 979	n/a	n/a	$1 677
Yearly				
1975 Volume (contracts)	14 428 380	3 482 258	137 884	n/a
Value ($ millions)	$6 423	n/a	n/a	n/a
1974 Volume (contracts)	5 640 480	—	—	—
Value ($ millions)	$1 658	—	—	—
1973 Volume (contracts)	1 026 803*	—	—	—
Value ($ millions)	$374*	—	—	—

* For 7½ months only in 1973.

† PRW figures since June 1975.

‡ MOCC figures since 15 September 1975 only.

FOREIGN INVESTMENT IN THE US

Foreign Portfolio investors at the end of 1974

Country	$bn
Germany	14.0
Switzerland	11.6
Canada	11.1
UK	9.1 (against $588 million in 1941 when UK at top of list)

Total foreign portfolio investment in US now stands at between $80 and $85 billion. Oil-exporting countries remain small investors in US stocks, bonds and Government paper accounting for no more than 3 per cent of all foreign holdings.

Foreigners' purchases and sales in US stocks reached a record $26 534 million in 1972.

Overseas investors' net purchases of US stocks reached a record $2785 million in 1973, only eight years after the record net outflow of $413 million in 1965.

Direct Investment

Country	$bn
UK	6.0
Canada	5.0
Holland	3.0
Switzerland	2.2
Germany	1.0
Other	4.5
Total	21.7

This figure is a fifth of the $120 billion worth of direct foreign investment owned by American corporations outside the US.

TOP TEN MARKET CAPITALISATIONS OF US STOCKS

The table overleaf shows the ten highest market capitalisations of stocks quoted on the New York Stock Exchange on 21 April 1976, when the Dow Jones Index closed at 1011.02.

Top Ten Market Capitalisation of US Stocks

Rank	Stock	Price $ at 21/4/76	No of shares outstanding (million)	Market capitalisation ($m)
1	IBM	260½	148.638	38720.2
2	ATT	57⅛	561.922	32099.8
3	Exxon	96	223.633	21468.8
4	General Motors	70⅛	286.745	20108.0
5	Eastman Kodak	114¼	161.342	18433.3
6	Sears Roebuck	74¼	157.854	11720.7
7	Dow Chemical	111	92.575	10275.8
8	General Electric	54⅝	182.868	9989.2
9	Proctor and Gamble	89¾	82.418	7397.1
10	Du Pont	153¼	48.158	7380.2

The greatest aggregate equity market value of any corporation was $54.4 billion, assuming a closing price of $365¼ multiplied by the 149 million shares of IBM outstanding on 9 February 1973.

AMERICAN SHAREHOLDERS

A shareholder census published by the New York Stock Exchange showed that the number of Americans (as opposed to institutions and foreigners) owning stocks and shares in the USA reached a peak of 32.5 million in 1972, a fivefold increase since 1952, when one in 20 Americans held stock. The number has fallen by 18.3 per cent to 25.2 million between the start of 1970 and mid 1975. As the population has increased during that period, the Stock Exchange calculates that one American in eight now owns stock, compared with one in seven in 1970. They are not only fewer but also older. Their average age has risen from 48 in 1970 to 53 in 1975.

The over-the-counter (OTC) shares which are traded between brokers as opposed to on an exchange, enjoyed massive popularity in the late 1960s as investors sought relatively inexpensive shares of the new IBMs. In the past five years the OTC market has suffered the most and shareholders have dropped from 6.7 million to 3.3 million.

The total worth of all shares declined from $1 200 000 million at the end of 1972 to $700 000 million at the end of 1974. Individuals took about three-quarters of the losses.

The average individual stockholding is about $10 500, but most personal stock is still held by an élite few.

It has been estimated that 10 per cent of the population own 75 per cent of individually owned shares.

New York Stock Exchange companies with the largest number of common stockholders of record and institutional following in 1975

Rank	Company	Stockholders	Institutional holders
1	American Tel and Tel	2991620	710
2	General Motors	1283260	725
3	Exxon Corporation	707000	806
4	IBM	589214	1301
5	General Electric	530000	711
6	General Tel and Electronics	476000	351
7	Gulf Oil	372415	339
8	Ford Motor	352000	404
9	Texaco Incorporated	330000	548
10	Consolidated Edison	302817	36

A stockholder of record is a name or nominee listed in the transfer books of a corporation. The total of stockholders of record differs from the total of individual share owners because some individuals may appear under more than one name or on more than one company's list, and some individuals may hold their stock in the name of a nominee such as a bank, or in a 'street' or broker's name.

MOST SPECTACULAR FINANCIAL CRISIS

Historically, it is fair to say that financial troubles have followed every period in which boom conditions have encouraged excessive speculation, be it in bonds, stocks, commodities or other financial instruments.

SOUTH SEA BUBBLE

The South Sea Bubble has a good claim to rank as the first, and for two centuries, the most spectacular of financial crises. The South Sea Company was formed in 1711 principally to trade with Central and South America. The original capital issued was increased in 1714 and 1717, and speculative dealings in the company's shares began in earnest in 1719, when the Directors suggested that they might take over the responsibility of gradually paying off Britain's National Debt. A Bill was passed through Parliament in 1720, with Government support, and before it reached the House of Lords the company's stock was being dealt in at a price of four times the nominal value of £100. The public saw this new road to quick riches and indulged in a speculative orgy of a degree of madness never again to be matched. The speculative fever that attacked the investing public, and the general feeling of optimism that came from the rapid rise of South Sea's stock, led to the starting up of other concerns with strange projections. The most often cited – 'for an undertaking which shall in due time be revealed' – caricatures a period in which investors, convinced that fortunes lay waiting in stocks, queued to join every new company that appeared. There were 190 new issues, with a total nominal capital of £220 million between September 1719 and August 1720.

At the height of the boom Change Alley and Cornhill in the City of London were almost impassable. The Directors of South Sea, taking advantage of this boom, issued a further £1 million of stock at three times its nominal value, and later another £1 million worth was all bought up in a few hours at four times its nominal value.

As Secretary of the South Sea Company, John Blunt ingeniously manipulated the stock to rise to its peak price of £1050 in September 1720. The South Sea Bubble then 'burst' and the prices of the company's stock and other speculative undertakings collapsed. Thousands were ruined, including a good proportion of the well-to-do, for virtually all London society had been involved. The South Sea trade gave few opportunities of profit and when the company's exclusive trading rights were formally taken from it by Parliament in 1807 it was soon wound up.

LONDON STOCK EXCHANGE

BROKERS AND JOBBERS

The members of the Stock Exchange dealing in Government bonds and ordinary shares are divided into two categories – jobbers and brokers. Jobbers specialise in certain stocks and 'make the price' of the security balancing supply and demand. They trade on their own account and do not deal directly with the public. Brokers are agents for the public who want to buy and sell shares and are remunerated by a scale of commission.

Total membership of the Stock Exchange has remained steady at about 4000. However, there has been a gradual but consistent trend to fewer but larger brokerage firms from a peak of 475 in the 1920s to only 168 in 1972/3 but not at the expense of partners, whose numbers have increased from 1513 in 1920 to a peak of 2623 in 1974.

Jobbing firms have seen a sharp contraction from over 400 in the 1920s to only 21 in 1975. The number of partners has been reduced from 1465 to only 131 over the same period.

The biggest London Stock Exchange stock and share jobber is **Wedd and Durlacher Mordaunt Limited,** whose turnover in 1972 (defined as total value of sold bargains) reached a record £14300 million and £13000 million in 1975.

The most expensive 'hammering', i.e. default by a UK stockbroking firm, was that of

Chapman and Rowe on 1 April 1974. Losses are expected to exceed £1¼ million after realising all assets.

To minimise the losses of the general public through the failure of a Member firm, the Stock Exchange instituted a Compensation Fund in 1950. During the 1974/5 Tax year, Members paid a record £550 each to the Fund as five firms defaulted that year.

FINANCIAL TIMES INDEX

The Financial Times Industrial Ordinary Share Index (1 July 1935=100) is an unweighted geometrical average of the price changes of 30 leading UK ordinary shares. This widely quoted index (the 'FT Index') is calculated hourly and indicates the current mood of the equity market.

The constituents as at 1 April 1976 are listed below:

Allied Breweries	Grand Metropolitan Hotels
Associated Portland	Hawker Siddeley
Cement	Imperial Chemical
Beecham Group	Industries
Boots Pure Drug	Imperial Group
Bowater	London Brick
British Oxygen	Lucas Industries
Brown (John)	Marks and Spencer
Cavenham	Peninsular and Oriental
Courtaulds	Steam Navigation
Distillers	Plessey
Dunlop	Spillers
Electric and Musical	Tate and Lyle
Industries	Tube Investments
General Electric Company	Turner and Newall
Glaxo	United Drapery Stores
Guest, Keen and	Vickers
Nettlefolds	

The highest ever calculated figure of the FT index was 545.6 at 10.00 am on Monday, 22 May 1972, but the record closing level was 543.6 on 19 May 1972. The lowest figure was 49.4 on 26 June 1940.

The greatest absolute rise in a day was 23.7 points to 315.5 on 1 July 1975, and the largest percentage increase was 10.1 per cent to 217.0 on 24 January 1975. The greatest fall in a day was 24.0 points to 313.8 on 1 March 1974 on the unexpected formation of the fourth postwar Labour Government.

After the steepest declines not seen since the 1929 'crash', the FT Index bottomed out at 146.0 on 6 January 1975, when the liquidity problems of Burmah Oil were announced. This represented a 397.6 point fall since the 1972 closing peak. The subsequent recovery saw the FT Index rise a record 157 per cent to 375.7 by 31 December 1975.

FT All-Share Index

The Financial Times Actuaries All-Share Index (10 April 1962=100) is a weighted arithmetic average of the relative price changes of 650 shares and is published daily. The highest figure reached was 228.18 on 1 May 1972 and the low was 61.92 on 13 December 1974.

STOCK EXCHANGE EQUITY ACTIVITY

Daily records

The highest daily turnover figure for equities since February 1974, when daily records were started, was £234.88 million on 21 April 1975. The peak figure for the number of equity bargains in a day was 45 458 on 23 April 1975.

Before the Stock Exchange published daily turnover figures the number of 'marks' (i.e. prices recorded of about half the total number of transactions) gave some indication as to the amount of business done each day. Now with more detailed disclosure, the importance of the daily number of marks has diminished, but record figures are given for completeness.

Record number of marks

The highest number of markings received in one day on the London Stock Exchange was 32 655 on 14 October 1959 following the General Election. That era of no capital gains tax helped make October 1959 the record month with 527 565 bargains marked. The record for a year is 4 396 175 marks in the year ending 31 March 1960.

Monthly records

The record monthly turnover for equities was £2 088 414 000 in May 1972 and a record number of 732 309 transactions (called 'bargains') were done the same month.

London Stock Exchange. *(Popperfoto)*

Yearly record

The record year for turnover in equities was £20 065 647 000 in 1972.

ANALYSIS OF SECURITIES QUOTED IN LONDON

There were 8830 securities (Government and Public Stocks 1528, and Company Securities 7302) quoted in London at 31 December 1975 with a total market value of £250 446 million – a record high. The Government Stocks group is shown below:

Category	No of securities	Market value (£m)
British Funds	55	24 366
Guaranteed Nationalised Stocks (e.g. Brit. Electric)	14	728
Irish Government	82	879
Public Body	89	217
UK Corporations	782	2014
Foreign Stocks and Bonds	384	2221
Commonwealth Stocks, etc.	122	564
TOTAL	1528	30 989

The Company Securities group is split up as follows:

Category		No of securities	Market value (£m)
UK:	Loan	2329	3977
	Preference	1472	495
	Ordinary	2820	42 491
	Sub total	6621	46 963
Irish:	Loan	24	47
	Preference	68	9
	Ordinary	94	384
	Sub total	186	440
Overseas:	Loan	39	176
	Preference	69	213
	Ordinary	362	161 820
	US securities of no par value	25	9845
	Sub total	495	172 054
	Grand Total	7302	219 457

Assets of Investment Institutions
31st December 1974

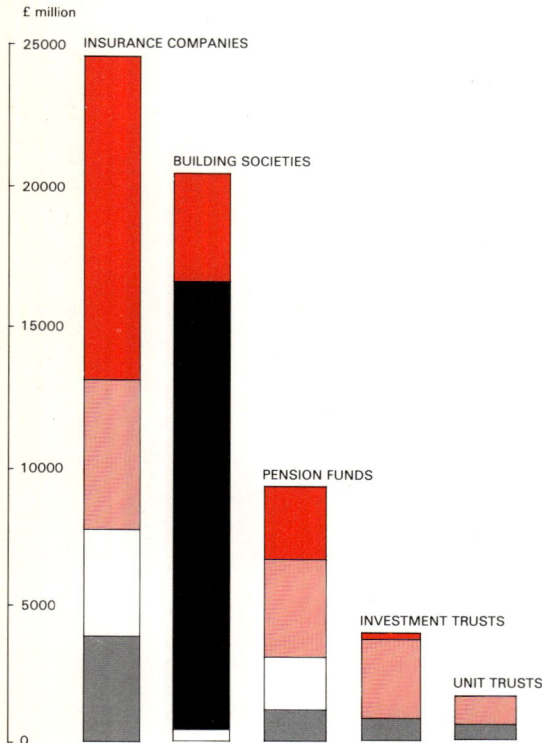

£ million

Key

FIXED-INTEREST

MORTGAGES

ORDINARY SHARES

PROPERTY

CASH &c

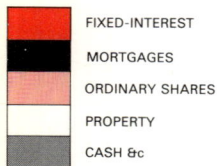

GILT-EDGED MARKET

Largest issue

A record nominal value of £2 553 814 699 **War Loan 5 per cent 1929/47** was issued on 16 February 1917 as a cash and conversion issue at a price of £95 per cent giving a gross redemption yield of £5 6s 6d (£5.32) per cent. This stock was converted into a

nominal value of £1 920 804 243 of **War Loan 3½ per cent** on 1 December 1932 at a yield of £3 10s 8d (£3.53) per cent. The new stock was to be redeemed no earlier than 1952 and even then redemption was to be at the Government's discretion. The price reached a record high of £110⅛ in 1935 and a low of £19⅞ on 12 December 1974. This dismal performance has resulted in the Government not exercising its discretion to redeem the stock. The lower coupon of 3½ per cent was accepted by investors in a patriotic attempt to reduce the cost of National Debt payments. Those patriotic investors have since lost about three-quarters of their capital in money terms or a staggering 98 per cent in real terms. That disastrous record reinforces the caution of this generation's investors when faced with the financing of the current large borrowing requirement.

The largest single cash issue was the £1 000 000 000 **Treasury 9 per cent 1980 Convertible** issued on 15 March 1973 at a price of £99½ per cent and a gross redemption yield of £9.110 per cent.

Least successful issue

The City of Lincoln issued a nominal £7 million 13 per cent 1980 on 21 February 1975 at a price of £99 per cent and a gross redemption yield of £13.397 per cent. Only 8.9 per cent of the stock was subscribed for by investors. The remaining 91.1 per cent of the stock had to be taken up by the underwriters, i.e. institutions who had earlier guaranteed to buy any unsold stock for a small underwriter's commission.

Turnover

Turnover in the gilt-edged market reached a massive £13.724 billion in January 1976 passing the previous record level of £8.4 billion twelve months earlier. The demand for stock was so great that the Government Securities Index continued to rise for a record 18 consecutive days – from 15 December 1975 to 13 January 1976.

Activity in the gilt-edged market reached a record £67.2 billion in 1975, due partly to the world-wide fall in interest rates and decelerating inflationary expectations.

TURNOVER IN ALL SECURITIES

Business in all securities quoted in London swelled to a record £16326 billion in January 1976 (mainly due to the gilt boomlet) implying total turnover of approximately £801 million per day.

Breakdown of turnover on the Stock Exchange 1975

Breakdown of turnover	Total for year £ million	Average day £ million
British Government short-dated stock	41218	162.3
British Government long-dated stock	26028	102.5
Irish Government securities	3963	15.6
Local Authority securities	3500	13.8
Overseas Government securities	222	0.9
Debentures and Preference	1558	6.1
Ordinary shares	17545	69.1
ALL SECURITIES TOTAL	94034	370.3

NEW MONEY RAISED BY STOCK EXCHANGE

The amount of new money raised in 1975 by the issue of securities with a Stock Exchange listing totalled almost £2000 million. The previous best total was in 1972, when the figure was £1096 million – and the amount raised in 1975 was, in fact, as much as for the whole of the three previous years added together.

The tables below and above right show the top ten brokers and issuing houses responsible

Top Ten Brokers

Rank	Broker	Amount raised £m
1	Cazenove	279
2	Hoare and Company Govett	210
3	Rowe Pitman, Hurst-Brown	200
4	J Sebag	100
5	W Greenwell	92
6	L Messel	86
7	Pember and Boyle	43½
8	Mullens	37½
9	De Zoete Bevan	33
10	Sheppards and Chase	29½

for raising money (gross, not net proceeds) on the London Stock Exchange to finance British industry and commerce in 1975. It includes rights issues, convertible loan stocks, fixed interest issues (e.g. finance for industry) but excludes Government, municipal and water-works stocks, foreign registered companies, sterling dollar convertibles and placings of old shares by third parties.

Top Ten Issuing Houses

Rank	Issuing house	Amount raised £m
1	Kleinwort Benson	178
2	Schroder Wagg	168
3	Lazard Brothers	165
4	N M Rothschild	129
5	Morgan Grenfell	126
6	Samuel Montagu	95
7	Hill Samuel	88
8	Baring Brothers	77
9	Bank of England	75
10	S G Warburg	54

RIGHTS ISSUES

A rights issue is a method by which companies can raise new funds from existing shareholders and a record £1583 million was raised in this way by the London Stock Exchange in 1975.

Largest Issue

On 13 May 1976 **Imperial Chemical Industries** announced a one-for-eight rights issue at 330p a share to raise £196 million after expenses of £7.8 million – the largest share issue ever launched in the London market.

Despatch of the prospectuses and circulars to ICI's 530000 shareholders involved 18 tons of paper. To handle this volume of material, without imposing undue burdens on the Post Office, the documents were supplied to the Post Office and posted in a phased programme over six days between 14 and 20 May 1976.

Hitherto, the biggest rights issue had been British Petroleum's £125 million on 14 October 1971, though some half of that was subscribed for by the Government.

Top ten UK Equity Market capitalisations

Rank	Stock	Price (pence)	No of Ordinary Shares outstanding	Market capitalisation (£m)
1	BP	663	386 070 116	2 559.7
2	Shell Transport and Trading	438	552 417 208	2 419.6
3	ICI	404	494 064 835	1 996.0
4	British American Tobacco	402	261 848 916	1 052.6
5	Unilever	490	183 067 266	897.0
6	General Electric Company	162	540 616 884	875.8
7	Marks and Spencer	97	649 005 200	629.5
8	Barclays Bank	300	201 079 375	603.2
9	Rio Tinto Zinc	235	250 145 640	587.9
10	Distillers	158	363 169 544	573.8

Largest Acquisitions in the UK

Rank	Victim	Net assets (£m)	Date	Acquirer
1	English Electric	251	Nov 1968	GEC
2	Watney Mann	236	June 1972	Grand Metropolitan Hotels
3	Associated Electrical Industries	196	Oct 1967	GEC
4	Courage	186	Aug 1972	Imperial Tobacco
5	International Publishing Corporation	122	Feb 1970	Reed International
6	Cadbury Group	106	Mar 1969	Schweppes

TOP TEN UK EQUITY MARKET CAPITALISATIONS

The table at the top of the page shows the ten highest market capitalisations of UK shares quoted in London on 4 May 1976, when the FT Index closed at 420.8.

MACABRE INVESTMENT

Buy 500 shares in **Dundonian,** the Cheam-based London quoted investment group, ex-Dundee Crematorium, and you can be buried for free. In what must rank as the investment world's most macabre fringe benefit, Dundonian promises that if you die after holding the shares for a year it will pay your widow £150 to cover funeral expenses. That will see you safely underground at today's prices and if inflation sends the cost up, it will index-link the terminal bonus.

TAKEOVERS AND MERGERS

Largest Takeover

The largest takeover by value in commercial history was the bid of £438 000 000 by **Grand Metropolitan Hotels Limited,** for the brewers Watney Mann on 17 June 1972. The value of the consideration was £378.3 million.

Largest Acquisitions in the UK

The table above gives the largest acquisitions in the UK (1948–72) as measured by the net assets of the victim in the last balance-sheet available before the acquisition.

Largest merger

The largest merger ever mooted in British business was that of the **Hill Samuel Group** (£768 million assets) and **Salter, Walker Securities** (£469 million) in April 1973 with combined assets of £1237 million. This plan was called off on 19 June 1973.

UK Shareholders

Rank	Company	No of shareholders (date)	Notes
1	Imperial Chemical Industries	577190 (16 April 1975)	
2	Shell Transport and Trading	399850 (Dec 1975)	Peaked 430000 in Oct 1972
3	Marks and Spencer	249332 (Nov 1975)	
4	Imperial Group	236572 (31 Oct 1974)	
5	General Electric Company	181421 (Aug 1975)	
6	Courtaulds	168956 (July 1975)	Peaked 205494 in July 1969
7	British American Tobacco	161000 (1974)	
8	British Petroleum	150000 (Oct 1975)	50% stake held by British Government 20% Bank of England
9	Rio Tinto Zinc	123613 (15 July 1975)	
10	Boots Pure Drug	113891 (Mar 1975)	

The largest successful merger in the UK was that between Leyland Motors (£146 million assets) and British Motor Corporation (assets £160 million) in May 1968 resulting in **British Leyland Motor Corporation.**

Peak of Activity

Takeover and merger activity in the UK reached a peak of £2531.6 million in 1972 when a record 1210 companies were acquired. The figures since 1969 are given in the table below.

Year	Acquiring No.	Acquired No.	Value (£m)
1969	686	846	1068.9
1970	629	793	1122.5
1971	687	884	911.1
1972	928	1210	2531.6
1973	929	1205	1304.3
1974	427	504	508.4
1975	276	315	290.8

UK SHAREHOLDERS

The number of different ordinary shareholders of Britain's ten most widely held companies are shown in the table above:

Imperial Chemical Industries Limited

ICI's Register of Members Ordinary Stock shows that over half the shareholders have a holding of up to only £250 and that the average holding is £841.

British Leyland which had a peak number of 210000 shareholders in May 1975 had only 107000 seven months later as a result of the Government takeover.

Analysis of Register of Members

Ordinary Stock: shown in the table below.

ICI's register of members Ordinary Stock

Size of Holding £	16 April 1970		17 May 1971		12 April 1972		17 April 1973		3 June 1974		16 April 1975	
	No of accounts	Amount £m	No of accounts	Amount £m	No of accounts	Amount £m	No of accounts	Amount £m	No of accounts	Amount £m	No of accounts	Amount £m
1–250	285470	33.9	306362	36.2	303262	35.4	297007	34.3	298131	34.4	294537	35.3
251–500	132722	49.9	138734	52.1	138323	52.0	135927	51.1	135316	51.1	134588	50.8
501–1000	89439	65.7	92358	67.3	91653	67.3	89904	66.1	89298	65.7	89692	66.1
1001–5000	62405	113.6	62356	113.0	60035	108.5	57253	103.1	55586	99.8	54884	98.4
5001–50000	3530	40.4	3474	40.1	3359	39.5	3165	38.1	3039	37.5	2924	36.1
50001–100000	409	80.8	431	88.7	450	93.1	505	99.9	501	101.5	522	104.4
Over 100000	27	63.7	29	70.8	32	78.4	36	85.6	40	90.2	43	94.8
All Holdings	574002	448.0	603744	468.7	597114	474.2	583797	478.2	581911	480.2	577190	485.9
Average Holding	£780		£776		£794		£819		£825		£841	

The Diamond Commission Report

	1969	1970	1971	1972	1973
Total Market Valuation					
UK Ordinary Shares	£38010	£35670	£50920	£60070	£40520
Persons	47.0%	45.0%	44.0%	43.0%	42.0%
	=£17860	=£16065	=£22396	=£25843	=£17010
Savings Institutions					
Life Assurance	12.4%	13.0%	13.7%	13.8%	14.2%
Pensions Fund	9.4%	10.4%	11.0%	11.3%	12.1%
Investment Trusts	7.0%	6.9%	7.0%	6.9%	6.5%
Unit Trusts	2.9%	2.9%	3.2%	3.1%	3.4%
SUB-TOTAL	31.7%	33.2%	34.9%	35.1%	36.2%
	=£12046	=£11862	=£17764	=£21095	=£14660
Other Institutions					
Charities	3.6%	3.8%	4.0%	4.2%	4.4%
Other Insurance	1.4%	1.4%	1.6%	1.7%	2.0%
Other Financial	3.6%	3.7%	3.5%	3.7%	3.3%
Non-Financial Companies	4.6%	4.7%	4.6%	4.7%	4.3%
SUB-TOTAL	13.2%	13.6%	13.7%	14.3%	14.0%
	=£5016	=£4856	=£6972	=£8580	=£5669
Public Sector	2.5%	2.4%	1.8%	1.9%	2.5%
	=£950	=£857	=£916	=£1140	=£1012
Overseas Holders	5.6%	5.8%	5.6%	5.7%	5.2%
	=£2128	=£2071	=£2850	=£3420	=£2106

Who is the market's majority shareholder? (£m)

The report of the Royal Commission on distribution of Income and Wealth (the Diamond Commission) showed that private investors are still the most important single component of the London capital market. Its conclusions are set out in the table above and indicate a slowly declining trend in the proportion of listed shares owned by individuals with a corresponding increase of those held by savings institutions.

The British Market Research Bureau found that in 1974/5 there were approximately 2.7 million individual shareholders, half of whom were aged 55 or more. Two-thirds of all shareholders had household incomes of less than £3500.

On 8 October 1975 the London Stock Exchange made an analysis of all transactions carried out in the market. Private investors did 79.8 per cent of all bargains by number and 32 per cent of the value of equity dealings.

SHARE PERFORMANCE

Attempting to name the most spectacular share of all time presents many problems, and so the price histories of a number of stocks are shown over varying time spans.

One-Day Wonder Tasminex

On the 27 January 1970 optimistic comments in Melbourne, Australia, by Mr W S Singline, Chairman of **Tasminex,** on the company's nickel find sent the 25 cent shares streaking up from £2 17s 6d (£2.87½) to £40 in London in a few hours before coming back to close at £21, valuing the small company at £42 million. Just a week later the shares were back to £6.

Each day the *Financial Times* 'marks' some of the bargains in particular stocks, i.e. records the prices of some of the transactions, although not necessarily in chronological order. The symbol Φ after a price means that the bargain was marked after 2.15 pm the previous day or was inadvertently omitted. The prices at which

		195	135	Roan Cons. K4	180	.....	‡Q16.0	4.7	₹
.2	6.5	175	140	Tanganyika 50p	142xd	.....	Q10.0	Φ	7.0
		68	65	Do. Pref. 80p	68	.....	Q9	18.0	11.1
.4	9.7	48	25	Wankie Col. Rh.1	28	.....	†Q6½c	1.3	10.0
.0	13.5	46	24	Zam.Cpr.$BD0.24	29	+1	QUS-c	3.2	7.1
.5	18.1								
.7	—								

AUSTRALIAN

2.2	—	26	18	Acmex 25c	22	.....			
		215	132	A. M. and S. 50c	209	.....	Q7c	Φ	2.2
.7	Φ	156	96	Bougainville 50c	145	+1	Q10c	Φ	4.5
.7	7.0	203	145	BH South 50c	190	+2	—	—	—
		75	30	G.M. Kalgoorlie $1	40	.....	—	—	—
		82	58	Hamptn Areas 50c	72	.....	1.18	4.2	2.5
.14	Φ	79	38	Metals Ex. 50c	79	+4	—	—	—
		20	13	Metramar 20c	15	.....	—	—	—
.9	Φ	294	200	M.I.M. Hldgs. 50c	275	-2	‡Q10c	1.8	‡
		105	70	Mount Lyell 25c	90	.....	‡Q5c	2.4	‡
		2½	2	Newmetal 10c	2½	.....	—	—	—
		182	138	North B. Hill $1	178	-1	Q9c	1.4	3.2
		9	5	Nth. Kalgurli	5	.....	—	—	—
.8	9.4	97	65	Oakbridge $A1	97	.....	tQ8c	1.3	5.4
.14		35	14	Pacific Copper 25c	32	.....	—÷	—	—
		£191½	725	Pancont'l 25c	£13	.....	—	—	—
.4	6.9	16	9	Paringa M&Ex.5p	13	.....	—	—	—
.0		615	430	Peko-Wallsend 50c	570	.....	Q15c	Φ	1.7
		285	140	Poseidon 20c	285	+10	—	—	—
		13	9	Vultan Min. 50c	10	~...	—	—	—
.0		9	4	Westmex 10c	7	.....	—	—	—
		*193	127	Westn. Mining 50c	193	+6	‡Q6.5c	0.8	‡
.8	15.4	54	36	Whim Creek 20c	45	.....	—	—	—
.0	3.9								

TINS

		45	28	Amal. Nigeria	41	+1	5.62	1.5	21.1
		265	160	Ayer Hitam	260	.....	†13.0	1.8	7.7
		30½	17	Berall Tin	27½	.....	1.75	Φ	9.8
		405	315	Berjuntai $M25	400	.....	Q$M15	Φ	7.6
		18	13	Ex Lands 10p	15	.....	15	3.8	15.4
		240	155	Geevor	230	.....	†12c	2.3	‡
		14	10	Gold & Base 12½p	10	.....			

The FT Share Information Service showing Poseidon at £2·85, 15 June 1976

speculators dealt in Tasminex shares around the time of the nickel discovery announcement are shown below.

Tuesday 27/1/70: £2½Φ £2¾Φ £2⅞Φ £2⅝Φ £2¹¹⁄₁₆₵ £10 £10½ £9 £9½ £15 £9⅝ £14 £35 £25 £9¾ £5⅝ £28 £11 £40 £18 £17 £19.

Wednesday 28/1/70: £38Φ £23Φ £26Φ £15Φ £13⅛Φ £21Φ £20Φ £22Φ £14½Φ £29Φ £37Φ £36Φ £34Φ £30Φ £27Φ £24Φ £21½Φ £32Φ £2? £21 £22 £23 £19 £15 £17 £24 £21½ £18 £23½ £17½.

Thursday 29/1/70: £16Φ £16½Φ £17 £14 £16 £18 £19 £20 £17½ £16½.

Friday 30/1/70: £20Φ £19½Φ £15½Φ £18 £18½ £19 £20 £16¼ £17½ £17.

Monday 2/2/70: £16Φ £15Φ £7 £11 £9½ £10 £10½ £11½ £12 £9 £8½.

Tuesday 3/2/70: £8 £7½ £6½ £6 £7 £6¼ £7¾.

Poseidon – everyone's dream

The staggering performance of **Poseidon**, the 12 cent Australian nickel share, which became the darling of speculators all over the world has had few challengers. The real take-off began on 29 September 1969, when the London price rose from £1.93 to £2.97 on the news of the West Australian nickel and copper find. Poseidon broke the £10 barrier on Friday, 3 October and closed above £100 for the first time on the last day of 1969. The highest price recorded in the *Financial Times* was £130 on 19 February 1970. Thus, in only a few months the stock had multiplied by about 2500 times – a truly magnificent rise. Then the bubble burst and the price continued to slide for six years, ruining thousands, to a low of £1.40 on 27 February 1976.

Mineral Securities

A report published in July 1974 on the Australian Securities Market had this to say of Mineral Securities: 'No company has had a more spectacular rise and fall than **Mineral Securities Australian Limited,** formed in 1965, and listed in 1967. After a comparatively small public issue of $A137500, the company had acquired assets in excess of $A100 million by the end of 1970 . . . Five weeks later, the shares were suddenly suspended from trading on the exchange as a preliminary to their formal removal from the lists forever as being worthless.'

INVESTMENT $ PREMIUM

Any UK resident buying foreign securities has to do so with 'investment security dollars' which stand at a premium because they come from a limited pool – the proceeds of the sales of similar stocks by UK residents.

The **dollar premium,** which is quoted daily like a price, is the percentage premium, payable in sterling, of a foreign price converted into sterling at the ruling rate of exchange. It reached a record high on 4 May 1976 of 127½ per cent, based on the old IMF middle parity rate of $2.60 = £1.

A UK resident wishing to buy foreign securities pays an **effective premium** for the privilege – the record figure of 91¼ per cent reached on 24 April 1975 implied that it would have cost a UK investor £191.25 for every £100 of foreign securities he bought.

On selling these securities, 25 per cent of the proceeds must be sold to the Treasury at the official rate, which normally entails the investor losing between 7 and 11 per cent of his capital. Thus on any one day, a UK buyer pays the full premium while a UK seller receives only 75 per cent of it. And the UK official reserves benefit by the difference.

EURODOLLARS AND EUROBONDS

A Eurodollar is a claim for a dollar in the hands of someone outside the USA who does not want to transfer the money to America. The market began when US regulations fixed the maximum rate of interest that could be paid on dollars owned by non-Americans. Eurodollars are constantly being changed into and out of many national currencies, to meet the needs of borrowers and lenders in the countries involved.

In the Eurobond market, Governments and industrial companies (many of them subsidiaries of American firms) borrow money over longer periods (5 to 15 years) by issuing bonds that are subscribed in dollars or in European currencies.

The volume of new Eurobond issues topped a record $2 billion in January 1976 (more than a full year's worth in 1974). It followed a good 1975, when a record $7.1 billion worth of issues were placed, two-thirds ending up in the hands of Swiss bank customers.

Eurobond business in 1975

Borrower	$m	%
Industrial and Financial Companies	3208.33	45.3
Government Agencies	1875.08	26.4
Central Governments	762.94	10.8
Municipalities	567.11	8.0
International and European Agencies	393.26	5.5
Convertibles	282.43	4.0
TOTAL	7089.15	100.0

Largest Eurodollar Loan

The largest single Eurodollar bank loan ever raised in the international capital markets was for $2.5 billion for the UK Government. It was announced in the Budget speech of March 1974 and signed at the Bank of England on 7 May 1974. The loan is for ten years and the rate of interest incorporates a margin over the cost on the London inter-bank market. The margin or 'spread' being $\frac{3}{8}$ per cent in the first two years, $\frac{1}{2}$ per cent in the next three, $\frac{5}{8}$ per cent in the sixth and seventh years and $\frac{3}{4}$ per cent in the last three. Repayment will be made in four equal instalments in the final four years.

Source of Funds	$m	%
France	1158.41	16.3
Japan	997.49	14.1
Canada	975.25	13.8
Sweden	527.39	7.4
Norway	456.18	6.4
Netherlands	395.03	5.6
International and European Agencies	393.29	5.6
UK	164.50	2.3
Others	2021.61	28.5
TOTAL	7089.15	100.0

Chosen Currency	$m	%
Dollars	3090.50	43.6
Deutsche Marks	1727.50	24.4
Dutch Guilders	586.78	8.3
Canadian Dollars	560.39	7.9
European Units of Account	381.13	5.4
French Francs	286.51	4.0
Sterling Deposit Receipts (SDRs)	173.62	2.4
Kuwaiti Dinars	123.40	1.7
Other Currencies	159.32	2.2
TOTAL	7089.15	100.0

Managers	No of issues	No of issues as Lead Manager
Kreditbank	83	12
Credit Suisse White Weld	60	16
Deutsche Bank	54	15
Union Bank of Switzerland (Underwriters)	54	4
Swiss Bank Corporation	45	—
Westdeutsche Landesbank	43	12
Société Générale de Banque	43	2
Dresdner Bank	42	12
Commerzbank	39	8
Banque de Paris et des Pays-Bas	32	5
S G Warburg	30	4

BUILDING SOCIETIES

Earliest

The first recorded building society in the world is the **Ketley Building Society** formed in 1775 at the Golden Cross Inn in Birmingham; it was known as 'Terminating Society'.

Oldest

The **Chesham Building Society** founded on 3 September 1845 has been called the oldest building society still in existence, but the Chelmsford and Essex Society is a few months older (see page 111).

Smallest

The smallest building society in the world, which some may argue as being the most exclusive, is the **Willingham and District Mutual Permanent Benefit Building Society** registered in 1890, having total assets of only £3.

Largest

The largest building society in the world is the **Halifax Building Society** of Halifax, West Yorkshire. It was established in 1853 and has total assets of £4 577 000 000, liquid assets of £904 300 000 and reserves of £115 900 000 in 1975. A record 123 584 mortgages were completed that year and the total number of accounts at 31 January 1976 was 4 618 732.

Fastest expansion

The **Britannia Building Society,** formerly the Leek Westbourne and Eastern Counties Building Society has successfully increased its total assets every year since 1945 from £8 726 210 to a staggering £688 443 000 at 31 December 1975 and is the ninth largest in the UK.

Mortgage rates

The lowest mortgage rate recommended by the Building Societies Association was 4 per cent before tax relief in September 1945 and continued unchanged until April 1951. The highest recommended rate was 11 per cent reached in September 1973.

Net inflow

The largest monthly net inflow of new savings into building societies was £406 000 000 in April 1975.

Net outflow

The largest monthly net outflow from building societies was £23 000 000 in March 1974 and the only other time there was a net outflow was the preceding month with £17 000 000.

Lending

The largest monthly mortgage lending was £553 000 000 in June 1976.

Building Societies expect to lend about £6 billion to some 700 000 home buyers in 1976.

UNIT TRUSTS

First unit trust

The first unit trust was the **First British Fixed Trust** of the M and G Group and was formed on 22 April 1931. (See also page 114.)

Biggest groups (Unit Trust)

Name	31 March 1976 value of funds £m	31 March 1976 number of unitholders	Peak value of funds £m	Peak number of unitholders
Save and Prosper	646.3	641.294	759.6 (November 1972)	792068 (May 1970)
M and G	321.0	142934	321.0 (March 1976)	142934 (March 1976)
Barclays Unicorn	298.7	282956	304.8 (February 1976)	293462 (March 1974)
Slater Walker	186.0	319297	203.5 (14 Feb 1976)	328462 (14 Feb 1975)

Oldest still running

The **Banking Insurance and Finance Unit Trust,** now part of the Slater Walker Group, which started in May 1936 is the oldest unit trust still running.

Largest unit trust

The largest fund is the **S and P Investment Trust Units** valued at £158.5 million on 31 December 1975 with 113000 unitholders. Its peak level was £190.6 million in November 1972, and the largest number of unitholders was 138980 in December 1970. In the recent bear market the value of the units fell to £76.4 million while the number of unitholders bottomed out at 114523 in October 1975.

Fastest growing unit trust

Barclays Unicorn Extra Income Unit Trust which was launched as a £2½ million fund in April 1972 had one of the fastest growth records ever. It attracted so much new money that its value at the end of April was £9.16 million and by the end of May 1973 the fund had grown to £20.72 million. The value of the units finally peaked at £21.66 million at the end of October 1973.

Total unit trust value

The total value of all unit trusts authorised by the Department of Trade first broke the £1 billion barrier in April 1968 with £1106150000. The peak of £2647520000 reached at the end of December 1972 was unsurpassed until the end of April 1976, when the record total value reached £2736000000.

Largest number of unitholders

The record number of unitholders was at the end of June 1970, when 2431920 people had an average holding of £520.

Record sales

The highest monthly sales of unit trusts was £44723000 in April 1972.

Record repurchases (sales by unitholders)

The highest monthly figure for repurchases by the Unit Trust movement was £21195000 in January 1973.

Record net new investment

The highest monthly level of net new instrument, i.e. the difference between sales and repurchases, was £33263000 in January 1969.

Unitholder Index

The Unitholder Index is an unweighted arithmetic average of the capital growth of all Unit Trusts with a base of 1000 at 1 January 1964, and reached an all-time low of 901.1 on 1 November 1966 and an all-time high of 2165.7 on 28 December 1972.

Performance records

On a calendar year basis and considering authorised unit trusts only, **Confederation Growth,** which is managed by Mr James Wellings, increased its unit offer price by 171.4 per cent in 1975 – more than any other unit trust on record. In the same period the FT Industrial Ordinary Share Index rose a record 143.2 per cent.

Although **Crescent Growth** fell by a record 62.8 per cent in 1974 it subsequently rose by 143.5 per cent in 1975, the fifth best performer that year.

James Wellings

INVESTMENT TRUSTS

Oldest and longest running

The Foreign and Colonial Government Trust (name changed to **Foreign and Colonial Trust** in 1891) which was formed in 1868 and became a company in 1879 has the distinction of being both the oldest and the longest running trust in England.

The first English investment trust company now part of Drayton Premier Investment Trust was the **Government Stock and Other Securities Investment Trust Company Limited** started in 1871.

The oldest investment trust in Scotland is the **Scottish American Investment Trust** formed in 1873, which became a company in the same year.

GROWTH OF THE INVESTMENT TRUST COMPANY MOVEMENT

31 December	Total assets £million	No of members
1933	not available	212
1949	619	255
1957	1142	280
1960	1989	283
1970	4469	266
1971	5758	263
1972	7515	268
1973	5814	262
1974	3708	247
1975	5671	236

Geographical Division (Investment Trusts)

	UK		US and Canada		Other Overseas	
	£m	%	£m	%	£m	%
1949	489	79	31	5	99	16
1957	674	59	354	31	114	10
1960	1429	72	458	23	102	5
1970	2781	65	1140	26	363	9
1971	4015	71	1229	22	414	7
1972	4829	64	1682	22	983	14
1973	3696	64	1351	23	761	13
1974	2206	59	996	27	506	14
1975	3509	62	1395	25	767	13

Portfolio Division

	Fixed interest %	Equities %
1949	38	62
1957	11	89
1960	8	92
1970	7	93
1971	9	91
1972	8	92
1973	16	84
1974	26	74
1975	13	87

New money raised

In the year to 30 August 1972 the Investment Trust movement raised a record £500 million in new money – £340 million in equity money, £20 million in debentures and £140 million in foreign currency loans. Some 40 new trusts were granted quotations in this period. In this period they raised more than four times the amount raised in 1968 under similar bull market conditions – itself an all-time high. The £500 million is also more than twice the comparable figure for the Unit Trust movement.

Highest capitalisation

The FT Investment Trust Index touched an all-time high of 245.79 on 25 April 1972, when the market capitalisation (as opposed to total assets) of all quoted trusts was £5478.43 million.

NUMBER OF SHAREHOLDERS

1957 The Radcliffe Committee evidence showed that there were 209684 *shareholdings* of which nearly 200000 were in the names of individuals.

1965 The Association invited members to circulate copies of a memorandum on the 1965 Finance Bill to all their shareholders; over 650000 were circulated.

1966 A Market Survey made on behalf of the Stock Exchange estimated that there were 200000 *shareholders,* i.e. excluding multiple holdings.

1971 Returns made by 151 members for the Page Committee evidence showed total *shareholdings* in 1971 of 670000 of which 604000 were personal holdings, accounting for 90 per cent of holdings and 46 per cent of shares held.

1974 Evidence submitted to the Royal Commission on the Distribution of Income and Wealth revealed the following figures for 80 member companies covering 90 securities. Shown in the table below.

The figures are interesting in that they show the preponderance of relatively small holdings by personal investors. The figures show a trend towards smaller personal holdings, even allowing for the fall in share prices between 1971 and 1974, and an overall increase in total personal shareholdings in trust companies from over 604000 on an 82 per cent sample in 1971 to more than 660000 on an 86 per cent sample in 1974. This demonstrates the role which trust

Breakdown of Shareholdings

	SHAREHOLDINGS				*SHARES HELD			
	Number '000		Propn %		Value £ million		Propn of Total %	
	1974	1971	1974	1971	1974	1971	1974	1971
Below £500	146	58	42	17	33	16	5	1
£500–£1000	68	60	20	18	44	45	6	2
£1000–£2000	48	76	14	23	58	111	8	6
£2000–£5000	31	75	9	22	73	238	10	12
Over £5000	11	38	3	11	84	490	12	25
TOTAL	304	307	88	91	292	900	41	46

* By market value at 31 December 1974 and 1971. Estimated size of sample: 42 per cent in 1974 and 49 per cent in 1971.

companies perform in attracting small investors to the UK equity market.

On the 31 December 1974 **Cable Trust** had a total of 27 833 shareholders consisting of 24 327 individual shareholders and 1427 institutional shareholders.

Discount

The discount of an investment trust is the percentage by which the price of the trust is below the value of the underlying portfolio expressed per share. The smallest average discount of 20 leading trusts was 4.0 per cent in mid April 1972 (the top of the 1972 bull market) and the largest average discount was 39.7 per cent on 19 December 1974 which corresponded closely with the bottom of the 1972–4 bear market.

Largest group

The largest identifiable investment trust group in England is that of **Touche Remnant and Company** with £501 million under management at 31 October 1975, and the largest in Scotland is **Baillie Gifford** with £216 million at the same date.

LANDOWNERS

World's largest

The world's largest landowner is the **United States Government,** with a holding of 760 204 000 acres (1 187 818 miles² (3.07 m km²), which is 12.5 times larger than the total area of the UK.

UK's private landowner

The UK's greatest ever private landowner was the third Duke of Sutherland, **George Granville Sutherland-Leveson-Gower, KG** (1828–92), who owned 1 358 000 acres (549 560 ha) in 1883.

Current UK landowners

Currently, the largest landholder in Great Britain is the **Forestry Commission** (instituted in 1919) with 2 982 158 acres

(1 206 818 ha) most of which is fairly barren or mountainous. The eight largest UK landowners are shown below:

Rank	Landowner	Area (acres)
1	Forestry Commission	2 982 158
2	Ministry of Defence	600 000
3	National Trust	400 000
4	Ninth Duke of Buccleuch (b. 1923)	335 000
5	Oxford and Cambridge Colleges	275 000
6	The late Countess of Seafield	213 000
7	The Crown	175 000
8	Church of England	170 000

USE OF AGRICULTURAL LAND IN THE UK

The total land area of the UK is approximately 59.5 million acres (24.08 million ha), of which some 47 million acres (19.02 million ha) are in agricultural use. Of this 47 million acres, 25 per cent is under crops, 12 per cent under temporary grass, 26 per cent under permanent grass and 36 per cent rough grazing.

Total land loss from agricultural usage is currently running at an average of 65 000 acres (26 304 ha) per annum (taken over the last ten years).

THE IMPORTANCE OF UK AGRICULTURE

In 1974–5 there were some 670 000 persons engaged in agricultural production in the UK. This total amounts to 2.7 per cent of the nation's work force. A lower proportion is engaged in agriculture in the UK than in any other country, and certainly much lower than in all other member countries of the European Economic Community.

The value added (gross product) per person engaged in agriculture in 1974–5 was about £2850 which was equal to the output per head for the economy as a whole. Over the last decade, agricultural productivity has risen by an average of 6 per cent per annum, more than double the national average increase.

For 1974–5 the value of final farm output was estimated at £4489 million, which was greater than the combined output of the agricultural industries of Australia and New Zealand; while Canadian farm sales amount to slightly less than two-thirds of the level of British farm output. The industry's final output is nearly three times the size of the total turnover of the coal industry (almost £1600 million in 1974–5) and six times that of British Rail receipts.

LAND VALUES

Highest

Currently the most expensive land in the world is that in the **City of London.** The freehold price on small prime sites reached £1950/ft² (£21 230/m²) in mid 1973.

The 600 ft (182.88 m) **National Westminster Bank** on a 2¼ acre (0.91 ha) site off Bishopsgate has become *pro rata* the world's highest valued building. At rents of £15/ft² on 500000 net ft² (46 452 m²) and on 18 years purchase, it is worth £135 million. The value of the whole site of 6½ acres (2.6 ha) was £225 million. In February 1964 a woman paid $510 (£212.50) for a triangular piece of land measuring 3 × 6½ × 5¾ in (7.6 × 16.5 × 14.6 cm) at a tax lien auction in North Hollywood, California, USA – equivalent to $365 182 470 (£152.1 m) per acre.

Agricultural land which cost £107 an acre in 1962–3 was selling for £197 in 1969–70. Peak prices of over £1000 an acre were briefly obtained during the land boom in 1972–3.

GREATEST AUCTION

The greatest auction was that at Anchorage, Alaska, on 11 September 1969 for 179 tracts 450858 acres (182455 ha) of the oil-bearing North Slope, Alaska. An all-time record bid of $72 277 133 for a 2560 acre (1036 ha) lease was made by the **Amerada Hess Corporation–Getty Oil** consortium. This £30 115 472 bid indicated a price of $28 233 (then £11 763) per acre.

HIGHEST RENT

The highest recorded rentals in the world are for modern office accommodation in the prime areas of the **City of London.** In mid 1975 figures of £24/ft² (£304/m²) were reached exclusive of rates and services. For main-thoroughfare ground-floor banking halls, figures up to £46/ft² (£494/m²) were under negotiation.

UNEMPLOYMENT

Highest

The highest recorded unemployment in Great Britain was on 23 January 1933, when the total of unemployed persons on the Employment Exchange registers was 2903065, representing 22.8 per cent of the insured working population. In percentage terms the worst month was May 1921, when 23.4 per cent of total insured workers in the UK were registered as unemployed.

The highest figure for Wales was 244579 (39.1 per cent) on 22 August 1932.

Lowest

In Switzerland in December 1973 (population 6.6 million), the total number of unemployed was reported to be 81. The lowest recorded peacetime level of unemployment in the UK was 0.9 per cent on 11 July 1955, when 184929 persons were registered. The peak figure for the total working population in the UK was 26290000 in September 1966.

Vacancies

The largest number of vacancies notified and remaining unfilled was 520000 in January 1948, and the smallest number was 141 200 in February 1963.

INFLATION

The world's worst inflation occurred in Hungary in June 1946, when the 1931 gold pengö was valued at 130 trillion (1.3×10^{20}) paper pengös. Notes were issued for szazmillio billion (100 trillion of 10^{20}) pengös on 3 June and withdrawn on 11 July 1946. Notes for 1000

Unemployed marchers in Hyde Park, 1934. (Popperfoto)

trillion or 10^{21} pengös were printed but not circulated.

On 6 November 1923 the circulation of Reichsbank marks reached 400 338 326 350 700 million.

The inflation in Chile from 1950–73 has been 423 100 per cent compared with 199 per cent in Great Britain in the same period. The inflation in the period spanned by the premiership of Sir Harold Wilson (1964–76) was such that the purchasing power of the £ sank to 37p, a process unarrested during the premiership of Edward Heath.

The UK's worst rate year on year has been for August 1974 to August 1975 when inflation ran at a rate of 26.9 per cent. The worst single rise in a month was May over April 1975 at 5.4 points to 134.5 (15 January 1974 = 100) or 4.18 per cent. In comparison, the largest annual fall in the rate of inflation was – 0.8 per cent from June 1958 to June 1959. The largest single fall in a month was – 1.8 per cent between June and July 1948.

ANNUAL BUDGET

United States

The greatest annual expenditure budgeted by any country has been $349 000 million (£171 000 million) by the US Government for the fiscal year ending 30 June 1976. The highest budgeted revenue in the USA has been $280 549 million (£121 977 million) in the calendar year 1974.

The greatest surplus was $8 419 469 844 in 1947–8, and the greatest deficit was $57 420 430 365 in 1942–3.

United Kingdom

The greatest budgeted current expenditure of the UK has been £42 587 million for the fiscal year 1975–6. The highest budgeted current revenue has been £43 778 million after the Budget changes of 15 April 1975.

NATIONAL DEBT

The largest National Debt of any country in the world is that of the USA, where the gross federal public debt of the Federal Government surpassed the half trillion dollar mark in 1975, reaching $509.7 billion (£221 600 million) in March 1975.

The UK National Debt, which became a permanent feature of Britain's economy as early as 1692, was £56 577 million or £1010 per person at 31 March 1976. Interest payments on the National Debt currently exceed £3.5 billion annually or £142 per worker.

U K BALANCE OF PAYMENTS

Every month the UK Balance of Trade statistics are published and have made dismal reading in recent years. The visible balance is simply the exports from the UK minus the imports from other countries. The current balance of payments figure is the visible balance

UK Balance of Payments

	Visible Current Balance £m		Current Balance of Payments (including invisibles) £m	
	Surplus	Deficit	Surplus	Deficit
Monthly	+68 (Aug 1971)	−600 (Nov 1974)	+137 (Aug 1971)	−429 (Nov 1974)
Quarterly	+172 (3rd Q 1971)	−1454 (4th Q 1974)	+380 (3rd Q 1971)	−1051 (4th Q 1974)
Annually	+285 (1971)	−5264 (1974)	+1093 (1971)	−3771 (1974)

plus invisibles, i.e. the net inflow of earnings from banks, insurance companies, the securities industry, shipping and tourism.

The table above summarises the small record surpluses and huge record deficits and clearly shows the importance of the invisible earnings in reducing the visible balance deficit.

GROSS NATIONAL PRODUCT

The estimated world aggregate of Gross National Products in 1975 was about $4000 billion or $1000 per head.

The country with the largest GNP is the USA with an estimated $1600 billion in 1976. The figure for the UK is estimated at £100 billion in 1976.

NATIONAL WEALTH

It has been estimated that the value of all physical assets in the USA in 1968 was $3078 billion or $15255 (£6633) per head. The comparative figure for the UK is £193.7 billion (1972) or £3472 per head.

The richest large nation in 1975, measured by real GNP *per capita*, is Kuwait with $11365 per head. The USA which took the lead in 1910 is now (1975) sixth and the UK just makes the top 20 countries with only $3640 per head.

The twenty countries with the highest per capita GNP

Rank	Country*	1975 GNP at Market Prices	
		US $ million (average 1975 exchange rate)	Per Capita (US $)
1	Kuwait	11 140	11 365
2	Switzerland	55 975	8 740
3	Sweden	69 140	8 420
4	Norway	29 730	7 425
5	Denmark	36 356	7 195
6	USA	1498 900	7 020
7	West Germany	423 745	6 855
8	France	351 548	6 665
9	Canada	152 115	6 660
10	Belgium	64 100	6 540
11	Luxemburg	2 156	6 040
11	Australia	83 145	6 120
13	Netherlands	80 354	5 885
14	Finland	24 412	5 205
15	Austria	37 606	4 980
16	Iceland	1 152	4 800
17	Japan	488 436	4 400
18	Saudi Arabia	36 500	4 055
19	New Zealand	12 500	4 040
20	Great Britain	203 943	3 640

* Only countries with populations over 1 million included, with exception of Luxemburg and Iceland.

U K INDUSTRIAL PERFORMANCE

UK MANUFACTURING INVESTMENT

The annual volume of gross UK manufacturing investment increased by over 30 per cent between 1964 and 1974 with peak expenditure of £2130 million in 1970. In terms of the proportion of GDP spent on manufacturing investment the UK has a poor record as the chart below clearly demonstrates.

Manufacturing Investment:

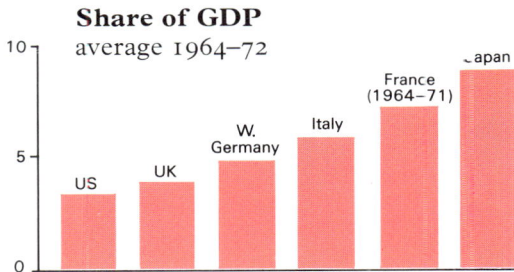

Share of GDP
average 1964-72

SOURCE *NEDC*

UK INDUSTRIAL PRODUCTION

The highest absolute yearly level of UK Industrial Production (1970=100) was 110.2 in 1973, over double the index figure of 25 years earlier. In the third quarter of 1975 the index fell to 99.8 indicating no growth in production in five years. During the miners' strike, industrial production fell a record 6.5 per cent between January and February 1972.

UK NEW CAR REGISTRATIONS

The highest yearly total of new car registrations for all vehicles was 2230183 in 1973, the record month being 255505 in August that year. The greatest yearly increase was 28 per cent in 1952-3 and the largest annual decrease was 22 per cent in 1973-4 as a result of the quadrupling of the oil price and petrol rationing.

BRITAIN'S DECLINING PRODUCTIVITY

The Central Statistical Office has calculated that in 1974, a massive 77 per cent of the wealth created by British industry went in wages and salaries against only 51 per cent in Japan. The difference between the money going out to buy raw materials and energy and the revenue flowing in from the sale of finished goods is the value added or wealth created by industry. The value added per employee in a sample of 416 Japanese manufacturing companies in the year to 31 March 1975 was £8859 (630 yen = £1) against a pathetic £2585 per employee in the UK. Each worker in Japan had assets totalling £27994 backing his skills, the British figure was only £9036.

At the moment the Japanese worker is enjoying 51 per cent of £8859, which is substantially more than his British counterpart's 77 per cent of £2585. The future prosperity of the country depends on how the extra wealth or value added is distributed between wages and salaries, interest on borrowed money, taxes, profit, depreciation and new capital expenditure. The Japanese were able to reinvest £1545 per employee in 1973, compared with reinvestment of £606 per employee in Britain.

For example, the value added per employee at British Leyland was £2929 in 1974 and wages, salaries and pension payments absorbed 91.6 per cent of that figure. (At another great beneficiary of taxpayer's money, Chrysler, the figure was more than 100 per cent.) Toyota employees added £7608 in the year and took out only 46.7 per cent in wages, salaries and pension payments. In 1975, the average price of a British Leyland product (buses, cars, lorries) was £2300, compared with an average price per vehicle of £1003 in Japan. This simple price comparison demonstrates that a series of small devaluations will not greatly affect Britain's competitiveness.

Britain's standard of living will, therefore, continue to slide relative to other industrialised nations, unless the wealth-creating capacity is increased. This increase will not be possible until a greater proportion of the wealth created each year is ploughed back into the economy.

UK TRADE IN MANUFACTURED GOODS

Britain is more dependent on its export trade than many other developed countries. It has, however, been less successful in holding on to its position in world trade. Over many years the share of manufactured goods in Britain's exports has remained at the high level of 80 per cent. But Britain has not succeeded in keeping or extending its share of world export markets for manufactured goods. This share has steadily diminished, as shown below.

Meanwhile imports of manufactured goods have made increasing inroads into the domestic market as shown in this chart. Traditionally Britain has been an importer mainly of raw materials and foodstuffs, and an exporter of manufactures, but now over half the UK's imports consist of manufactured goods.

Main manufacturing countries' shares of world exports of manufactured goods

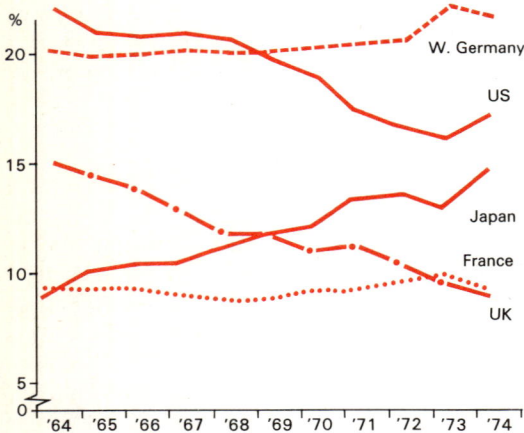

UK manufacturing imports as % of total final expenditure

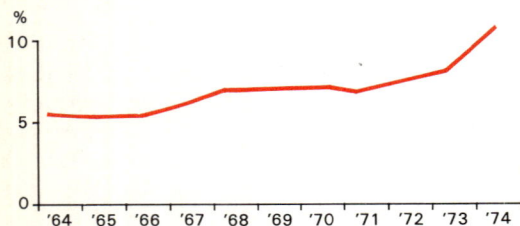

RETURN ON CAPITAL IN THE UNITED KINGDOM

The profitability of the industrial sector (industrial and commercial companies) has been in long-term decline. The chart below gives the rate of return on capital employed by industrial and commercial companies at current replacement cost and after provision for stock appreciation.

Rate of return on capital employed by industrial and commercial companies

(after providing for stock appreciation and on a replacement cost basis)

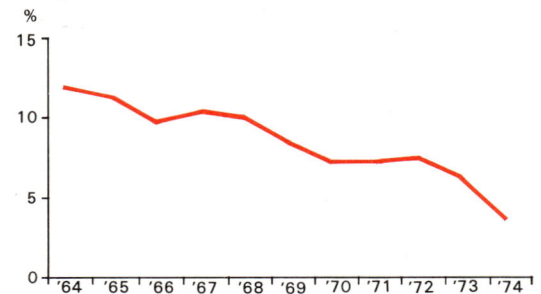

Profits and income from employment

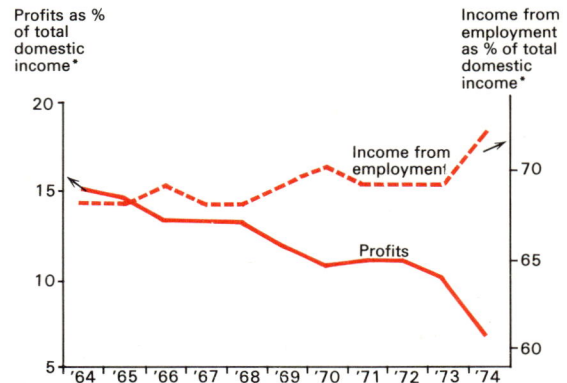

*Net of stock appreciation

The second chart illustrates the movement of gross trading profits (net of stock appreciation) of industrial and commercial companies as a proportion of (net) total domestic income. It can be seen that in 1974 the proportion was rather less than half of that ten years earlier. Income from employment has risen correspondingly, although the change in its share over the decade is far less.

LOCAL AUTHORITY SPENDING

Most profligate borough

In the fiscal year 1975–6 the borough of Camden's net rent (after rebates) was £6.5 million. This compares with housing management expenses of £4.9 million and maintenance costs of £3.6 million. Thus, with expenses *exceeding* revenue by a massive £2 million annually, Camden must be the most free-spending of all local authorities.

Debt charges

In 1975–6 debt charges for the borough of Camden reached the unbelievable level of £20.05 million out of a total current expenditure of £30.467 million.

Housing land

In 1973, at the top of the property boom, Camden Council in London paid £520000 for an acre of housing land – one of the highest prices ever. The site which is running up interest charges of £1500 a week still remains derelict.

Highest subsidy

Camden Council is proposing converting a terrace of nine Georgian houses in Bloomsbury, London, into two-bedroomed council flats costing £73000 each. This will mean a subsidy of more than £150 per week for each council tenant. Camden leads in subsidies to each council tenant at £639 against a national average of £237 per year.

Capital/Revenue spending

In 1975, on capital account Camden spent £218 for every man, woman and child in the borough – more than five times the national average. On revenue account the borough will spend £158 – more than four times the national average (and of this 93 per cent will be paid by taxpayers outside the borough).

Management costs

The highest management expenses in the country were in Camden at £174 per council flat, the national average being only £47 in 1975.

Highest rent arrears

Camden's rent arrears are by far the highest in the country, equivalent to nearly a third of 1975/6's anticipated rent-roll. Nearly 10000 of the 26000 tenants were in 'serious arrears' at the end of 1975. Camden's rent arrears reached a peak of £69 per dwelling against a national average of £6. Since then there has been some improvement.

STERLING

BREAKING THE $2 BARRIER

At 13.18 on Friday, 5 March 1976 the Reuter financial newstape announced that spot sterling was trading at $1.9995/2.0005, making a 1.40 cents fall from the $2.0135/45 overnight close. When it became apparent that the Bank of England did not strongly oppose sterling's decline to the psychological $2 level, selling became more hectic and widespread. The pound closed at $1.9815/35 in London for a 3.20 cent fall on the day and representing an effective sterling depreciation against other major currencies of a record 31.5 per cent from the Smithsonian level.

ALL-TIME LOW

Sterling touched an all-time low against the US dollar of $1.7010/20 during the morning of Thursday 3 June 1976 following Denis Healey's 'don't panic' message on television the night before. The pound recovered during the rest of the day and closed at a worst ever $1.7090/1.7105.

Sterling's trade weighted average depreciation since the Washington Currency Agreement, as calculated by the Bank of England, widened to a record low of 41.9 per cent in early dealings before closing at 41.6 per cent.

Sir Stafford Cripps's 1949 Budget. *(Popperfoto)*

DECLINE AND FALL OF THE £

The long slide in the dollar parity of sterling began in August 1914, when Britain went off the gold standard. The rate declined from $4.866 in July 1914 to $3.20 in 1920. The rate returned to $4.866 in the early 1920s and full gold convertibility was restored by Churchill in 1925. On 21 September 1931 Britain left the gold standard for the second time, which resulted in the parity reaching a low of $3.145 in November 1932. The effects of the Depression led to the US leaving the gold standard in March 1933, and the devaluation of the dollar enabled the pound to rise to a short-lived peak of $5.065 in November 1933. For the next six years sterling remained stable around the $4.80 level. On 1 September 1939 the pound was devalued to $4.03 where it remained throughout the war and during the early post-war years.

The first major post-war exchange crises came when Sir Stafford Cripps' determined resistance to devaluation was finally overcome by strong pressure from the US – resulting in a 30.52 per cent devaluation to $2.80 on 19 September 1949.

There were more runs on sterling in 1957, in 1961, and again in 1964 when the Labour Government entered office. The deep-rooted economic problems of the UK continued to put pressure on the exchange rate and in spite of Mr Harold Wilson's adamant opposition to

devaluation the battle to preserve the $2.80 parity was soon over. On 20 November 1967 the 14.3 per cent devaluation brought the parity down to $2.40. This sterling crisis set off a wave of currency disturbances which led to the collapse of the Bretton Woods System in 1971. The Smithsonian agreement at the end of 1971 brought a temporary realignment of currencies and on 22 June 1972 the pound was floated in the $2.45–$2.50 range. During the six trading days from 15 June 1972 a record $2600 million was spent defending sterling.

After further sharp falls in the first six months of 1973 the effective rate for sterling has declined at a slower rate to reflect the difference between inflation rates in the UK and other countries (in order to maintain the competitive position of UK exporters).

The five months to end February 1976 saw sterling relatively stable about the $2.03 in spite of the upsets in exchange markets caused by the weakness of the Italian lira. The fall in the Minimum Lending Rate (MLR) to 9 per cent on 5 March 1976, together with the reluctance of the British authorities to aggressively support the currency, resulted in widespread selling and sterling closing below the $2 level for the first time.

On Friday, 2 April 1976, the Treasury announced that Britain's Gold and Currency reserves fell by a record $1119 million in March to stand at $5905 million. Thus in one month 15 per cent of the country's reserves were lost attempting to support the pound.

The surprise announcement on Monday, 7 June 1976, of a $5.3 billion credit facility for the UK by major Central Banks, and the National Union of Mineworkers vote in favour of wage restraint had an immediate dramatic effect on sterling. It rose 3 cents within half an hour of the stand-by announcement from the Bank of England. After closing in London at $1.7572½, wiping out virtually the whole of the previous week's fall, the pound made further ground in New York to finish nearly 5½ cents higher than Friday's close. The European markets, the centre of much speculative activity, were closed on the Monday and so during early Tuesday morning dealings sterling raced up to $1.8015/25 indicating a fierce bear squeeze in operation as speculators attempted to cover their commitments by buying pounds.

FOREIGN EXCHANGE LOSSES

In 1974 a series of substantial foreign exchange losses by leading banks confirmed that international banking was a risky business. Floating exchange rates and the consequent larger movements in currency values transferred the risks formerly borne by the central banks to the commercial banking sector. In many cases the full extent of the losses have not been reported and hence best estimates are given.

Loser's League Table

Rank	Bank	Country	Loss ($m)
1	I D Herstatt	Germany	160
2	Westdeutsche Landesbank Girozentrale	Germany	114
3	Banque de Bruxelles	Belgium	100
4	Lloyds Bank	UK	77
5	Union Bank of Switzerland	Switzerland	56
6	Franklin National Bank	USA	46

THE LUGANO AFFAIR

A special place in the history of foreign exchange dealings must be given to Marc Colombo, aged 30, who was able to lose £32 million at the **Lloyds Bank International** branch office in Lugano, Switzerland. The dealer had speculated madly in an effort to recover an initial loss on foreign exchange dealings sustained early in 1974 of SF7 million and had continued until the loss mounted to SF222 million (then £32 million), when, on 8 August 1974, high officials from Lloyds Bank International in London arrived hot foot in Lugano, suspended him from his post, and set in motion the investigation which revealed the full and appalling size of the liability. Colombo was subsequently convicted of violating Swiss banking law and of falsifying documents. He was fined only SF2000 (then approximately £365) and received an 18-month suspended sentence as he was a first offender. Similar penalties were given to the Branch Manager Egidio Mombelli, aged 42.

GOLD

From 1934 the USA guaranteed the gold price by aggreeing to buy or sell from or to central banks at a price of $35 a fine ounce, plus or minus handling charges. Thus, the owner of dollars could always exchange them for gold. During the dollar crisis of March 1968 a two-tier gold market was started – central banks continued to buy and sell gold at the official price, but the private market price was allowed to find its own level. It was the weakness of the dollar as a result of increasing balance of payments deficits that forced President Nixon to suspend convertibility on 15 August 1971. With the distrust of paper currencies and the fear or world-wide inflation the price of gold started to increase dramatically.

Gold first broke the $100 an ounce barrier on 11 May 1973 and climbed to its all-time-high closing level of $195.5 on 27 December 1974.

The highest London Gold Fixing was $197.5 on 30 December 1974, having traded at about the $200 level during early dealings.

Largest one-day rise and fall

Gold rose a record $8.5 an ounce on three occasions – from $92.5 to $101 on 28 November 1973, from $154.5 to $163 on 5 June 1974 and from $149.5 to $158 on 29 July 1974. The largest one-day fall was $11.5 to $174.5 on 2 January 1975, as the end of the gold-holding ban in the USA on 31 December failed to produce the great gold-rush many had predicted.

The world's deepest gold-mine, the Western Deep Level Mine at Carletonville, South Africa

US GOLD AUCTION

The US Treasury put on sale 2 million ounces from its official reserves on 6 January 1975, but less than half the metal offered was even bid for and only 750 000 ounces eventually found buyers. The average auction price was $165.67 an ounce.

West Germany's Dresdner Bank applied to buy up to 401 000 ounces at prices between $158 and $171.5 an ounce.

BIGGEST MANIPULATION OF THE GOLD MARKET

The outstanding speculative event in the history of the Gold Exchange was Black Friday, 24 September 1869. For several years the US had been on a paper-money basis, with gold running at a premium. The fluctuations in the gold price of paper money caused much speculation in gold. Congress had made laws aimed at restricting speculation in gold, but these resulted only in higher premiums and did not stop the speculation. The restrictions were repealed in 1864 and gold-dealers were then free to establish an organised market for gold. It was during 1869 that Jay Gould and James Fisk attempted to engineer a corner on gold. Gould had employed more than 40 brokers; a pool had been formed to put up gold; and President Grant had been lavishly entertained and carefully instructed as to the desirability of maintaining a relatively high premium on gold for the good of the export business, of the country in general, and of the farmer in particular. It was Gould's and Fisk's plan to buy all the gold available. On 24 September their brokers were instructed to buy as much gold as possible. Gold was run up to $162\frac{1}{2}$, when President Grant learned what was happening and instructed the Treasury to sell gold. This burst the bubble as everyone scrambled to sell. The price tumbled to 133. The gold transactions of the day amounted to well over $400 million. Losses were tremendous and many brokerage houses failed.

KRUGERRANDS

The highest price attained by Krugerrands was $229 – 234 ($97\frac{3}{4}$–99\frac{3}{4}$) on 27 December

1974, and the highest premium over the gold value reached $33\frac{7}{16}$ per cent on 1 May 1974, when Chancellor Mr Healey stopped the import of foreign gold coins. The lowest premium on domestic coins was 1.61 per cent on 1 September 1975.

GOLD RESERVES

The country with the greatest monetary gold reserve is the USA, whose Treasury had $11 652 million (£5006 million) on hand in January 1975 (if valued at $42.22 per fine ounce). The United States Bullion Depository at Fort Knox, 30 miles (48 km) south-west of Louisville, Kentucky, USA, is the principal Federal depository of US gold.

The greatest accumulation of the world's central banks $49 795 million of gold bullion is now in the Federal Reserve Bank at 33 Liberty Street, New York City, NY, USA. Some $17 000 million or 14 000 tons is stored 85 ft (25.90 m) below street-level.

United Kingdom

The lowest published figure for the Sterling Area's gold and convertible currency reserves was $298 000 000 (then £74 million) on 31 December 1940. The peak figure was the June 1973 amount of £2716 million (valued at $2.582 to £ and $42.22 to fine ounce).

WHERE IS THE WORLD'S GOLD?

The table below, based on figures published by the International Monetary Fund (IMF), shows the value of gold holdings of Central Banks (excluding China, USSR and associated countries) at 30 June 1975.

Rank	Central Bank	Gold holdings (million fine ounces)
1	USA	275.23
2	IMF	153.43
3	Western Germany	117.60
4	France	100.94
5	Switzerland	83.20
6	Italy	82.49
7	Netherlands	54.31
8	Belgium	42.17
	Rest of World	264.46
	TOTAL	1173.83

GOLD-MINES INDICES

The **Financial Times Gold Mines Index** (= 100 on 12 September 1955) is based on 30 South African gold-mines quoted in London. It reached an all-time low of 43.5 on 26 October 1971 and an all-time closing high of 442.3 on 22 May 1975. However, if the dollar premium element of the Index is stripped out, the adjusted ex-premium Index reached a peak of 336.9 on 3 April 1974. The largest one-day rise in the FT Gold Mines Index was 24.9 on 5 June 1974, and the worst fall was 29.6 on 19 November 1974. The all-time high of the South African Gold Mines Index was 460.9 on 16 August 1974. The Canadian Gold Mines Index topped out at 617.61 on 2 April 1974.

GOLD-MINES CAPITALISATION

Highest capitalised gold share

At its peak price of £55 a share-cum-premium **West Driefontein,** with a total of 14 082 160 shares issued, was capitalised at a massive £774.5 million on 22 May 1975. This was over half the capitalisation of Britain's largest company – **Imperial Chemical Industries.**

Total market capitalisation

The highest total market capitalisation of South African gold-mines (for the quarter ending 31 March 1974) was Rand 10 471 642 000 (£6.5 billion).

GOLD-MINES

Largest area

The largest gold-mining area in the world is the **Witwatersrand** gold-field extending 30 miles (48 km) east and west of Johannesburg, South Africa. Gold was discovered there in 1886 by George Harrison, and by 1944 more than 45 per cent of the world's gold was mined there by 320 000 Bantu and 44 000 Europeans. Currently 78 per cent of the Free World's supply comes from this area, whose production reached a peak 999 857 kg (984 tons) in 1970.

Largest in the world

The largest gold-mine in area is the **East Rand Proprietary Mines Limited** whose 8785 claims cover 12 100 acres (4900 ha). The largest measured by volume extracted is **Randfontein Estates Gold Mine Company Limited** with 170 million yd³ (129 million m³) – enough to cover Manhattan Island to a depth of 8 ft (2.4 m). The main tunnels, if placed end to end, would stretch a distance of 2600 miles (4184 km).

UK and Ireland

The most productive gold-mine in Britain was **Clogan St David's,** Powys, Wales, in which county gold was discovered in 1836. This mine yielded 120 000 fine ounces between 1854 and 1914. Alluvial gold deposits are believed to have been worked in the Wicklow Mountains, Ireland, as early as 1800 BC.

Richest gold-mine

The richest gold-mine has been **Crown Mines** with nearly 45 million ounces (1275 million g) and still productive. The richest in yield per year was **West Driefontein,** which averaged more than 2½ million ounces (71 million g) per year, until disrupted in November 1968 by flooding. The only large mine in South Africa yielding more than 1 ounce per ton (28.8g/tonne) milled is **Free State Geduld.**

Deepest gold-mine

The world's deepest gold-mine is the **Western Deep Level Mine** at Carletonville, South Africa. A depth of 12 600 ft (3840 m) (2.38 miles) was attained by May 1975. At such extreme depths where the rock temperature attains levels of 126°F (52.2°C) refrigerated ventilation is necessary. The other great hazard is rock bursts due to the high pressures.

Earliest listed gold-mine

The first listed gold-mine was the **Witwatersrand (Knight) Gold Mining Company Limited** which was founded in September 1886.

WORLD SUPPLY AND DEMAND OF GOLD

Metric tons	1971	1972	1973	1974	1975
Net Investment	45	—50	615	825	420
Bar	—5	—110	560	540	215
Coin	50	60	55	285	205
Industrial Demand	1340	1285	785	430	735
Jewellery	1060	995	490	225	450
Other	280	290	295	205	285
TOTAL Demand/Supply	1385	1235	1400	1255	1155
New Output	1235	1170	1220	1015	965
South African	975	910	850	760	715
Other	260	260	270	255	250
Russian Sales	55	215	275	220	120
Other official sales (purchases)	95	—150	5	20	70

SILVER

Highest prices

On Tuesday, 26 February 1974 London bullion spot silver rose by a record 33p an ounce to the all-time-high morning fix of 293p, while three-month silver spurted by the same amount to reach the high of 303p an ounce. These morning levels were not sustained and LME spot and three month silver closed at 267.5p and 276.5p respectively.

Biggest one-day fall

At the London bullion fixing on Thursday, 28 February 1974 spot silver collapsed 35.5p to 246.5p and the three months quotation by 34.4p to 255.6p an ounce.

Largest number of 'up the limits'

In 1974 the price of silver futures on the New York market was only allowed to move up or down by a maximum of 15 cents per ounce. From Friday, 8 February until Wednesday, 27 February 1974 the price of silver rose 'up the limit', i.e. 15 cents, every day except one to an all-time-high of $6.00 an ounce.

Largest silver-mine

The world's largest silver-, lead- and zinc-mine is the Kidd Creek Mine of **Texasgulf Canada Limited,** located at Timmins, Ontario, Canada.

GREATEST ATTEMPTED 'CORNER' OF THE SILVER MARKET

The force behind the meteoric rise in silver prices was in the buying power of Mr Nelson Bunker Hunt, the Texan multi-millionaire. By taking physical delivery of his purchases, estimated between 20 million and 50 million ounces, at prices of about $3 an ounce, prices rocketed to $6 giving him a paper profit of between $60 million and $150 million. At the time, explanations as to why he should take delivery of such a huge amount of silver were rampant. One interesting scenario was that Hunt would ensure a profitable exit from the silver market by purchasing enough of the metal (50 million ounces would exceed the photographic and electronic industries annual consumption) to put the squeeze on the main consumers (i.e. Eastman Kodak which has two years' supply in stock) and force them to meet his selling price.

COPPER

Highest price

The highest closing prices for cash wirebars (long bars of 99.9 per cent pure copper for immediate cash settlement) on the London Metal Exchange (LME) was £1400 per metric ton on 1 April 1974. For three months wirebars, i.e. forward settlement in three months, the highest price was £1286 on 6 May 1974.

Largest fall

In half an hour on Wednesday, 27 February 1974, waves of speculative selling resulted in copper prices falling £100 per tonne but prices closed well above the worst. The following day cash wirebars fell by £73 per tonne to close at £1075.5 per tonne and the three months wirebars by £86 to close at £1030.

Copper stocks

From an all-time low of 9750 tonnes on 29 March 1970 LME copper stocks have increased to an all-time-high of 559900 tonnes on 30 August 1976. World stocks of refined copper rose to a record 1583720 tonnes at the end of 1975. After adding several hundred thousand tonnes of unrefined copper (much of it in Japan) the Free World's stocks could be over 2 million tonnes – equivalent to about four months supply.

Backwardation and Contango

A backwardation occurs when the cash price exceeds the three months price, say in the case of a shortage of near-by supplies, and reached a peak of £222 per tonne on 5 December 1973. A contango arises when the cash price is less than the three months forward price and reached a peak of £25 per tonne on 2 August 1974.

Metal trading company failure

On Wednesday, 24 April 1974 it was announced that **Aaron Ferrer and Sons Company,** an international American-based metal-trading company failed to provide sufficient funds to cover an outstanding commitment of 22000 tonnes of copper. Copper prices jumped sharply, with the three month wirebars quotation gaining £41.5 to £1263, while cash wire-

bars rose by £55 to £1332.5 a tonne. The next day potential losses from the failure of the firm to meet its commitment on the LME were estimated at £3.5 million even though 75 per cent of the outstanding 'short' positions had been covered. This news pushed three months copper to its all-time inter-day high of £1290 in early trading but closed at £1274.

Most productive copper-mines

Historically the world's most productive copper-mine has been the Bingham Canyon Mine, 30 miles (48 km) south of Salt Lake City, Utah, USA belonging to the **Kennecott Copper Corporation.** Over 9000000 short tons (=8000000 tonnes) have been mined in the 65 years 1904–68.

Currently the most productive is the **Chuquicamata Mine** of the Anaconda Company, 150 miles (240 km) north of Antofagasta, Chile with more than 300000 tonnes. The world's largest underground copper-mine is at El Teniente, 50 miles (80 km) south-east of Santiago, Chile with more than 200 miles (320 km) of underground workings and an annual output of nearly 11000000 tons (11176 tonnes) of ore.

COPPER CONSUMERS AND PRODUCERS

The top ten consumers of refined copper in 1975 is shown below.

Rank	Country	Consumption '000 tonnes	% world
1	USA	1350.0	18.4
2	USSR	1200.0	16.4
3	Japan	795.0	10.9
4	German Federal Republic	620.0	8.5
5	UK	450.0	6.1
6	France	320.0	4.4
7	Italy	300.0	4.1
8	China	270.0	3.7
9	Canada	195.0	2.7
10	Belgium	174.2	2.4
	Rest of World	1644.3	22.4
	TOTAL	7319.2	100.0

The top ten producers of copper in 1975 is shown below.

Rank	Country	Production '000 tonnes	% world
1	USA	1280.0	17.4
2	USSR	1200.0	16.3
3	Chile	793.0	10.7
4	Canada	712.9	9.7
5	Zambia	668.9	9.1
6	Zaire	460.0	6.2
7	Poland	270.0	3.7
8	Philippine Republic	215.0	2.9
9	Australia	211.1	2.9
10	South Africa Republic	178.9	2.4
	Rest of World	1384.2	18.7
	TOTAL	7374.0	100.0

OTHER COMMODITIES

SUGAR

Highest price

Rising from about £50 a tonne in 1971 the London daily price of sugar reached a peak of £650 per tonne on 21 November 1974.

Sugar trading loss

On Wednesday, 4 December 1974, the local Paris commodity brokers association announced it had struck off the **Nataf** trading-house which had been unable to meet its margin commitments on an estimated 1660 of the 3000 lots outstanding (which had a 'paper' value of some £60 million) on the market. The financial liability of M Maurice Nataf's company was estimated at about Frs 100 million (£9 million).

Closure of Paris sugar market

After the Paris Sugar Market had suffered seven successive limit-down sessions, trading was suspended by the French authorities on Tuesday, 3 December 1974. Only after ten days of confused argument as to how to close open positions did normal trading begin.

Throughout this débâcle both the London and New York markets remained open.

COCOA

Highest prices

Rising from a cyclical low of about £200 per tonne in 1971 the cocoa price rose to a cyclical high of £1250 per tonne on 3 May 1974. This record level was exceeded in June 1976, due mainly to the depreciation of sterling.

Losses

The volatility of the cocoa market has claimed many victims, the most spectacular being the disclosure by the **Rowntree Mackintosh** confectionary group of losses of about £20 million on 12 July 1973. After being suspended for one and a half hours, while Rowntree made the details public, the shares slumped 36p to 184p when trading resumed in London. However, by September the total cost of the disastrous speculation reached £32.5 million due to the need to liquidate positions taken on the cocoa terminal market at prices significantly above those ruling when the first announcement was made on 12 July.

Another significant cocoa débâcle was that of the Swiss subsidiary of the **United California Bank,** which lost $40 million in 1970 because of unauthorised commodity dealings by employees.

REUTER'S COMMODITY INDEX

The Reuter's Commodity Index (18 September 1931 = 100) is a geometric average of the sterling prices of 17 primary commodities weighted by their relative importance in international trade.

Rising from a low of 538.9 in January 1972 the Index rose during the world commodity boom to a cyclical high of 1497.7 on 26 February 1974. The subsequent world recession saw prices weaken and the Index fell to a low of 1051 in June 1975 before starting its upward climb on the back of world economic recovery and the depreciation of sterling. The old record was broken on 9 June 1976 when the Index closed at 1500.5.

US COMMODITY FUTURES TRADING

Trading on all US Commodity exchanges in 1975 amounted to a record 32.2 million contracts (+16 per cent over 1974), valued at $598 027 million (+5 per cent over the 1974 performance).

Commodity	VOLUME		VALUE	
	Million contracts 1975	% change over 1974	$m 1975	% change over 1974
Maize	5 637 222	+3.63	73 185	−2.91
Soyabean	4 570 936	+39.00	120 105	+12.03
Silver	5 300 195	+54.30	110 825	+22.85

SALARIES, WAGES AND INCOMES

Highest salary

The highest salary paid in the United States in 1973 was to the Chairman of **Johnson and Johnson,** the drug company with $975 000 (£407 500).

The highest salaried woman executive in the US was believed to be **Mary Wells Lawrence,** Chairman of the advertising firm Wells, Rich, Greene, Incorporated of New York, $385 000 (£160 400) in 1973. She is the mother of five and has an earning husband – Harding L Lawrence, Chairman of Braniff Airways.

United Kingdom

Britain's highest paid executive is **Mr Richard Tompkins,** Chairman of Green Shield Trading Stamp Company which he founded in 1958. His service agreement entitled him to 15 per cent of profits, which for the year ending 31 October 1971 would have earned him £395 000. He waived £135 000. On 1972/3 full standard taxation rates it has been calculated that £185 600 of the £260 000 would be payable in income tax and surtax. His 1973/4 salary is believed to have been less than £100 000 gross.

Alphonse Capone. *(Popperfoto)* (see page 246)

The highest straight salary paid in British business is the £91 842 payable to the Managing Director of Shell Transport and Trading, **Mr F S McFadzean** in 1975.

Highest wage

The highest recorded wages in Britain are those paid to long haulage lorry-drivers and tower-crane drivers on bonuses. A specific case of £350 a week has been cited.

Wage inflation

The largest ever annual rise in UK wage rates was 33.5 per cent from May 1974 to May 1975.

The highest annual rise in UK earnings was 33.9 per cent from February 1974 to February 1975.

The smallest annual rise since 1963 was 1.5 per cent from May 1966 to May 1967.

Highest incomes

The greatest incomes derive from the collection of royalties per barrel by rulers of oil-rich sheikhdoms, who have not abrogated personal entitlement. Before his death in 1965, **H H Sheikh Sir Abdullah as-Salim as-Sabah GCMG, CIE.** (b 1895), the eleventh Amir of Kuwait was accumulating royalties payable at a rate of £2.6 million per week or £145 million a year.

The highest gross income ever achieved in a single year by a private citizen is an estimated $105 million (then £21½ million) in 1927 by the Sicilian-born Chicago gangster **Alphonse** ('Scarface Al') **Capone** (1899-1947). This was derived from illegal liquor trading and alky-cookers (illicit stills), gambling establishments, dog tracks, dance-halls, 'protection' rackets and vice. On his business-card Capone described himself as a 'Second Hand Furniture Dealer'.

DISTRIBUTION OF INCOME IN THE UK

The table on page 247 shows that the top half of income recipients in 1972/3, whose income ranged from £1338 upwards, received over three-quarters (76.0 per cent) of the total income before tax.

The differences in the shares of each group comparing the distribution of income before and after tax are relatively small; the share of the top 10 per cent fell from 26.9 to 23.6 per cent and the share of the bottom 20 per cent increased from 5.8 to 6.8 per cent.

In general, changes in the distribution of income since 1959 have not been particularly pronounced, but there has been a continuing decline in the share of the top 5 per cent (from 19.9 per cent of income before tax in 1959 to 17.2 per cent in 1972/3), accounted for largely by the drop in the share of the top 1 per cent (from 8.4 per cent in 1959 to 6.4 per cent in 1972/3).

Taking all sources of income into account, some 214000 couples or single people had gross incomes of £10000 or more in 1974/5. However, only 65000 people earned £10000 or more from employment in the 1974/5 tax year, accounting for just 2.1 per cent of the nation's earnings. The really high-powered earners – £50000 or more – totalled only 300. Only one in 50 of the high paid are

women, three-quarters are over 50 years old and 85 per cent have university degrees.

If salaries were restricted to a maximum of £10000 a year and the 'excess' of £387 million redistributed, the other 25 million working people would be only £15 a year better off. However, with a £10000 income one is already paying tax at the 60 per cent rate and so if the Treasury is not to lose out the effective share out would be only about £5 a head.

Moreover, it has been calculated that if graduated rates of income tax above the basic 35 per cent were completely abolished for the 65000 people earning at least £10000 only £183 million a year gross tax revenue would be lost – about 14p a week for each of the 25 million work force. After taking into account the costs of collection, etc from our comparatively underpaid innovative business leaders, it is hard to see any justification for keeping penally graduated rates of income tax – which can only destroy incentive.

TAXATION

Most taxed

The major national economy with the highest rate of taxation (central and local taxes, plus social security contribution) is that of France with 53.0 per cent of her National Income in 1970 (latest data). The lowest proportion for any advanced national economy in 1973 was 19.5 per cent in Japan, which also enjoyed the highest economic growth rate. In the UK in 1971 current taxation receipts were 48.7 per cent of GNP.

Least taxed

There is no income tax paid by residents on Lundy Island off north Devon, England. This 1062.4 acre (429 ha) island issued its own unofficial currency of Puffins and Half Puffins between the wars for which offence the owner was prosecuted.

Highest taxation rates

The country with the most confiscatory taxation is Norway where in January 1974 the

DISTRIBUTION OF PERSONAL INCOME

Percentage shares of income, before and after income tax, received by given quantile groups; 1949 to 1972/3. United Kingdom.

Income unit: tax unit.

Quantile group (%)	Before income tax 1949	1959	1964	1967	1972/3	Income range 1972/3 (lower limit)	After income tax 1949	1959	1964	1967	1972/3	Income range 1972/3 (lower limit)
	%	%	%	%	%	£ pa	%	%	%	%	%	£ pa
Top 1	11.2	8.4	8.2	7.4	6.4	6236	6.4	5.3	5.3	4.9	4.4	4162
2–5	12.6	11.5	11.3	11.0	10.8	3512	11.3	10.5	10.7	9.9	9.8	2853
6–10	9.4	9.5	9.6	9.6	9.7	2857	9.4	9.4	9.9	9.5	9.4	2398
Top 10	33.2	29.4	29.1	28.0	26.9	2857	27.1	25.2	25.9	24.3	23.6	2398
11–20	14.1	15.1	15.5	15.2	15.8	2289	14.5	15.7	16.1	15.2	15.8	1988
21–30	11.2	12.6	12.6	12.6	13.1	1937	11.9	12.9	12.9	13.0	13.2	1679
31–40	9.6	10.7	10.9	11.1	11.0	1626	10.5	11.2	11.1	11.0	11.2	1421
41–50	8.2	9.1	9.2	9.1	9.2	1338	9.5	9.9	8.8	9.7	9.5	1187
51–60	23.7 (51–100)	7.5	7.4	7.7	7.5	1065	26.5 (51–100)	7.2	8.0	7.7	8.0	978
61–70		5.9	5.8	6.0	5.9	837		6.6	5.6	7.1	6.5	801
71–80		4.4	4.3	4.8	4.8	644		5.2	5.1	4.9	5.5	637
81–90		(5.3) (81–100)	5.2	3.4	(5.8) (81–100)	—		(6.0) (81–100)	6.5	7.1 (81–100)	(6.8) (81–100)	—
91–100				2.2		—						—
	£ pa											
Median	£259	£514	£679	£843	£1338		£250	£477	£596	£758	£1187	

Source: Pre-1972/3 figures derived from Blue Book; 1972/3 figures derived from provisional Central Statistical Office income distribution table.

Note. In some years the income share of the lower quantile groups cannot be estimated with any degree of confidence as the published range tables have too few income ranges at the lower end of the distribution to permit successful interpolation.

Labour Party and Socialist Alliance abolished the 80 per cent limit so that some 2000 citizens have to pay more than 100 per cent of their taxable income. The shipping magnate Hilmar Reksten was assessed at 491 per cent. The highest marginal rate in the United Kingdom, is the 1975–76 rate for taxable incomes over £20000 at 83 per cent with an additional surcharge on investment income in excess of £2000 of 15 per cent making a rate of 98 per cent. In 1967–8 a 'special charge' of up to 9s (45p) in the £ additional to surtax brought the top rate to 27s 3d (136p) in the £ on investment income. A married man with two children earning £5000 per year in 1938 would, in June 1975 have to have earned £113500 to have enjoyed the same standard of living.

Highest and lowest rates in UK

Income tax was introduced in Great Britain in 1799 at the standard rate of 2s (10p) in the £. It was discontinued in 1815, only to be re-introduced in 1842 at the rate of 7d (3p) in the £. It was at its lowest at 2d (0.83p) in the £ in 1875, gradually climbing to 1s 3d (6p) by 1913. From April 1941 until 1946 the record peak of 10s (50p) in the £ was maintained to assist in the financing of the Second World War. Death Duties (introduced in 1894) on million-aire estates began at 8 per cent (1894–1907) and were raised to a peak of 80 per cent by 1949. Capital Transfer Tax rates have yet to be enacted.

TOP RATES OF INCOME TAX FOR A SINGLE PERSON

Rank	Country	Top rate (%)	Starting level for top rate (£)
1	Burma	99	—
2	UK	83	20000*
3	Ireland	77	10350
4	Italy	72	344827
5	Netherlands	71	25604
6	USA	70	47619†
7	France	60	11279
8	Belgium	60	48781‡
9	Luxembourg	57	8465
10	West Germany	56	23636

* Maximum of 98 per cent on unearned income.
† Maximum of 50 per cent of total earned income.
‡ Maximum of 50 per cent of total income.

PERSONAL WEALTH

The measurement of extreme personal wealth is beset with intractable difficulties. Apart from understandable reticence and the element of approximation in estimating the valuation of assets, inflation and exchange rate changes make comparisons complicated.

The term 'millionaire' was invented about 1740 and 'billionaire' in 1861. The earliest dollar billionaires were **John Davison Rocke-feller** (1839–1937); **Henry Ford** (1863–1947) and **Andrew William Mellon** (1855–1937). In 1937, the last year all three were alive, a billion US dollars were worth £205 million but that amount of sterling would today have a purchasing power in excess of £1600 million.

Wealthiest man in real terms

In 1915 **John Davison Rockefeller** was perhaps the wealthiest man the modern world had ever known. His personal fortune was equal to 2 per cent of the total Gross National Product of the USA (then $425 billion) and this did not include the vast fortune passed on to the rest of his family which then controlled banks, railways and newly created philanthropic foundations. His monopoly of oil would even make the sheikhs blush as his Standard Oil Companies then refined more than 90 per cent of the oil sold in America and most of that of the rest of the world.

Wealthiest UK Citizen

The wealthiest UK citizen, at the time of his death, was **Sir John Reeves Ellerman**, second Baronet (1909–73), whose fortune was estimated at £600 million (then $1500 million).

Other Billionaires

Jean Paul Getty (b Minneapolis, Minnesota, 15 December 1892) died a multi-billionaire at his Guildford home in Surrey, England on 6 June 1976. He controlled more than 60 per cent of the parent Getty Corporation, which had 1975 sales of $2984 million (then £1480 m), net income of $257 million (then £127 m) and net recoverable oil reserves of 2440 million barrels and 3369 billion ft² of natural gas. Shortly before Getty's death his total wealth

Howard Robert Hughes (b Houston, Texas, 24 December 1905), the billionaire recluse died on 5 April 1976. *Fortune* assessed Mr Hughes at $1200 million in December 1973. His will has not yet been found and thus a realistic figure for his wealth is not known.

However, following the sale of his 75 per cent state in Trans World Airlines in 1966, Hughes received a banker's draft for $546 549 771 – probably the largest sum ever to fall into one man's hand in one day, which made him, in cash terms, the richest man at the time.

Richest man in the World?

Following the death of Getty, experts suggest that **Daniel K Ludwig** (b South Haven, Michigan, June 1897) would be a leading contender for the title of the richest man in the world. He is a self-made man and owns the following: National Bulk Carriers, a shipyard in Japan, a large share in the National Mortgage Bank in America, a deep-water port in Florida, a big interest in potash in Ethiopia, iron ore in India, oranges in Panama, a million acres (0.41 million ha) of Venezuela, 3 million acres (1.22 million ha) of Brazil and large areas of Australia and United States.

Richest man in Great Britain

The richest man in Great Britain is reputed to be **John Moores,** the football pioneer in 1923. In 1973 he was estimated to be worth about £400 million (then $1000 million). His first job after leaving school at 14 was as a telephone-operator. He was born in Eccles, Lancashire in 1896.

Billion dollar loser

Only one man has the distinction of making and losing $1000 million in less than two years. **H Ross Perot,** aged 46, founder and Chairman of Electronic Data Systems (EDS) of Dallas saw the value of his 9 million shares rise from $150 million when issued in September 1968 to $1476 million in March 1970. Then in only six months the share price fell from $164 to $33 giving him a paper loss of $1179 million equivalent to $75 per second. Ironically, even after such a staggering fall, his personal

Jean Paul Getty. (Popperfoto)

Howard Robert Hughes. (Popperfoto)

was put at between $2000 and $4000 million (£1130 and £2260 million with £1 = $1.77). Getty's $650 million estate (£368 m) was shared among family, close friends and a J Paul Getty Museum, which contains his art collection estimated to be worth $200 million (£113 m).

US PERSONAL WEALTH

Top wealth-holders by age and sex

Number of Top Wealth-holders ('000)	Total				%			
	1953	1958	1962	1969	1953	1958	1962	1969
Male[1]	1330	1936	2539	5643	67.2	64.3	61.4	62.6
Under 50 years	491	741	988	2657	36.9	38.3	38.9	45.3
50–60 years	648	923	1173	2329	48.7	47.7	46.2	41.3
70 years and over	151	232	332	666	11.4	12.0	13.1	11.8
Female[1]	648	1073	1594	3370	32.7	35.7	38.6	37.4
Under 50 years	197	299	471	932	30.4	27.9	29.5	27.6
50–60 years	306	530	758	1630	47.2	49.4	47.6	48.4
70 years and over	120	209	324	726	18.5	19.5	20.3	21.5
TOTAL	1979	3009	4132	9013	100.0	100.0	100.0	100.0

Top wealth-holders by size of gross estate

Number of Top Wealth-holders ('000)	Total				%			
	1953	1958	1962	1969	1953	1958	1962	1969
$60 000–$99 999	(NA)	1193	1593	3341	(NA)	39.6	38.6	37.1
$100 000–$199 999	(NA)	1179	1627	5214	(NA)	39.2	39.4	57.8
$200 000–$499 999	(NA)	488	692		(NA)	16.2	16.7	
$500 000–$999 999	(NA)	102	149	311	(NA)	3.4	3.6	3.4
$1 000 000–$9 999 999	(NA)	45	69	143	(NA)	1.5	1.7	1.6
$10 000 000 or more	(NA)	2	2	4	(NA)	0.1	(z)	(z)

Top wealth-holders by asset composition

Number of Top Wealth-holders ($bn)	Total				%			
	1953	1958	1962	1969	1953	1958	1962	1969
Real estate	81.8	132.6	158.0	428.0	23.0	24.5	25.0	27.1
Bonds	35.6	35.6	47.9	85.0	9.9	6.6	6.4	5.4
Corporate stock	140.9	231.1	325.8	551.4	39.6	42.6	43.3	34.9
Cash	33.8	45.9	70.7	189.7	9.5	3.5	9.4	12.0
Notes and mortgages	12.5	20.5	30.4	59.4	3.5	3.8	4.0	3.8
Insurance equity	7.1	10.8	15.6	31.0	2.0	2.0	2.1	2.0
Other	44.2	65.5	73.5	235.7	12.4	12.1	9.8	14.9
Debts	31.8	49.6	82.7	203.6	8.9	9.2	11.0	12.9
Net worth (less deficit)	324.1	492.4	669.3	1377.0	91.1	90.8	89.0	87.1
TOTAL ASSETS	355.9	542.0	752.0	1550.6	100.0	100.0	100.0	100.0

NA   Not available.   Z   Less than 0.05 per cent.   [1] Includes persons of unknown age.

Source: US Internal Revenue Service. *Statistics of Income, 1969*, Supplemental Report, *Personal Wealth*.

holding was worth about $300 million, which still put him amongst the wealthiest few. Worse was still to come. At its low point in 1974 EDS was trading at about the $13½ level thus reducing Mr Perot's worth by another 67 per cent to $100 million. However, with EDS closing at $13 on 5 April 1976, he is again attempting to remake that 'lost' billion dollars.

Richest families

It has been tentatively estimated that the combined value of the assets nominally controlled by the **du Pont** family of some 1600 members may be of the order of $150000 million. The family arrived penniless in the USA from France on 1 January 1800. Europeans with family assets in excess of the equivalent of a billion dollars, include the **Wallenburg** family in Sweden.

The largest number of millionaires estates in one family in the British Isles is that of the Wills family of the **Imperial Tobacco Company,** of whom 14 members have left estates in excess of £1 million since 1910. These totalled £55 million of which Death Duties (introduced in 1894) have taken over £27 million.

US PERSONAL WEALTH

In the US there was little change between 1958 and 1969 in the overall distribution of wealth, but the increase in the proportion of males under 50 in the top wealth-holders' category indicates an ability to accumulate capital out of earned income. Relatively low tax rates on income is probably an important factor.

INDEX

Index compiled by Gertrude Mittelmann, BA, MIL